Understanding

SECOND EDITION

Moyra Grant

An A Level Course Companion

Stanley Thornes Publishers Ltd

First published in 1992 by:
Stanley Thornes (Publishers) Ltd
Ellenborough House
Wellington Street
CHELTENHAM
GL50 1YW
UK

Second Edition 1999

A catalogue record for this book is available from the British Library.

ISBN 0 7487 4433 9

99 00 01 02 03 / 10 9 8 7 6 5 4 3 2 1

Typeset by The Florence Group, Stoodleigh, Devon
Printed and bound in Great Britain by Redwood Books, Trowbridge, Wiltshire

Contents

Acknowledgements   v

Chapter 1   **Studying A-level Politics**   1

             Key points   1
             The right approach   1
             Study skills   1
             You and the examiner   9
             What *not* to do   16

Chapter 2   **Basic principles of British government and politics**   17

             Key issues   17
             Topic notes   17
             Essays   29
             Guide to exercises   32
             References   36

Chapter 3   **Voters and elections**   37

             Key issues   37
             Topic notes   37
             Essays   52
             Guide to exercises   57
             References   60

Chapter 4   **Members of Parliament and political parties**   61

             Key issues   61
             Topic notes   61
             Essays   77
             Guide to exercises   81
             References   84

Chapter 5   **Parliament: House of Lords and House of Commons**   85

             Key issues   85
             Topic notes   85
             Essays   103
             Guide to exercises   107
             References   109

Chapter 6   **Executive: monarchy, Prime Minister and Cabinet**   110

             Key issues   110
             Topic notes   110
             Essays   124
             Guide to exercises   129
             References   130

Chapter 7	**The civil service**	**131**
	Key issues	131
	Topic notes	131
	Essays	142
	Guide to exercises	149
	References	150
Chapter 8	**Local goverment and devolution**	**151**
	Key issues	151
	Topic notes	151
	Essays	163
	Guide to exercises	168
	References	168
Chapter 9	**The legal system and civil rights**	**169**
	Key issues	169
	Topic notes	169
	Essays	186
	Guide to exercises	192
	References	193
Chapter 10	**Public opinion, pressure groups and the media**	**194**
	Key issues	194
	Topic notes	194
	Essays	205
	Guide to exercises	215
	References	216
Chapter 11	**The European Union**	**217**
	Key issues	217
	Topic notes	217
	Essays	230
	Guide to exercises	232
	References	233
Chapter 12	**British parliamentary democracy: A revision chapter**	**234**
	Some key issues	234
	Revision exercises	234
	Essays	238
	Guide to exercises	250
Chapter 13	**Countdown to the exam**	**256**
	Key points	256
	Before the exam	256
	In the exam	260
	After the exam	261
	Glossary	**263**
	Recommended reading	**269**
	Index	**271**

Acknowledgements

The author and publishers are grateful to the following organisations for permission to reproduce material:

Times Newspapers Ltd, News Group Newspapers Ltd, The Independent, The Week; The Conservative Party, The Labour Party, The Liberal Democrat Party; Press Association (Dave Cheskin, Sean Dempsey, Robert Paul, Stefan Rousseau, John Stillwell), Guardian Media Group plc (Martin Argley, Merrily Harpur), Icon Books Ltd; The Associated Examining Board, Joint Matriculation Board, London Examinations, a division of Edexcel Foundation, Oxford and Cambridge Local Examinations Council, University of Cambridge Local Examinations Syndicate, University of Oxford Local Examinations Syndicate.

Edexcel Foundation, London Examinations accepts no responsibility whatsoever for the accuracy or method of working in the answers given.

Every effort has been made to contact copyright holders, and we apologise if anyone has been overlooked.

Key words and phrases emboldened in the text are defined in the Glossary on pages 263–8.

1 Studying A-level Politics

KEY POINTS

▶ The right – and wrong – approaches
▶ Study skills:
  Note-taking
  Hints on factual learning
  Keeping a current events diary
▶ You and the examiner: Writing Politics essays
▶ What *not* to do

THE RIGHT APPROACH

Take the practical approach: you are not aiming to learn everything there is to know about Politics; you are aiming for a good A-level grade. The first is a matter of weighty learning and deep thought; the second is simply a matter of technique. As the examiners say repeatedly, it is seldom lack of knowledge which fails students, but poor application of good knowledge. What you should *not* be doing is passive reading, parrot-learning and irrelevant regurgitation of facts; the key to success is *active study* which focuses as much on technique as on content.

STUDY SKILLS

Focus on the exam from start to finish. Read your syllabus carefully and break it down into a list of topics; ensure that your course is covering them fully, and tick them off as you go.

Obtain as many past exam papers as you can – order them directly from the exam board if your teacher cannot supply them. Make sure that you are thoroughly familiar with the *current* 'rubric', i.e. that you are familiar with the total time allowed for each paper, the number of sections on each paper, the type and number of questions which you must do, etc.

The types of question may include *essays*, *stimulus response questions* (questions on and around a passage or piece of data) or *short answer questions*. Each requires a different technique and different timing; they may be worth different marks and feature in different sections of the exam, and your work schedule should allow for this. The different techniques and timing are simply a matter of frequent practice, but it is clearly not enough just to 'learn a topic'.

If your teacher is not already doing this for you, go through every past paper after each topic that you do, and list every past question on that topic. Go through the list carefully and critically; look at the 'angle' of each question. You will find that there are only four or five angles on every topic. Look at the examples below from the London Board.

Past questions on the Prime Minister and Cabinet

(from the London Board: A-level Government and Politics, Paper 1)

Jan. 1999: Stimulus response question
Study the source material below and then answer questions (a), (b) and (c).

SOURCE A

"The Cabinet"
'The Cabinet is not a place where decisions can be formulated. It's bound to be a place where decisions that have been formulated by smaller groups, maybe of ministers and party people together, or maybe parliamentary groups outside, and then put to ministers or maybe the Prime Minister and her advisers quite separately, are then tested and validated and argued about.'

(Source: Peter Hennessy, The Cabinet, *Blackwell, 1986)*

SOURCE B

Cabinet Changes, 1990
'The Chief Whip came in. He argued strongly that William Waldegrave – who was on the left of the Party – should join the Cabinet. I had never kept talented people out of my Cabinets just because they were not of my way of thinking, and I was not going to start even now. I asked him to take on the Department of Health.

But I still wanted a new face at Education, where John MacGregor's limitations as a public spokesman were costing us dear in an area of great importance. So I appointed Ken Clarke – again not someone on my wing of the Party, but an energetic and persuasive bruiser, very useful in a brawl or an election. John MacGregor I moved to Leader of the House. The appointments were well received. My objective of uniting the Party seemed to be succeeding.'

(Adapted from: Margaret Thatcher, The Downing Street Years, *Harper Collins, 1993)*

> **SOURCE C**
>
> **Newspaper headlines on Labour's New Cabinet, May 1997**
> 'Women swell Cabinet team'
> 'The Prime Minister puts his old team on new trial'
> 'Blair has been constrained in his choices'
>
> *(Source: The Times, 5 May 1997)*

(a) With reference to the sources, outline the role of the Cabinet.

(b) With reference to the sources, what factors do Prime Ministers take into account when constructing their Cabinets?

(c) To what extent does collective cabinet government operate in the UK?

June 1998: Essay
'Prime Ministerial power is a myth.' Discuss.

Jan. 1998: Essay
'The Prime Minister has to all intents and purposes turned into a President.' Discuss.

June 1997: Short answer question
Outline the functions of the Prime Minister.

Jan. 1997: Stimulus response question
Study the following diagram and then answer questions (a) to (c).

> **A Model of Prime Ministerial Power**
>
> **External factors**
> for example, (a) Economic conditions
> (b) Policy successes/failures
> (c) International factors
> (d) Level of popular support
> (e) Level of Parliamentary support
>
> **Prime Minister's resources**
> for example, (a) Patronage
> (b) Cabinet
> (c) PM's Office/Cabinet Office
> (d) Personal authority
> (e) Media
>
> **Minister's resources**
> (a) Personal authority/political support
> (b) Department/civil servants
> (c) Knowledge
> (d) Links with outside bodies
> (e) Policy successes
>
> *(Adapted from: M.J. Smith, 'Reassessing Mrs Thatcher's Resignation', in Politics Review, Vol. 3, No. 4, 1994, Philip Allan Publishers)*

(a) With reference to the diagram, explain the resources available to a Prime Minister.

(b) With reference to the diagram, explain the resources available to a minister.

(c) How can changing circumstances affect the power of the Prime Minister?

June 1996: Essay

'The Cabinet has increasingly become a reporting and reviewing body, rather than a decision-taker.' Discuss.

Jan. 1996: Essay

To what extent is British government becoming presidential?

June 1995: Stimulus response question

Study the following extract and then answer questions (a) to (c).

> ### The Scott Inquiry
>
> 'The inquiry was told that the guidelines limiting defence-related exports to Iran and Iraq were originally drawn up in late 1984 but ministers and civil servants decided not to announce them publicly in a high profile way, opting instead to let them "trickle out". They were finally made public after a parliamentary question in October 1985. Lady Thatcher conceded: "It might have been better if we had published earlier".
>
> Despite asking to be kept informed of "all relevant decisions", Lady Thatcher said she was never told formally that the guidelines were subsequently revised in 1988 . . . "It may have been mentioned to me by one of my secretaries. I have no recollection if it was . . . I had 19 departments of government and 83 ministers . . . if I had seen every copy of every minute when I was in government I would have been in a snowstorm" . . . She said that she only got involved if policy matters arose. Administrative details did not concern her. Her ministers only bothered her with the "big issues".'
>
> *(Adapted from:* The Independent, *9 December 1993)*

(a) Use the extract to illustrate the limitations on the power of the Prime Minister.

(b) What does the extract tell us about 'responsible government' in Britain?

(c) How could ministers and civil servants be made more accountable?

Jan. 1995: Essay

Explain the nature of the relationship between Prime Ministers and their parties.

June 1994: Essay

Discuss the relationship between the office of Prime Minister and Parliament.

When you come to revise each topic, look for relevant points on key 'angles' as you re-read your material, and re-note that topic under the key headings. This will help to ensure relevance in your essay answers, rather than writing 'all you know about . . . '.

RELEVANCE IS ALL

London ▶

GOOD, honest competence characterised the quality of work submitted for this paper, with a few really weak candidates but also a limited number of outstanding answers. Many candidates displayed up-to-date political knowledge but too many candidates were dependent on 'current affairs' information, offering too little depth in their answers. As usual, the main weaknesses were a failure to read and accurately interpret the questions, and time wasted on irrelevancies and repetition. Too many candidates still seem unable to integrate political concepts with political institutions. The principal regional differences of Scotland, Wales and Northern Ireland is an area of the syllabus which appears to cause some difficulty, as also is order and disorder. The overall standard of candidates' approaches to the questions improved significantly again this year, although the importance of including examples to gain extra credit in Question 1 still needs to be stressed.

Examiners' comments from subject reports

The examiners' subject reports contain some useful hints on how to improve your marks in the exam – look at these reports.

THE best candidates...answered questions explicitly, backed up their arguments with appropriate, well-selected evidence and reached logical, sustainable conclusions. There was evidence of self-disciplined study, wide reading, hard work, good understanding and genuine interest.

As always, though, a significant minority of candidates gained marks which were probably below their potential...

(a) Handwriting, spelling and syntax presented a significant problem. If an examiner cannot read or understand a sentence, the candidate will not gain the marks that might otherwise have been awarded. Some candidates did not seem to understand the idea of paragraphs...Where a line had been left blank between paragraphs, this made the whole page more 'readable'...

(b) Many candidates seemed to have great difficulty allocating their time evenly across the four questions...

(c) More candidates than usual seemed to try to write all they knew on a chosen topic without paying attention to the specific requirements of the question...

(d) Candidates need to be more ready to embrace policy developments and current debates...For example...John Prescott's transport policy...the Jenkins Commission...or the intention to incorporate the European Convention on Human Rights into UK law...

(e) Some quite strong answers produced pertinent and sophisticated answers to the first part of a question but then largely ignored the second part...

(f) Examiners also noted a potentially serious deterioration in the conceptual awareness of candidates...e.g. the terms 'bipartisan'...'gridlock'...'accountable'...'power', 'authority'.

◀ AEB

THE overall impression of this year's entry is a favourable one. If anything the general standard was higher than in previous years and the recent improvement in answers to questions in Section A was sustained. Common and traditional faults, however were again frequently in evidence and prevented many candidates from deploying their often considerable knowledge of the subject to maximum effect.

It is frequently the case that, in answering questions, candidates take too much for granted. Answers to Q.2, for example, were sometimes seriously weakened by a failure to define an interest group. Similarly, it is difficult to argue rigorously and coherently about the role of an M.P. (Q.6) without explicit consideration of the distinction between a delegate and a representative. Again a full and critical discussion of Q.9(b) on the democratic credentials of the authors of the *The Federalist* requires some investigation of the concept of democracy. Its meaning ought not to be assumed, since so much hinges on it. An argument, for example, which is informed by a concept of totalitarian democracy will be very different from one which is informed by a concept of liberal or constitutional democracy.

One very obvious and wholly predictable fault is the failure of candidates to focus clearly and consistently on the specific issue raised by a question. Often Ideally that issue should structure the argument from beginning to end. Often candidates either raise the issue immediately only to lose sight of it within the first page of the answer or greatly delay its introduction. In either case the argument inevitably loses much of its impact. This fault was evident, for example, in many answers to Q.11(a) on the relation between the Bourgeoisie and Proletariat. A general summary of Marx's though, however competently ...could not be regarded as an adequate response to the question. ...many well informed answers to Q.9(b) allowed the specific issue of ...become submerged in a general discussion of the problem of ...he neglect of the question is partial rather than total, as ...answers to Q.11(b) on the state as capitalist machine ...phrase 'no matter what its form'.

Oxford and Cambridge ▶

THERE were some outstanding answers on this paper. However, more often than in previous years, many candidates seemed to be relying on question-spotting and prepared answers. This was reflected in lower marks on some questions where good but irrelevant material was included and little, if any attempt, made to adapt material to the question as asked. This was particularly clear in answers to three questions; on Cabinet government; on the two/three/multi-party system in Britain; and on local government. Conversely, two questions which required thought elicited some interesting and thoughtful answers: those concerned, firstly, the relative powers of resistance to central government enjoyed by local government and Parliament and, secondly, the contribution of civil servants, backbenchers, and judges to the law-making process. Overall the standard was pleasing and this was also reflected in some good performances by S-level candidates. The fact that the examination took place on the day of the election did not seem to have unduly influenced candidates – with the exception of those who had presumably made a case study of the campaign and wished to employ this material even when it was irrelevant.

◀ Cambridge

Note-taking

Do take brill notes throughout your course, from your reading and class discussions. Brill notes are:

▶ **b**rief

▶ **r**elevant

▶ **i**temised and well-organised

▶ **l**aid-out clearly

▶ **l**egible.

> Do not note as you read.
>
> Read a whole section first; re-read and mark key points; then note them in 'potted' form.

Organise your notes in ring-binder files with section dividers.

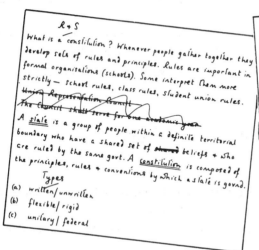

▲ *Bad notes*   ▲ *Good notes*

Ten hints on factual learning

1 Write your own revision 'quizzes' on key definitions, events, dates, issues, examples, quotes and names.

2 Write lists – quotes on the left and names on the right, or events on the left and dates on the right, etc. – so that you can cover one side with a sheet of paper and reveal the answer once you have tested yourself.

3 Write lists and stick them on mirrors.

4 Photocopy sheets of information with blanked out sections for self-testing on names, dates and examples.

5 Keep a box file of small index cards with key concepts and definitions to revise on the bus or in the bath (don't drop them!).

6 Draw picture diagrams showing 'factors influencing . . . (for example, policy-making)' or 'methods used by . . . (for example, pressure groups)'.

7 Work with a friend doing the same subject – test each other.

8 Make up sentences using the initials of key names as the first letter of each word (the more silly or rude the sentence, the more memorable).

9 Tape key facts and play them back to yourself on your portable stereo Walkperson.

10 Try putting them to music!

Keeping a current events diary

▶ Use a good-sized notebook.

▶ On a daily basis, take brief notes from TV news and documentaries, and from the quality press. Always note the source and date.

▶ You may want to organise it under topic headings for easy revision: PM/pressure groups/Parliament/EU, etc.

▶ Concentrate on relevant events and issues; if your exam is purely on British politics, skip the foreign news items.

▶ Include not only key facts, but arguments and opinions too, with names and sources.

▶ Feel free to add your own comments and opinions on events and arguments – it helps you to remember them, it makes your diary more interesting to re-read during revision, and it clarifies your own ideas for essay-writing.

▶ If you include newspaper cuttings, mark the key points in the margin for easy re-reading and revision – do not just stick them in unmarked (or unread!).

▶ Do not save all the newspapers up for a week before going through them – it can ruin your Sundays!

See the example overleaf.

March 1999

Elizabeth Dole considering standing
for US presidency (vs George W. Bush)

80% increase in govt. press releases
(18,300) since Major's admin. -
reinforces spin-obsessed image of
lab. govt.

Creation of Northern Ireland
executive postponed till Good Friday
because of deadlock over
decommissioning.
Hardline republican plot to kill
Gerry Adams due to 'betrayal'.

Michael Howard to stand down from
Shadow Cab. in next reshuffle. May
imply Cons. pessimism about the next
election.

Hague tells party to focus on 'kitchen table' politics -
bread and butter issues - which strike a chord with voters,
to admit past mistakes and look forward.

Lab MP Mohammed Sarwar acquitted of fraud in '97 election;
other charges still pending.

BUDGET AT A GLANCE

- 10p tax rate on first £1,500 next month
- 1p off basic income tax rate, down to 22p from April 2000
- New children's tax credit to replace married couple's allowance
- Mortgage interest relief (Miras) abolished from April 2000
- Pensioners' winter allowance up from £20 to £100
- Cut of £55 in excise duty for cars with engines below 1,100 cc
- New 10p corporation tax rate for small firms
- Share ownership scheme for workers to take stake in their firms
- £60-a-week credit for over-50s moving off welfare into jobs
- New energy tax on business from April 2001
- Extra £1.1 billion for schools,
- Stamp duty up 0.5 per cent on properties over £250,000
- Duty on spirits, beer and wine frozen
- Cigarettes up 17.5p, cigars by 7.5p
- 4.25p on litre of unleaded petrol, 3.79p on unleaded and 6.14p on diesel
- 900,000 taken out of national insurance, those earning over £26,000 to pay more
- New research and development tax credit for small businesses
- Child benefit up to £15 for the first child, £10 for others, from April 2000
- Company car tax reform to remove incentive to increase mileage

Hot praise

The Chancellor was praised by the Tory leader's mother, who welcomed his £80 rise in winter fuel payments for pensioners. Stella Hague, 71, whose Yorkshire home has gas central heating, said: 'It is very nice to have. The £100 will be very acceptable.'

Met. Commissioner Sir Paul Condon questioned by Commons Home Affairs select committee
over Macpherson report on Stephen Lawrence case - says recommendation of criminal
offence of racial language in private homes would be unworkable.

Law lords rule - despite public order laws - that 1995 Stonehenge ('85 anniversary)
protesters had right to protest on public highway (if not obstructive); so positive
legal right to protest for first time - case law. Lord Irvine (Lord Chancellor) was
the leading judge.

▲ *An example page from a current events diary*

YOU AND THE EXAMINER

Writing politics essays

ANSWER THE TITLE, NOT JUST THE TOPIC

The essay question

▶ *Answer the question, the whole question and nothing but the question*. This is the most common source of failure among students. Read the question, slowly and carefully, three times. Underline or circle all key words and phrases, for example:

To what extent does Britain still have a system of Cabinet government?

This question does not ask, 'Write down everything you know about Cabinet'. Unasked-for information will gain no extra marks, however accurate it may be.

▶ Do not parrot-learn 'model answers', or you may answer the question you wanted to get rather than the one you were asked.

▶ Practise writing timed essays as much as possible before the exam.

▶ Learn to assess your own strengths and weaknesses, and make a concentrated effort to eliminate those weaknesses one by one.

The essay plan

▶ Writing an essay plan may feel unduly time-consuming, but – second only to reading the question carefully – it is the most important part of the whole process.

▶ Divide the essay up into appropriate sections; this helps to plan the timing of the essay as well as the content. It is especially necessary if the essay title is divided into parts – (a) and (b) – because the answer *must* be similarly divided. If total marks are shown for each part of a question, obviously use them as a guide to the relative timing and length of each section.

▶ Write a very brief skeleton outline of the main headings and sub-headings for each section; then if necessary re-arrange them in logical order – *structure* is as important as *content*.

▶ Leave spaces to add to the plan as new points come to mind.

▶ Feel free to question the question, for example, to point out and discuss ambiguities in the wording or examine critically any assumptions made in the title. If there is more than one possible interpretation of the title, plan to answer all angles.

▶ If you consult the plan frequently and tick off each point as you go, it will help you in writing the essay; and it will also enable the examiner to see what you intended to say if your actual essay is unfinished or goes astray.

▶ Be sure that you have a clear and explicit conclusion before you start the essay; and structure the essay accordingly – always put your own case last.

▶ Head it 'Essay plan' or 'Rough work' and put a line under it before you begin your essay.

Sample essay plan

Q? To what extent does Britain still have a system of Cabinet government?

A✓ *Intro*: —— Cab. govt. – def . . . coll. resp . . .

Hist: —— 'Still' – implies did have: Bagehot

Case for: —— Still now – Jones, St John Stevas; constraints on PM: party, hire/fire (Macmillan), econ., EU and other internat. insts. and events, media, pressure groups, domestic events, personality (Major), need for authority . . . Thatcher's forced resignation by colleagues . . .

Case against: —— 'PM govt': Crossman, Mackintosh, Benn, Heseltine . . . PM's powers of patronage, etc. (Blair and Gus MacDonald); Cab. committees (Hennessy 'engine room'), PM Office/Cabinet Office, PM policies and examples: Falklands, GCHQ, Libyan bombing, poll tax, GLC, Gulf War, Formula One . . . Blair's 'control freakery' and 'presidentialism' . . .

Not new: Attlee quote . . . Callaghan/Wilson 'nukes' . . .

Other constraints on Cab.: EU, other internat. bodies and events, party, media, pressure groups, domestic events . . . examples . . .

Conc: —— To some extent but less now. Not pure PM or Cab. govt: depends on PM, circumstances, economy, majority, war/peace, external constraints . . . 'Central exec. territory' (Madgwick)

Not dem./accountable enough . . .

Reforms: PM powers in law (Benn), transfer patronage to Commons, more min. advisers (Kinnock)

The essay

▶ Waffly introductions are pointless – literally – and give the examiner a bad first impression. A useful way to introduce the essay is to define key terms – learn the precise definitions of political terms and concepts. A 'constitution' is not 'the laws of a country'. Imprecise definitions are usually plain wrong – at best they will lose marks, and at worst they will put you off course for the whole essay. Where necessary, give your interpretation(s) of the title in the introduction. Do not give your conclusion in the introduction – reserve it for the end.

✗ 'Before answering this title we must first consider what is meant by the key concepts in the title, such as Cabinet government, and who actually says we do still have cabinet government, and who says we don't and why. I would agree with critics that we have Prime Ministerial government.'

> 'Cabinet government means policy-making and responsibility by all senior minis-
> ters as a collective body, with the Prime Minister *primus inter pares*. The word
> "still" in the title implies that Britain used to have Cabinet government – but this
> is debatable, as we shall see.'

▶ Every paragraph in the essay should refer explicitly to (some part of) the title, using the wording of the title.

▶ Use structure and language (paragraphs and wording) so that each point is clearly made.

▶ Think out each sentence before you write it to avoid messy errors or ambiguities.

▶ Make your point once, clearly, then move on to the next. Avoid repetition – it gains no extra marks and wastes valuable time – yours and the examiner's. A good, concise answer will gain more marks than a long rambling one.

▶ Use the correct terminology – 'constitutional monarchy' rather than 'a Queen who can't actually do much', etc. Show that you know your subject.

▶ Use concrete evidence and examples to illustrate every general point made, so that the examiner knows that you understand what you are saying and have not just parrot-learnt a list of notes.

▶ Mere assertion, without factual evidence, gains no marks.

▶ Whenever possible make your examples topical rather than out-dated or hypothetical – this obviously means keeping abreast of current political events.

▶ Avoid slang, colloquialism and an over-personal approach. (Write 'Public opinion polls indicate that the monarchy is a popular institution' rather than 'I think the Queen is great'.)

▶ Style should be ABCD – **a**ccurate, **b**rief, **c**lear and **d**irect.

▶ Consult your essay plan frequently and review your time periodically throughout the essay. Devote an appropriate amount of time to each section of the essay to give a balanced answer. You should always put your own case last – and do not leave less time for it than the case you have rejected.

▶ Write legibly and neatly. The examiner cannot give you credit for something she or he cannot read, and will not appreciate having to struggle to understand your work (which may be script number 149 on the pile).

▶ Spell political terms and names correctly; if you are unsure of any, drill them until you are sure. Any student of Politics who cannot spell such words as *sovereignty*, *independence*, *committee*, *bureaucracy* or *biased* evidently has not done enough reading and does not know the subject.

Spellcheck

allege	Cranborne	hierarchy
amendment	criticism	ideological
argument	Crossman	independent
Attlee	deferential	influential
Bagehot	deterrent	irrelevant
bourgeois	dissension	Irvine
Brittan	eligible	libel
by-election	Falklands	manifesto
coercion	fulfil	precedent
commissioner	Gaitskell	privilege
consensus	Gilmour	toe the line

▶ Re-read the title before you write your concluding paragraph. The conclusion must explicitly answer every part of the title, using the precise wording of the title, and it should follow logically and predictably from the structure of the essay.

▶ If you run out of time, give a skeleton answer, i.e. a full and detailed answer, with evidence and conclusion, in note form.

▶ Do not write three paragraphs and 'Sorry, ran out of time' – you will probably get three marks. Never omit any questions – remember that no answer at all means no marks at all.

▶ A further point to remember is that first marks are easier to earn than last marks, i.e. it is harder to increase the value of an answer from, say, 12 to 15 marks than to earn the first 5 marks on the next question.

▶ Finally, always try to allow time to read over your work – often a painful process, but worthwhile. Careless errors like omitting a 'not' can be crucial. And if, in the exam, you do finish early, do read over your work – do not sit staring into space and do not leave early.

Common essay formats

'Quote – discuss'

Q? 'Local democracy is now dead.' Discuss.

(London, June 1998, Paper 1)

Q? 'In theory monarchy is indefensible in modern government; in practice no one has invented a better system.' Discuss.

(Oxford, Summer 1986, Paper 1)

This kind of question is asking, 'Do you agree with this contentious statement wholly, partially or not at all? Weigh up the arguments and evidence for each side of the case(s), and say in conclusion which view(s) you support and why'.

Evaluation of every part of the title statement is required, based on sound reasoning and evidence. Note that you can agree with one part of the statement and disagree with another part. If it is famous quotation, the first sentence of the essay should say who said it. Otherwise, it may express a clear political or philosophical viewpoint, for example, socialist, conservative, anti-'PM government', etc.; point this out. If the statement is ambiguous, point this out explicitly and say in the introduction, 'I shall consider each interpretation in turn'.

'Should . . . ?'

Q? Should party leaders respond more to their parties or to the voters who might support them?

(Oxford, Summer 1989, Paper 1)

Q? Should there be fixed-term Parliaments?

(London, Specimen Paper, 1997, Paper 2)

This type of question requires a balanced evaluation of both sides of the argument, based on topical evidence, coming down explicitly on one side in conclusion – yes or no.

'Compare and contrast'

Q? Compare and contrast the powers exercised by British Prime Ministers since 1976.

(Oxford and Cambridge, June 1997, Paper 1)

Q? Compare and contrast the contributions of the Commons and Lords to the operation of parliamentary government.

(Cambridge, June 1989, Paper 1)

These questions require direct and explicit comparison of similarities and contrasting of differences. Every paragraph (or two paragraphs) should link both items. If you write half of the essay on one, and half of the essay on the other, with no linkage, you will not have answered the question, and you will fail outright (no matter how accurate the factual content).

The conclusion should say whether, on balance, there are more similarities or contrasts.

'State a case for and a case against'

Q? State (a) a case for and (b) a case against the introduction of a Bill of Rights.

(London, Jan. 1996, Paper 1)

Q? Make a case for the activities of pressure groups, and a case against them.

(London, Jan. 1981, Paper 1)

Questions like these require 'empathy' – the ability to argue either side of a case persuasively. The answer must be balanced. It can be done either point-for-point, for and against in successive paragraphs (unless (a)/(b) essay structure); or all points for, then all points against (or vice-versa) in two separate halves.

The conclusion should say whether, on balance, the case for or against is stronger and why. Put your own case last throughout the essay, whichever format you adopt.

'Is Z X or Y?'

Q? Is it the function of the media to reflect public opinion or to form it?

(Oxford and Cambridge, July 1984, Paper 0)

Q? Are senior civil servants too powerful, or are they too pliable?

(London, June 1984, Paper 1)

There are four possible answers:

► Z is only X
► Z is only Y
► Z is both X and Y
► Z is neither X nor Y.

You must reach one of these four conclusions.

You could point out in the introduction that the title implies either/or, but that this is not necessarily so – could be both or neither.

Structure:

► First, is it X, yes or no . . .

► Then, is it Y, yes or no . . .

► Conclusion . . .

'Does A lead to B?'

Q? Does nationalism lead to racialism?

(London, June 1978, Paper 3)

Q? Examine the view that freedom consists in the silence of the law.

(Oxford and Cambridge, July 1980, Paper 1)

Consider:

► A → B

► B → A

► A alone (leading to factors other than B)

► B alone (stemming from factors other than A).

The conclusion is usually 'Sometimes – not always'.

'If . . . then . . . ?'/'Since . . . then . . . '

Q? 'If the quality of work of departmental select committees is maintained, their influence is bound to increase.' Is it?

(Oxford, Summer 1989, Paper 1)

Q? 'Since one of its consequences is to weaken the link between the government and the electorate, a system of proportional representation is less rather than more democratic.' Discuss.

(Oxford and Cambridge, July 1986, Paper 1)

Both parts of the title require critical scrutiny.

Structure:

► First part of title: case for/against (or vice versa) – conclusion, true or not.

► Second part: case for/against, and does it follow from first part or not – conclusion, yes or no.

► In final paragraph, explicitly conclude on both parts of the question, and say whether one does or does not always follow from the other.

'To what extent/how far/how true is it to say . . . ?'

To what extent do the results of recent elections support the case for electoral reform in Britain?

(Oxford and Cambridge, June 1997, Paper 1)

Q? How effective is Parliament in controlling the executive?

(London, Jan. 1997, Paper 1)

Answer is invariably 'To some extent . . . '.

Structure:

▶ First, outline how far it is the case and why, with evidence . . .

▶ Then, how far it is not the case and why, with evidence . . .

▶ Summary conclusion: 'It is true to the extent that . . . but not to the extent that . . .' – be explicit and concrete.

Key words in essay titles

In essence, some key words in essay titles seek mere description; others require critical evaluation.

Descriptive key words	**Evaluative key words**
Define	Discuss
Outline	Examine
Describe	Comment on
Explain	Evaluate
Give an account of	Account for
Compare	Compare and contrast
Illustrate	Explore
Enumerate	Analyse
List	Assess
State	Criticise
Summarise	Interpret
	Justify
	Relate
	Review

▶ Obviously, A-level questions usually seek evaluation rather than mere description; but often they are combined: 'Describe and account for . . . ', 'Define and discuss . . . ', 'Explain and comment on . . . '.

▶ If you are short of time for your final question in the exam, it might be a good idea to seek out a descriptive title; they tend to be shorter or at least simpler than evaluative titles.

▶ If you are short of time on any evaluative question, do not waste time on a lengthy descriptive introduction. Go straight to the core of the question – arguments and evidence for and against – and give an explicit conclusion to the title asked.

▶ Some evaluation in answer to a descriptive question will always gain extra credit; mere description in answer to an evaluative question will probably fail.

Examiners are human too

Put yourself in the place of the examiners: try marking your own (or friends') scripts – pretending that you have already marked a couple of hundred, that it is hot and sunny outside, that you still have shopping to do or next term's teaching to prepare and that you are only human! Marks will be awarded if:

▶ the script is legible

▶ it is clear what section of what question you are answering

▶ the answer bears some relation to the examiners' marking scheme. ('In checking the marking scheme care is taken to ensure that the anticipated answers match the questions and that account has been taken of acceptable different answers. Marks are not allocated to answers which are not relevant to, or required by, a question.' AEB)

▶ the structure is logical

▶ arguments are backed up with evidence

▶ the facts are relevant and accurate

▶ the wording is clear and concise

▶ the title is explicitly addressed throughout

▶ the conclusion answers the question asked.

WHAT NOT TO DO

Do not:

▶ overwork

▶ underwork

▶ parrot-learn

▶ try 'topic-spotting' or 'question-spotting'

▶ cheat at patience, for example, announcing loudly to the family, 'Well, I'm off to do some work now', then retreating to your room to read Jeffrey Archer

▶ try last-minute cramming, or think 'It'll be all right on the day' – it will not, without some help from you.

2 Basic principles of British government and politics

KEY ISSUES

▶ The concept of democracy
Power and authority
What is liberal democracy?
The nature and extent of democracy in Britain
Pluralist, elitist and Marxist theories
▶ The British constitution: principles and practice
Unconstitutional and anti-constitutional activity
British parliamentary government
Parliamentary sovereignty and its limits
The power of the executive – elective dictatorship?

TOPIC NOTES

Key facts and concepts

A **state** is an independent entity with ultimate political power – **sovereignty** – over all the individuals and groups within its territorial boundaries. It is made up of all the formal institutions of political power such as the Crown, legislature, executive, judiciary, army and sometimes the Church. It has a legal monopoly on the use of violence, but will often use consensus – agreement – as well as **coercion** – force – to keep order.

The **government** is the agent of the state; it enforces the rulings of the state and acts under its authority. Whereas the state is said to be a permanent, abstract entity (for example, the Crown), the people and the institutions of government come and go (for example, the monarch).

Society is the body of people within and under the power of the state – both individuals and informal power bodies, such as pressure groups.

A **nation** is a group of people who share a sense of common culture, based on common ties of language, religion, race, territory and/or history. One state may embrace many nations: for example, the Scots, Irish, Welsh and English in the United Kingdom all have a distinct sense of nationhood; or one nation may be spread across many states: for example, the Jews were a nation without a state until the creation of Israel in 1948.

The concept of democracy

Like most countries, Britain claims to be a democracy. Democracy – from the Greek *demos* and *kratos* – literally means 'people power', or self-government of the people, by the people, for the people. Britain is not, therefore, a direct democracy in the full sense of the term. Britain claims to be an indirect or representative democracy. This involves the election by qualified citizens of representatives who govern over, and on behalf of, the people. All representative democracy therefore entails **oligarchy** or **elitism**: rule by the few.

Nevertheless, all modern states – whatever their type of economic or political system – have some valid claim to call themselves democratic if they contain elements of one or more of the following:

▶ *people-power*, for example, referenda, effective pressure groups, trade unions, etc.

▶ *participation*, for example, through voting, standing for political office, political meetings, demonstrations, etc.

▶ *representation* – this can mean different things:

  – The political power-holders may carry out the views and *wishes* of the voters. If they act as instructed by the voters they are called delegates. This view of representation is associated with the radical French philosopher Jean-Jacques Rousseau (1712–78), and applies within many trade unions. It does not apply to British MPs

  – The political power-holders may act in what they see as the best *interests* of the voters. This weaker view of representation is associated with the British conservative Edmund Burke (1729–97). It may apply to British MPs, but they are also closely tied to their parties

  – The political power-holders may be *typical* of the voters in terms of social background, for example, the same proportions of women, ethnic minorities, young people, etc. British MPs are now more representative of the wider public in this sense than ever before, but are still more conspicuous for their a-typicality

▶ *responsibility* – this, too, can mean different things:

  – The main interpretation of **responsible government** is *accountable or answerable* for its actions, ultimately to the voters

  – Responsible government may also mean wise and sound government in the best *interests* of the voters, i.e. the same as the second point under representation, above.

▶ *consent* – most modern states, even some dictatorships and military juntas, rest on the general agreement of the people that the governors have the right to govern (even if many people do not agree with what they are doing).

Power and authority

A system of government without this minimum criterion of consent rests solely on **power**: the ability to make people do things by the threat or use of punishment, force or violence. Such a system cannot claim to be democratic. Most political systems, however, rest on a substantial degree of **authority**: the ability to make people do things because they think the power holders have that right. Authority involves legitimate power based on consent, respect and support. It is the basis of any democracy. It may derive from election, but also from tradition, personal popularity (**charisma**), efficiency, or other sources.

What is liberal democracy?

Representative democracies take many forms: one-, two- or multi-party systems, etc. Britain, like the United States and most European countries, claims to be a **liberal democracy**. This is a representative system embodying the concepts of diversity, choice and individual **rights** and freedoms (as opposed to collective equality or mass participation). It involves the following principles.

▶ *Pluralism*: diverse centres of economic and political power; thus private ownership in the economy and two or more parties in the political system, together with many pressure groups. This should generate competition and hence freedom of choice and effective representation of different views and interests.

▶ *Constitutionalism*: government within clear and enforceable rules which set limits to political power.

▶ *Limited government*: checks and constraints by various other bodies on the power of government, for example, the courts and pressure groups, to safeguard individual liberties.

▶ *Open government*: non-secretive government, to ensure that government is representative and accountable to the people.

▶ *The **rule of law***: a fair, just and impartial legal system which should include legal equality and an independent judiciary.

▶ *Civil rights* and *liberties*: essential freedoms, preferably enshrined in **law**.

The nature and extent of democracy in Britain

Supporters of Western liberal democracy, such as Schumpeter and Dahl, argue that any other system is undemocratic. However, many essay questions ask how far the above principles apply in the practice of British government and politics. Critics of the system would point, for example, to:

▶ the high concentrations of wealth, income and economic power

▶ the election of strong, single-party governments with a minority of votes cast

▶ the lack of effective opportunities for minority parties and independents in the British electoral system

▶ the lack of effective power of many pressure groups, and most individuals, in politics, work, education, etc.

▶ the lack of balanced debate and discussion about alternative political ideas, for example, **communism**, **fascism**, **anarchism**

▶ the lack of separation of powers in Britain between legislature, executive and judiciary

▶ the centralisation of government, and relative weakness of Parliament, opposition, the courts and local government

▶ the exceptional secrecy of British government

▶ alleged injustices in the legal system, ranging from expense of litigation for ordinary citizens to social and political **bias**

▶ the lack of guaranteed civil liberties in law, together with with legal constraints on free speech, movement, assembly, protest, etc.

▶ the concentration of media ownership and control

▶ the impact of professional lobbying on politicians and civil servants

▶ international constraints and controls – EU, NATO, IMF, etc.

Pluralist, elitist and Marxist theories

The strongest critics of British liberal democracy fall into three main camps:

▶ *radical liberals*, for example Bottomore and Hain, who argue that the system needs substantial reform to make it more liberal and democratic. They have long advocated, for example, a written constitution, Bill of Rights, devolution, freedom of information, and the reform of legislation on secrecy, terrorism and police powers. The 1997 Labour government has now enacted some of these reforms

▶ *classical or single elitists*, for example, Pareto and Mosca in the 1920s and Guttsman in the 1960s. They argue that all effective political power is concentrated in the hands of a single self-serving elite, comprising: the leaders of the main political parties, the government, MPs and peers, top civil servants, judges, police, church and military leaders, businessmen, academics and scientists and a few key pressure group leaders. Guttsman estimated that the British **political elite** totals around 11,000 people, all of whom, regardless of party label, share a common interest in preserving the existing power structure. Single elitists are pessimistic about the prospects for change

▶ *radical socialists and Marxists,* such as Miliband. They argue that the present power structure and political system serve and protect the interests of a dominant economic **class** (as opposed to a political elite), while depriving the majority of effective

economic or political power. They also apply their critique to all of the major political parties. They believe, however, that fundamental and progressive economic and political change will happen, and that minor reforms to the system merely prop it up temporarily.

Short answer questions

Short answer questions are a compulsory part of some examinations, for example, on the London Board, and they are a useful revision exercise even if they are not a feature of your particular examination. On the London Board they require around ten minutes' worth of concise, precise, relevant, factual definition, detail and example. They should not be miniature essays. Aim for maximum information in the minimum space; avoid waffle, repetition or messy errors. Think before you write; quality is more important than quantity.

Short answers are a valuable aid to essay revision because they help you to learn precise terms, definitions and facts, and to express them briefly and clearly.

Sample short answer question

Q? Distinguish between two different types of democracy.

(London, June 1989, Paper 3, part (a) of question (x))

A✓ *Good answer:*

In a direct democracy, political decisions are made by all qualified citizens, as in the ancient Greek city-states. However, even there, women and slaves were not allowed to participate; and it is often argued that this system is not feasible in large modern states. Therefore most societies today have a system of indirect or representative democracy, where representatives are elected to govern on behalf of voters. This may be pluralist (for example, Britain) or single-party (for example, former USSR), but is inevitably oligarchic or elitist.

Bad answer:

Direct democracy is where people do it themselves, whereas with indirect democracy other people do it for them, which isn't really democratic at all.

Bad answer:

In direct democracy, everyone votes for everything, like in ancient Greece, though actually women and slaves didn't, so it wasn't really very democratic, and anyway it's not possible in big, complicated societies, whereas in Greece it was only in small cities, so it doesn't really happen now except in some African tribes, and referenda like on the EU in 1975 are a bit like direct democracy. Instead voters vote for representatives to represent them, i.e. indirect, usually in a party system like Britain's two-party system which is called pluralist, or the old Soviet Union's one-party system which isn't democratic anyway, but anyway only a few people are doing the ruling, which is oligarchy.

---

1 Say why the above examples are good or bad. If you were the examiner, how many marks (out of 10) would you give to each?

More sample short answer questions and answers

Q? Distinguish between 'power' and 'authority'.

A✓ Power is the ability to dictate others' behaviour through sanctions or coercion. Authority is the ability to shape others' behaviour through consent, respect and support, i.e. authority is rightful, legitimate power, and a feature of representative democracy. The nineteenth-century German sociologist Max Weber distinguished three types of authority: traditional (for example, House of Lords), charismatic (for example, Churchill) and legal-rational (for example, MPs). Power may exist without authority (tyranny), or authority without much power (for example, the British monarch). Authority tends to generate power, but power may generate authority through indoctrination. Conversely, misjudgment or misuse of power may lose authority, for example, Thatcher's downfall in 1990. In a democracy, power should rest on authority.

Q? What is meant by 'pluralism'?

A✓ A pluralist society is one with a diffusion of power among many divergent groups. Political pluralism implies a multi-party system and competing pressure groups, and economic pluralism implies competing centres of ownership and control. Genuine pluralism requires a wide distribution of property and wealth, a distinction between the roles of government, society and individual, and checks and balances between the different sources of power. Many writers, especially Marxists – for example, Miliband – question the extent to which power in 'liberal democracies' like Britain is really diffused.

---

2 Write short answers to the following questions (simulated examples).

a) (i) Distinguish between 'the state' and 'the government'.

(ii) What is the 'organic' theory of the state?

b) (i) Define the concept of 'a political elite'.

(ii) Explain the theory of single elitism.

c) (i) Distinguish between a delegate and a representative.

(ii) How far may British MPs be described as 'representative'?

d) What is meant by 'pluralist democracy'?

e) (i) What is meant by 'sovereignty'?

(ii) How far can Parliament be said to be sovereign?

The British constitution

A **constitution** is the set of rules and principles by which a state is governed. If a constitution is outlined in a single, legal document it is described as written or codified, for example, the American constitution. The British constitution is described as **unwritten** or **uncodified**, because its rules derive from many different sources – some written and some not, some with the force of law and some not:

▶ Acts of Parliament (statute law), for example, the Crime and Disorder Act 1998

▶ EU law (since 1973): takes precedence over domestic law, for example, the beef ban

▶ **case law** (judge-made law): judicial interpretations of common and statute law, for example, giving Diane Blood the right to use her dead husband's sperm for fertility treatment (1997); the General Pinochet extradition case (1998)

▶ **common law**: ancient, unwritten law, for example, the powers of the Crown

▶ **conventions**: unwritten customs which are traditionally regarded as binding, but which have no legal force, for example, the practice that the Queen chooses as Prime Minister the leader of the majority party in the House of Commons

▶ historical documents and constitutional writings: for example, Magna Carta (1215), Walter Bagehot's *The English Constitution* (1867). Not legally binding; merely interpretive.

The British constitution is also **flexible**, i.e. it requires no special procedures for amendment, but can be changed by an ordinary Act of Parliament. Thus there is no distinct body of **constitutional law**. This does not necessarily mean that the constitution is quick or easy to change; some critics (such as Ponton and Gill) have argued that the British political system is too static and outdated in many respects. A **rigid constitution**, by contrast, requires a special process for change: for example, the USA requires two-thirds of Senate and House of Representatives votes, plus three-quarters of the state legislatures; and the Australian constitution requires a **referendum** for major change. Note that a constitution may be written but also flexible, for example, New Zealand.

The British constitution is also **unitary**, i.e. it has one sovereign legislature. Although there is local government and there are now also local Parliaments throughout the UK, these bodies are still subordinate to the centre and their existence and powers are wholly determined by Westminster which can limit the powers of local bodies or, indeed, abolish them altogether at any time. (This does not mean that the law must be uniform throughout the whole country; but differences are only those permitted, if not decreed, by the centre.) This contrasts with a **federal** constitution, such as the USA or Australia, where the local executive and/or legislative bodies have strong and autonomous powers within their own defined areas of responsibility. The centre has decision-making power over matters such as national security, defence and foreign affairs but it cannot impinge on the powers of the local bodies (nor vice versa) – they are, in theory, equal and autonomous and there are mutual checks and balances between them.

In theory – *de jure* – therefore, the British constitution is unwritten, flexible and unitary. In practice – *de facto* – however, all of these features are changing.

The British constitution is, in practice, becoming more written and legally codified, mainly because of the growing quantity and impact of EU laws and regulations, which take legal precedence over all other sources of the constitution; and also because of the large number of constitutional reforms introduced by law since 1997, for example, **devolution**, reform of the Lords, a domestic **Bill of Rights**, etc. This trend will continue.

Again, in practice rather than theory, the British constitution is gradually becoming more rigid as the principle becomes increasingly accepted and expected that referenda should be held on issues of major constitutional change such as electoral reform, devolution and joining the euro. Although such referenda in the UK are invariably merely 'advisory' to maintain the semblance of **parliamentary sovereignty** (see later), no government could, in reality, ignore a referendum result.

Finally, the unitary nature of the UK is already challenged by the power of the EU over Parliament; and it is likely to come under more challenge from below as the Scottish, Welsh and Northern Ireland assemblies consolidate their roles.

The changing constitution since 1997 – a ten point plan

1 Devolution to Scotland, Wales and Northern Ireland (subject to referenda)

2 Creation of Greater London Authority and elected mayor (subject to referendum)

3 Regional Development Agencies for England

4 Reform of the House of Lords

5 Bill of Rights for the UK

6 Freedom of Information Act

7 Opting in to EU Social Chapter

8 Proportional representation (closed party lists) for elections to EU Parliament

9 Referendum on joining the single European currency

10 Referendum on electoral reform for Westminster Parliament

The box above lists only the *de jure* changes promised or enacted by the Labour government. Other, perceived, *de facto* changes, such as centralisation of the executive, politicisation of the civil service and Blair's growing 'presidentialism', may be less legitimate.

Unconstitutional action

An action is **unconstitutional** if it breaks any part of the constitution. It may break a law: for example, Labour's ban on the sale of beef on the bone was ruled illegal in 1998. Or it may break a convention: for example, in 1998 Prime Minister Tony Blair appointed Scottish media tycoon Gus MacDonald as a junior industry minister although he was neither an MP nor a peer, breaching the rule that government ministers should be chosen from within Parliament. Also in 1998, when electoral reform for Westminster was under discussion, the government threatened to delay a referendum on the issue until after the next election, despite a **manifesto** promise to the contrary. However, manifesto promises – like many of the important rules of the constitution – are not legally binding. It is therefore often hard to know what is unconstitutional. Similarly, a rule of the constitution may itself break the 'spirit', if not the letter, of the constitution; for example, the draconian new anti-terrorism laws passed through Parliament in a single day in 1998 were, though perfectly legal, severely constraining of citizens' civil liberties. Similarly, retrospective law, for example, the backdated closure of an offshore tax loophole in Gordon Brown's 1998 Budget, breaches the principle that the law should be 'knowable' at the time we are breaking it. The British constitution is thus, in many ways, uncertain and even unknowable. For this reason, Alexis de Tocqueville in the nineteenth century said that Britain had no constitution.

Anti-constitutional action

An action is **anti-constitutional** if it aims to destroy the whole constitution, whether to replace it or not. Anarchists would not replace it, whereas the IRA would set up a united, independent Ireland, the neo-Nazi British National Party would create a one-party state and the Trotskyist Socialist Workers Party would seek a socialist republic. The action itself may be illegal and violent, for example, IRA bombs, or legal and peaceful,

for example, an SWP meeting. It is the aim – the ultimate overthrow of the whole system – which makes it anti-constitutional.

British parliamentary government

Any system of government has three branches:

► a *legislature*, which makes the laws
► an *executive*, which implements the laws and policies
► a *judiciary*, which interprets and enforces the laws.

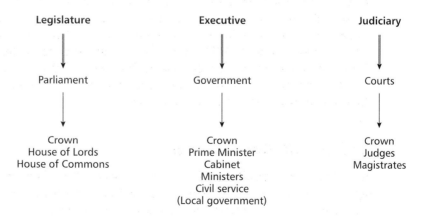

Legislature	Executive	Judiciary
↓	↓	↓
Parliament	Government	Courts
↓	↓	↓
Crown House of Lords House of Commons	Crown Prime Minister Cabinet Ministers Civil service (Local government)	Crown Judges Magistrates

▲ *The British system of government*

If the three branches of government are completely united, the system may be a tyranny. Liberal democratic theory advocates the **separation of powers**, to ensure checks and balances between the different parts of the system and hence freedom for the citizen. The United States has a substantial degree of separation between the legislature (Congress), the executive (President and Cabinet) and the judiciary. Britain, however, does not practise extensive separation of powers (see the diagram below).

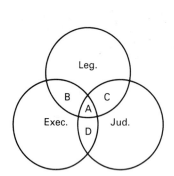 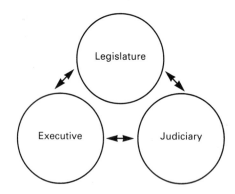

▲ *Contrasting structures of government*

---

3 List the institutions and individuals which are located in the overlapping areas A, B, C and D in the diagram above left.

The main overlap in the British system is between the legislature and the executive (see the diagram on page 27). The term **parliamentary government** refers to this overlap between Parliament and government: the executive is chosen from within the legislature (MPs and peers), and is, in theory, subordinate to the legislature. For example, an important convention of the constitution is that, if a government is defeated in a vote of no confidence by the House of Commons, it should resign. Government is also responsible, i.e. accountable, to Parliament through Question Time, debates, votes, committees, and financial scrutiny. Thus, through its link with Parliament – and especially with the elected House of Commons – Britain is said to have both representative and responsible government. Many essay questions ask about these key concepts, and their limits in practice.

The United States and many other countries, by contrast, have a **presidential system**. This does not refer to the fact that they have a President and Britain does not. It means that the executive is separately elected from Congress, is outside of the legislature and is in theory equal to the legislature with mutual checks and balances.

Parliamentary sovereignty and its limits

There are said to be two pillars of the British constitution; but both are questionable. One is the legal sovereignty or supremacy of Parliament. This suggests that Parliament is the supreme law-making body in the UK, and that no institution in the country can override its laws. Thus no Parliament can bind its successors, i.e. a future Parliament may amend or repeal any previous statute. Also, Parliament is not bound by its own statutes, but instead by a special body of law known as **parliamentary privilege**. This exempts MPs from much ordinary law; for example, they cannot be sued for slander for words spoken in Parliament.

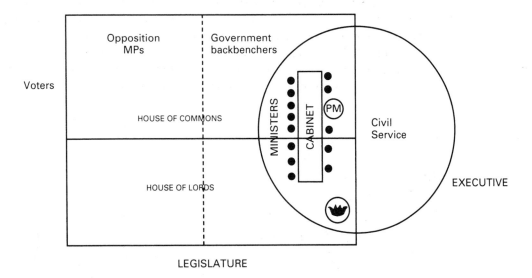

▲ *Parliamentary government in Britain*

However, parliamentary sovereignty is limited in practice, mainly by the EU whose laws have formal sovereignty over all member states, for example, fishing quotas and the 48-hour working week. There are many other, informal, constraints on parliamentary sovereignty: for example, other international courts and laws, such as the European Court of Human Rights (for example, in 1998 the Labour government was ruled illegal for trying to prohibit pressure groups from issuing leaflets about party candidates' personal views on matters such as abortion). Parliament is also constrained by **pressure groups**, business, the City and other economic power bodies, the media, and ultimately by the political sovereignty of the electorate, who choose the MPs in the Commons.

The power of the executive – elective dictatorship?

Internally, Parliament tends to be dominated by a majority government which, with party discipline and backbench support, can usually ensure that its legislative proposals are passed by Parliament. No majority government has been forced to resign by a vote of no confidence in the House of Commons since 1880.

In his 1976 Dimbleby Lecture, Lord Hailsham therefore used the term '**elective dictatorship**' to suggest that a majority government, in control of a sovereign Parliament, with a flexible constitution, could effectively change the constitution at will. This thesis gained renewed strength after the general election of 1997 when Labour won a massive 179 majority of seats over all of the other parties combined in the House of Commons (on a minority of the votes cast) and seemed, to many critics, virtually unstoppable. Thus, for example, within its first year in office Labour had pushed through many unpopular policies which were not in its manifesto, such as lone parents' benefit cuts, students' tuition fees, a five-year public sector pay squeeze, giving the Bank of England independence to set interest rates, increasing taxation of pension funds, etc.

The – rare – exceptions to this balance of power within Parliament are:

▶ a backbench revolt – for example, the second VAT rise on domestic fuel, 1996

▶ defeat by the House of Lords – for example, Sky TV sports coverage, 1996

▶ a **minority government** – for example, Conservatives, April 1997.

The second pillar of the British constitution – according to Dicey in 1885 – is 'the rule of law' (see Chapter 9, page 170). Again, this is an ideal principle which is often breached in practice (see below).

Sample short answer questions and answers

Q? What is meant by sovereignty?

A✓ Sovereignty resides in that body which has supreme or ultimate decision-making power. It also implies authority, i.e. consent and **legitimacy**. The state has sovereignty over all individuals and groups within its boundaries. In Britain, Parliament is said to have legal sovereignty, i.e. it can pass, amend or repeal any law without challenge. In practice it is subject to constraints, for example the EU, other international bodies, economic and business powers, pressure groups, media and the electorate who have ultimate political sovereignty. Thus 'sovereignty' is divided between state (exercised by the executive), Parliament and electorate; it is therefore debatable where, or whether, it exists at all.

Q? What is meant by calling British government 'parliamentary government'?

A✓ In British parliamentary government the executive is chosen from the majority party in the legislature, and is therefore dependent on its support and hence in theory subordinate to it (unlike the US presidential system, where the executive is separately elected and in theory equal to the legislature with mutual checks and balances, and the principle of separation of powers is generally followed). In practice in Britain, the executive tends to dominate the legislature because the party and electoral systems usually produce a strong majority government; Lord Hailsham has described this as 'elective dictatorship'.

Q? Define the word 'control' in the phrase 'parliamentary control of government'.

A✓ In 'parliamentary government', the executive is chosen from within the legislature and is in theory subordinate and accountable (responsible) to it. Parliament is therefore supposed to examine, debate, criticise and check the activities of government, publicise executive actions, convey public opinion to government, and authorise the raising and spending of money by government – through, for example, debates, votes, Question Time and committees. However, some see parliamentary control as inadequate – 'elective dictatorship' (Hailsham).

Q? Distinguish between Conservative and Liberal Democrat views on the constitution.

A✓ The Conservatives strongly uphold the existing constitution, because of their stress on tradition, parliamentary sovereignty, strong government, gradual 'organic' evolution and the *status quo*. Thus they defend the monarchy, House of Lords and 'rule of law'. The Liberal Democrats, however, advocate a written, federal constitution and a Bill of Rights, together with devolution, PR, reform of the second chamber and greater protection of individual rights and liberties. They fear the concentration of power which can result from a flexible constitution and ('the myth of') parliamentary sovereignty.

Q? What is meant by 'the rule of law'?

A✓ The 'rule of law' (Dicey, 1885) is a principle of the constitution which seeks to equate law and **justice**: everyone should be equally subject to the same laws – but, for example, the

Crown, diplomats, MPs, etc., are not. There should be a clear statement of people's legal rights and duties, fair and consistent trial and sentencing, and no arbitrary law or government. Justice should be an end in itself and always impartial. However, all of these principles are breached in practice, for example, by ambiguous laws, 'sus' laws, remand, inconsistent sentencing, high legal costs and police and judicial 'bias' (J.A.G. Griffith).

---

4 Say what is wrong with each of the following statements, and why.

   a) The legislature – Parliament – is elected by the people.

   b) The two elements in 'parliamentary government' are the House of Commons and the House of Lords.

   c) In parliamentary government the executive is elected from the majority party in the legislature.

   d) In parliamentary government the Cabinet and ministers are taken from the House of Commons.

   e) The legislature is often, in theory, subordinate to the executive.

   f) The British constitution is unwritten, therefore flexible.

   h) The British constitution is flexible, therefore Britain has no constitutional laws.

   h) A minority government has a minority of the votes but a majority of the seats.

   i) A coalition government is where two or more parties have merged to form a single governing party.

   j) A manifesto is what the government proposes to do, and the mandate is what they actually do when they get in.

ESSAYS

Most of the essay titles relevant to this chapter are wide-ranging questions on the British constitution and British democracy, which require material covered in later chapters. See also revision Chapter 12 for a more detailed summary of the broad themes raised in essay questions, including:

► representative and responsible government

► pluralism in British politics

► the role of the executive, Prime Minister and civil service

► secrecy in British government

► 'the rule of law'

► the role of pressure groups and media

► the impact of the European Union

► constitutional reform.

1 *Theme:* 'Elective dictatorship' of the executive

Q? Has the executive's dominance of the legislature weakened over recent years and, if so, why?

(Simulated question)

A✓ Short plan for guidance

Note: This is not, of course, the sort of plan which you should write in exams. Instead, use it to write a full essay; or, alternatively, write another plan for an essay on the same title which arrives at a different conclusion.

a) 'Parliamentary government' – define

b) Aims: representative and responsible government – define both

c) Methods of Parliamentary control of executive – brief list, including key conventions

d) With weakening of parliamentary control in this century, changing view of British parliamentary government, which sees Parliament's tasks as scrutiny and legitimising of executive, rather than control

e) 'Executive dominance of legislature' – electoral system, **party system**, parliamentary procedures, weak second chamber, executive secrecy, **delegated legislation** and retrospective law, control of civil service: hence 'elective dictatorship' (Hailsham). Topical examples . . .

f) Changes in last twenty years which may have weakened executive dominance ('rise of Parliament' – Norton thesis, etc.):

   i) Minority governments in 1970s. But they were not necessarily weak, for example, nationalisation of shipbuilding 1977; and they were exceptional; large majority governments in 1980s and most of 1990s, especially 1997 (179 majority)

   ii) Backbench revolts increasing (Norton): Nationality Act 1982, Shops Bill 1986, VAT 1996. But not treated as issues of confidence

   iii) Specialist select committees 1979, for example, British Aerospace/Rover inquiries. But they are relatively weak, and often ignored by government, for example, 1999 Foreign Affairs committee report on arms to Sierra Leone. Civil service and ministerial responsibility limited, for example, Osmotherly memorandum 1980 (listing many issues and areas where civil servants should not answer questions); arms to Iraq 1995

   iv) Other Parliamentary reforms: **Ombudsman** (since 1967) – lacks power and publicity; Special Standing committees – rare; Estimates and Opposition Days – few; Public Accounts Committee and National Audit Office – useful, not powerful

   v) Less secrecy: **Green** and **white papers**, etc. But still: Ponting 1984; Westland 1986; Zircon 1987, sale of Rover to British Aerospace 1990, BSE, arms to Iraq, arms to Sierra Leone – information withheld from Parliament. Freedom of information law delayed and watered down by Labour government

   vi) House of Lords defeats of government, for example, GLC abolition 'Paving Bill' 1984, Sky TV sports coverage 1996; but still weak (justifiably, since non-elected) – for example, closed party list system for EU elections forced through in 1998 despite six rejections by Lords

   vii) Lords select committees; useful, but often ignored

   viii) **Influence** of pressure groups on Parliament and government: for example, trade unions forced withdrawal of Industrial Relations Bill 1969 and National Industrial Relations Court 1974; Countryside Alliance 1998. But trade unions in 1980s and 1990s weak – recession, unemployment, new laws, governments anti-corporatist

g) Conclusion: Recent structural changes should have weakened the executive's dominance of the legislature over recent years: parliamentary reforms have improved Parliament's scrutiny of the executive, and changing attitudes among backbenchers – until 1997 – increased parliamentary control to some extent. However, writers like Johnson argue that the changes are only marginal. Labour's massive (179) majority in 1997, together with the leadership's authoritarian tendencies, have increased the potential for 'elective dictatorship'. Further reforms are needed for more representative and responsible government: for example, PR (to lessen the likelihood of one-party government); an elected second chamber which could then be given more powers of control; freedom of information legislation; and more powerful select committees (along the lines of the US Congressional committees).

2 *Theme:* Pluralism and elitism in the British power structure

Q? Some people believe that parliamentary government actually restrains democracy. State the cases for and against this view.

(London, Feb. 1976, Paper 1)

A✓ **Examiners' comments**

'The simplest and barest pass answer will be in terms of popular direct democracy versus parliamentary indirect democracy. The better answer will add to the arguments for and against the revolutionary socialist, or sometimes the radical liberal, view that the working of the two-party system and the conventions of parliamentary procedure stifle extreme and allegedly popular solutions. Some empathy should be displayed for this viewpoint, but a formal rebuttal in the form of either "it is so that the present system restrains, but it should be so" or "it is not so, the present system could be used for revolutionary policies if anyone wanted them" would be acceptable.'

Additional essay tips

▶ 'Some people': for example, who? Give political viewpoints/groups/names.

▶ 'Parliamentary government': define and discuss theory versus practice of representative and responsible government through Parliament.

▶ 'Democracy': define and discuss broad and narrow interpretations, from 'people-power' to consent; including the extent to which Britain lives up to the principles of its own 'liberal democratic' theory.

▶ 'State the cases for and against': this format requires balanced argument for a pass grade. However, even where they sound merely descriptive, A-level essay questions always (as the examiners' comments indicate) require your own informed, reasoned arguments, critical analysis and conclusions.

This is a very broad-ranging title; your answer could include discussion of, for example:

▶ the effective degree of popular participation in the system, beyond mere vote-casting

▶ the party system, and the extent to which the parties in Parliament – especially the governing party – reflect 'public opinion' (choice of parties and candidates, manifestos, the doctrine of the **mandate**, differences between England, Scotland, Wales and Northern Ireland, etc.)

▶ the electoral system, and the extent to which it reflects 'public opinion' – including the disproportions between votes and seats, regional imbalances, and the range of power bodies which are not elected

▶ the degree of executive accountability to Parliament and the people – power and influence of backbench MPs, committees, Ombudsman, etc., 'elective dictatorship', secrecy, collective and individual ministerial responsibility, etc.

▶ contrasts with presidential system – pros and cons of US separation of powers and direct election of executive

▶ the degree of centralisation of the British parliamentary system

▶ the Marxist and/or elitist arguments that the parliamentary system protects the economic and political power of a small ruling class or dominant elite

▶ arguments against 'democracy' – that people may be ill-informed, selfish, fickle, inconsistent; that a more 'democratic' system may be inefficient, bureaucratic, etc.

---

5 Write at least *one* of the following essays. Always write a brief plan first.

a) The British constitution is 'something we make up as we go along'. Discuss.

(London, Jan. 1998, Paper 1)

b) What are the respective merits and demerits of the Marxist and pluralist theories of politics? Have the actions of British governments since 1974 provided any evidence for or against these theories?

(Cambridge, June 1986, Paper 1)

c) Using such terms as 'power', 'authority' and 'legitimacy', outline the main characteristics of political culture in the UK. How far, and in what ways, do the values of the political culture change over time?

(AEB, Summer 1998, Paper 2)

d) (i) By what means is the executive held accountable to Parliament?

(ii) How effective is this accountability?

(London, June 1997, Paper 1)

e) Can sovereignty be divided?

(Oxford, Summer 1990, Paper 4)

GUIDE TO EXERCISES

Page 21

1 Note that the 'bad' short answers are not factually wrong. The first is much too short and skimpy; it would be lucky to get one mark. The other is long-winded, repetitive, clumsy and colloquial in style, and contains unsubstantiated value-judgements; but it would gain 5–6 marks for factual detail.

Page 22

2 a) (i) *Distinguish between 'the state' and 'the government'.*

The state is an independent, territorial entity with ultimate sovereignty over all individuals and groups within its boundaries. It is a permanent and abstract institution with power to use consensus where possible and coercion where necessary – it has a legal monopoly on the use of violence. The government is the agent of the state which enforces its rulings and acts under its authority. It is a finite and regularly changing institution.

(ii) *What is the 'organic' theory of the state?*

This theory likens state and society to a living organism (rather than to a machine). Like any living organism, it has different components, each with a different and specific place and role (brain v. hand, rulers v. ruled), and all must work together in a harmonious and co-ordinated way; and therefore the whole entity is more than the sum of its parts, and the society as a whole is more important than the individual within it. There is a natural and desirable inequality within the organic state – the different parts perform different roles. Often this theory stresses tradition and resists radical change on the grounds that society cannot be severed from its roots if it is to survive; for example, the theory of political conservatism.

b) (i) *Define the concept of 'a political elite'.*

A political elite is a small, privileged group who dominate the decision-making processes in society. Any representative democracy generates political elitism – 'oligarchy'. Classical elite theorists (Pareto, Mosca and Michels) say that elite rule is inevitable and desirable; so does Toryism. Plural elitists or democratic elitists (for example, Dahl) see diverse and competing elites as good; they disagree with Marxists (for example, Miliband) who perceive a single ruling class in Britain and the USA, and with radical elite theorists (for example, Guttsman) who perceive a single self-serving power elite.

(ii) *Explain the theory of single elitism.*

The theory of classical or single elitism was first advanced by Pareto, Mosca and Michels in the 1920s. They argued that apparently diverse and competitive power holders in fact share common social origins, aims and interests, above all the aim of preserving their own political and economic power. Together they form a single self-serving elite. Guttsman identifies an elite of around 11,000 in Britain: top businessmen, academics, ministers, MPs, civil servants, judges, church and military leaders, etc. This elite does not represent the people, but dupes them by the facade of elections, etc. into believing that the country is a democracy.

c) (i) *Distinguish between a delegate and a representative.*

A 'representative', once elected, exercises his/her own judgement, supposedly in accordance with the best interests of the electors as the representative sees them; whereas a 'delegate' acts on particular issues according to the specific wishes of the electors. Rousseau advocated a system of delegates; Burke argued in 1774 that MPs should be representatives rather than delegates. A trade union leader at a conference is often a delegate with a specific 'mandate' from the members, i.e. she or he is instructed on how to vote on each issue. A representative may also be 'typical' of the voters in terms of social background.

(ii) *How far may British MPs be described as 'representative'?*

MPs are not representative of the voters in the sense of 'typicality' of social background: they are predominantly middle class (over 60 per cent professionals and under 10 per cent manual workers); university-educated (60 per cent compared with 30 per cent of the adult population); white and male. Only 18 per cent of MPs are women and only six are black (1997). Nor are MPs delegates of their voters (and it would be very hard in practice for them to refer back to their constituents on every issue). They sometimes exercise independent judgement in the Burkean sense – notably in free votes and backbench revolts in the Commons; but more often they toe the party line and are sometimes perceived as mere 'lobby fodder'.

d) *What is meant by 'pluralist democracy'?*

Pluralism advocates a diffusion of political and economic power, in order to prevent tyranny and to enhance individual freedom, choice, representation and power. In the economic sphere this means diverse, independent and competing centres of economic power and influence – implying private property and a competitive market economy with a wide distribution of ownership and wealth. In the political sphere it means a choice of political parties (formalised in Britain in Her Majesty's Opposition) and pressure groups, with checks and balances between the different parts of state and society, including active local government. In this way, all diverse views and interests should be represented, and the system is thus 'democratic'. A one-party system, from this viewpoint, is by definition not 'democratic'.

A modified version of pluralist theory is 'plural elitism' or 'democratic elitism' (for example, Schumpeter, Dahl). This accepts that power is not equally dispersed from top to bottom in society; indeed, it argues that full pluralism would be inefficient, and is therefore not desirable. Instead it accepts that power is concentrated at the top, but is divided among competing elites – parties, pressure groups and economic power bodies. These effectively represent the diverse interests and views of the rest of society, and the system therefore provides the ideal combination of representative democracy and efficiency.

e) (i) *What is meant by 'sovereignty'?*

Sovereignty means ultimate power – the capacity to decide, to do, or make others do what you wish through threat or use of sanctions such as rewards, punishment, force or violence. It is widely seen also to require authority, i.e. consent and legitimacy. A state has sovereignty over all groups and individuals within its boundaries. In Britain, Parliament is said to have legal sovereignty (Dicey, 1885). In practice it is subject to constraints, for example EU, pressure groups and the 'political sovereignty' of the electorate. The nominal sovereign – the monarch – now has little *de facto* power. Thus sovereignty is divided between state (exercised by the executive under the 'royal prerogative'), Parliament and electorate; it is therefore debatable where, or whether, sovereignty exists at all. Pluralist theory says this is as it should be.

(ii) *How far can Parliament be said to be sovereign?*

'Sovereignty' means ultimate or supreme power and authority. In Britain, Parliament (legislature – Commons, Lords and Crown) has legal sovereignty, i.e. in theory it can pass, amend or repeal any law without limit or challenge from any domestic body – unlike, for example, USA and Supreme Court. Thus Parliament itself cannot be ruled illegal or unconstitutional. It can for example 'legalise illegality' through retrospective law – often passed in support of the executive, for example. Ridley v. GLC 1985 over funding of London Regional Transport. Ascherson and others therefore argue that 'absolutism' has shifted from the Crown to the Crown-in-Parliament. In practice there are constraints: the EU (for example, beef ban, fishing quotas) as long as Parliament chooses to remain a member; pressure groups, international bodies such as NATO and IMF; media; and the 'political sovereignty' of the electorate (Dicey) as long as the Commons submits to periodic elections and ultimately reflects the political will of the voters. Moreover, a majority government with strong party loyalty and discipline can usually effectively control Parliament from within – 'elective dictatorship' (Hailsham).

Page 26

3 A: Crown, Lord Chancellor, Home Secretary, Attorney General and Solicitor General

   B: PM, Cabinet and other ministers; some local councillors who are also MPs

   C: Law Lords

   D: Judges who are appointed to chair executive inquiries; magistrates who are also councillors; executive functions of judges and magistrates (for example, pub licensing)

Page 29

4 a) Only the House of Commons is elected; not the Lords or Crown.

   b) The two elements in 'parliamentary government' are the legislature and the executive.

   c) The executive is not elected; it is appointed by the Crown.

   d) Ministers may be taken from the Lords as well as from the Commons.

   e) The legislature is often, in practice, subordinate to the executive; but always sovereign in theory.

   f) There is no necessary connection between an unwritten and a flexible constitution.

   g) Britain does have constitutional laws, though they are enacted in the same way as other laws.

   h) A minority government has under 50 per cent of the seats in the House of Commons; its percentage vote is irrelevant.

   i) A coalition government consists of two or more parties (either in a 'hung' Parliament or in a crisis, such as war) – they do not merge to form a single party.

   j) A manifesto is the list of policy proposals issued by any party prior to a general election. A 'mandate', strictly, is the assent and authority, or even duty, given to the government by the electors to govern along the policy lines indicated in the manifesto. However, voters often do not read manifestos, and cannot choose between specific policies; while governments usually win under 50 per cent of the votes cast, and often do not adhere to their manifestos. They may claim a 'Doctor's Mandate' to do as they see fit in changing circumstances. The 'doctrine of the mandate' is therefore a myth (Marshall).

REFERENCES

Ascherson, Neal (1988) *Games With Shadows*, Radius

Bagehot, Walter (1963) *The English Constitution* (1867), Fontana

Bottomore, T.B. (1964) *Elites and Society*, Watts

Burke, Edmund (1774) Letter to his Bristol Constituents, in Bredvold and Ross (eds) (1961) *The Philosophy of Edmund Burke: A Selection of His Speeches and Writings*, Cresset Press

Dahl, R.A. (1963) *Modern Political Analysis*, Prentice-Hall

de Tocqueville, Alexis (1956) *Democracy in America* (1840), Mentor

Dicey, A.V. (1961) *Introduction to the Law of the Constitution* (1885), Macmillan

Griffith, J.A.G. (1985) *The Politics of the Judiciary*, Fontana

Guttsman, W.L. (1964) *The British Political Elite*, MacGibbon & Kee

Hailsham, Lord (1976) 'Elective Dictatorship', The Dimbleby Lecture, in *The Listener*, 21 October

Hain, Peter (1983) *The Democratic Alternative*, Penguin

Johnson, Nevil (1980) *In Search of the Constitution*, Methuen

Marshall, G.W. (1971) *Constitutional Theory*, Oxford University Press

Mosca, G. (1936) *Histoire des doctrines politiques*, Payot

Miliband, Ralph (1969) *The State in Capitalist Society*, Quartet

Norton, Philip (1982) *The Constitution in Flux*, Basil Blackwell

Pareto. V. (1966) *Sociological Writings* (ed. S.E. Finer), Pall Mall

Ponton, G. and Gill, P. (1982) *Introduction to Politics*, Blackwell

Rousseau, J.J. (1968) *The Social Contract* (1762), Penguin

Schumpeter, J.A. (1977) *Capitalism, Socialism and Democracy*, Allen & Unwin

3 Voters and elections

KEY ISSUES

▶ Merits and demerits of electoral systems: first-past-the-post; various types of PR; other democratic reforms

Implications of each for:

- political equality: one person, one vote, one value
- the doctrine of the mandate
- parliamentary government
- representative and responsible MPs/government

Constitutional consequences of different reforms

▶ Factors influencing voting behaviour, including:

- declining influence of class on voting behaviour
- changing national/regional patterns of voting behaviour
- reasons why people may abstain from voting

TOPIC NOTES

Key facts and concepts

The extension of the **franchise** (the right to vote) dates from the 1832 Reform Act. Only half a million of the male middle-class population were given the vote, but the principle of electoral sovereignty was established, then later extended.

1867   Representation of the People Act: reduced property qualification to £5. Electorate = two million male voters

1872   Ballot Act: introduced the secret ballot and made intimidation of the voters illegal

1884   Representation of the People Act: extended the franchise to all male householders. Electorate = five million

1918   Representation of the People Act: extended the franchise to all men over 21 and all women over 30. Electorate = 21 million

1928   Representation of the People Act: extended franchise to all women over 21 – 'universal adult suffrage'

1948   Plural voting abolished (previously holders of business premises and Oxbridge degrees had two votes)

1969   Voting age reduced to 18. Electorate now around 42 million

Voting is not compulsory in Britain as it is in, for example, Australia. To be eligible to vote, a person must be on the register of electors, and resident in the constituency on the qualifying date (though there is provision for postal voting). Those not allowed to vote are peers, non-British citizens, under-18s, certified mental patients, prisoners under sentence and people disqualified for corrupt electoral practices (for example, bribery).

There are 659 single-member parliamentary constituencies in the UK: England 529, Scotland 72, Wales 40 and Northern Ireland 18. A general election, involving all constituencies, must be held when Parliament has run its full five-year term (under the Parliament Act 1911) or is dissolved. A **by-election** is held in a single constituency if the MP dies, retires, is expelled or disqualified by accepting a peerage or paid Crown office.

Electoral systems

First-past-the-post (FPTP)

Britain has a single-vote, first-past-the-post electoral system: one vote per person; and the one candidate with the most votes wins the constituency, with *or without* an absolute majority (meaning more than 50 per cent of the votes cast).

Advantages

▶ The first-past-the-post system is simple, quick and cheap.

▶ One person, one vote is a basic form of political equality.

▶ It is said to favour the two-party system as it usually produces single-party, majority government and one strong Opposition party in the House of Commons; hence strong and stable government which is clearly accountable to the voters. However, this must be qualified: the system produced minority governments – with under 50 per cent of the seats in the Commons – in the 1970s; and a two-party system has both advantages and disadvantages – the latter including lack of choice and diversity (especially in **safe seats** which one party is virtually certain to win every time), unfair representation of minority parties and voters, and a majority-seat government with a minority of votes cast. The rise of the Liberals in the 1970s and the new centre parties in the 1980s for a time undermined the two-party system; as have the marked regional differences in party support, for example, in Scotland and Northern versus Southern England – producing a clear north-south, Labour–Conservative political divide and, critics say, two Britains.

▶ It is also sometimes said (for example, by Duverger) that the two-party system created by first-past-the-post electoral systems reflects a natural political divide between conservatism and radicalism. However, the substantial third-party vote in the 1970s and 1980s belied this argument, as did the substantial policy similarities between the two main parties in the 1997 election.

▶ Finally, it is said that contact between MP and constituents is closer than in large, multi-member constituencies. In principle there is a one-to-one relationship; but in practice MPs need not even live in their constituencies and contact is often negligible, especially in safe seats (though these are now declining as voters become more volatile).

Disadvantages

▶ Since any vote for a losing candidate is wasted, i.e. not directly represented at all in the Commons, all votes do not carry equal weight; i.e. the system does not grant one person, one vote, *one value*, and political equality is denied. Voters may therefore be discouraged from voting for minority parties, or from voting at all.

▶ Because many or most MPs have fewer than 50 per cent of the votes cast in their constituencies, no government since 1935 has had an absolute majority of votes cast, though most have had an absolute majority of seats in the Commons. This usually produces a powerful government which the majority of people voted *against* – arguably an elective dictatorship (to use Lord Hailsham's phrase) of an unrepresentative kind. Opinion polls suggest that around 60 per cent of voters now favour a system of **proportional representation** (PR).

▶ Until the 1997 general election when the Conservatives were under-represented in the Commons, the two main parties had been consistently over-represented, while the Liberal Democrats especially – because of the geographical dispersal of their votes – have been consistently under-represented.

▶ Occasionally, a government may have more seats but fewer votes than the losing party: for example, the Conservatives in 1951 and Labour in February 1974 (because of unequal constituency sizes and winning margins).

▶ Independent candidates have very little chance of success. Martin Bell in the 1997 election was a rare exception who won largely because Labour and the Liberal Democrats did not stand candidates in his Tatton constituency. This may exclude quality and diversity from the system.

▶ Finally, in the period of economic boom from the 1950s to mid-1970s, the two-party system was based on **consensus politics**, when the two main parties shared very similar, centrist policies in support of the mixed economy, **welfare state**, full

employment and nuclear defence. This was praised by some for producing moderation and stability, but was criticised by others for its lack of innovation and choice. Conversely, the recessions of the 1980s were said to have produced **adversary politics** with more right-wing Conservative governments and a more influential left wing in the Labour Party. The opposite pros and cons were advanced – more diversity and choice, but also more risk of a pendulum swing, i.e. sharp policy reversals between different governing parties. However, after four successive election defeats, the Labour Party in the 1990s shifted increasingly to the right in pursuit of disaffected Conservative voters. The post-1997 period witnessed a new kind of consensus – in terms, at least, of economic policy – centred on a conspicuously right-wing agenda of cuts in taxation, inflation, public spending and welfare.

The 1997 General Election

659 seats	% Votes	% Seats	No. of seats	Gains	Losses
Labour	43.2	63.6	419	146	0
Conservatives	30.7	25.1	165	0	178
Liberal Democrats	16.8	7.0	46	28	2
Others:	7.0	4.3	29	5	0
of which:					
SNP			6		
Plaid Cymru			4		
Independent			1		
UUP			10		
DUP			2		
SDLP			3		Northern Ireland
Sinn Fein			2		
Robert McCartney			1		

Notes and novelties

- Overall Labour majority: 179 seats
- Record number of Labour seats
- Swing from Conservative to Labour: 10 per cent
- Turnout: 71.2 per cent – the lowest since 1935
- Record 120 women MPs (including Labour: 101; Conservatives: 14)
- Record five Asian and four black MPs (all Labour)
- Three openly homosexual MPs
- First independent MP (Martin Bell) since 1950
- Youngest MP in this Parliament is aged 24
- The youngest Prime Minister this century
- The Conservative Party's most disastrous result since 1906
- No Conservative and Unionist MPs in Scotland, Wales or Northern Ireland
- Liberal Democrat tally of seats highest by a third party since 1929
- The Referendum Party (James Goldsmith's anti-EU party) spent an estimated £20 million on 547 candidates for 810,778 votes (3 per cent) and lost all of their deposits
- The last seat to be announced – Winchester – was lost by the Conservatives to the Liberal Democrats by two votes – the smallest majority for 87 years

Why did the Conservatives lose?

Why did the Conservatives lose, especially at a time of economic recovery?

- Forced withdrawal from ERM in 1992 (which, paradoxically, helped recovery)
- Unpopular policies, for example, rail privatisation, VAT
- Air of arrogance and hubris, for example, sleaze, cheating on pairing on fishing quotas (1996), arms to Iraq, prison escapes, BSE, judicial reviews, reluctance of ministers to accept responsibilities and resign
- Minority government by end of 1996. Government dependent in Commons on Unionists; abandonment of IRA ceasefire early in 1996.
- February 1997 Wirral South by-election: 17 per cent swing to Labour. (Unhappy irony: the Conservative candidate's name, Leslie Byrom, is anagram of 'loser by mile')
- Manifest and bitter party disunity over Europe, especially smack-of-firm-compromise 'wait and see' approach to a single European currency
- Longest post-war electoral campaign – backfired. Boredom and further sleaze
- Sniping from the wings by James Goldsmith's Referendum Party and Alan Sked's Independence Party
- Defections by pro-Europeans such as Alan Howarth and Emma Nicholson
- Unpopularity of Major versus Blair
- Conservative Norman Lamont said government gave the impression of being 'in office but not in power'
- Inept campaigning, for example, 'demon eyes' and 'weeping lion' posters ridiculed
- Conservative press largely turned against them
- Time for a change – widely held public sentiment

Why did Labour win?

Labour benefited by:

- Internal reforms, for example, some reduction in trade union power; OMOV
- John Smith's death in 1994 allowed creation of new Labour by the more modernising Blair – notably, abandonment of Clause IV in 1995
- Rapid centralisation of party and presentation around leader and spin-doctors at Millbank election headquarters and a highly polished campaign
- Abandonment of traditional socialist – or even social democratic – principles and acceptance of market economics, low inflation and interest rates, cuts in taxation, spending and welfare. Pre-election commitment to maintain existing tax levels for a five-year term and present spending levels for two years, welfare to work, tough law and order especially for juvenile offenders. Difficult for the Conservatives to criticise what were, largely, their own policies
- Desire for power, combined with growing party discipline, largely silenced left-wing Labour dissidents
- New, radical proposals for constitutional reform

Lack of 'clear blue water' between the two main parties threatened to squeeze the Liberal Democrats but – despite a lower vote than in 1992 – they won over twice as many seats due to careful targeting of their limited resources and skilful tactical voting by anti-Conservative voters.

1 Write the following short answer:

a) Summarise the results of the 1997 General Election.

b) What factors help to explain the Conservatives' defeat?

Non-proportional voting systems

Alternatives to first-past-the-post are many and varied; they need not involve proportional representation.

The alternative vote (AV)

Voters list candidates in order of preference – the last candidate(s) are struck out and their votes are redistributed among the second choices marked on their ballot papers until one candidate has an absolute majority (over 50 per cent) of the votes (for example, in Australia).

The supplementary vote

Similar to the above – preference voting; all candidates except first and second are eliminated and the one with the most first and second preferences combined is the winner. Labour's Plant Commission on electoral reform recommended this system in 1993 but it is only a very limited change from the present system.

The second ballot

Voters put one cross against one candidate; the last candidate(s) are struck out and new ballots are held until one candidate has an absolute majority (for example, in France).

		Mark order of preference in space below
DALEY, James	Lib. Dems	3
FOSTER, Mark	Labour	
LEEDS, Mary	Labour	
PAUL, John	Green Party	
POWELL, Jim	Conservative	1
RADCLIFFE, Susan	Lib. Dems	4
THOMPSON, Simon	Conservative	2

▲ *A preferential ballot paper*

Proportional representation

This label covers a wide variety of electoral systems where seats are more or less in proportion to votes cast. PR, in one form or another, is used throughout Europe, has long been advocated by the Liberal Democrats and support for it has grown in Britain since the 1970s. This is partly because the first-past-the-post system failed in the 1970s to produce majority governments, and partly because the increasing third-party vote since the mid-1970s has highlighted the distortions of the present voting system. The 1997 Labour government promised a referendum on the issue, but the referendum itself was delayed and the amount of choice offered to the electorate was bound to be very limited.

All forms of PR are said by supporters to share the same basic advantages.

▶ They are more representative of voters' wishes as expressed at the ballot box.

▶ Fewer votes are 'wasted', therefore greater participation may be encouraged.

▶ Minority parties are more fairly represented.

▶ There are more opportunities for independents.

▶ There are less likely to be 'safe seats' with low turn-outs and poor quality MPs.

▶ Voters may have more choice and therefore candidates may be of better quality.

▶ The two-party system (which may have both pros and cons) is usually eliminated and the end result is more 'pluralist'.

▶ The possibility of single-party elective dictatorship is greatly diminished.

It is sometimes argued against PR that it generally demands more knowledge and activity of the voters (for example, to rank candidates in order of preference), and hence may discourage participation. Conversely, however, voters may welcome the opportunity to be better informed and to exercise greater choice, and turnout may actually increase.

PR cannot be used where there is only one seat to be filled, for example at by-elections, but this is not a major problem.

Above all, if there are more than two main parties competing, a proportional allocation of seats to votes will tend to produce a 'hung Parliament' where no party has 50 per cent of the seats. In the British system of parliamentary government, the choice between first-past-the-post and PR is therefore often presented as a choice between single-party, 'majority' government or a 'fair' reflection of the votes. This, however, is too simplistic: PR may produce an absolute majority government (as, for example, in Spain in October 1982); and first-past-the-post may produce a hung Parliament (as in Britain in February 1974).

Moreover, the consequences – and pros or cons – of a hung Parliament are not clear-cut. For one thing a hung Parliament in post-war Britain is relatively rare; and, given the nature of the British constitution, when it happens the 'rules' are uncertain, for example, who may become Prime Minister, when and whether a fresh election should be called, etc.

A hung Parliament need not result in **coalition** government (i.e. two or more parties in executive office). More often in Britain the result has been single-party, minority government with under 50 per cent of the seats in the Commons. For example, in February 1974 Labour under Harold Wilson hung on for eight months as a minority government, boosting its own popularity with pension increases and rent freezes before calling a new election in October 1974 and winning a small overall majority. By 1977 Labour had lost this majority through by-election defeats, and therefore entered the 15-month Lib-Lab pact. This was not a coalition government – there were no Liberals in the executive – but an informal agreement on Liberal support for the Labour government in the House of Commons in return for consultation on policy. This minority Labour government pushed through a lot of contentious legislation: the Aircraft and Shipbuilding Industries Act and the Race Relations Act, for example. It was not, in that sense, a 'weak' government, any more than majority governments are always and in every sense 'strong'. By late 1995, for example, John Major's government was not strong in the face of persistent opposition from its own backbenchers (for example, on VAT, Post Office privatisation, family law, etc.).

The Liberal Democrats argue that single-party majority government is normally 'weak' in that it rests on a minority vote and therefore lacks consent; it may also lack power in relation to interest groups, such as business or the trade unions. They prefer to call a hung Parliament a 'balanced Parliament'; they favour a centrist coalition, arguing that it would curb 'elective dictatorship', encourage moderation and continuity, promote greater stability of national direction and policy and therefore be more efficient than the present 'swing of the pendulum'. Certainly a hung Parliament usually ensures better attendance in the Commons and harder working MPs, while coalition governments can draw on a wider pool of talent, and may be quite stable. Equally, one-party government may be 'unstable' if it adopts sudden policy changes: for example, Major's forced withdrawal from the ERM in 1992. (It could be argued, of course, that all of the main parties are, anyway, coalitions of diverse **factions** and political tendencies; 'single-party' versus 'coalition' government is therefore just a matter of organisational structure and labelling.)

The case against this argument and against PR is that no one votes for a real coalition; there is no **mandate** for compromise politics. Coalition government may also give disproportionate power to small parties, and therefore be as unrepresentative, in its own way, as the first-past-the-post system. Nor is there any inherent virtue in centrism which, from a critical standpoint, may be seen as stagnation. If the Blair project and Liberal Democrats' goal of a permanent, centre-coalition and consensus was to be achieved, it could amount to a new 'elective dictatorship' and a retreat from pluralism.

It is now necessary to examine the main types of PR individually, because each has its particular characteristics, merits and demerits; beware of generalising in essay answers.

The single transferable vote (STV)
This is based on multi-member constituencies. Voters list candidates in order of preference. Any candidate obtaining the necessary quota of first preference votes is elected. (The quota is a formula designed simply to ensure that there are not more winners than there are seats available within each constituency.) Any surplus votes are redistributed among the other candidates in proportion to the second choices on the winning candidates' ballot papers and so on until all seats are filled. If too few candidates achieve the quota, the last candidate(s) are dropped and their votes redistributed in proportion to their second preferences (for example, used in Ireland; advocated by the Liberal Democrats.)

The party list system
This is the most common form of PR. The elector votes for a particular party list of candidates, and seats are allocated to each party in proportion to votes received. They are then allocated to specific candidates (for example, USA, Switzerland, Israel).

There are two varieties of the party list system.

▶ *Bound/closed list*: The elector simply votes for a party label and then the party chooses the candidates to fill the seats. The obvious criticism of this system is that the voter has no say in who are the actual MPs, who are likely to be loyal party placemen.

Shortly after it came to power, the Labour government proposed the closed party list system for future elections to the EU Parliament, generating loud protest from some left-wing Labour MPs who feared that they would be frozen out by the process. The Labour leadership sought to silence them (an unconstitutional action, according to critics). The House of Lords rejected the closed list system for EU elections a record *six* times, but the government in the Commons pushed it through nevertheless. By 1999, some independent-minded and popular Labour MEPs, for example Christine Oddy (Coventry and North Warwickshire), were pushed so far down the party lists as to be effectively deselected by the leadership, with the voters having no say in the process.

▶ *Free/open list*: The elector may have several votes, and may vote for specific candidates on one party list or across different party lists. Seats are then given to candidates with the most personal votes. This may be complicated, but allows the voter considerable choice together with close proportionality.

Closed list	Free list
Place a cross in one box only	**You may cast up to five votes for different candidates**

		LIBERAL DEMOCRATS	CONSERVATIVE	GREEN	LABOUR
Conservative Party........	[X]	Ben Osbourne..	Matt Gee...........	Janet Young...........	Marni Singh.....
Green Party	[ ]	Bob Pawson ..X.	Andrew Hunt....	Calum Thomson....	Vince Meate..X..
Labour Party..................	[ ]	Meg Nelson......	Brian Leeds	Sally Green ...X....	Mike Pettavel.X
Liberal Democratic Party	[ ]		David Lewis......	Peter Myer..............	Carol Reld ..X...
National Front	[ ]				
Workers' Party...............	[ ]		Lucy Johns.......		Sue Smith ....

▲ *Party list systems*

Mixed proportional systems

Additional member system (AMS)

Sometimes referred to as a mixed proportional system, this combines first-past-the-post and PR. The ballot paper has two parts and the elector has two votes. One vote is cast for a candidate to win a seat in a single-member, first-past-the-post constituency. The second vote is cast for a party label and a number of set-aside seats in the legislature (perhaps up to 50 per cent) are filled by non-constituency candidates – additional members – chosen

```
┌─────────────────────────────────────────────────┐
│  Place a cross in one box only                   │
│                                                  │
│  Jane Dean (Cons)............................ │X│ │
│                                                  │
│  Michael Taylor (Lab)....................... │ │ │
│                                                  │
│  Raj Rajah (Lib Dem)........................ │ │ │
│                                                  │
│  Max King (Green)........................... │ │ │
├─────────────────────────────────────────────────┤
│  Place a cross in one box only                   │
│                                                  │
│  Conservative Party......................... │X│ │
│                                                  │
│  Labour Party............................... │ │ │
│                                                  │
│  Liberal Democratic Party................... │ │ │
│                                                  │
│  Green Party................................ │ │ │
└─────────────────────────────────────────────────┘
```

▲ *AMS ballot paper*

through the party list system in proportion to the votes cast for each party on the second part of the ballot paper. This retains single-member constituencies but also provides top-up proportionality for parties which would otherwise be under-represented by first-past-the-post alone (used, for example, in Germany on a ratio of 50/50 constituency and PR MPs). The Scottish Parliament is elected by AMS but on a ratio of 56 per cent first-past-the-post MSPs (73 out of 129) to 44 per cent (56) top-up MSPs elected from closed regional party lists using the eight European parliamentary constituencies.

Alternative vote plus (AV+)

This is a novel combination of electoral systems, advocated by the Jenkins Commission in 1998 for future Westminster parliamentary elections. It combines the Alternative Vote for about 80 per cent of the (single-member constituency) seats at Westminster, with 20 per cent of (non-constituency) top-up PR seats to be chosen by a regional list system. This only contains a very limited element of PR because Tony Blair's aides urged Roy Jenkins to water down his original ideas; and the promised referendum on the issue was delayed despite a manifesto promise.

1997 General Election: estimated results using diverse electoral systems (number of seats)

	FPTP	AV	AV+	STV	AMS	Party List
Labour	419	436	368	342	303	285
Conservative	165	110	168	144	203	202
Lib. Dem.	46	84	89	131	115	110
SNP/Plaid Cymru	10	10	15	24	20	46
Others	19	19	19	18	18	18

Note: The examiners do not want to see detailed descriptions in essays of every type of electoral system; they do want to see an informed assessment of the advantages and disadvantages of the various systems, without sweeping and simplistic generalisations.

2 Make a list of the potential merits and demerits of each of the systems outlined above; then answer the questions below.

a) Which system seems to give the most power to the parties in choosing MPs?

b) Which system seems to produce the closest proportion of seats to votes?

c) Which system does not have single-member constituencies? List three advantages and three disadvantages of multi-member constituencies.

d) Which system(s) produce one winning candidate with more than 50 per cent of the votes cast?

e) Which system(s) produce two types of MPs, one with a local constituency and one without? Suggest two advantages and two disadvantages of this arrangement.

f) Which system requires the electorate to turn out to vote more than once? Give one advantage and one disadvantage of such a system.

g) Which system(s) allow for cross-voting between parties and/or candidates? Give two possible advantages and two disadvantages of cross-voting.

h) Which system(s) are likely to give more accurate representation to minority parties? Give two advantages and two disadvantages of such systems.

i) Suggest one reason why STV is not purely proportional.

j) List four *alternative* reforms to the present first-past-the-post system which may make it more democratic.

3 How representative is proportional representation? Complete the exercise below by filling in the blanks.

Diverse definitions of representative: **a)** ....

b) ....

c) ....

Some forms of PR are less proportionately representative of votes cast than others, for example, ... is less proportional than ....

Generally, PR is likely to produce hung parliaments and coalition governments. Compared with first-past-the-post, these may be more representative of voters' views as expressed at the ballot box because:

d) ....

e) ....

f) ....

However, coalition governments may be seen as less representative of voters' views, despite basic proportionality, because:

g) ....

h) ....

i) ....

However well proportional coalition governments may represent voters' views, there is no guarantee that they will be any better than first-past-the-post in representing either voters' .... or ....

Assessing specific types of PR:

j) AMS and AV+ are the least representative form of PR in the sense that ...., but because they retain single-member constituencies they are representative in the sense of ....

k) STV's main characteristic is multi-member constituencies. These may enhance representation of voters' views and interests because ....
....

The alternative danger with multi-member constituencies is that ....
....

Another problem about representation of voters' views arises out of the system of preference voting, namely that ....
....

l) The party list system is broadly the most representative of voters' views in that ....
but the bound list system (as introduced by Labour for EU parliamentary elections) is unrepresentative in that ....
.... The free list system is technically the most representative of all but, precisely because it is the most proportional, it may undermine representation in the sense that ....

Factors influencing voting behaviour

Social class and occupation

These have long been the most important influences on voting behaviour in Britain. Historically, the wealthier upper and middle classes were more likely to vote Conservative and the working class were more likely to vote Labour; while centrist parties such as the Liberal Democrats have suffered from their lack of class identity. However, there have always been exceptions. Lower-income Conservative voters used to be classified by sociologists either as deferential voters (regarding the Conservatives as superior governors) or as secular or instrumental voters (seeking personal advantages such as tax cuts [McKenzie and Silver]).

This analysis is now regarded as too simplistic. Since the 1970s voters have become more volatile and quicker to change sides, and the old class allegiances are weakening – a process known as class or partisan dealignment. There are several suggested reasons for this process.

▶ The traditional manual working class has declined in size with structural changes in the economy and rising unemployment. Trade union membership has also fallen for the same reasons, and with it some of the traditional working-class values of equality, **collectivism**, solidarity and Labour support. Rising living standards for those in work, increasing home and share ownership, geographical mobility (often due to the break-up of traditional working-class communities, for example, after pit closures), population shifts to the south, privatised and non-unionised work have also weakened traditional working-class values and voting patterns.

▶ Many workers looked to the Conservatives in the 1980s for promised tax cuts and council house sales. Other key policy issues, for example, defence, law and order and local government, also caused problems for Labour.

▶ As the Conservative and Labour parties were seen to be polarising throughout the 1980s, growing support for the centre parties increased the distortions of the first-past-the-post system, giving the Conservatives 52 per cent of the seats in 1992 on their lowest winning proportion of the vote since the war.

▶ In the 1997 election, as new Labour adopted wholesale the Conservatives' tax and spend policies, they won over many middle-class voters for the first time.

1997 General Election, voting by class (% change on 1992 in brackets)

	Conservative	Labour	Lib. Dem.
Electorate	31 (–12)	44 (+9)	17 (–1)
AB	42 (–11)	31 (+9)	21 (–1)
C1	26 (–22)	47 (+19)	19 (–1)
C2	25 (–15)	54 (+15)	14 (–4)
DE	21 (–8)	61 (+9)	13 (0)
Home owners	35 (–12)	41 (+11)	17 (–3)
Council tenants	13 (–6)	65 (+1)	15 (+5)
Trade union members	18 (–9)	57 (+7)	20 (+2)

Other important factors cut across class divisions.

Regional variations

Labour is stronger in inner-city areas, and in Scotland and Wales where the Conservatives won no seats at all in 1997. The Conservatives are stronger in rural areas and in southern England. These patterns are linked to both class and local culture. The Liberal Democrats have pockets of support in Wales, south-west England and the Scottish Isles and borders.

Sex, age and race

Historically, women tended to vote Conservative more than Labour but, by 1997, the figures were almost identical. More young people in 1997 voted Labour: 57 per cent of first-time voters as opposed to 19 per cent for the Conservatives and 18 per cent for the Liberal Democrats. Surveys of ethnic minorities consistently showed around 70 per cent support for Labour, 25 per cent for the Conservatives and 5 per cent for the Liberal Democrats.

Religion

Roman Catholics and non-conformists tend to be less conservative than Anglicans; but this influence is declining and, again, may be linked to class.

Mass media

TV and newspapers both create and reflect public opinion and can highlight a particular political issue (for example, inflation, unemployment), party images and personalities as a basis for voting. For several decades the national press in Britain was largely Conservative (hence *The Sun*'s notorious front-page headline after the 1992 Conservative victory, 'It was the Sun wot won it'). Uniquely, however, Blair courted and won over the Rupert Murdoch stable – *The Sun*, *The Times*, *The Sunday Times* and the *News of the World*, as well as Sky TV and other international broadcasting media – before the 1997 election. Whether they helped to swing the result or simply anticipated the inevitable is a matter of conjecture.

Personal experience

Family, friends and work associates can help to form political opinion; parental influence is particularly strong (and is, of course, linked to social class).

Party image and party policy

Because of the first-past-the-post and parliamentary systems – when we vote for a single, local MP we are indirectly voting for a national government – electors tend to vote for a party more than for an individual candidate. Some voters look closely at the parties' past records and present policies; many vote on the basis of a broad party image (united or divided, pro-spending or cutting, pro- or anti-welfare, helping the poor or the wealthy, etc.), although this may not correspond to the parties' actual policies when in power. For example, much is made of the economic 'feel good' factor; but, paradoxically, the economy was in serious decline when the Conservatives won again in 1992 and was recovering well when they lost in 1997.

Growing emphasis has been put upon the image and popularity of the party leaders – especially in the 1997 election when the main parties' policies were quite similar. In 1992, the 'Kinnock factor' clearly put off a significant number of voters who felt that he lacked stature and gravitas; he was also the object of a sustained campaign of character assassination by *The Sun* newspaper. Conversely, in 1997 Blair was perceived to be leading an increasingly moderate and disciplined party in contrast to the feuding Conservatives; and he was careful not to repeat Kinnock's over-exuberance and premature triumphalism.

Abstentions

Qualified voters may abstain from voting for many reasons:

▶ lack of information about, or interest in, the election (especially in local council elections, by-elections and European elections, and also in safe seats where campaigning may be minimal and the outcome is a foregone conclusion)

▲ *At the end of the 1990s, Tony Blair is perceived as a (too?) strong, authoritarian leader; in contrast William Hague is considered to have no strength of leadership*

▶ dislike of all available parties or candidates or lack of effective choice (again, especially in safe seats)

▶ difficulty in getting to the polling station (though the local parties may provide transport for some voters), i.e. apathy, disillusionment, protest or practical difficulties.

The young, the poor, ethnic minorities and the unemployed are the most likely to abstain – or not to register at all – which tends to hit the Labour vote hardest. (In London in 1998, for example, 24 per cent of blacks were non-registered compared with 6 per cent of whites.)

4 True or false?

   a) Candidates lose their deposits if they win under 12.5 per cent of the votes cast.

   b) A safe seat is one which a particular candidate is virtually certain to win.

   c) The Boundary Commissions usually report every ten to fifteen years.

   d) Once elected, MPs may not resign.

   e) The party which wins the most votes always wins the general election.

ESSAYS

1 *Theme:* Electoral systems

Q? Examine the view that far from being a weakness in the case for electoral reform in the UK, the possibility that such reform might lead to a coalition government should be regarded as a positive advantage. How far does the experience of other countries justify the use of proportional representation in national elections and suggest that coalitions can be beneficial?

(AEB, Summer 1998, Paper 1)

A✓ Examiners' comments

'This was a very popular question, though a significant number of candidates tried to use it as an opportunity to use an answer they had prepared to a different question. A proportion of candidates completely ignored the second part of the question. Some of those who did respond made the mistake of thinking that Italy had abandoned PR rather than going over to a German-style AMS system in which 475 members are elected from single-member constituencies and the remaining 155 seats are filled from lists and awarded so as to make the overall result more proportional. Another popular misconception was that France operates a PR rather than a second ballot system. Most of those who did focus on the question as set were aware that some political commentators see the coalition governments that are likely to come with PR as a positive strength. It was also noted that some Labour politicians clearly do not fear a possible Lib-Lab administration if the Jenkins Commission recommends a form of PR and if it is supported in a referendum. It is most unlikely there will be an outright winner in the elections for the first Scottish Parliament, yet perceptive candidates noted this had not been argued as a weakness. In spite of fears often expressed in the UK, the coalitions experienced in, for example, Eire and Germany, were not thought to have led to the government of either country to be weakened, though the same could certainly not be said of Italy or, perhaps, Israel, where (a majority of candidates pointed out) governments are often unstable and sometimes beholden to fanatical extremist minorities.

Most answers noted that electoral reform, particularly PR, is often criticised on grounds of leading to unstable governments. Most candidates were aware that such a view had been challenged by writers and academics such as Vernon Bogdanor, S.E. Finer and Joe Rogaly who have argued that coalition governments which denied any one party total power would be beneficial for the political system, avoiding the danger of what Finer called "zig zag" politics before the Conservatives installed themselves in power for 18 years. The long-standing coalition between Christian Democrats and Free Democrats in Germany was often cited as an example of how coalition government can engineer stability, though a weakness even of the German example has to be the fact that in the past the small number of Free Democrats changed sides and abandoned the Social Democrat government to install the Christian Democrats in their place. There were also frequent references to Eire where coalitions of one sort or another seem to shift into and out of power. Thoughtful candidates carefully evaluated the case for both proportional representation and coalition government. They were able to distinguish between PR and other forms of electoral reform such as alternative vote or second ballot, and many discussed the activities and likely impact of the Jenkins Commission. A few candidates went on to deploy the Adonis argument that while Tony Blair's government has a large majority, they might wish to have the support of the Liberal Democrats as an insurance policy against the more "extreme" Labour MPs, just as the Conservatives depended on the Lib Dems to help them get the Maastricht Treaty through the House of Commons. The Lib Dem-Lab Cabinet Committee was regarded by the candidates who mentioned it as evidence of a bipartisan approach to some constitutional or related issues, just as the Scottish Constitutional Convention was another grand alliance for reform. They concluded that perhaps a co-operative model of politics may be emerging with which coalition government could easily become compatible.'

5 Answer the following question.

To what extent do the results of recent elections support the case for electoral reform in Britain?

(Oxford and Cambridge, June 1997, Paper 1)

Use the figures below in your answer.

General election results 1970–1997

Date	Party	Votes (millions)	% Votes	Seats	% Seats
1970	Cons*	13,145	46.4	330	52.4
	Lab	12,179	42.9	287	45.6
	Lib	2,118	7.5	6	1.0
	Others	903	2.2	7	1.1
1974 (Feb)	Cons	11,869	37.9	297	46.8
	Lab*	11,639	37.1	301	47.4
	Lib	6,063	19.3	14	2.2
	Others	1,762	5.6	23	3.6
1974 (Oct)	Cons	10,465	35.8	277	43.6
	Lab*	11,457	39.2	319	50.2
	Lib	5,347	18.3	13	2.1
	Others	1,920	6.6	26	4.2
1979	Cons*	13,698	43.9	339	53.4
	Lab	11,510	36.9	268	42.2
	Lib	4,314	13.8	11	1.7
	Others	1,700	5.5	17	2.7
1983	Cons*	13,103	42.4	397	61.0
	Lab	8,462	27.6	209	32.2
	Lib/SDP	7,776	25.3	23	3.6
	Others	1,420	4.6	21	3.2
1987	Cons*	13,760	42.3	376	59.4
	Lab	10,030	30.8	229	36.1
	Lib/SDP	7,341	22.6	22	3.5
	Others	1,398	4.3	23	3.5
1992	Cons*	14,092	42.0	336	51.6
	Lab	11,560	35.4	271	41.6
	Lib Dem	5,999	17.9	20	3.1
	Others	1,998	5.6	24	3.7
1997	Cons	9,593	31.5	165	25.0
	Lab*	13,517	44.4	419	63.6
	Lib Dem	5,243	17.2	46	7.0
	Others	2,513	8.5	29	4.4

(* governing party)

Note: Unless an essay question on electoral reform specifies 'PR', do not confine your answer to PR. Read the following examiners' comments carefully.

Q? Would a more democratic electoral system be compatible with strong and stable cabinet government?

(London, Feb. 1976, Paper 1)

A✓ **Examiners' comments**

'Firstly, there must be a clear discussion of what "more democratic" could mean. Merely to plunge into proportional representation would be a poor beginning. Credit could be gained by anyone who sees that initiative, recall, referenda and fixed-term elections have also been called "more democratic". An A grade can only be awarded if the discussion ranges more widely than proportional representation, but this alone if very well done could be awarded a grade B. Either conclusion can (and must) be reached. If both conclusions are reached then, for a candidate to progress beyond grades D and C, the difficulties must be faced. For example, the likely result is minority government or coalition, but these are not necessarily weak or unstable as this would depend on the circumstances, for example, wartime crises, and other countries. If conclusions are not reached, the candidate is unlikely to score beyond a D or C grade, particularly if s/he cannot see that simple majority government is not always strong. An A grade candidate will realise that "strong" and "stable" can work against each other.'

Additional essay tips

Key words:

▶ 'Initiative': where a new law (or repeal of an existing law) can be proposed directly by voters through a petition, and then put to a referendum, for example, USA, Switzerland.

▶ 'Recall': where a representative can be removed from office between ordinary elections by a vote of the people, for example, former USSR.

Note: In 1987, PR (party list system) in Portugal produced a single-party majority (Social Democratic) government with over 50 per cent of both votes and seats. Coalition governments produced by PR may be stable and strong, for example, Sweden, Germany. Some would argue that PR may produce a near-permanent, centrist coalition which could be too static. Equally, some would argue that a single-party majority government may be *too* strong – 'elective dictatorship' – especially if it rests on a minority of votes.

However, a 'majority' government with a minority of votes may be deemed weak in terms of popular support (former MP Roy Jenkins' argument); or relative to **extra-parliamentary** interests such as the EU, pressure groups, or other financial and international power bodies. Alternatively, it may only be stable within 'safe' policy limits, beyond which its own backbenchers may defeat it. Finally, 'stable' may mean different things: a secure majority, consistent policy and/or stable ministerial team, etc.

Q? Discuss the proposition that electoral systems are meant to shape political attitudes rather than reflect them.

(London, June 1985, Paper 1)

Note: This title has very little to do with first-past-the-post versus PR, and any answer which did not recognise that would fare badly.

A✓ **Short plan for guidance**

a) (i) The orthodox argument is that elections are intended to choose representatives in accordance with the wishes of the people. Hence, in Britain, convention that Queen chooses leader of *majority* party as PM; or in PR, principle that seats match votes . . .

(ii) *But:* electoral results are rarely an arithmetical reflection of votes; not in first-past-the-post, alternative vote, second ballot, *nor* sometimes in PR (for example, Spain, 1982: Socialists won 57 per cent of seats on 46 per cent of votes).

Problem with PR: no one votes for a coalition.

Nor, in most electoral systems, can people usually vote for specific policies.

Even votes themselves may not wholly reflect political attitudes, either at election, for example, tactical voting, or after it.

Fringe candidates and small parties are often deliberately excluded: for example, by £500 deposit in Britain; and 5 per cent minimum threshold of votes required to gain seats in Germany, which was ruled illegal by the German courts in 1990.

b) The British electoral system is clearly not meant to mirror political attitudes; it is meant to produce a workable government from within Parliament – the constitutional emphasis is more on 'responsible government' than on 'representative democracy'. Radical critics of Western electoral systems, for example, single elitists and Marxists, would argue that a limited vote-casting system was introduced in order to *prevent* a more radical degree of 'people-power' or stronger representation of people's views.

c) 'Electoral systems are meant to shape political attitudes': for example, through electoral campaigns: use of media, posters, etc. Key function of all political parties: education, propaganda, organising/shaping political opinion into cohesive blocks. Some parties produce their own opinion polls (or use others') to manipulate opinion, not merely to measure it.

Dismissive treatment (for example, by media and main parties) of minority parties during elections probably reduces their support; may be meant to do so.

d) Also, all electoral systems shape political attitudes in the wider sense by *legitimising* government at home and abroad: 'rigged' elections, for example, Marcos in the Philippines; Britain's 'mythical' mandate (Marshall); elections in 'totalitarian' systems, for example, Nazi Germany.

But, once political attitudes are 'shaped', they may then be 'reflected' by an electoral system.

e) 'Rather than': implies either/or. Title implies the very strong and cynical view that all electoral systems are deliberately intended to indoctrinate rather than to represent the voters. More accurate to say that all electoral systems both shape and reflect political attitudes to varying degrees; some are meant to do one more than the other.

2 *Theme:* **Voting behaviour**

Q? How true is it to say that voting behaviour in Britain is becoming more volatile?

(JMB, June 1984, Paper 1)

---

6 Write an essay on the title above, using your own notes, the contents of this chapter, and the points below – which are not in any logical order.

Note carefully the examiners' comments below.

Write a brief plan first.

▶ Influence of opinion polls . . .

▶ 'Deferential' v. 'secular' voting – outdated theory?

▶ 46 per cent of Labour and Conservative voters expressed 'very strong' allegiance in 1964, versus 23 per cent in 1997

▶ Changes in voting population . . .

▶ Changes in relative class sizes: increasing public service sector and white-collar workers, etc. . . .

▶ 1945–55, governments lost only one seat in a by-election; 1988–97 they lost every single one

▶ Images of party leaders (for example, 1997 Blair versus Major)

▶ In 1983, for the first time, less than half of the voters – one-third of the electorate – voted for their 'natural' class party, compared with two-thirds in 1966 (47 per cent v. 66 per cent)

▶ Very different regional patterns of voting, for example, Scotland

▶ Special factors, for example, the miners' strike 1974, the 'Falklands factor' 1983, Gulf war before 1992

▶ Rise of third party – cause or consequence of class dealignment?

▶ Increasing fragmentation rather than volatility of electorate?

▶ Changing regional voting patterns

▶ Previously 'safe' seats' have changed hands: for example, seven Cabinet ministers lost their seats in 1997

▶ Influence of media on voting attitudes . . .

▶ 'Consensus politics' versus 'adversary politics'

▶ Percentage of middle-class voting Cons. has fallen from over 60 per cent in 1945 to under 55 per cent in 1987 and 34 per cent in 1997

A✓ Examiners' comments on above question
'This most popular question very effectively discriminated the abilities of candidates. Answers varied from the poor and imprecise recital of theories now dated and no longer relevant to contemporary British politics to those that applied the recent work of Crewe and Rose. These better answers offered evidence from recent elections to show that there has been considerable class and partisan dealignment, and that also there has been the development of more distinct regional voting patterns.'

---

7 Write at least one of the following essays. Always write a brief plan first.

a) 'Since one of its consequences is to weaken the link between the government and the electorate, a system of proportional representation is less rather than more democratic.' Discuss.

(Oxford and Cambridge, July 1986, Paper 1)

b) If there were electoral reform, what other constitutional changes do you think would have to follow?

(London, June 1978, Paper 1)

c) Are 'democracy' and 'majority rule' the same thing?

(Oxford, Summer 1985, Paper 4)

d) Discuss the links between voting behaviour and the economy.

(London, Jan. 1998, Paper 2)

e) Examine the view that while most people tell friends, colleagues, party canvassers and the pollsters about their opinions, when they vote it is their interests which are in the forefront of their mind. Consider whether the shift towards market structures in the 1980s and 1990s has had a greater impact on interests than opinions.

(AEB, Summer 1998, Paper 2)

GUIDE TO EXERCISES

Page 42

1 a) *Summarise the results of the 1997 General Election.*

Labour won the election with a massive majority of 179 seats, i.e. 64 per cent, on 44 per cent of the votes cast – potential for elective dictatorship (Hailsham). The Conservative Party got 31 per cent of the votes and only 25 per cent of the seats (i.e. under-represented for the first time in living memory), with no gains anywhere and no seats at all in Scotland, Wales or Northern Ireland. They got the smallest number of seats since 1906 and their lowest share of the poll since 1832. The Liberal Democrats got 17 per cent of the votes and 7 per cent of the seats – under-represented as usual, but less so than before, i.e. 46 seats, the most for a third party since 1945 (on a lower vote than 1992 because of tactical voting and party targeting of seats). There were more women and black MPs elected than ever before, and one independent (non-party) MP, Martin Bell, who stood against Neil Hamilton on an anti-sleaze ticket. However, the turn-out was low (71 per cent) after a long and uninspiring campaign.

  b) *What factors help to explain the Conservatives' defeat?*

- Despite most economic indicators looking good, the voters were ready for a change after 18 years of Conservative power.

- New Labour had shifted well to the right, especially on taxation and public spending, and were widely regarded as safe by business and the middle-classes. Labour's accusation of 22 Tory tax rises hit home. Labour's more right-wing policies on law and order also hit a populist nerve.

- Blair's image was more popular than Major's.

- While Labour maintained a disciplined facade of unity, the Conservatives looked very divided, especially on Europe. Major had lost his majority and could not control his party, and was dependent on the Unionists for survival to the detriment of the Northern Ireland peace process. There were back-bench revolts (for example, over fishing quotas), defections (for example, Emma Nicholson and Alan Howarth) and dissension even within Cabinet.

- The Euro-sceptic Referendum and UK Independence Parties took some crucial votes from the Conservatives.

- Sleaze was a big factor: the arms to Iraq and cash for questions scandals lingered, and when Neil Hamilton refused to resign as MP it made Major look weak. Other Conservative MPs were behaving embarrassingly: for example, David Willetts (a former whip who improperly influenced the cash for questions committee); Nicholas Scott (drunk in gutter), Jerry Hayes (rumoured sex with under-age boy); and David Evans (racial and sexual remarks to a group of sixth-formers).

- The government itself acted unconstitutionally when it paired three MPs twice on a crucial Commons vote.

- Some privatisation policies were unpopular, notably British Rail.

- The Tories were particularly unpopular in Scotland because of the poll tax fiasco and growing voter support for devolution.

- Overall, the Conservatives looked tired and directionless but also arrogant and complacent, despite a rapidly declining membership (with an average age of 64) throughout the country.

- Their massive defeat in a by-election in February 1997 was a sign of things to come.

Page 47

2   a)   The 'bound' party list system.

b)   The party list system (both types).

c)   STV; and the party list system may be based on multi-member, regional constituencies, or may treat the whole country as a single constituency (for example, Israel).

Advantages of multi-member constituencies:

- Voters have a choice of MPs to represent them.

- Competing MPS may work harder for their constituents.

- Different shades of thinking in one party can be represented by different MPs in one constituency.

Disadvantages:

- Constituencies would probably be larger, less homogeneous and less easy to represent.

- Blurring of accountability between different MPs.

- MPs may work less hard if others are there to do the work.

d)   The alternative vote, AV+ and the second ballot.

e)   AMS and AV+.

Advantages:

- Non-constituency MPs can concentrate on 'national' issues and on parliamentary versus constituency work (for example, committees).

- Maintains one-to-one relationship between constituency MPs and voters, whilst also giving a greater degree of proportionality.

Disadvantages:

- Non-constituency MPs are not elected by voters.

- Closed party list element gives greater power to party machines.

f) The second ballot.

Advantage: Produces one winner with absolute majority of votes, while also allowing sophisticated re-casting of votes, or second thoughts.

Disadvantage: Prone to apathy and low turnout on second ballot.

g) Alternative vote, second ballot, STV, 'free' party list, AMS and AV+.

Advantages:

- More choice for voters
- Allows electorate to vote for personalities as well as parties – may improve quality of representatives.

Disadvantages:

- Complexity
- Undermines 'the doctrine of the mandate' – theory that the link between voters and policies is party.

h) STV, party list and AMS.

Advantages:

- Fairer and more representative
- More 'pluralist'

Disadvantages:

- May produce coalitions where small parties have disproportionate power.
- May produce fragmented and inefficient legislature.

i) Second and third preference votes are given the same weight as first preference votes; minority parties may have disproportionate balance of power.

j) Initiative, recall, referenda, fixed-term elections, primaries, votes for 16–18-year-olds, a presidential system, an elected second chamber, lower (or no) deposit, devolution . . . and many others.

Page 47

3 *How representative is proportional representation?*

Diverse definitions of representative: a) Reflecting voters' views.

b) Reflecting voters' interests.

c) Reflecting voters' social background.

Some forms of PR are less proportionately representative of votes cast than others, for example, STV is less proportional than party list.

Generally, PR is likely to produce hung parliaments and coalition governments. Compared with first-past-the-post, these may be *more* representative of voters' views as expressed at the ballot box because:

d) seats accurately reflect the voting arithmetic

e) an over-represented, single-party government cannot dictate all policy

f) coalitions may be more moderate, consensual, broad-based and talented.

However, coalition governments may be seen as *less* representative of voters' views, despite basic proportionality, because:

g) there is no mandate for compromise, coalition policies

h) small parties may hold a disproportionate balance of power

i) the one-to-one relationship between MP and voter may be lost.

However well proportional coalition governments may represent voters' *views*, there is no guarantee that they will be any better than first-past-the-post in representing either voters' best interests or social backgrounds.

Assessing specific types of PR:

j) AMS and AV+ are the least representative forms of PR in the sense that they contain at least 50 per cent non-proportionality, but because they retain single-member constituencies they are representative in the sense of maintaining the one-to-one link between MP and voter.

k) STV's main characteristic is multi-member constituencies. These may enhance representation of voters' views *and* interests because voters have a choice of MPs to approach and the MPs may be more hard-working because competitive. The alternative danger with multi-member constituencies is that MPs may 'pass the buck', be *less* hard-working and less directly accountable.

Another problem about representation of voters' views arises out of the system of preference voting, namely that second preferences have the same weight as first preferences.

l) The party list system is broadly the most representative of voters' views in that it is the most arithmetically proportional, but the bound list system (as introduced by Labour for EU parliamentary elections) is unrepresentative in that the party machine, and not the voters, decides who will be the MPs. The free list system is technically the most representative of all but, precisely because it is the most proportional, it may undermine representation in the sense that it is most likely to raise the problems of hung Parliaments and coalitions.

Page 51

4 a) False – now 5 per cent

b) False – it is one which a particular party is virtually certain to win, regardless of candidate

c) True

d) True – they must disqualify themselves for example, by taking a paid Crown office

e) False – for example, 1951 and Feb. 1974

REFERENCES

Butler, D. and Kavanagh, D. (1997) *The British General Election of 1997*, Macmillan
Crewe, I. (1992) 'Why did Labour lose (yet again)?', *Politics Review*, Autumn
Duverger, Maurice (1964) *Political Parties*, Methuen
Marshall, G.W. (1971) *Constitutional Theory*, Oxford University Press
McKenzie, R.T. and Silver, A. (1968) *Angels in Marble*, Heinemann
Rose, Richard (1982) *Understanding the United Kingdom*, Longman

4 Members of Parliament and political parties

TOPIC NOTES

Key facts and concepts

Despite significant improvements in the 1997 general election, parliamentary candidates and MPs are still by no means 'representative' of the electorate in their social background; as some essay questions put it, they are still predominantly white, male and middle class. This is partly because of discrimination in the process of selection of candidates (the controversy over the selection of the black candidate John Taylor in the Cheltenham Conservative Constituency Party in 1990 still serves as a good example); and partly because working-class people, women and ethnic minorities are slower to come forward as candidates (because of pressures of work, financial constraints, lack of political background, contacts or self-confidence). In the early 1990s, Labour adopted a policy of all-women short-lists in many constituencies, but this was ruled illegal in 1996, though not before a large number of women candidates had been chosen. Since the 1997 election, active thought has been given to possible reforms of the House of

Commons – such as fewer late-night sittings and even the number of available toilets – which might make it easier for women, especially, to serve as MPs. Whether MPs must be 'typical' of voters in order to represent them adequately is, however, debatable. Traditional Tory philosophy would argue that MPs should be socially 'superior' to the mass of voters in order to represent their best interests.

Parliamentary candidates are chosen by their local constituency parties (unless they are standing as independents). In 1993 the Labour Party introduced a new method of selection based on 'one member, one vote' (OMOV) in the local party. This is similar to the American system of closed **primary elections** for political candidates. However, there have been some rows within Labour when the central party leadership has **vetoed** a candidate whom they perceived to be too left-wing (for example, Leeds North East candidate Liz Davies in 1995). In the Conservative Party, candidates are selected by local constituency associations.

British MPs must be British subjects, over 21 years of age, and must deposit £500 with the election Returning Officer which is forfeited if they obtain under 5 per cent of the votes cast in the constituency. Those disqualified from membership of the Commons include those disqualified from voting, plus undischarged bankrupts, clergy of the established churches, judges, civil servants and other Crown officials, heads of nationalised industries and directors of the Bank of England and those convicted of corrupt practices at elections. For example, Labour MP Mohammed Sarwar (the first Muslim MP) was tried in 1999 for electoral fraud and perverting the course of justice, for allegedly trying to bribe another candidate against campaigning.

Technically, MPs can be expelled from the party (as was Mohammed Sarwar), but cannot be sacked as MPs by the parties, because liberal democratic theory suggests that only the voter should have the power to select or reject an MP (though none of the parties allows the voters to select parliamentary *candidates*).

Many essay questions ask about the diverse roles and conflicting loyalties of MPs; the key concepts of 'representation' and 'responsibility' should be addressed in essay answers. Who – or what – should MPs represent? How feasible or valuable are different theories of representation? To whom should MPs be accountable? Thus, in a parliamentary system, what is – or should be – the theory and practice of representative and responsible government in Britain? (Bear in mind that the question of 'what should be' raises issues of both principle and practicality.)

Diverse roles of an MP

Legislator

MPs are elected to a national legislative assembly. They debate and vote on parliamentary bills in the House of Commons and in standing committees. They are constrained by party discipline from speaking or voting against the party line on a two- or three-line whip, on pain of suspension from the party. However, backbenchers may assert themselves by rebelling collectively against a bill. This usually happens where MPs see the bill as contrary to the basic principles of their party. Norton argues that backbenchers have been more ready to revolt since the 1970s, and that this increases both the power and the authority of the House of Commons.

1 Read the paragraph above, then complete the following exercises.

    a) Find and list *three* important examples of backbench revolts.

    b) Were any of these issues 'contrary to the basic principles of the party' and, if so, how?

    c) From Norton or elsewhere, find figures to support – or to refute – Norton's argument.

    d) Explain why backbench revolts may increase (i) the power and (ii) the authority of the Commons. What is the difference between the two?

Backbenchers may initiate legislation in the form of **private members' bills**: for example, Labour MP Michael Foster's anti-fox hunting bill in 1998, which was defeated because the government squeezed it out of the parliamentary timetable – arguably an 'unconstitutional' action on their part since a private member's bill should be purely a matter for Parliament. There is usually little time set aside for private members' bills anyway and in procedural terms they are easily defeated (especially those introduced after Question Time under the Ten Minute Rule). Therefore few are passed (though good publicity may be won for the issue): on average, over 50 are introduced in each parliamentary session but only around half a dozen are passed.

Controller of executive

According to the theory of parliamentary government, MPs – regardless of party – are supposed to scrutinise, check and publicise the activities of the government, through, for example, debate, Question Time, **standing** and **select committees**, voting on bills, adjournment motions, the Ombudsman and control of government finance as well as via the media, etc. Some MPs have made their mark in this role: for example, radical Labour MPs such as Dennis Skinner are a constant thorn in the flesh of the Labour government. They are, however, constrained in this role by:

▶ the power of a majority government to push through bills: for example, in 1997, cuts in lone parents' benefits were forced through despite a 47-strong revolt by Labour MPs

▶ lack of time available to backbenchers in the Commons

▶ lack of information granted to Parliament by government in Britain's highly secretive system: for example, the Conservative government's arms to Iraq scandal, the BSE scandal in the 1980s and early 1990s, and Labour's arms to Sierra Leone scandal in 1998

▶ lack of office, research and secretarial facilities available to MPs (though new building is underway to help remedy this).

Labour MP Austin Mitchell once wrote that trying to control the executive was 'as useful as heckling a steamroller'. However, although only a backbench rebellion has the real *power* to defeat a majority government, MPs of all parties may have *influence* on government, by publicising embarrassing information or by conveying public opinion to government. The Labour leadership was genuinely shocked by the scale of the 1997 revolt on lone parents' benefit cuts and subsequently raised child benefit substantially as a concession.

To this end, MPs also use early day motions and points of order with growing frequency: for example, in 1998 139 MPs, mostly Labour, signed a parliamentary motion backing a private member's bill against age discrimination, where the government wanted only voluntary curbs.

Trainee minister

All ministers should, by convention, be selected from either the Commons or the Lords. (In America, by contrast, the executive may be drawn from the ranks of big business, the army, lawyers, academics, state governors, etc., as well as Congress.) Parliamentary work – in debate, in committee, and in the constituency – may provide some useful training for future executive office. However, since ambitious MPs may hesitate to offend their party leaders, MPs who see themselves as trainee ministers may do little to control their own governing party. The parliamentary system thus creates role conflict for some backbenchers.

Representative

MPs are also elected to express the views of their constituents, individually or severally.

Diverse responsibilities of an MP

MPs have wide-ranging, and sometimes conflicting, loyalties. To whom MPs are – or should be – responsible is a matter of debate; the answer depends on political **ideology**, party structure and personal inclination. The demands on an MP's loyalty include the following.

The parliamentary party

Disraeli said 'Damn your principles! Stick to your party.' The 'doctrine of the **mandate**' suggests that electors vote for a package of party policies as outlined in a manifesto, and therefore MPs are most effectively representing the voters' wishes if they toe the party line. The Conservative Party, especially, historically had a strong philosophical emphasis on party unity and loyalty to the leadership, but since the 1997 election the

Labour leadership has become markedly more disciplinarian. For example, in 1998 they expelled two Euro-MPs (Hugh Kerr and Ken Coates) from the party for public dissent.

Party conference

Whereas the Conservative conference is not a policy-making body, the Labour conference is – or, at least, was. Democratic socialists such as Tony Benn argue that Labour MPs should pursue conference policy, even if that means defying the whips. They argue that conference is a more broadly democratic forum than is the party leadership; though right-wing critics would point out that the conference, unlike the party leadership, tends to support radical, democratic socialist, 'Bennite' policies. For this reason it has been increasingly sidelined as a policy-making forum by internal party reforms (the so-called Partnership for Power) which gave a stronger voice to loyalists within the party.

Constituency party

The local party selects the MP and provides the electoral campaign back-up; rank-and-file activists may also have a good understanding of constituency needs. Many MPs therefore pay special heed to the local party, even where this may jeopardise their standing with the national leadership.

Constituents

Total subservience to the national party would negate the role of constituency MPs; and the strict theory of liberal democracy does not recognise party at all – it perceives a one-to-one relationship between the individual MP and voter. Thus, an MP who leaves one party and joins another need not stand for re-election, for example Conservative defectors such as pro-European Peter Temple-Morris who joined Labour in 1998. MPs' local role may cause difficulties where special constituency interests conflict with the 'national interest' (if there is such a thing) or with national party policy. For example, in 1997, Conservative MP John Gorst nearly left the party over the threatened closure of a local hospital. It may also be difficult to serve diverse local interests: for example, farmers versus farm-workers; and it is hard for an MP to gauge the views of constituents as a whole.

Interest groups

Many MPs have special personal interests (for example, deaf Labour MP Jack Ashley campaigns on behalf of disabled people). They are often sponsored or lobbied by pressure groups and private companies to act on their behalf. About one-third of Labour MPs are sponsored by trade unions (for example, Dennis Skinner by the National Union of Mineworkers); here, the trade union pays some of the candidate's campaign costs in return for a voice in Parliament where possible.

Many other MPs, especially Conservatives, are paid personal fees (ranging from £1,000 to £20,000 per year) as consultants or directors by pressure groups, private individuals and companies seeking to promote their own interests. There had long been a Register of MPs' Interests and loose guidelines about how such arrangements should operate, but the rules were unclear and often flouted. This generated the 'cash for questions' scandal of the 1990s.

(The Sunday Times)

In 1994, two Conservative MPs – Graham Riddick and David Tredinnick – and, more importantly, three Conservative ministers – Tim Smith, Neil Hamilton and Jonathan Aitken – were alleged to have tabled parliamentary questions in return for money from outside interests, notably from Harrods owner Mohamed Al Fayed. Tim Smith promptly and honourably resigned; Neil Hamilton and Jonathan Aitken clung to office for as long as possible and even tried to sue the media before having to make humiliating climbdowns (after which *The Guardian* described Hamilton on its front page as 'a liar and a cheat', and Jonathan Aitken in 1999 pleaded guilty to perjury and conspiracy to pervert the course of justice). Then Prime Minister John Major set up a Commission on Standards in Public Life (or commission on 'sleaze' as it was popularly described by the media) under senior judge Lord Nolan. When his recommendations for curbs on MPs' outside economic activities were debated in the Commons, John Major unwisely supported the many Conservative MPs who opposed any such constraints. The Commons' vote went against them and even strengthened some of Nolan's suggestions. In 1996 the following rules were agreed.

▶ MPs must register all outside interests with a Parliamentary Commissioner for Standards (originally Sir Gordon Downey, then [1999] Elizabeth Filkin).

▶ MPs must disclose sources and amounts of outside earnings.

▶ MPs are forbidden from tabling questions on behalf of outside paying interests and must declare such interests when speaking in debates.

▶ A new Commons' Committee on Standards and Privileges has been established to enforce the new rules.

The 1997 Labour government was later ordered by Lord Neill (who had replaced Lord Nolan) to return a £1 million donation from Formula One boss Bernie Ecclestone – which had coincided with an exemption for motor racing from a ban on tobacco sponsorship; and Prime Minister Tony Blair was personally rebuked by the Commons Standards Committee for not declaring a foreign trip financed by Formula One.

National interest

Burke argued in 1774 that an MP was a member of 'a deliberate assembly of one nation with one interest, that of the whole,' and that MPs should pursue the 'general good' according to their personal judgement. The concept of a 'national interest' is central to traditional political conservatism, but is denied by liberals (who perceive diverse individual interests) and by socialists (who perceive conflicting class interests). However, all governments bring the concept into play when it suits their policy objectives.

Conscience

This is the second feature of Burke's theory of the role of an MP: 'Your representative owes you not his industry only, but his judgement; and he betrays instead of serving you, if he sacrifices it to your opinion'. Private conscience is given expression particularly in free votes in the Commons (for example, on capital punishment, abortion and homosexuality laws), in private members' bills and in backbench revolts. It may obviously conflict with party, constituency and other interests outlined above.

Political parties

A party system implies political decision-making and representation on the basis of formal, organised groups of (more or less) like-minded people who stand candidates for election on a common policy programme. This may be a one, two or multi-party system. A party system, of any type, has merits and demerits as compared with, for example, representation and political decision-making by independent individuals. This is the subject of many essay questions: such as 'Could Britain be well-governed without a party system?' (London, June 1978 Paper 1). The issues involved include representative and responsible government, 'elective dictatorship' and pluralism.

The parties listed overleaf took part in the 1997 general election.

Advantages of a party system
▶ Parties provide the basis for a coherent and comprehensive body of policies for government.
▶ Parties organise and crystallise public opinion into coherent blocks.
▶ Parties educate public opinion via their activities in Parliament, the media, etc. (though they may also try to manipulate and mislead public opinion for party advantage).
▶ Parties provide effective organisation, financing and campaigning for parliamentary candidates.
▶ According to the 'doctrine of the mandate', an elected government is authorised, or even obliged, to implement the policy proposals contained in its party manifesto; the party system is therefore essential for representative government.

1997 GENERAL ELECTION

Major Parties: C.- Conservative; Lab - Labour; Lab Co-op - Labour & Co-operative; LD - Liberal Democrat; PC - Plaid Cymru; SNP - Scottish National Party; Ref - Referendum Party; Green - Green; UUP - Ulster Unionist Party; DUP - Democratic Unionist Party; SDLP - Social and Democratic and Labour Party; SF - Sinn Fein; Alliance - Alliance.

Minor parties: 21st Cent - 21st Century Independent Foresters; Albion - Albion Party; ANP - All Night Party; Alt LD - Alternative Liberal Democrat; Embryo - Anti Abortion Euthanasia Embryo Experiments; ACA - Anti Child Abuse; ACC - Anti-corruption Candidate; AS - Anti-sleaze; AS Lab - Anti-sleaze Labour; B Ind - Beaconsfield Ind, Unity Through Electoral Reform; Bert - Berties Party; BHMBCM - Black Haired Medium Build Caucasian Male; BDP - British Democratic Party; BFAIR - British Freedom and Individual Rights; Home Rule - British Home Rule; BIPF - British Isles People First Party; BNP - British National Party; Fair - Building a Fair Society; By-pass - Newbury By-pass Stop Construction Now; Care - Care in the Community; Rights - Charter for Basic Rights; Ch D - Christian Democrat; Ch Nat - Christian Nationalist; Ch P - Christian Party; Ch U - Christian Unity; CSSPP - Common Sense Sick of Politicians Party ; Comm Lge - Communist League; Comm Brit - Communist Party of Britain; CRP - Community Representative Party; CASC - Conservatives Against the Single Currency; CVTY - Conservatory; Constit - Constitutionalist; CFSS - Country Field and Shooting Sports; D Nat - Democratic Nationalist; EDP - English Democratic Party; Ind Hum - English Independent Humanist Party; EUP - European Unity Party; FDP - Fancy Dress Party; Fellowship - Fellowship Party for Peace and Justice; Dynamic - First Dynamic Party; NIFT - Former Captain NI Football Team; FP - Freedom Party; FEP - Full Employment Party; Glow - Glow Bowling Party; GRLNSP - Green Referendum Lawless Naturally Street Party; Stan - Happiness Stan's Freedom to Party Party; Heart - Heart 106.2 Alien Party; Hemp - Hemp Coalition; HR - Human Rights '97; Hum - Humanist Party; Ind - Independent; Ind AFE - Independent Against a Federal Europe; IAC - Independent Anti Corruption in Government/TGWU; Anti-maj - Independent Anti-majority Democracy; Ind BB - Independent Back to Basics; Ind C - Independent Conservative; Ind CRP - Independent Conservative Referendum Party; Consult - Independent Democracy Means Consulting The People; Ind Dem - Independent Democrat; Ind ECR - Independent English Conservative and Referendum; Ind F - Independent Forester; Ind Green - Independent Green: Your Children's Future; Ind Lab - Independent Labour; Ind No - Independent No to Europe; Ind OAP - Independent OAP; Ind Dean - Independent Royal Forest of Dean; Barts - Independent Save Barts Candidate; Beaut - Independently Beautiful Candidate; IZB - Islam Zinda Baad Platform; Ind Isl - Island Independent; Juice - Juice Party; JP - Justice Party Ind; JRP - Justice and Renewal Independent Party; KBF - Keep Britain Free and Independent Party; Lab Change - Labour Time for Change Candidate; LCP - Legalise Cannabis Party; Lib - Liberal; Loc C - Local Conservative; LGR - Local Government Reform; Loc I - Local Independent; Logic - Logic Party Truth Only Allowed; Byro - Lord Byro versus The Scallywag Tories; LC - Loyal Conservative ; Mal - Male Voice of the People Party; Meb Ker - Mebyon Kernow; Miss M - Miss Moneypenny's Glamorous One Party; Loony - Monster Raving Loony Party; MRAC - Multi-racial Anti-corruption Alliance; Musician - Musician; Nat Dem - National Democrat; NF - National Front; NLP - Natural Law Party; N Lab - New Labour; New Way - New Millennium New Way Hemp Candidate; NPC - Non-party Conservative; None - None of the Above Parties; NIP - Northern Ireland Party; NI Women - Northern Ireland Women's Coalition; O Lab - Old Labour; Pacifist - Pacifist for Peace, Justice, Co-operation, Environment; PF - Pathfinders; Slough - People in Slough Shunning Useless Politician; Choice - People's Choice; PLP - People's Labour Party; PP - People's Party; Plymouth - Plymouth First Group; Shields - Pro Interests of South Shields People; ProLife - ProLife Alliance; PUP - Progressive Unionist Party; PAYR - Protecting All Your Rights Locally Effectively; R Alt - Radical Alternative; Rain Isl - Rainbow Connection Your Island Candidate; Dream - Rainbow Dream Ticket Party; Rain Ref - Rainbow Referendum; R Lab - Real Labour Party; Ren Dem - Renaissance Democrat; Rep GB - Republican Party of Great Britain; RA - Residents Association; Rizz - Rizz Party; Ronnie - Ronnie The Rhino Party; Route 66 - Route 66 Party Posse Party; SCU - Scottish Conservative Unofficial; SLI - Scottish Labour Independent; SLU - Scottish Labour Unofficial; SSA - Scottish Socialist Alliance; Scrapit - Scrapit Stop Stratford Ring Road Now; SIP - Sheffield Independent Party; Soc Dem - Social Democrat Socialist; SEP - Socialist Equality Party; Soc Lab - Socialist Labour Party; Soc - Socialist Party; SPGB - Socialist Party of Great Britain; Beanus - Space Age Superhero from Planet Beanus; Spts All - Sportsman's Alliance: Anything but Mellor; SFDC - Stratford First Democratic Conservative; SG - Sub-genius Party; Teddy - Teddy Bear Alliance Party; FP - The Fourth Party; Mongolian - The Mongolian Barbecue Great Place to Party; NLPC - the New Labour Party Candidate; PPP - The People's Party Party; Speaker - The Speaker; Third - Third Way; Top - Top Choice Liberal Democrat; UK Ind - UK Independence Party; UKPP - UK Pensioners Party; UKU - United Kingdom Unionist; UA - Universal Alliance; Value - Value Party; Wessex Reg - Wessex Regionalist; WCCC - West Cheshire College in Crisis Party; Whig - Whig Party; WP - Workers' Party; WRP - Workers Revolutionary Party.

(The Times Guide to the House of Commons (1997) Times Books)

▲ *The major and minor parties taking part in the 1997 general election*

▶ The convention of collective responsibility, whereby government is accountable to Parliament and hence to the electorate, assumes an executive united around a common body of policy. The party system is therefore essential for responsible government.

▶ The party system provides stability and consistency of government.

Disadvantages of a party system

▶ A single-party, majority government based on strong party discipline may amount to 'elective dictatorship'.

▶ Parties may encourage partisan conflict for its own sake, undermining effective government.

▶ Voters have no choice between the policies of any one party.

▶ Voters have no say in the parties' candidates (though 'open primaries' could be introduced, as in the USA).

▶ The party system discourages close, personal contact between MPs and voters.

▶ The party system undermines MPs' independence and **individualism**.

▶ The national or local party machines may have excessive power, for example, over MPs, at the expense of the voters.

▶ The party system may permanently exclude some minority views, or may neglect important issues which cut across orthodox party lines (for example, moral issues, such as abortion or capital punishment).

▶ The party system excludes able independents.

Britain is often also described as a *two-party system*.

---

2 a) Define a two-party system.

b) Give three reasons for, and three reasons against, describing Britain as a two-party system. On balance, do you think Britain is a two-party system or not?

c) Suggest three likely advantages, and three likely disadvantages, of a two-party system.

By the late 1990s, when the Conservative Party had been in government for 18 consecutive years and for two-thirds of the post-war period, commentators increasingly began to speak of Britain as a *dominant party system*, i.e. one where a single party is in power over long periods of time for most of the time (whether with a small or large majority). The main disadvantages of such a system are that:

▶ the governing party becomes complacent, arrogant and even corrupt

▶ government becomes stagnant and runs out of useful ideas

▶ alternatively, government casts around for new ideas for their own sake, which may generate policy instability

▶ the Opposition lacks information and experience over the long term, especially in a system as secretive as Britain's

▶ institutions such as the civil service, police and judiciary may become 'politicised'

▶ large sections of the electorate are long excluded from representation by government and may become apathetic or angry; they may turn to direct action, etc. Even supporters of the governing party may tire and develop the 'time for a change' sentiments so evident in the 1997 election.

Principles and policies of the major parties

The Conservative Party

The Conservative Party (the oldest of the three main parties) under Thatcher was led by economic conservatives who emphasise private property, the free market, individual enterprise and self-help, reducing inflation, public spending and taxation (at the expense of employment, if necessary). Paradoxically, the stress on 'rolling back the frontiers of state' in the economy was combined with growing political centralisation and state control, for example, of education and local government. They tend also to be strongly Euro-sceptical. There is also, however, still an older school of more traditional political conservatives in the party (for example, the late Lord Whitelaw) who emphasise social stability and consensus, traditional institutions (for example, monarchy, Church and Lords), the nuclear family, Christian **morality** and public duty. The 'wets' (a derogatory label coined by Mrs Thatcher) combine traditional Toryism with a Keynesian approach to economic policy, favouring some state intervention, a mixed economy, public spending and welfare and strongly pro-Europe – for example, Michael Heseltine and Kenneth Clarke. John Major and especially William Hague have leant more towards the Thatcherite wing of the party which has caused continuous intra-party conflict especially over Europe. All Conservatives advocate private property, hierarchy, strong defence and law and order.

William Hague had a profoundly difficult task after the 1997 election in trying to reassert or redefine the party's identity, with rather ambiguous slogans such as 'the British way'. The voters had, apparently, pushed the Conservatives so firmly out of their hearts and minds that, in October 1998, 67 per cent of voters polled could not name a single Shadow Cabinet minister. Also, the average age of Conservative party members at that time was 64; one of Hague's main aims was therefore to attract more young people into the party.

The Labour Party

The Labour Party (founded in 1900) was historically similarly divided between a more right-wing, social democratic leadership which favoured 'market socialism' – freedom, fairness and fraternity in a mixed, mainly private enterprise, economy – combined with some state control and planning, welfare and multilateral nuclear disarmament within international bodies such as NATO and the EU; and the more radical left-wing demo-cratic socialists (for example, Tony Benn), who seek extensive collective ownership, workers' democracy, welfare, social equality, greater political participation and political reform (for example, of the House of Lords), unilateral nuclear disarmament and with-drawal from NATO and the EU.

In 1995 Labour abandoned Clause IV of its founding constitution about common owner-ship, the most sacred symbol of old Labour values. This was the most symbolic moment of the shift from 'old' to 'new' Labour, pioneered by Neil Kinnock and then John Smith before Tony Blair took over as leader. As DTI Secretary Stephen Byers said in 1999, 'new' Labour is about 'wealth creation, not wealth distribution'. Blair's 'third way' is more right-wing than either of the old Labour schools of thought: although it has elements of social democracy within it, it has chosen largely to continue Conservative **New Right** economic, fiscal and law and order policies, combined with the pro-European stance of the 'wets' and a radical liberal programme of constitutional reforms. Senior Conservative Lord Onslow said of the Labour government in its early days, 'They're buggering up the constitution and ruining fox hunting. Otherwise, it's a perfectly sound Tory government.'

Examples of 'old' Labour policies enacted by the post-1997 Labour government include:

▶ Amsterdam Treaty: opted into the EU Social Chapter, for example, minimum wage – although it was set at a low £3.60 – and lower for under-21s – and was there-fore criticised by the trade unions

▶ restoration of trade union rights at GCHQ and compensation for sacked workers

▶ Employment Relations Act 1999: enhanced workers' rights of trade union recognition and parental leave – although it was watered down from the original Freedom at Work white paper and was criticised as inadequate by the trade unions

▶ shocked by the revolt over cuts in lone parents' benefits, the government restored them as family child care benefits in the March 1998 budget

▶ increased spending on education and health

▶ March 1999 budget: further increases in child benefit, help for pensioners and abolition of MIRAS, i.e. mortgage interest tax relief.

Examples of 'new' Labour policies enacted by the post-1997 Labour government include:

▶ Tony Blair's 'project': to create a centre-left alliance over the long term, excluding both radical left and radical right

▶ appointment of Liberal Democrats and Conservative 'wets' such as David Mellor, Michael Heseltine, Kenneth Clarke, Chris Patten to various official jobs, **quangos** and committees in pursuit of Labour's 'third way'

▶ privatisation (whole or part) of air traffic control, the; London underground, etc.

▶ putting out 'failing' state schools to private management tender

▶ Crime and Disorder Act 1998: introduced Britain's first child jail for 12–14-year-olds, curfews for under-10s, etc.

▶ extension of US-style 'three strikes' policy to increase minimum sentences for burglary, etc.

▶ 1998 cuts in lone parents' benefits

▶ 1999 welfare to work reform policies: similar to the US Workfare system with compulsory interviews and job offers

▶ Radical constitutional reforms: devolution, local government, Lords, Bill of Rights, etc.

The Liberal Democrats

The Liberal Democrats emerged out of the break-up of the SDP/Liberal Alliance after the 1987 election and the merger of most of its members under the leadership of Paddy Ashdown. They are much the same, philosophically, as the old Liberal Party. They favour a private enterprise economy but with positive state intervention to promote positive individual freedom through, for example, the provision of welfare and legislation to promote freedoms such as access to official information and the prevention of discrimination. They were historically the party most enthusiastic about civil rights and liberties, and issues of constitutional reform – notably a written constitution and Bill of Rights, proportional representation, devolution and a reformed second chamber. 'New' Labour has stolen many of their ideas – indeed, Tony Blair brought Paddy Ashdown into a Cabinet committee on constitutional reform soon after the 1997 election and steadily extended consultation with the Liberal Democrats on education, welfare, foreign and defence policy until Ashdown's resignation as party leader in June 1999. However, the Liberal Democrats' ideas on constitutional reform go further than Labour's to include proportional representation for Westminster and local authorities, an elected second chamber with appointed **cross-benchers**, fixed term parliaments, regional government for England and a Supreme Court able to veto legislation and resolve disputes within a federal UK with a codified constitution.

Conservatives – You can only be sure with the Conservatives

Economy

❒ Cut public spending to less than 40% of GDP over five years
❒ Aim for a 20p basic rate of income tax; maximum should be no more than 40p.
❒ Reduce families' tax bills by transferring personal allowances of people at home looking after children or relatives
❒ Privatise Parcelforce, London Underground; more competition in gas and water industries.

Welfare

❒ Increase NHS expenditure on a yearly basis.
❒ Begin to phase out State Earnings Related Pension Scheme (SERPS) by providing personal pensions for all employees.
❒ Extend Project Work Programme to get jobless off benefit and into work.
❒ Raise £25 million for housing estates by encouraging tenants to transfer to housing associations or private landlords.
❒ Guarantee school standards through national targets and the publication of test results for 7, 11 and 14 year olds.

Law and order

❒ Install 10,000 CCTV cameras in town centres and public places by 1999.
❒ A voluntary identity card scheme based on new photographic licence.
❒ Courts to impose a Parental Control Order on those parents failing to discipline children.
❒ Automatic life sentences for anyone convicted of second serious sexual or violent crime.

Environment

❒ New taxes to penalise water pollution.
❒ Reduce out of town shopping centres.
❒ End over-fishing in the North Sea.
❒ Cut carbon dioxide emissions by 10% by 2010.

Constitution

❒ Resist moves towards European federal state, safeguard national interest by staying out of a single European currency, maintain opt-out and 'wait and see'.
❒ Oppose rivals' plans for devolution for Scotland and Wales.

▲ *The Conservative Party's 1997 general election manifesto*

Labour – Britain deserves better

Economy

☐ No increase in basic (23p) or top (40p) rates of income tax over five year period.
☐ Keep Conservative spending plans for first two years of office.
☐ Maintain inflation target of 2.5% p.a.
☐ Keep trade union reforms of 1980s; grant unions recognition where this is the wish of the majority of the workforce.
☐ Establish a minimum wage – precise amount unspecified.
☐ Opt into the Treaty of Maastricht's Social Chapter.

Welfare

☐ Increase share of national income spent on education over five years.
☐ Cut class sizes for 5–7 year olds to a maximum of thirty – financed by abolition of assisted places scheme.
☐ Parental ballots on future of selective secondary schools.
☐ 250,000 young unemployed people to be taken off benefit and placed in work – financed by windfall tax on privatised utilities.
☐ Cut NHS waiting lists by 100,000 by reducing administrative costs by £100 million.

Law and order

☐ Fast track punishment for persistent young offenders.
☐ Reform Crown Prosecution Service to convict more criminals.
☐ Put more policemen on the beat.
☐ Crack down on petty crimes and neighbourhood disorder.
☐ Fresh parliamentary vote to ban all handguns.

Environment

☐ Cut carbon dioxide emissions by 20% by 2010.
☐ Promote energy saving schemes in housing.
☐ Increase amount of renewable energy.
☐ Improve public transport.

Constitution

☐ A plethora of referenda to decide upon: a Scottish Parliament; a Welsh Assembly; a Greater London Authority and Mayor; the method of electoral system for Westminster elections.
☐ European Convention of Human Rights to be incorporated into British law.
☐ Freedom of Information Act to replace Official Secrets Act.
☐ House of Lords: remove rights of hereditary peers to sit or vote in the Chamber; review the system of life peers.
☐ Single European Currency to be adopted following approval by referendum.

▲ The Labour Party's 1997 general election manifesto

Liberal Democrats – Make the difference

Economy

- ❐ Remove 0.5 million low earners from income tax by increasing personal allowance threshold by £200 to £4,245.
- ❐ Increase basic rate by 1p.
- ❐ New higher rate of 50p for those earning over £100,000.
- ❐ Aim to create a flexible labour market with a regionally variable minimum wage.

Welfare

- ❐ An additional £2 billion funding in education per year.
- ❐ Reduce class sizes to a maximum of thirty for 5–11 year olds.
- ❐ An additional £540 million for the NHS per year financed by an extra 5p levied on a packet of cigarettes.
- ❐ Free eye tests and dental checks on the NHS.

Law and order

- ❐ Put 3,000 more police officers on the beat; expansion of community policing.
- ❐ Require parents to participate in support projects where their children have been involved in juvenile crime.
- ❐ Give police and Customs and Excise support to stop importation of drugs.
- ❐ Strengthen criminal justice system.

Environment

- ❐ Cut road tax from £145 to £10 for cars under 1600 cc.
- ❐ Increase cost of petrol.
- ❐ A 30% reduction in carbon dioxide emissions.
- ❐ A carbon tax on fossil fuels.
- ❐ Greenfield tax to discourage development in the countryside.

Constitution

- ❐ Referendum on electoral reform for Westminster elections.
- ❐ Create a democratic second chamber.
- ❐ Establish a Bill of Rights.
- ❐ Introduce Home Rule for Scotland and Wales.
- ❐ A fixed-term parliament (four years).

▲ *The Liberal Democrats' 1997 general election manifesto*

Organisation and financing of the major parties

The structure of the major parties used to reflect their different philosophies and principles. For example, traditional conservative ideology stressed political hierarchy, 'natural governors' and loyalty to leadership; the Conservative leader – elected only by Conservative MPs from 1966 until the late 1990s – was therefore responsible for policy-making, party headquarters and internal appointments (for example, the chairman and Shadow Cabinet). The conference was not a policy-making body, but a political rally intended to demonstrate unity and loyalty to the leader. The Labour party's philosophy, by contrast, demanded greater intra-party democracy: the Shadow Cabinet was elected by the MPs; conference was a policy-making forum; and the National Executive Committee (NEC) – elected by conference – directed policy and controlled the party machine. The Labour leader had much less formal power – until Tony Blair.

The positions are now almost reversing. As Hague democratises the machinery of the Conservative Party, Blair centralises that of the Labour Party. Conservative leaders are now elected by all party members (one member, one vote) from a short-list of two candidates drawn up by MPs and – following the 'sleaze' of the 1990s – the Conservatives have set up their own Ethics and Integrity Committee.

Labour, by contrast, in 1995 set up Millbank Tower as a centralised campaigning and media centre. It has reduced the more radical input of activists and trade union **delegates** on policy in favour of the more moderate constituency members, and has downgraded conference in favour of the largely loyalist National Executive Committee (through their 1997 restructuring programme called 'Partnership in Power'). In sum, it has transformed the party from an 'activist-delegatory' organisation into an 'elite-plebiscitory' organisation where a largely quiescent membership periodically vote through leadership policy initiatives. It has also pushed through changes in the process of selection – from one member, one vote to an electoral college – of key candidates, for example, for London mayor and Welsh First Secretary, to exclude old Labour favourites like Ken Livingstone and Rhodri Morgan. There have been signs of rebellion within the party against this 'control freakery': for example, the election of four radical left-wingers to the NEC in 1998 despite the whips giving the MPs pre-named ballot papers on Blair's orders. There was also a decline in Labour membership in 1998 from 405,000 to 391,000.

The Conservative Party is financed largely by private firms and individuals, whereas the Labour Party was previously always financed largely by trade unions. However, this, too, has changed, with Labour looking increasingly to private donations, even setting up a 'Thousand Club' for wealthy individual donors like Bernie Ecclestone of Formula One. By 1997, only 46 per cent of Labour funding came from the unions, a 20 per cent fall from 1987. Both parties are also helped by free party political broadcasts and electoral postage, as well as by membership fees and fund-raising events staged by the local parties.

There were several scandals about party funding in the 1990s: for example, the Conservatives took money from what their critics called 'foreign crooks' such as fugitive businessman Asil Nadir; and Labour had its Ecclestone affair. Labour asked the Committee on Public Standards – chaired by Lord Neill since Lord Nolan's retirement – to establish clear rules about party funding. Embarrassingly for them, Neill first obliged Labour to return the £1 million to Ecclestone. In 1998 the following rules were proposed:

▶ foreign donations banned

▶ blind trusts abolished

▶ all national donations of £5,000+ and local donations of £1,000+ to be made public

► anonymous donations of £50 or more banned. (NB How?!)

► £20 million ceiling on each party's national election campaign spending

► tax relief on donations up to £500

► increased state funding for opposition parties

► shareholders to approve company donations and sponsorship

► equal state funding for both sides in referenda campaigns, and government should remain neutral

► an Electoral Commission to oversee the rules with the power to impose heavy fines.

The government almost immediately rejected the idea that it should remain neutral in forthcoming referenda such as on the single European currency, but said that it would legislate on the rest of the proposals in 1999.

Controversial issues, requiring balanced discussion, i.e. case for and case against, in relevant essays, include:

► What should be the main role(s) of an MP?

► Should MPs be full-time or part-time?

► Should MPs be allowed to accept any fees or payments beyond their salaries?

► Have curbs on 'sleaze' gone far enough?

► Does factionalism within the parties threaten to split them apart?

► What exactly is Tony Blair's 'third way'?

► How far have the main parties' policies converged in the 1990s, and why?

► Is new Labour too centralised and disciplinarian?

► Intra-party democracy in theory and practice: does it necessarily decline when a party is in office?

► The relative power of Labour and Conservative leaders, in and out of office: does the power and authority of prime ministerial office outweigh formal party differences?

► What sort of controls should there be on party funding?

► Should the trade unions' voice in Labour party affairs be further reduced or reformed?

---

3 Write short answers to the following questions.

a) (i) Distinguish between two types of party system.

(ii) Outline the nature of Britain's party system.

b) (i) How has the role of MPs changed in recent years?

(ii) Is this change undermining the representative nature of Parliament?

c) Distinguish between 'representative' and 'responsible' government.

ESSAYS

1 *Theme:* Role of MPs

Q? State a case for and a case against backbench MPs more frequently initiating legislation in the House of Commons across party lines.

(London, June 1978, Paper 1)

A✓ Short plan for guidance

Introduction: descriptive outline of 'parliamentary government', the party system and private members' bills.

Case for:

▶ To represent special interests of constituents in accordance with liberal democratic theory of MPs' role; or to promote sponsors' interests.

▶ To gain publicity for an issue – or for the MP – even if the bill is not passed. (Bills introduced under the Ten Minute Rule are most relevant here.)

▶ Thus to increase support for MP/party.

▶ To enhance parties' awareness of constituency needs and of MPs' opinions.

▶ Burkean concept of role of MP: to use independent judgement and conscience.

▶ Thus to make up for the loss of independents in the party system.

▶ To give more power to MPs and Parliament, versus executive, in accordance with the theory of parliamentary sovereignty.

▶ To reduce the danger of 'elective dictatorship' of single-party, majority government based on strong party discipline.

▶ To pursue important issues neglected by the parties (for example, moral issues, minority interests, or those where an MP has special expertise).

▶ To produce more active MPs.

▶ To enhance the Commons' role as as a deliberative chamber.

Case against:

▶ Need for strong party system to produce effective government in Parliament.

▶ 'Doctrine of the mandate': MPs are elected and expected by voters to support party manifesto policies.

▶ Government should be allowed to govern; trivial, obstructive or unsuccessful private members' bills may simply waste valuable Commons' time (and money).

▶ MPs depend on party for election, and owe loyalty to party, besides their natural sense of loyalty and support for party.

▶ Focus on narrow sectional or local interests may undermine 'national interest' which national party is pursuing.

▶ May produce conflicting body of statute law.

▶ MPs' power to abstain or rebel against government legislation is adequate.

▶ May antagonise party and jeopardise MP's promotion prospects within it.

▶ Practical difficulties of drafting bill, etc. may deflect MP from more important and productive tasks – for example, select committee work, constituency surgeries, etc.

Additional essay tips

▶ The format 'state a case for and a case against' requires balanced argument, but also a reasoned conclusion; the above structure leads to the conclusion that, on balance, the 'case against' is stronger; if you favour the 'case for', put it last.

▶ Consider whether the number of points in a plan is the crucial factor in deciding how to conclude, or whether some points have more weight than others, for example, do constitutional principles matter more than practical pros and cons?

▶ Note also that the phrase 'initiating legislation' does not imply that the private members' bills are necessarily passed.

▶ Finally, as an optional extra, if your syllabus includes coverage of other countries, for example, the USA and the role of members of Congress, you can use that information to make comparisons in this essay.

---

4   What other arguments, and topical examples, can you add to the above plan? For example, does it make any difference whether the MP is a government or opposition backbencher, or to which party the MP belongs?

---

2 *Theme:* The party system and 'elective dictatorship'

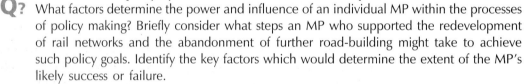

What factors determine the power and influence of an individual MP within the processes of policy making? Briefly consider what steps an MP who supported the redevelopment of rail networks and the abandonment of further road-building might take to achieve such policy goals. Identify the key factors which would determine the extent of the MP's likely success or failure.

(AEB, Summer 1998, Paper 1)

A✓ Examiners' comments

'Answers generally recognised that an MP may influence the policy-making of her or his party through backbench committees and conceivably through effective performances in select or standing committees. Seniority in the party, which wing of the party the MP comes from, how strong the party is in Parliament, how persuasive a publicist the MP is, were all identified as significant factors in helping to determine the extent of an MP's influence. Sadly, a number of weaker answers, which seemed to be based on a very superficial understanding of Parliament and the work of its members, argued that an MP might seek to win Parliamentary approval for his proposals during time allocated to private members' legislation. Only stronger answers went on to add that to have any chance of success the MP needs to enjoy government and wide cross-party support; even then, as Michael Foster, MP for Worcester, found in 1998, a determined minority can even thwart measures enjoying clear majority support.

Candidates generally recognised that an MP supporter of the government party who has been in Parliament for ten years or so is well placed to be a member or chairman of committees which may help her or him to advance any cause she or he supports. An MP's demeanour and style of working are important in the sense that someone who is regarded as sincere, honest and trustworthy may be seen as a valuable figurehead to play a leading role on an all-party committee; an opposition MP who has no capacity to gain support from other parties, including like-minded people in the government party, is unlikely to achieve success. Better informed candidates sometimes pointed out that the government is most sensitive to backbench pressures when its majority is small.

It was claimed that Macclesfield MP, Nicholas Winterton, got the government to agree to keep £8 million of new road schemes for his constituency in the programme as a result of threats to vote against the Major government if they decided otherwise. Thoughtful candidates pointed out that if the road/rail debate is relevant to any legislation, the MP will wish to be involved in the standing committee; he may even wish to promote a private member's bill, though the chances of success (particularly if the government is hostile or unpersuaded) are poor. Some answers suggested that the MP may be able to gain a place on the Transport departmental select committee, though if the party whips are opposed to the MP's point of view, other "safer" MPs are likely to be appointed instead. Answers adopting such a line sometimes went on to discuss the opportunities MPs have to engage with civil servants/ministerial advisers at select committee hearings. It was also recognised that if the MP is concerned with a specific project in a particular part of the country she or he is more likely to succeed than if they are trying to change policy in general for all the country, in which case, the MP in this example would certainly attract the wrath of the roads lobby. The best answers were able to relate the general or hypothetical points they made to tangible examples, perhaps from the areas in which they lived themselves.

Essentially, this question was about the "power" and opportunities open to MPs and the more answers reflected the "real" world of Westminster, the better they did. Unfortunately, though, examiners found little awareness of John Prescott's policy to encourage greater use of rail, nor did there seem to be much real knowledge of the work of MPs and Parliament.'

---

5 List ten opportunities, techniques and methods available to government opponents to challenge or influence the government. Give one effective, and one ineffective, example of the use of each (ensure that your examples are topical). Consider, as you do this exercise, what you take to mean by 'effective'.

---

3 *Theme:* **Parties, power and pluralism**

 Does the alternation of parties in government make any real difference to economic and political life in Britain?

(Cambridge, June 1985, Paper 1)

---

6 First, write brief notes on how you would answer this essay question; then read the notes below; then write a concise but comprehensive plan incorporating both sets of notes.

A✓ **Notes for guidance**
This title is open to broad and diverse interpretations:

► Single elitist or Marxist theory: the arguments that all major parties serve the interests of a single dominant elite or ruling class, and therefore a change of party makes no significant difference to the economic or political power structure.

► Consensus politics: the narrower argument that the two main parties in Britain share similar, centrist policies, despite their rhetoric of opposition. This argument was popular during the boom years, but from the late 1970s to early 1990s the opposite thesis of 'adversary politics' was more often advanced. There is now, again, substantial policy consensus between the two main parties, for example, on taxation, law and order, etc.

▶ Limits to the power of government: arguments contrary to the thesis of 'elective dictatorship', suggesting that even a radical government is constrained by, for example, Parliament, opposition parties, civil service, pressure groups, the international economic climate and international bodies such as the EU, IMF, NATO and USA. A comprehensive answer would include the cases for and against all of these arguments, with persuasive evidence about (lack of) changes in economic and political life in Britain at least since the war, and some attempt at value-judgement – is (lack of) change good or bad?

Q? 'In a successful system of Parliamentary government, the parties should agree on fundamentals and differ only over details.' Discuss, with reference to the present state of British Parliamentary government.

(London, June 1984, Paper 1)

A✓ **Examiners' comments**

'Candidates who answered this question largely ignored the words "successful", "fundamentals" and "details" that appeared in the quotation. Many candidates concentrated on differences in policy between the Conservative and Labour Parties, but few discussed whether the alleged post-war consensus was itself successful or a condition of success. Other fundamentals, which might include agreement about the basic rules underlying the political system, went largely unnoticed.'

Additional essay tips

▶ The core of this question is the problem that too little choice and diversity between parties undermines the freedom of electoral choice which is central to the pluralist theory of liberal democracy; while too much divergence and polarisation may produce deadlock, weak government, excessive conflict or even breakdown of the system. A balanced approach is necessary here.

▶ These points must be related to the theory and practice of 'parliamentary government' (as opposed to separation of legislature and executive).

▶ Go beyond discussion of 'consensus' and 'adversary politics' to consider all of the parliamentary parties, major and minor – including the Irish, Scottish and Welsh parties.

▶ Bear in mind that the Thatcher government was often described as 'Radical Right': how true was this description, and is there any risk of 'extremist' government or opposition ever threatening British 'parliamentary democracy' itself?

---

7 Write at least one of the following essays. Always write a brief plan first.

a) Should a backbench MP try to follow his or her party, the wishes of his or her constituents, or his or her own judgement?

(Oxford, Summer 1986, Paper 1)

b) Outline the reasons for the internal splits in the Labour, Liberal Democrat (previously the Liberals and SDP) and Conservative parties since 1979 and assess the effects of such divisions on the UK party system.

(AEB, Summer 1997, Paper 1)

c) Explain the disadvantages of a party system that is dominated by a single party.

(London, Jan. 1997, Paper 1)

d) Is participation through political parties a necessary condition of representative government?

(London, Jan. 1991, Paper 1)

e) Examine the view that Tony Blair has been responsible for dramatic changes in the Labour Party's principles, internal organisation and electability.

(Oxford and Cambridge, June 1997, Paper 1)

GUIDE TO EXERCISES

Page 63

1 a) Shops Bill 1986; second VAT rise on domestic fuel 1996; lone parents' benefit cuts 1997

  b) The Shops Bill neglected the traditional conservative stress on Christian morality and family unity; the VAT rise would have hit pensioners hard; traditional Labour principles seek to protect disadvantaged groups such as single parents.

  c) 'The 7-year period from April 1972 to April 1979 witnessed a total of 65 Government defeats on the floor of the House of Commons. To find a similar number in a 7-year period one has to go back to the 1860s . . . This new attitude was not confined to the 1974–9 Parliament. It carried over into the current Parliament' (Norton, p. 112). Update these figures.

  d) Backbench revolts may force Government to abandon a proposal – power; and may increase respect for MPs who are seen to be performing their constitutional functions effectively – authority.

Page 69

2 a) A system in which two major parties dominate the political scene, and no other single party is able to win executive power.

  b) For:

  • Balance of seats in Commons (give current figures)

  • Labour/Conservative single-party governments since 1945

  • 'Her Majesty's Government' and 'Her Majesty's Opposition', plus salary for Opposition Leader and Chief Whip, Commons' procedures such as Opposition Days, etc.

  Against:

  • Balance of votes in country (give current figures): for example, a 1998 poll in Scotland on voting intentions for the Scottish assembly produced the following result: SNP: 48 per cent, Labour: 34 per cent, Liberal Democrats: 9 per cent, Conservatives: 9 per cent

- Regional factors – for example, Northern Ireland parties
- Nine parties in House of Commons
- All parties are coalitions – for example, factions within the Conservative Party (for example, the Tory Reform Group) and within the Labour Party (for example, The Fabian Society).
- Britain as a dominant party system…
- Britain as an 'elective dictatorship'…

c) Advantages:

- Effective and accountable government and Opposition
- Clear choice for voters in system of parliamentary government
- Reflects 'natural divide' in population between conservatism and radicalism (Duverger).

Disadvantages:

- Over the long term it may create a dominant party system
- Strong, single-party government may mean 'elective dictatorship'
- Narrow choice for voters, contrary to 'pluralist' theory
- Tends either to consensus politics – lack of choice and innovation – or to adversary politics – excessive polarisation and 'swing of the pendulum' between policies of different governments.

Page 76

3 a) (i) *Distinguish between two types of party system.*

A party system implies political decision-making and representation on the basis of formal, organised groups of (more or less) like-minded people who stand candidates for election on a common policy programme. A one-party system means that only one party is allowed to put up candidates for election; all other parties are banned. This is a non-liberal democratic system and it operated in the former Soviet Union, Nazi Germany, etc. A dominant party system, on the other hand, means that many parties exist and more than one party may have the chance of winning power, but one party is in power over long periods of time – for example, the Conservatives in Britain for two-thirds of the post-war period and especially 1979–97.

(ii) *Outline the nature of Britain's party system.*

At electoral and regional level, Britain has a multi-party system: over one hundred parties stand candidates in general elections, there are nine parties in the House of Commons, the Liberal Democrats won 17 per cent of the votes in 1997 and the Scottish Nationalists are prominent in the Scottish polls. However, only two parties are dominant in the House of Commons with almost 90 per cent of the seats between them and most Commons' procedures – for example, pairing – assume two main parties. In some ways, Britain is even less than a two-party system: it was a dominant party system at least until 1997, and is now an 'elective dictatorship' (Hailsham) with Labour's massive 179 majority of seats – though on only 44 per cent of the votes.

b) (i) *How has the role of MPs changed in recent years?*

MPs are elected legislators in a national assembly with the additional task of scrutinising the executive in Britain's system of 'parliamentary government'. Thus their essential roles – making law, representing the people and controlling the executive – are unchanged. MPs today probably seek increasingly to represent their constituents' views and not simply their interests as the MPs judge them (i.e. they are delegates and not just representatives in the Burkean sense) – hence most hold regular surgeries to meet their constituents and take up their grievances. However, in recent years they have tended to see themselves more as professional politicians pursuing a long term career, often fulltime (rather than treating politics as a part-time hobby). British MPs average 20 years in the Commons, far longer than in most comparable countries. They also have increasing links with outside bodies such as businesses and pressure groups.

(ii) *Is this change undermining the representative nature of Parliament?*

As MPs become increasingly careerist, they are more likely to heed their party leadership and toe the party line, since their jobs may depend on the party. Thus they may be less independent-minded, less likely to revolt and more likely to be 'lobby fodder' for the national and/or local party, which may mean that they represent voters' views or interests on controversial issues less well (for example, only one Labour MP – Dennis Canavan – rebelled in 1998 over the government's unpopular policy on Scottish university tuition fees). Their growing links with outside interests fuelled the 'cash for questions' scandals of the 1990s (Smith, Hamilton, Aitken, etc.) and prompted the Nolan Inquiry and subsequent curbs on paid advocacy. Heavy lobbying of MPs by outside interests may distract MPs from focusing on their own constituents' interests. However, they have become more 'representative' of the voters since the 1997 election in terms of social background – for example, record numbers of female, black and Asian MPs.

c) *Distinguish between 'representative' and 'responsible' government.*

'Representative government' implies government of the people: elected or accredited by them; typical of them in social background; reflecting their views as a delegate, or their interests. 'Responsible government' implies government for the people: being responsive and ultimately accountable to them; governing wisely and sensibly but perhaps not popularly; or governing in the interests of the electors as perceived by the governors (Burke). In Britain the Labour Party stresses representative government, while the Conservative Party stresses responsible government. The constitutional arrangement of parliamentary government involves both: by convention, the executive is appointed from the majority party in the Commons in order to make it representative. The doctrines of **collective** and **individual ministerial responsibility** are intended to make ministers answerable to Parliament and the people for government policy and for departmental and individual errors. Ultimately Parliament can dismiss government on a vote of no confidence, as it did in 1979. The 'doctrine of the mandate' seeks to link party, policy and people and thus make government representative of the views of the voters. However, in practice there are flaws: the electoral system usually means that a 'majority government' in fact has a minority of votes cast. The strict doctrine of the mandate cannot apply when voters do not read manifestos or do not support all of the policies in them. The doctrines of collective and individual responsibility are not always applied – for example, William Waldegrave and Nicholas Lyell did not resign over the arms to Iraq scandal in 1996. Critics therefore seek reforms such as PR and devolution to enhance representative and responsible government in the UK.

Page 79

5 'Effective opposition' may come from ministers themselves, backbenchers, the House of Lords, select committees, the civil service, the courts, pressure groups, media and international bodies, especially the EU. Methods may include: Commons debates and votes, early day and adjournment motions, Opposition Days, cross-party criticism by the select committees, votes of censure, lobbying, the Ombudsman, ministerial speeches, leaks to the media or resignation, backbench committees, press or TV criticism, civil service obstruction, domestic or overseas courts ruling the government ***ultra vires***, EU regulations, directives and court rulings, etc. Find and list topical examples of each.

REFERENCES

Duverger, M. (1964) *Political Parties*, Methuen

Mitchell, Austin (1986) 'The seven roles of an MP: a personal view', *Social Studies Review*, May

Norton, Philip (1982) *The Constitution in Flux*, Blackwell

5 Parliament: House of Lords and House of Commons

KEY ISSUES

▶ Functions, (in)effectiveness and reform of Parliament

▶ Lords:

Power and authority

Criticisms and reform/abolition

Reasons for lack of reform

▶ Commons:

Procedural issues: for example, timetable, Question Time, facilities for MPs, televising debates and committees

Substantive issues: for example, representativeness: electoral system, two-party system, role of the Opposition, parliamentary privilege, devolution

'Elective dictatorship': delegated legislation, devolution, MPs' control of finance, access to information

Assessment of past reforms: for example, departmental select committees

TOPIC NOTES

Key facts and concepts

Note that essay questions on Parliament cover the Commons, Lords and monarchy (legislative functions only, for example, royal assent).

Functions of Parliament

Parliament has the following functions:

- ▶ making the law
- ▶ controlling the executive
- ▶ representing the people.

Subsidiary functions

It also has the following subsidiary functions:

- ▶ debate and deliberation
- ▶ controlling government finance
- ▶ channel of communication between government and electorate.

These could provide a useful framework for general essay questions, such as 'Discuss the role which Parliament plays in British democracy' (London, Jan. 1996, Paper 1). Such broad essay questions on the role of Parliament cover the electoral system, party system, practice of 'parliamentary government', nature of MPs and impact of the EU and devolution – all of which, critics say, combine to limit Parliament's effectiveness in carrying out its functions today. Essay answers should be very broad-ranging, concise and topical.

House of Lords

---

1 The House of Lords usefully illustrates the difference between the key political concepts of power and authority. Complete the passage below, using either 'power' or 'authority' as appropriate.

Under the Parliament Acts of 1911 and 1949, the .... of the Lords to delay legislation was limited to one year. It has no .... over money bills; but it has the .... of absolute veto over (a) any bill seeking to extend the life of Parliament, (b) private bills and (c) delegated legislation. However, the Lords derive .... from tradition, expertise and responsible use of their legal .... Television broadcasting of their proceedings since the mid-1980s may also have enhanced their ....

The 1997 Labour government came to power with a manifesto commitment to reform the Lords; they promised to abolish the hereditary peers, but were conspicuously vague about any degree of reform beyond that. They were accused of seeking simply to create a prime ministerial super-quango which Tony Blair could pack with his own appointees. In 1999, Blair voluntarily gave up his prerogative power to veto the names of Conservative and Liberal Democrat nominees and announced a new appointments commission to nominate cross-bench peers – but the Prime Minister retains control of the *numbers* of new peers from each party, which is clearly the most significant power, and Blair said he would ensure that Labour has a working majority of life peers in the Lords after the hereditary peers were abolished. Blair also cleverly appointed senior Conservative Lord Wakeham to chair a Royal Commission on long-term reform of the Lords, making it difficult for the Opposition to criticise any resulting recommendations.

▲ *The Chamber of the House of Lords on the State Opening of Parliament 1994*

Essay questions on the House of Lords usually centre on one of the following themes:

▶ How useful is it?

▶ Should it be reformed and, if so, how?

▶ Why has it not been substantially reformed since 1911?

Note the following points:

▶ Arguments in support of a second chamber do not necessarily justify *this* second chamber: i.e. it is not enough to say 'there must be a check on the Commons'; an essay in defence of the traditional House of Lords must defend a non-elected chamber, the hereditary principle (until they were abolished), prime ministerial **patronage**, the long-standing Conservative majority, the legislative role of senior judges and Church of England bishops and the low rate of attendance (a product of other factors listed above).

▶ A defence of the hereditary principle (and hence also non-election) was available from former Conservative MP John Stokes: 'They are trained for the job from youth onwards and they are truly independent, being answerable to no constituents' (speech in House of Commons, 10 April 1981). However, as long ago as 1909, Lloyd George criticised the hereditary peers in the following terms: 'They do not even need a medical certificate. They need not be sound in either body or mind. They only require a certificate of birth – just to prove that they were the first of the litter. You would not choose a spaniel on those principles.'

▶ Although Conservatives had a numerical majority in the pre-reformed second chamber, they did not only seek to obstruct or amend Labour legislation. By the

1987 election they had blocked 100 items of Conservative legislation, including the restrictive Protection of Official Information Bill 1979; the 1984 'Paving Bill', i.e. the Local Government (Interim Provisions) Bill paving the way for abolition of the Metropolitan councils by replacing them with nominated bodies; the sale of council houses built for the elderly (1984 and 1986); and the retention of corporal punishment in state schools (1986) against the spirit of a European Court ruling. This may be because Conservative peers tend to be old-style, traditional Tories rather than New Right; and also because they perceive a duty to provide effective opposition to strong government as the Conservatives were in the 1980s. During John Major's Conservative government, the Lords successfully blocked a bill allowing Rupert Murdoch's Sky TV to buy up many prominent TV sports programmes, because Major's government was by then very weak. Also, Conservative peers tend to follow the principle that, if a bill was not in the government's manifesto, it does not have a mandate (the so-called 'Salisbury Doctrine'). Many – especially the hereditary Conservative 'backwoodsmen' – rarely attended at all. Finally, the 250 or so cross-benchers, including Law Lords and bishops, provide a relatively independent element which is absent from the Commons (though most, in practice, usually vote with the Conservative whip).

▶ By 1999 the Lords had attempted 37 significant defeats of the Labour government – for example, on Scottish university tuition fees. All of these were overturned in the Commons – clear examples of 'elective dictatorship'. The Lords did succeed in forcing the government to drop the lowering of the age of homosexual consent from 18 to 16 (so that Labour could get the rest of its Crime and Disorder Bill 1998 through), but the government simply re-introduced the measure as a self-contained Bill in 1999 (as they were obliged to do by a ruling of the European Court of Human Rights). A major constitutional clash occurred in 1998 when the Lords *six times* tried to change the proposed 'closed party list' voting system for EU elections into an 'open list' system – an interesting example of an 'undemocratic' chamber, still containing the hereditary peers, fighting a rearguard battle for greater democracy in the British political system. However, the government ultimately won on this as well, by doing a secret deal with the Conservative leader in the upper house, Lord Cranborne, to retain 91 hereditary peers in return for smooth passage of bills through the upper house – for which William Hague promptly sacked Lord Cranborne.

▶ The Lords can also help the government and Commons by giving detailed consideration to bills which the Commons, with its crowded timetable, may skimp. For example, the government itself introduced 500 amendments to the Financial Services Act 1986 while it was going through the Lords. Many non-controversial bills, and some controversial ones, are introduced first in the House of Lords, for example, the Shops (Sunday Trading) Bill 1986. This delays scrutiny by the 'democratic' chamber, and can be an unpopular tactic with the Opposition. The Lords also relieve the Commons of much detailed work especially on delegated legislation, private bills and EU law.

▶ Textbooks sometimes cite, as advantageous, the fact that 'the Lords is a place where the Prime Minister can honourably dispose of unwanted MPs', and that 'peers do not have to look to constituency opinion'. Is there also a case against these points?

▶ 'Expertise' is often cited as a merit of the Lords; ensure that you can give topical examples in essays, from press and TV coverage of Lords' debates (for example, 'Lord Hives is an expert on beekeeping, and contributed usefully to the Bees Act 1980'). This point can be related particularly to the Lords' select committees – for example, on finance, science and technology. The Lords' science and technology committee in 1998 advocated the legalisation of cannabis for medical use and the government announced the first medical trials early the next year. Remember, however, that the Commons also contains experts in many diverse fields, i.e. election does not preclude expertise – though it may render it less permanent.

▶ The views of the parties:

– The Conservatives by 1999 had no official policy on reform of the Lords. Obviously, traditional Tories supported the old-style chamber; but, in the face of the inevitable abolition of most hereditary peers in 1999, some Conservatives such as Ted Heath and John Major suggested more radical reforms – such as full election to a stronger second chamber – in an attempt to out-manoeuvre the Labour government.

– The Labour Party advocated complete abolition of the Lords in its 1983 manifesto, together with reform of the Commons to make it more efficient. However, the more 'moderate' 1987 manifesto did not mention the Lords at all. Then in its 1989 policy review Labour advocated a Charter of Rights, i.e. a number of specific statutes (rather than a Bill of Rights) legally guaranteeing freedom of information, a **right** to privacy, freedom from discrimination, devolution and stronger controls on the executive and security services. These would be protected by an elected second chamber, replacing the House of Lords, which would have the power to delay for the lifetime of a full Parliament any legislation which seemed to contradict the Charter. The 1997 proposal for the abolition of hereditary peers was considerably less radical.

▶ Finally, the judicial function of the Lords – as highest UK court of appeal – should not be included in discussion of the 'parliamentary' (legislative) role of the Lords.

---

2 True or false?

a) The Lords can veto legislation curbing their own powers.

b) There is no party discipline in the House of Lords.

c) Tony Benn was the first peer to renounce his title.

d) Women cannot inherit peerages in England.

e) The Law Lords do not take part in debates on legislation.

Reform of the Lords

Past proposals include:

▶ **Functional representation** of pressure and interest groups, rather than a party system (suggested by Mackintosh)

▶ Phasing out of hereditary peers (last proposed by Labour in 1969 – when it was defeated by a combination of left-wing Labour and right-wing Conservative MPs for whom it was too little and too much, respectively)

▶ Complete abolition (Labour, 1983)

▶ Indirect election of representatives from regional bodies (Alliance, 1987 manifesto)

▶ A directly elected second chamber based on proportional representation (Lord Hailsham in his 1976 lecture 'Elective dictatorship').

3 a) Select any three of the above, and write two paragraphs on each: a case for, and a case against.

   b) Now, decide whether you would advocate reform of the Lords in an essay and, if so, how. Think about its functions, powers and composition, and be as specific and detailed as possible. Remember that the kind of second chamber you want (if any) depends on what you want it to do (if anything).

   c) Consider any possible problems arising from your proposal; how would you counter or overcome them?

   d) If you reject reform or abolition of the Lords, write a reasoned and persuasive defence of the present second chamber.

House of Commons

This section attempts to provide only a selective outline of some current controversies, under the headings of Parliament's three key functions listed earlier.

Making the law

▶ A major challenge to Parliament's law-making function has come from the UK's membership of the European Union (EU), whose legislation takes precedence over the laws of member states. The assent of Parliament is not required. This effectively negates parliamentary sovereignty; although, technically, Parliament could legislate to withdraw from the EU at any time, in practice this is most unlikely. The more policy areas that are transferred to the decision-making of the EU – for example, by the Single European Act 1986 and Treaty on European Union 1993 – the less law-making power rests with Westminster.

▶ Devolution – especially the creation of a fairly powerful Scottish Parliament – will also lighten the load of Westminster considerably and may ultimately threaten its national sovereignty.

▶ The timetable of the House of Commons – 2.30 p.m. to 10.30 p.m., with some late or even all-night sittings – is often said to be inefficient. Morning sittings from 9.30 a.m. have been introduced on Wednesdays and Thursdays, but are opposed by many MPs, especially those with jobs outside Westminster. MPs also need time for committee work, and ministers need time for departmental work. Periodic surveys find strong support amongst MPs for a fixed 10.00 p.m. adjournment and a fixed parliamentary year; both would make life easier for MPs and more difficult for the government, which often manipulates the timetable to suit itself.

▶ Although usually the law-making process is slow and cumbersome, occasionally it may move too fast: for example, draconian new anti-terrorism laws were passed through Parliament in a single day in 1998, despite a significant backbench revolt.

▶ It is a matter of debate whether Parliament today actually 'makes the law' or merely endorses laws created by the executive. The latter view – the 'Westminster model' of parliamentary government – sometimes understates the legislative function of both Lords and Commons in amending and even defeating government proposals and initiating other types of bill.

There are two types of bill:

– *public bills*, which concern the general public interest. These may be:

government bills

money bills (a special type of government bill, which cannot be amended by the Lords)

private members' bills (usually public bills);

– *private bills* which concern individual or group interests: these breach the 'rule of law' and the principle of legal equality; they are therefore subject to special procedures and scrutiny. For example, the Felixstowe Dock and Railway Act 1987, extending the harbour area (over which Labour MPs staged a 'filibuster', trying to talk the bill out in an all-night sitting).

Hybrid bills concern both public and private interests: for example, the Channel Tunnel Act 1987.

The Speaker decides classification of bills.

Public bills lapse if they have not completed all stages at the end of a parliamentary session; this forces the government to organise its legislative programme carefully, and allows a rethink of controversial bills, but it may also waste time.

▶ In the committee stage of bills, if discussion is protracted the government may introduce the '**guillotine**' – a time limit. Early clauses may therefore be debated at length, and later clauses not considered at all. Ministers blame opposition MPs for time-wasting; the opposition argue that the guillotine negates the parliamentary process. One recent example was the guillotine imposed on the Amsterdam Treaty (1997).

▶ Special standing committees were introduced in 1980: these can investigate the issues behind a bill and may examine witnesses and experts. MPs are more informed as a result, but the process has only been used half-a-dozen times (for example, for European legislation); more frequent use is often advocated.

▶ **Delegated legislation** is controversial (and could equally come under the heading of 'controlling the executive' below). It is also known as indirect or secondary legislation, because it allows ministers, local authorities and others to make detailed regulations – for example, statutory instruments or by-laws – under powers delegated by Parliament in a parent Act. It thus turns ministers into lawmakers, breaching the principle of 'separation of powers'. It has grown up because it allows more time, detail, expertise and flexibility in the law-making process. However, parliamentary scrutiny is inadequate. The Joint and Select Committees on Statutory Instruments have a heavy workload – around 2,000 items a year to examine, each ranging from a couple of paragraphs to a hundred pages or more. Delegated legislation passes through Parliament much more quickly than primary legislation; it can only be challenged if it is incomprehensible or seems illegal under the parent Act – its underlying principles cannot be questioned; and it can only be accepted or rejected as a whole, not amended. The restrictive regulations for board and lodging payments under the Social Security Act 1986, for example, were repeatedly rejected by both the Commons and the courts, but were simply rewritten and re-introduced by the government.

Controlling the executive

This is the most controversial issue of all. Some commentators argue that the task of Parliament is simply to scrutinise and sustain government rather than 'control' it. Others, such as Stuart Walkland, say that Parliament should control government but cannot, for the following reasons:

▶ majority governments

▶ party discipline

▶ government control of parliamentary time

▶ government secrecy and obfuscation, especially on finance

▶ government control of civil service personnel and information

▶ the growth of delegated legislation

▶ the lack of power of parliamentary committees and the Ombudsman

▶ lack of resources and facilities for MPs

▶ the growing influence on government of extra-parliamentary bodies such as the EU, business, pressure groups and media.

For all of these reasons – but, above all, because of the power of a majority government in control of a sovereign Parliament with a flexible constitution – Lord Hailsham's phrase 'elective dictatorship' is commonly used to describe the British system of government.

▶ *Her Majesty's Opposition* – the second largest party in the Commons – is a formal part of the constitution: the leader, chief whip and two deputies of 'Her Majesty's Opposition' are paid a special salary; they have four civil servants to assist their parliamentary work, and are given special time and opportunities in Commons' procedures which are unavailable to other parties. The Leader of the Opposition is traditionally consulted on bipartisan matters (for example, the 1998 Northern Ireland peace deal), and is given a chauffeur-driven car. Since 1985, 20 Opposition Days are set aside in the Commons' yearly timetable for debate and criticism of government (replacing the old Supply Days); on 17 days, the topic is chosen by the leader of the Opposition, and the remaining three days are allocated to the leader of the second largest opposition party.

Nevertheless, the Opposition is clearly weak against a majority government. Occasionally the Commons does persuade the government to back down on an issue – for example, the taxing of disabled people's benefits in 1998 – but invariably this is under pressure from the government's own backbenchers. The Opposition alone cannot 'control' the executive; its main function now is to present itself to the electorate as 'the alternative government'. Frustration is demonstrated by low attendance of MPs (though committee work also takes its toll, with only about 70 MPs attending no committee meetings at all; and the mutual convenience of 'pairing' also allows MPs to absent themselves regularly from the Commons). Another outlet for MPs' frustration is rowdiness in the chamber; but this is not confined to the opposition, and anyway is not nearly as bad as it was in the nineteenth century (today it is publicised and exaggerated by selective broadcasting). Lively debate may be seen as a legitimate tradition of the House.

For some commentators, however, MPs' 'bad' behaviour is a symptom of the crisis of legitimacy developing in an unrepresentative, adversarial, executive-dominated House of Commons where the parliamentary process is slowly breaking down.

▶ *Question Time* – the noisiest and most publicised part of the Commons' day – epitomises government's accountability to Parliament. Around 50,000 questions are asked each year, and about 3,000 oral answers are given (the rest are written) at a cost of over £2 million in administrative effort; but many question the usefulness of the whole exercise, and it has been described as 'ritualised combat' and 'a punch and

judy show'. The 48 hours' notice required for oral questions undermines their topicality; supplementary questions can be topical and also have the element of surprise, but they do not allow detailed discussion of an issue. Prime Minister's Question Time wastes precious minutes on formula questions and answers, about the PM's engagements that day, as a prelude to the supplementaries. Other ministers appear only about once a month under the rota system; and their chief skill often seems to lie in evading the question, unless it is a 'plant' by the minister or by a supportive colleague to prompt an announcement or an opportunity for self-congratulation. In 1997 Blair reduced PM's Question Time to once instead of twice a week. By late 1998 things had reached such a low that a parliamentary correspondent wrote, 'We also heard Prime Minister's Question Time – but this is now so dreary, so predictable, so scripted and so empty of any useful content, that I will not inflict it upon you' (Simon Hoggart, *The Guardian*, 29 October 1998).

▶ *Select committees* (investigative committees) provide better opportunities for scrutiny, if not control, of government. Students of British government must be able to provide a topical assessment, especially of the departmental committees set up in 1979 by Norman St John Stevas. Peter Hennessy has called them the single most important weapon of increased parliamentary influence this century. Their members are chosen by the House on the recommendation of the Commons Committee of Selection, though the whips do try to manipulate membership. Their expenditure is controlled by the Commons, not by the Treasury. They run for a whole Parliament, not just for a session. They attract growing media attention (for example, the Foreign Affairs committee's 1998 investigation of the arms to Sierra Leone affair), absenteeism is low, and they have been able to extract valuable information from government: for example, the Foreign Affairs Committee won access to the 'Crown Jewels' – classified documents on the sinking of the *Belgrano* during the Falklands conflict of 1982. Serving MPs have thus become better informed and more specialised. The government has sometimes acted on their recommendations: for example, Downing Street staged a highbrow summit with the Arts establishment after the Culture Committee complained that new Labour was obsessed with lowbrow 'cool Britannia'; and in 1999 the government took up the Home Affairs Committee's suggestion of more use of electronic tagging and other community sentences to reduce prison overcrowding. The government also consulted the Social Security Committee on its pension reform proposals in 1998. The Treasury Committee produced ground-breaking new rules on the relationships between ministers and their civil servants and has introduced US-style 'confirmatory hearings' to approve members of the Bank of England Monetary Policy Committee, and other departmental committees are following suit in other areas.

Departmental Select Committees (1999)

Agriculture	Public Service
Culture	Science and Technology
Defence	Scottish Affairs
Education and Employment	Social Security
Environment	Trade and Industry
Foreign Affairs	Transport
Health	Treasury
Home Affairs	Welsh Affairs
Northern Ireland	

Often, however, the government simply ignores the criticisms and recommendations of the committees: for example, the Health Committee's attack on the government's handling of the Formula One tobacco sponsorship affair was ignored until Lord Neill stepped in; also the arms to Iraq affair in the 1990s before the Scott Inquiry (see page 97); and in 1999 the government contemptuously dismissed the Foreign Affairs Committee's highly critical report on arms to Sierra Leone some hours before it was even published. This prompted a minor scandal about a number of select committee reports being leaked to the government by loyalist committee members before publication. The committees lack adequate research and administrative resources, and – in practice – they lack the power to demand to see persons and papers; for example, Alan Clark simply refused to answer questions from the Trade and Industry Committee's inquiry into the Supergun affair and Foreign Secretary Robin Cook was accused of being very obstructive over the arms to Sierra Leone investigation.

The government is particularly likely to ignore the committees when they divide on party lines, for example, the Employment Committee on the treatment of miners sacked during the 1984–5 strike; and when they are united, they are criticised by radical MPs like Dennis Skinner for their 'sloppy consensus'. The whips certainly try to manipulate them through patronage, bribes and threats. For example, when the Health Committee, chaired by Tory Nicholas Winterton, was critical of the Conservative government's NHS reforms, the whips invented the 'Winterton rule' preventing a committee chairman serving more than two parliaments. Michael Foot dislikes the whole structure of select committees, arguing that they detract energy and attention from the debating chamber as a whole. The Lord Chancellor's department is wholly excluded from committee scrutiny.

In sum, most commentators agree that they have done little to shift the balance of *power* between executive and legislature, though they do have *influence* and provide more information, detailed scrutiny and public criticism of government. Reformers say that they need bigger budgets, stronger powers, and more capacity to conduct research, initiate debates and interrogate ministers and civil servants more rigorously. Such solutions lie largely in the committees' own hands.

▶ *Control of finance*: The Lords play no part in this major aspect of executive accountability. The Commons has three days set aside in each session for discussion of government estimates of how much money is required by each department. The annual Budget and Finance Act provides the necessary government revenue through taxation and borrowing. The departmental committees examine the spending of each department (the old Expenditure Committee was thus abolished in 1979). The Comptroller and Auditor General has, since the National Audit Act 1983, been independent of the Treasury; he audits government expenditure and reports to the Public Accounts Committee (PAC). This is a senior and influential backbench committee, traditionally chaired by an Opposition member. It can question civil servants and other witnesses, and is assisted by over 900 auditors and staff in the National Audit Office. It reports to the House, and its findings are publicised in the press. Many suggest that the PAC should be the model for the departmental select committees to emulate.

Nevertheless, the Public Accounts Committee has itself said that the Commons' control of government finance – 'Parliament's key constitutional function' – is 'largely a formality'. This is partly because a majority government can dominate the Commons, but also because the estimates and accounts provided by Whitehall are both too vague about key financial categories and objectives, and too complex on minor details. Often the committee can only criticise after the event, to little effect; for example, its 1998 report on the underpriced privatisation of the Atomic Energy Authority which the committee described as 'a staggering waste of public money'. The budgets of the security and intelligence services – an estimated £1,000 million per year – are not subject to parliamentary scrutiny; nor are the (few remaining) nationalised industries. The Comptroller and Auditor General has also accused apathetic MPs of ignoring his many critical reports about government waste and mismanagement.

---

4 Complete the blank spaces in the following passage (score out of a total of 35).

Every state has three functions to perform: making laws, executing policies and enforcing the law of the land. The body within a state which makes the law is generally known as the ....; in the USA this body is called ....; in the UK it is called .... and is, in turn, made up of three institutions: ...., ... and .... When voters go to the polls in a General Election in Britain they are electing a single .... to represent a single .... as a member of the national legislature. The other two institutions of Parliament are not elected.   (8)

Whilst a piece of legislation is going through Parliament it is called a ....; once passed it is called an .... or statute. No other institution in the British state can challenge or veto the law of Parliament, in other words Parliament is legally .... There are, however, external constraints upon Parliament, including ...., ..., ... and ....   (7)

The executive in Britain – otherwise known as the .... – has the task of carrying out policy (which should, of course, be in accordance with the laws of Parliament). The Crown appoints the .... as head of the executive and she or he then appoints her or his .... and other .... Britain does not practise Montesquieu's principle of .... of .... The electorate does not, therefore, directly elect the .... Instead, ... is chosen from within .... and is, in theory, subordinate and accountable to Parliament. Procedures by which Parliament holds government to account include ...., ... , ... and .... Recent examples where government has been forced to back down include ....

(13)

However, the British electoral system usually produces a government with over 50 per cent of the seats in the House of Commons, i.e. a .... government – even though no government since 1935 has had a majority of votes cast in the country. This means that the government cannot be defeated in the Commons except by a backbench .... The House of Lords may occasionally succeed in blocking or amending a bill, for example, ..., but usually lacks the power and authority to do so because it is not elected. This, combined with parliamentary sovereignty and a .... constitution which can be changed by the ordinary legal process, makes it potentially easy for a government to push through any bill, even in the face of public unpopularity. This was why Lord Hailsham described the British system of parliamentary government as ....

Examples where government has been able to push through unpopular policy include ....

(6)

At the present time the government has a majority of .... seats and is therefore very strong.   (1)

5 a) What constitutional issues were raised by the arms to Iraq affair and the Scott Inquiry? (See pages 97–8.)

b) What reforms might help to prevent such events recurring?

Representing the people

▶   The pros and cons of the electoral system (discussed in Chapter 3) are obviously central to this issue. So is the question of 'elective dictatorship' when the government can use its majority to dominate the Commons: for example, the Labour government effectively killed off Michael Foster's private member's bill seeking to ban fox hunting, even though it had nothing to do with the executive and opinion polls indicated substantial majority support for the bill.

Arms to Iraq: the facts, the Inquiry and the quotes

'Arms to Iraq' is the common, if misleading, label commonly given to the scandal arising from the sale of defence-related equipment to Iraq in the 1980s. In 1985 the Conservative government issued guidelines barring the sale of defence-related equipment to both Iraq and Iran because of the military tensions of the time. In 1988 three ministers – William Waldegrave (Foreign Office), Alan Clark (Trade and Industry) and Lord Trefgarne (Defence) and their senior civil servants – revised the guidelines to allow a more liberal policy on defence-related exports to Iraq, but agreed that no publicity should be given to the changes. Parliament and the public were repeatedly told that there had been no change in policy. William Waldegrave signed 27 letters to MPs to that effect. Customs and Excise were not told of the policy change, nor that ministers were approving Matrix Churchill company's sales of equipment to Iraq (despite Iraq's invasion of Kuwait in 1990), nor that MI6 was receiving intelligence information about Iraq from company director, Paul Henderson, in the process.

In 1992 Customs prosecuted the three company directors of Matrix Churchill for breaking the guidelines; they were thus faced with the threat of imprisonment for exporting goods with secret government approval, and the government was apparently prepared to let them go to prison rather than reveal that ministers had misled Parliament and the public. The government's Attorney General Sir Nicholas Lyell told four ministers – Kenneth Clarke, Michael Heseltine, Malcolm Rifkind and Tristan Garel-Jones – to sign Public Interest Immunity Certificates (PIICs) withholding documents which would have helped the defence; Heseltine objected and his PIIC was changed, but Lyell did not pass on those objections to Judge Smedley. However, Alan Clark gave candid testimony, Judge Smedley rejected the PIICs and the case collapsed – as did the Matrix Churchill company, with the loss of 660 jobs. In 1992 Prime Minister John Major set up a judicial inquiry into the affair, led by Sir Richard Scott. His report was published in 1996.

William Waldegrave told Scott that he believed the policy had not changed but was simply being more flexibly interpreted. Had the policy been changed, Prime Minister Margaret Thatcher would have to have been told; since she was not told, the policy had not been changed. Scott accepted that Waldegrave did not have any duplicitous intentions but said 'that underlines, to my mind, the duplicitous nature of the flexibility claimed for the guidelines'.

Of Lyell's attempted and improper use of secrecy orders Scott said, 'I accept the genuineness of his belief that he was personally, as opposed to constitutionally, blameless for the inadequacy of the instructions. But I do not accept that he was not personally at fault.'

Scott also noted that a 1988 MI6 document referring to Matrix Churchill's heavy involvement in exports to Iraq was sent to, and initialled by, Prime Minister Margaret Thatcher. However, Thatcher famously said, 'If I had seen a copy of every document made in my government, I'd have been in a snowstorm'.

John Major was told about the changed guidelines on his first day as Foreign Secretary in 1989. However, he told the Inquiry, 'There has been a view expressed that, as Foreign Secretary and then as Chancellor and then as Prime Minister, I should have known what was going on. . . . Something that I was not aware had happened suddenly turned out not to have happened.'

Alan Clark admitted to having been 'economical with the actualité . . . The guidelines were so obviously drafted with the objective of flexibility . . . You can no more break a guideline than you can break a blancmange.'

Geoffrey Howe said that there was 'nothing necessarily open to criticism in incompatibility between policy and presentation of policy'.

Tristan Garel-Jones said that he signed the PIIC because release of the documents could cause 'unquantifiable damage' to the security and intelligence services. Challenged by Scott's dismissal of this as 'risible', he said, '"Unquantifiable damage" could mean unquantifiably large or unquantifiably small'.

Cabinet Secretary Sir Robin Butler redefined a key constitutional convention as follows: 'A distinction must be drawn between ministerial responsibility and ministerial accountability. A minister should not be held to blame for a departmental action about which he knew nothing. But he should be accountable for it, i.e. should be forthcoming to Parliament with information about the incident.' It also transpired that, in 1995, John Major had changed the written rules about ministerial responsibility (Questions of Procedure for Ministers, paragraph 27) from ministers having an absolute obligation 'not to deceive or mislead Parliament and the public' to 'ministers must not *knowingly* mislead Parliament and the public'.

No ministers resigned over the arms to Iraq affair. As *The Independent* newspaper put it, 'The old doctrine of ministerial responsibility, which has looked so haggard for so long, can be declared dead'. Or, as one academic writer has put it:

> 'The Nolan Report on standards of conduct in the House of Commons and the Scott Inquiry into ministerial conduct during the arms to Iraq scandal both demonstrated the almost daily infringement of constitutional conventions, so much so that no knowledgeable academic or political commentator continues to take these conventions seriously; they act merely to distract us from the realities of power and policy making in the British state.'
>
> *(Mark Evans, 'Democracy and constitutionalism in Britain', Politics Review,*
> *Vol. 7, No. 2, Nov. 1997)*

There were also, incidentally, some memorable examples of civil service parlance during the Scott hearings:

▶ Eric Beston (DTI official): 'The avoidance of controversy was not an uncommon concern in the non-presentation of policy', and 'I quite simply misled myself on what I thought the situation was'

▶ Sir Robin Butler (Cabinet Secretary): 'This was all happening below my eyesight level', and 'Half the picture can be true'.

The Inquiry cost over £3 million. More than £750,000 of taxpayers' money was also spent on lawyers hired by ministers to advise them on how to defend themselves against the Scott Report after they saw the first draft – which was subsequently watered down.

▶ A further point to consider is the issue of *devolution*: the delegating of some legislative or executive powers from central to regional bodies. Britain has a system of local government but, until 1999, no local parliaments. In the 1997 election the Conservatives won no seats at all in Scotland or Wales and some nationalists therefore argued that Westminster and Whitehall had no authority to control Scottish or Welsh affairs. The 1997 Labour government came to power with a manifesto commitment to hold referenda on the question of legislative devolution. A Northern Ireland assembly was re-established in 1998 and new Scottish and Welsh assemblies were set up in 1999 (see Chapter 8). These are widely seen as representing the regions better than Westminster did, not least because they are elected on at least partial proportional representation.

▶ *Parliamentary privilege* is the exemption of MPs from some ordinary laws under the special laws and customs of Parliament. It is therefore a special category of constitutional law, which breaches 'the rule of law' and principle of legal equality. It was originally a defence against the power of the Crown, and is now justified on the grounds that MPs can better represent the people if, for example, they have complete freedom of speech. Thus they are immune from slander or libel actions for words spoken in Parliament. This may be used to expose wrongdoing – for example, Peter Wright's allegations about MI5 in his banned book *Spycatcher* were repeated in the Commons in 1986 by Labour MP Dale Campbell-Savours, allowing the press to report them under the same cloak of privilege. Similarly, Labour MP Stuart Bell used parliamentary privilege to raise the issue of 'cash for questions' in the 1990s. However, this freedom may be abused by MPs: in 1998, Brian Sedgemore made the allegation that *Sunday Telegraph* editor Dominic Lawson was an MI6 agent although all concerned denied it. In 1999, Unionist MP Ian Paisley accused a Mr Eugene Reavey of being an IRA killer although the police said that the man was an innocent farmer.

Despite this 'absolute' freedom of speech, Gerry Adams MP was permanently barred from the Commons by the Speaker after his election in 1997, because he refused – as a republican – to take an oath of allegiance to the Crown.

Other privileges – for example, freedom from arrest – may now seem anachronistic or excessive. The right of Parliament to control its own proceedings is reasonable, but its right to try and to punish outsiders for 'contempt of Parliament' is controversial. This crime includes refusing to answer questions (for example, media mogul Robert Maxwell's sons Ian and Kevin Maxwell in 1991–2 before the Social Services Committee); 'pressurising' MPs to vote in a certain way; publishing Commons papers without permission; and speeches or articles which 'bring the House into odium, contempt or ridicule or lower its authority' (Rory Bremner, beware!). The 'trial', by the Committee of Privileges, is secret and invariably party political, with no procedural safeguards for the accused. The 'punishment' is usually just a public rebuke in the House by the Speaker, but technically Parliament can fine or imprison offenders. Barrister Geoffrey Robertson is one critic of this aspect of parliamentary privilege, likening it to a 'kangaroo court'.

▶ *Televising of the Commons* (and its committees) was regularly debated in the House, and finally accepted in 1988. It enhances open government and freedom of the media; and many Labour MPs believe that TV – with its statutory duty of **impartiality** – will present a more balanced and fair view of party politics than does much of the British press. However, some MPs argued that it would encourage bad behaviour by MPs and public in the House, while others feared that selective broadcasting may trivialise, sensationalise or distort proceedings and undermine the authority of the Commons. Minority parties are under-represented in televised proceedings as

they are in the Commons itself – thus the Liberal Democrats initially opposed the idea. However, the 'experiment' of televising the Commons and its committees is clearly now here to stay.

▶ A related issue is the *lobby system*, which involves the briefing of specialist TV and press correspondents by MPs and ministers in Westminster and Whitehall, often on an unattributable basis, i.e. the media cannot name their sources. However, since 1997 this has become more open – for example, Tony Blair's spokesman, Alastair Campbell, is allowed to be named – and therefore the lobby system is now less often perceived as a channel of media manipulation, misinformation and propaganda.

---

6 Quick quiz. Briefly answer the following questions.

  a) When did a monarch last refuse assent to a bill?

  b) What is a White Paper?

  c) Who is responsible for drafting government bills?

  d) List the stages of legislation for public bills.

  e) What is a joint committee?

  f) What is *Hansard*?

  g) Once elected, does the Speaker cease to be an MP?

  h) List three functions of the Speaker.

i) Who is the present Speaker of the Commons?

j) What are Standing Orders?

k) What is a 'simple closure'?

l) What are 'the usual channels'?

m) List three functions of the whips.

n) What is 'pairing'?

o) What is meant by 'withdrawing the whip' from an MP?

p) Why might an MP seek a written rather than oral answer at Question Time?

q) What is the function of the Ombudsman?

r) What is the Consolidated Fund?

s) When was a Government last defeated in the Commons on a vote of no confidence?

t) What is (i) the PLP and (ii) the 1922 Committee?

Sample short answer question and answer

Q? Distinguish between the legal and the actual powers of Parliament.

A✓ Power is the ability to do, or make others do, something regardless of their consent, based on the capacity to coerce, i.e. to reward or punish. Parliament's power is supposed to be based on authority, for example, from elections for the House of Commons and tradition for the House of Lords.

In theory – *de jure* – the British Parliament has legal sovereignty: i.e. it can make, amend or repeal any law and no domestic institution can override its laws. Thus it cannot be ruled illegal or unconstitutional, it can pass retrospective law to legalise illegality, for example, sperm donors, and no Parliament can bind its successors, i.e. a future Parliament may amend or repeal any previous statute. Also, Parliament is not bound by its own statutes, but instead by a special body of law known as parliamentary privilege which exempts MPs from much ordinary law; for instance, they cannot be sued for slander for words spoken in Parliament. For example, Labour MP Stuart Bell used parliamentary privilege to expose the cash for questions scandal in the 1990s.

Also in theory, according to the British system of parliamentary government, Parliament should have the power to scrutinise and hold to account the executive, through for example, debates, votes, Question Time, select committees, the Ombudsman, etc. This holds particularly true when the executive does not have a majority in the Commons, for example, Major's government before the 1997 election.

Parliament is also given the authority and power to represent the people through the first-past-the-post system of election for the Commons, for example blocking the second VAT rise on domestic fuel. Though the Lords are not elected and therefore have limited power – one-year delay, for example, War Crimes Act 1991 – they derive authority from such factors as tradition and expertise, at least in the eyes of traditional Tories, for example, blocking Sky TV's dominance of TV sports coverage.

However, the actual – *de facto* – powers of Parliament are limited, first by a majority government within Parliament, for example, Labour (179 majority) killing off Foster's private member's bill on fox-hunting and pushing through cuts in lone parents' benefits despite a large revolt. The executive can effectively dominate Parliament due to party loyalty and discipline, control of the timetable, guillotine, and the weaknesses of the select committees, Ombudsman, Lords, etc., i.e. 'elective dictatorship' (Hailsham).

The European Union can, since 1973, override Parliamentary law, for example, fishing quotas and the beef ban. This also means that both the European and British courts can override Parliament's law where it conflicts with EU law, for example, on the 48-hour working week. Other international bodies such as the IMF and NATO also have influence.

Other constraints on the actual power of Parliament are pressure groups, for example, Snowdrop on the gun ban and the fox-hunting supporters; the media, for example, on the Dangerous Dogs Act and sleaze in the 1990s; the City and other economic power bodies, for example Britain's fallout from the ERM in 1992; and ultimately the political sovereignty of the electorate, who choose the MPs in the Commons and who may occasionally simply refuse to obey the law of Parliament, for example, the poll tax.

---

7 Consider the possible reforms of the Commons listed (in no particular order) below.

a) First, decide whether each is merely *procedural* or involves a *substantive* change in functions or powers. Now, decide which you would and would not advocate in an essay on the subject, and why.

b) Consider whether one reform may require, generate or preclude another, i.e. ensure that your choices are consistent and compatible.

c) Consider any possible problems arising from your chosen reforms; how would you counter or overcome them?

d) Can you add any suggested reforms to this list?

- **i)** Ombudsman: broader role (for example, over police); more staff; more power over Whitehall; more publicity

- **ii)** Fixed-term elections

- **iii)** Full-time MPs

- **iv)** Abolition of external fees and payments for MPs

- **v)** Push-button or proxy voting for MPs in the House

- **vi)** Reform of electoral system (Specify, and consider consequences.)

- **vii)** Freedom of information for MPs and committees

- **viii)** More free votes in the House

- **ix)** Fewer MPs, for example, 400, for a more efficient and professional House

- **x)** Prohibition of retrospective law

- **xi)** More use of special standing committees

xii) Regional Parliaments for England

xiii) More morning sittings

xiv) Fixed ten o'clock adjournment

xv) Better pay, research and office facilities for MPs

xvi) More power (to scrutinise people and papers) and more publicity for select committees

xvii) Abolition of all/obsolete parliamentary privileges

xviii) Abolition of the 'guillotine'

xix) Bills to be carried over from one session to the next

xx) Less control by whips of committee appointments

xxi) Abolition of pairing

xxii) More opportunities and (legal) assistance for private members' bills

xxiii) Reduction/abolition of notice for oral questions

xxiv) Better parliamentary scrutiny of delegated legislation

xxv) Separation of powers – the executive elected separately from Parliament

ESSAYS

1 *Theme:* **House of Lords**

Q? Should the House of Lords be abolished? Why have attempts at comprehensive reform of the House of Lords always failed?

(Simulated question)

A✓ Notes for guidance

This is a two-part question; unless otherwise stated, assume half marks for each part.

▶ Part 1 – 'Should the Lords be abolished?' – is evaluative; decide your conclusion at the planning stage and structure accordingly, putting your own case last.

▶ Part 2 – 'Why . . .?' – is largely descriptive; your answer should centre on a list of examples and reasons – 'Because . . .'.

There is some scope for overlap between the two parts of the question; decide at the planning stage where best to put each point, and avoid repetition.

Essay plan
Part 1:

a) 1983 Labour proposal: **unicameral** legislature

b) Crits. of Lords pre-1999 (case for abolition or mere reform):

Non-elected, undemocratic, unaccountable, hereditary principle, prime ministerial patronage, unrepresentative, Conservative majority, low attendance, little power, poor check against 'elective dictatorship'. Thus, if House lacks power, it is inadequate; if it has power, it is illegitimate. Opinion polls suggest majority support for reform, but not for abolition.

c) Abolition:

Case against:

▶ Would lose constitutional check: esp. veto over extending life of Parliament, and dismissal of judges. (Monarch's veto unsatisfactory.)

▶ Delaying power valuable.

▶ Double scrutiny of bills is valuable safeguard; checks and balances in lib. dem., for example, USA, France, etc. **bicameral**.

▶ Would require major reform of Commons for efficiency and constitutional checks.

▶ Would lose independent, leisurely and expert debate and scrutiny of Lords.

▶ What about the judicial function of the Lords?

▶ Traditional authority of Lords.

▶ 'Representative' claims of Commons and government are also questionable.

Case for:

▶ Constitutional check inadequate; majority government could change law to remove veto, or second chamber, first.

▶ Delaying power rarely used since 1949; and not legitimate anyway.

▶ Commons should scrutinise bills properly. Should reform Commons. Denmark, Sweden, New Zealand and others unicameral.

▶ Commons in need of major reform; abolition of Lords would provide impetus.

▶ Should not be 'independent' of voters. Again, Commons should have more time and expertise.

▶ Judicial function should be separated out, as per liberal democratic theory.

▶ No inherent virtue in the past.

▶ True: should have PR, written and rigid constitution and Bill of Rights subject to referenda, instead of non-elected Lords.

Therefore, yes, Lords should be abolished.

Part 2:

a) Attempts have not 'always failed': 1911 . . .

Reforms since: 1949, 1958, 1963, 1999 . . . not 'comprehensive'

Failed attempt: Labour, 1969 . . .

(Conservative proposal, 1978 – not attempted)

b) Reforms have largely failed because:

▶ Arguments in favour of present chamber – case against abolition, above. Useful functions – veto, delay, amendment, debate, etc. Especially since Lords are active against Conservative as well as Labour governments

▶ Lack of cross-party and intra-party consensus regarding functions, powers and composition of a reformed chamber

▶ Democratised chamber could be rival to Commons, or obstructive

▶ All governments are reluctant to increase constraints against themselves.

▶ Would be time-consuming and difficult – involving Commons, judiciary, Church and even monarchy. Governments have higher priorities, for example, economic policy. Little public concern.

▶ Prime Ministers of all parties find power of patronage useful.

▶ Conservatives not enthusiastic about reform; minority parties (for example, Liberal Democrats) have lacked opportunity.

▶ Conclusion: Lack of political will and consensus for wholesale reform, though strong case for it; and abolition viable if alternative constitutional safeguards were introduced.

2 *Theme:* Authority of Parliament

Q? Are there factors which are undermining the authority of Parliament in Britain?

(London, June 1980, Paper 1)

A✓ **Plan**

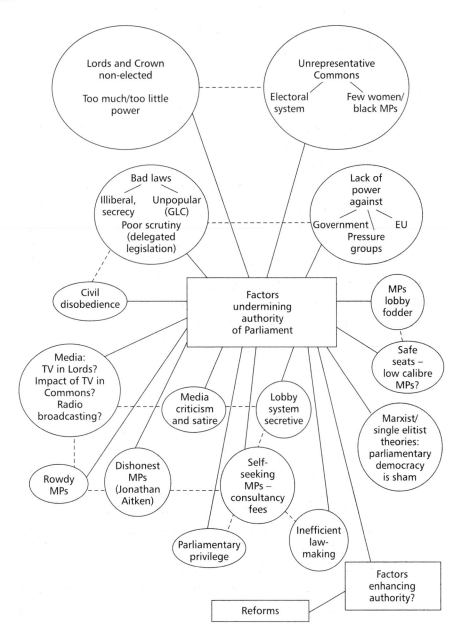

Additional essay tips

The key word in the title is *authority*. If you write an answer about Parliament's lack of *power* – for example, over the executive – it will often not be relevant. Instead, concentrate on factors which may be reducing the legitimacy, reputation and status of Parliament, for example, in the eyes of the electorate. Authority may shape power, or vice versa; be absolutely clear in defining and distinguishing the two concepts. Note: Crown, Lords and Commons are all relevant here.

8 Try to write a timed, structured essay using the diagrammatic plan on page 105.

9 Write at least one of the following essays. Always write a brief plan first.

a) Discuss the implications of an elected second chamber.

(London, June 1996, Paper 1)

b) Does the continued expansion of delegated legislation threaten the survival of the rule of law in Britain?

(Cambridge, June 1985, Paper 1)

c) Why was a new system of departmental select committees introduced in the House of Commons in 1979–80? How successful has this development been?

(JMB, June 1986, Paper 1)

d) What reforms would strengthen the accountability of government to Parliament?

(London, Jan. 1998, Paper 1)

e) It is sometimes suggested that those with large sums of money to spend can 'buy' the election results they favour or 'persuade' Parliament and the government to support the political outcomes that they desire.

Assess the accuracy of such a view and the adequacy of restrictions on such political funding. In what ways might expenditure by a company, individual or pressure group influence an election result or the decisions of Parliament or the government?

(AEB, Summer 1998, Paper 2)

f) In what ways does the Commons seek to control finance? How effective are its procedures?

(Oxford and Cambridge, June 1990, Paper 2)

GUIDE TO EXERCISES

Page 86

1   Power; power; power; authority; power; authority

Page 89

2   a) False

b) False

c) False – Lord Home was the first to renounce his peerage

d) True

e) False

Page 95

4   Every state has three functions to perform: making laws, executing policies and enforcing the law of the land. The body within a state which makes the law is generally known as the legislature; in the USA this body is called Congress; in the UK it is called Parliament and is, in turn, made up of three institutions: Commons, Lords and Crown. When voters go to the polls in a General Election in Britain they are electing a single MP to represent a single constituency as a member of the national legislature. The other two institutions of Parliament are not elected.   (8)

Whilst a piece of legislation is going through Parliament it is called a bill; once passed it is called an Act or statute. No other institution in the British state can challenge or veto the law of Parliament; in other words Parliament is legally sovereign. There are, however, external constraints upon Parliament, including the EU, business and City, pressure groups and the electorate.   (7)

The executive in Britain – otherwise known as the government – has the task of carrying out policy (which should, of course, be in accordance with the laws of Parliament). The Crown appoints the Prime Minister as head of the executive and she or he then appoints her or his Cabinet and other ministers. Britain does not practise Montesquieu's principle of separation of powers. The electorate does not, therefore, directly elect the executive. Instead, government is chosen from within Parliament and is, in theory, subordinate and accountable to Parliament. Procedures by which Parliament holds government to account include debates and votes on government bills, Question Time, select committees and the Ombudsman. Recent examples where government has been forced to back down include the second VAT rise on domestic fuel (1996).   (13)

However, the British electoral system usually produces a government with over 50 per cent of the seats in the House of Commons, i.e. a majority government – even though no government since 1935 has had a majority of votes cast in the country. This means that the government cannot be defeated in the Commons except by a backbench revolt. The House of Lords may occasionally succeed in blocking or amending a bill, for example, Sky TV sports coverage, but usually lacks the power and authority to do so because it is not elected. This, combined with parliamentary sovereignty and a flexible constitution which can be changed by the ordinary legal process, makes it potentially easy for a government to push through any bill, even in the face of public unpopularity. This was why Lord Hailsham described the British system of parliamentary government as an 'elective dictatorship'.

Examples where government has been able to push through unpopular policy include lone parents' benefit cuts (1997). (6)

At the time of writing the government has a majority of 179 seats and is therefore very strong. (1)

Page 96

5 The arms to Iraq affair and Scott Inquiry

    a) Constitutional issues raised:

- Government misleading Parliament and public about their knowledge of events and their actions
- Breaches of individual ministerial responsibility – especially Waldegrave and Lyell
- Political involvement of civil servants
- Loss of neutrality and anonymity of civil servants
- Breach of separation of powers in role of Attorney General
- Government secrecy and improper use of PIICs in trial
- Role of Judge Smedley in upholding freedom of information and rule of law
- Political involvement of Judge Scott in heading Inquiry
- Government rewriting the constitutional framework which regulates its own accountability

    b) Possible reforms:

- Clear duty in law for ministers to announce policy changes to Parliament for approval and to take responsibility for errors and malpractice – or sheer incompetence
- Freedom of Information Act (not then in existence)
- Statutory code of conduct for civil servants to protect them from having to lie for ministers (not then in existence)
- Civil Service Ombudsman (not then in existence)
- Severe curtailment of PIICs, and their use should be sanctioned by non-governmental officials or lawyers
- Legal post of Attorney General should cease to be a government minister
- Reforms of Parliament itself – for example, PR or even separation of powers – to make it more willing and able to hold government to account

Page 100

6   a) 1707 – Queen Anne, the Scotch Militia Bill

    b) An outline of proposed legislation, before publication of a Bill

    c) The Parliamentary Counsel of thirty lawyers – part of government, not Parliament

    d) First reading, second reading, committee stage, report stage, third reading, amendments in the Upper House, royal assent

e) A committee of MPs and peers combined

f) The official record of proceedings in the Commons

g) No

h) i) Decides allocation of time to parties and MPs

   ii) Exercises casting vote on a bill where votes are tied; by convention, arranges for vote to be taken again

   iii) Selects chairmen for, and allocates bills to, standing committees

i) Currently Betty Boothroyd (1999)

j) Written rules on the conduct of Commons business

k) A time limit on debate in the Commons; the Speaker decides whether to allow a vote on it, and 100+ MPs must win a majority vote for motion to be carried

l) The Government and Opposition chief whips, who between them arrange special debates, etc.

m) i) Circulate weekly notice of Commons business to MPs

   ii) Arrange pairing, ensure that MPs vote as required, and count the votes

   iii) Convey backbench opinion and recommendations for promotion to the party leadership

n) Government and Opposition backbenchers arrange permanent 'pairs' at the beginning of each Parliament; they can then be mutually absent on important votes (with the permission of the whips)

o) Suspending or expelling the MP from the party (not from Parliament)

p) More detailed information

q) To investigate citizens' complaints of maladministration by government departments

r) The government's account at the Bank of England

s) 1979 – a minority Labour government

t) i) The Parliamentary Labour Party – all Labour front and backbenchers in the Commons

   ii) All Conservative backbenchers; not frontbenchers

REFERENCES

Hennessy, Peter (1995) *The Hidden Wiring*, Gollancz

Mackintosh, John, cited in Gwyn, W.B. and Rose, R. (eds) (1980) *Britain: Progress and Decline*, Macmillan

Robertson, Geoffrey (1983) 'Out of court', in *The Guardian*, 24 January

Walkland, Stuart in Walkland, S.A. and Ryle, Michael (1977) *The Commons in the Seventies*, Fontana

Young, Hugo (1987) 'The thud of heads against a brick wall', in *The Guardian*, 17 November

6 Executive: monarchy, Prime Minister and Cabinet

KEY ISSUES

▶ Parliamentary government: elective dictatorship?

▶ Monarchy:

Legal versus actual powers

Arguments for and against the monarchy

Uses/abuses of the royal prerogative

▶ Cabinet:

Ministerial responsibility – to whom: the Crown, Prime Minister, Parliament or voters?

Effectiveness of conventions of collective and individual responsibility

Sources of Cabinet power; constraints and influences

▶ Prime Minister:

Powers and limitations

Cabinet or Prime Ministerial government?

Is British government becoming presidential?

TOPIC NOTES

Key facts and concepts

The executive consists of the Crown; the political policy-makers: Prime Minister, Cabinet and other ministers (around 100 altogether); and the administrators: the civil servants – a hierarchy of non-elected, permanent, impartial and professional 'bureaucrats' who administer the policies and machinery of government. The work of government is divided into around 50 government departments – defence, employment, education, etc. – and the ministerial heads of the 20 or so major departments are usually in the Cabinet.

In the British system of parliamentary government, the ministers are accountable to Parliament, and thus to the electorate, for the policies of government and the actions of government departments.

The monarchy

The Crown is the permanent, abstract institution which embodies the supreme power of the state. It is the formal head of all three branches of government – legislature, executive and judiciary – and all acts of state are done in the name of the Crown. The monarchy is the institution of hereditary, royal rule (as opposed to a republic, which is usually headed by an elected president). The sovereign or monarch is the person upon whom the Crown is conferred. In Britain, succession to the throne is determined by the Act of Settlement 1701; this states, for example, that male heirs take precedence over females, and that the monarch may not be, or marry, a Roman Catholic – outdated and offensive rules, according to some critics.

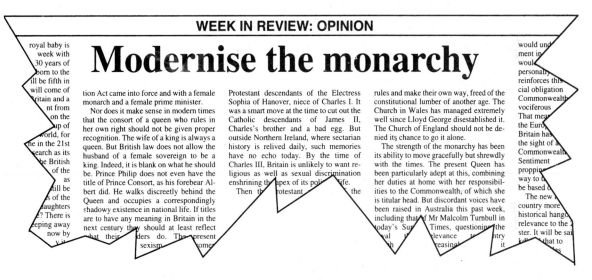

(Sunday Times, 31 January 1988, © Times Newspapers 1988)

The **royal prerogative** is the term given to the formal powers of the Crown. They are part of common law, and in theory are substantial (see page 112). However, Britain no longer has an absolute monarchy, but a **constitutional monarchy**: an impartial (non-party political), largely symbolic head of state whose powers are exercised by, and on the advice of, ministers, in theory subordinate to the will of Parliament, the people and the rules of the constitution. This is meant to 'democratise' the powers of the Crown and to keep the monarch out of political controversy. In the nineteenth century Bagehot classed the monarchy as a 'dignified' rather than 'efficient' part of the constitution, with much symbolic and ceremonial authority but little real power. Except in times of constitutional crisis, therefore, 'The Queen reigns, but does not rule'.

The royal prerogative

▶ Appointment and dismissal of the Prime Minister. *In practice*, usually governed by convention: the monarch chooses the leader of the majority party in the House of Commons, and the PM resigns if defeated in a general election or a vote of no confidence. However, if there is a 'hung Parliament' (as in February 1974) or if the PM refuses to resign according to convention, the rules are unclear, and the monarch may exercise some real choice and power of appointment and dismissal.

▶ Other appointments and powers of patronage, for example, ministers, peers, senior Church of England clergy, judges, civil servants, heads of the BBC and IBA, all honours and titles, etc. *In practice*, all are chosen by the Prime Minister; only the Order of the Garter and Order of Merit are at the personal disposal of the monarch.

▶ Opening and dissolving of Parliament, and approval of statute law. *In practice*, the PM chooses the date of the election within the five-year term; the Queen simply participates in the ceremonies and reads the Queen's Speech at the beginning of each parliamentary session – an outline of the government's legislative proposals, written by the government. No monarch has refused royal assent for a Bill since Queen Anne in 1707 (the Scotch Militia Bill).

▶ The granting of pardon and some sentencing powers: *in practice*, exercised by the Home Secretary. For example, in 1997 Home Secretary Jack Straw confirmed killer Myra Hindley's 'whole life' sentence (seemingly a judicial role).

▶ Declarations of war, treaties, etc. may be made under the royal prerogative by proclamations or orders in council, without reference to Parliament. *In practice*, exercised by the PM acting in the name of the Crown: for example, the banning of trade unions for civil servants at the government's intelligence-gathering centre, Government Communications Headquarters (GCHQ) in 1984 (Thatcher); the Maastricht Treaty in 1992 (Major); the bombing of Iraq in 1998 (Blair). Such actions do not require the approval of the monarch, and may also by-pass democratic accountability to Parliament.

Crown immunity

The monarch, in her private capacity, is above the law. The legal immunity conferred by the royal prerogative may extend to institutions and servants of the Crown: for example, in the trial of the Matrix Churchill directors arising out of the arms to Iraq crisis in 1995, ministers tried to claim immunity to prevent the release of key documents, but they were overruled by Judge Smedley. There is constitutional and legal debate among senior judges about whether Crown immunity extends to MI5 officers, allowing them to 'bug and burgle' without fear of prosecution.

Case for the monarchy

As the actual powers of the monarchy have declined, its symbolic and ceremonial functions have increased. The monarch is an impartial head of state, and thus a symbol of national unity, stability and continuity. As head of the Church of England she or he promotes Christian morality and family life. The British monarch is also head of many Commonwealth countries; she or he promotes good international relations and trade, while the pomp and ceremony of royal pageantry is good for tourism. The link with the Crown – royal assent, prerogative, etc. – lends authority and legitimacy to Parliament and government. The Queen has long experience and exceptional knowledge of British

The Royal Prerogative as a threat to the rule of law

Patrick McAuslan on a revived power that circumvents democracy

THE SUGGESTION, confirmed by the Prime Minister, that bugging and burgling by MI5 may be justifiable under the Royal Prerogative has clearly come as a surprise to many people, including Lord Denning and Merlyn Rees, both of whom vigorously repudiated such a notion in the letters column of this newspaper. It seems, however, that they are wrong.

The conventional view of the Royal Prerogative is that, following the Glorious Revolution of 1688, it was made subject to parliamentary control; and our constitution, based on parliamentary government under rule of law, dates from that time. How then can any actions which at first sight appear illegal, be justifiable, ie, legally supportable, by reference to this Royal Prerogative?

The fact is that the Royal Prerogative is alive and well and living for the most part in 10 Downing Street.

The authoritative jurist Albert Dicey defined the Royal Prerogative as "the residue of discretionary power left at any moment in the hands of the Crown, whether such power be in fact exercised by the Queen herself or by her ministers". It derives from the days before elected governments, when monarchs ruled the country and exercised powers over the citizenry. These powers, unique to the monarch, were his or her "prerogative" powers. Servants of the monarch, acting on his or her behalf, could also exercise the prerogative powers.

Modern elected governments govern in the Queen's name. Most of their powers are derived from the statute, and the constitutional struggles of the seventeenth century, confirmed by later judicial decisions, determined that prerogative powers could be displaced by Acts of Parliament and not vice versa, and that their use by elected governments was subject to parliamentary control and limited judicial supervision. But prerogative powers still exist and are still used by governments.

Much of the conduct of foreign affairs is carried on under the authority of the Royal Prerogative: for example, the declaration of war and the making of peace. Other examples of prerogative powers exercised by, or on the advice of, the government of the day are the granting of honours and the exercise of mercy. What currently gives cause for concern is that the Government appears willing to use such powers to circumvent actual or anticipated opposition to its policies; and the courts, though indicating a willingness in principle to control exercises of prerogative power, have in practice not done so.

The GCHQ case first alerted lawyers and others to the revived and aggressive use of prerogative powers by the Government. In January 1984, the Prime Minister unilaterally altered the terms of service of civil servants working in the GCHQ, forbidding them to be members of trade unions. In so acting, she exercised powers under the Royal Prerogative, for all civil servants are, *au fond*, servants of the Crown. She thus avoided the need for parliamentary approval.

The legality of her action was challenged in the courts, but the Lords, when the case eventually came before them, upheld her right to act, as she had done so on the grounds of national security. The decision provided powerful support for the use of the catch-all 'national security' argument as a justification for the use of prerogative powers.

Three years later, another unusual use of prerogative powers was sanctioned by the courts. In 1986, The Home Secretary issued a circular to chief constables inviting them to go behind the backs of their police authorities and obtain the support of HM Inspector of Constabulary, to try and bounce the authorities into agreeing to the chief constables' stocking supplies of plastic bullets and CS gas. In the event of any authority still being unwilling to allow such equipment to be stocked, the circular made it plain that the Home Office would nonetheless supply it.

The Northumbrian Police Authority challenged the lawfulness of this circular and the proposed action under it in the courts. The Divisional Court and the Court of Appeal found both to be lawful. The proposed action was justified as being an exercise of power under the Royal Prerogative: the prerogative of the maintenance of peace within the kingdom.

The judges gave the narrowest possible interpretation to the fundamental constitutional principle that where statute law and prerogative power cover the same subject matter, statute law always prevails. They said that since the 1964 Police Act did not specifically state that the Home Secretary could not supply police forces with equipment, it followed that the Act did not cover the whole subject, and prerogative powers were available to the Home Secretary to justify supply of equipment against the wishes of the police authority.

Legislation does not, and indeed cannot, cover absolutely all possible eventualities. The judgments in this case seem to be saying that if ministers find that they do not have power under a statute to take a certain action, they can nonetheless take action and justify it by reference to the Royal Prerogative. If they can in addition claim that the action taken is necessary in the national interest, then they will be free of any effective scrutiny.

Given these judicial decisions, it is easier to understand the claim that MI5 can justify its actions by reference to the Royal Prerogative. Officers of the security services could even be empowered to kill their fellow citizens, for one aspect of the Royal Prerogative is the defence of the realm. If there were any doubt, it should have been dispelled by the decision, announced yesterday, not to prosecute police officers who covered up unlawful killings in Northern Ireland. National security considerations were cited by the Attorney General as one reason for this.

Support may also be derived from the remarkable statement by Lord Donaldson, Master of the Rolls, in the Court of Appeal last Friday, that where members of the security services do commit illegal acts, there is always a prerogative power not to pursue criminal proceedings. This statement was confirmed by the Prime Minister herself in the House of Commons on Monday.

The present state of affairs is not consistent with any notion of constitutional democracy under the rule of law. The Government's willingness to use prerogative powers to get its way and national security to block scrutiny of what it is doing is as much a threat to parliamentary control of the executive as ever was James II's use of prerogative powers. It is, indeed, alarming that exactly 300 years after the Glorious Revolution, the executive is reviving the use of the prerogative to extend its powers over the citizenry.

(The Independent, 27 January 1988)

and international politics which may be a valuable source of advice to governments and Prime Ministers. She does her job conscientiously and competently, and both monarch and monarchy are currently relatively popular.

Case against the monarchy

Approval of the symbolic role of the monarchy is a conservative view which favours the *status quo* and fears progressive change. The monarchy has an ideological role in promoting class hierarchy, hereditary privilege, snobbery and deference, and its existence reduces British citizens to mere subjects. It is also anachronistic to have one established church in the modern, multicultural age. Heredity is no guarantee of merit, and the aristocracy and patronage perpetuated by the institution of monarchy are undemocratic. 'New' Labour's arguments against hereditary peers should, logically, apply equally to the monarchy. The popularity of the monarchy is said by critics to be largely a product of **socialisation** by the media, which trivialises the royal family whilst neglecting any pluralist debate about the political institution of the monarchy itself. The scandals and salacious gossip which surrounded the lives and deaths of some of the minor royals have, anyway, seriously undermined the symbolism and popularity of the whole institution. The formal powers of the monarch, such as the royal assent, are redundant and should be abolished. The powers and immunities conferred on the Prime Minister and others by the royal prerogative are dangerously undemocratic, by-passing Parliament and breaching the 'rule of law'. In 1996, senior members of the royal family themselves formed the 'Way Ahead Group' to debate on-going reforms to make the monarchy more open and populist and in 1998 Buckingham Palace appointed its first spin doctor.

The Civil List – an annual grant from Parliament, by 2000 almost £8 million – pays for the personal income and households of leading members of the royal family, but not for the upkeep of the royal estates, train, plane, horses and carriages, travel, etc. which bring the total cost close to £100 million. The monarchy is therefore sometimes criticised on grounds of cost; but it also generates revenue – for example, through tourism – and any alternative, such as an elected president, may have similar financial costs and benefits. Nevertheless, in the 1990s the Queen herself opted to start paying income tax and to limit the Civil List and in 1998 the royal finances were opened to parliamentary scrutiny by the Public Accounts Committee and National Audit Office.

---

1 Briefly answer the following questions.

    a) Suggest why the powers of the Crown have not been formally transferred to the Prime Minister and other ministers.

    b) Suggest three exceptional circumstances in which the monarch may exercise real power.

    c) Since the monarch usually has little real power, give reasons why the royal prerogative – the power of the Crown – is still controversial.

    d) Should the monarchy be left alone, reformed or abolished?

The Cabinet

The 20 or so most senior Government ministers form the Cabinet, which grew out of the body of policy advisers to the monarch in the eighteenth century. According to current constitutional theory (since Bagehot), we have **Cabinet government**: collective policy-making by a united team of senior ministers with the Prime Minister *primus inter pares* (first among equals). All Cabinet ministers are MPs or peers, and most are heads of major government departments such as the Foreign Office and Treasury. The Prime Minister decides the size and composition of the Cabinet, and allocates portfolios, i.e. departmental responsibilities.

The Ministers of the Crown Act 1937 gives ministers (together with the Opposition Leader and Chief Whip) a special salary and the Ministerial and Other Salaries Act 1975 sets an upper limit of 22 paid Cabinet members; but the Cabinet's composition, functions and powers are otherwise governed entirely by conventions. The two most important of these are the doctrines of collective and individual ministerial responsibility.

Collective responsibility

This doctrine rests on the assumption that ministers make policy decisions collectively and that they should therefore publicly support and defend all government policy, and should be accountable for it to Parliament and thus to the electorate, for example, through Question Time and votes of censure in the Commons. If ministers disagree so strongly with a policy that they cannot defend it in public, they should resign, as did junior minister Malcolm Chisholm in 1997 over Labour's cuts in lone parents' benefits. A united front – even if it is sometimes a facade – increases public confidence in the government and gives it strength and stability. More importantly, collective responsibility is central to the democratic accountability of government to Parliament and thus to the people.

In recent years this convention has been weakening; because of the rise of prime ministerial power, adversary politics in the 1980s and intra-party divisions in the 1990s, ministers have often disagreed publicly with government policy but have not resigned over it, most notably John Major's Eurosceptics. Heseltine said that he resigned in 1986 because the Westland affair was not collectively discussed in Cabinet due to Thatcher's 'prime ministerial dictatorship', and therefore he would not be bound by collective responsibility. However, the resignations of Nigel Lawson and Geoffrey Howe in 1990 were clear examples of collective responsibility in operation. It even applies to shadow ministers in the House of Lords, as was demonstrated by William Hague's sacking of Lord Cranborne – Conservative leader in the Lords – when Cranborne did a secret deal with Blair in 1998 to save some of the hereditary peers from abolition.

Occasionally, the Prime Minister has been obliged to allow ministers to disagree publicly over an issue so controversial that the enforcement of collective responsibility would have risked mass resignations and the collapse of the government. Such 'agreement to differ' occurred in 1975 over the EEC referendum under Harold Wilson, and again in 1977 under James Callaghan over the European Assembly Elections Bill.

Individual responsibility

This doctrine rests on the assumption that ministerial heads of department are the chosen representatives of the people, while the non-elected civil servants who administer policy within each department are impartial, anonymous bureaucrats carrying out political orders. All ministers with portfolio should therefore be publicly accountable for all the actions of their department, and should resign in the event of serious error – whether departmental or personal.

However, this convention is also weakening. The last minister to resign over a relatively minor error was Thomas Dugdale in 1954 over Crichel Down (farmland taken over by the Ministry of Agriculture during the war and not returned to the owner afterwards). Foreign Secretary Lord Carrington resigned over the Falklands conflict in 1982, and Trade and Industry Secretary Leon Brittan took the blame for the leak of a confidential letter and resigned during the Westland affair; but in both of these cases, the very survival of the Prime Minister and government was at stake. Chancellor Norman Lamont had to be sacked in 1993 – belatedly and reluctantly – over the UK's forced withdrawal from the European Exchange Rate Mechanism in 1992. In other cases, civil servants are becoming more accountable to Parliament (for example, to the Ombudsman and select committees), while ministers have not resigned. Conservative Home Secretary Michael Howard sacked top civil servant Derek Lewis rather than resign over a series of prison crises in the 1990s; no ministers resigned over the arms to Iraq affair despite heavy criticism in the Scott Report; and, again, in 1998, civil servants were blamed over the arms to Sierra Leone affair and Foreign Secretary Robin Cook remained in office. This may undermine the democratic accountability of government ministers and openly embroil civil servants in controversial political matters.

Individual responsibility also covers personal impropriety: for example, Labour's Welsh Secretary Ron Davies resigned in 1998 over sexual impropriety on Clapham Common; and at the end of that year, Peter Mandelson and Geoffrey Robinson resigned over a large, undeclared loan from Robinson to Mandelson, while Mandelson's Trade and Industry department was investigating Robinson's personal financial affairs. John Major's government lost a catalogue of ministers over 'sleaze', most notably Neil Hamilton, Jonathan Aitken and Tim Smith over the 'cash for questions' scandals. Ministers resign far more frequently over personal indiscretion (since there is no one else to blame) than over departmental error, although the latter seems constitutionally more important.

2   Write the following short answer: When do ministers resign?

3   Cabinet authority: sources and constraints.

   Which factors do you think are the most important? Can you add any others?

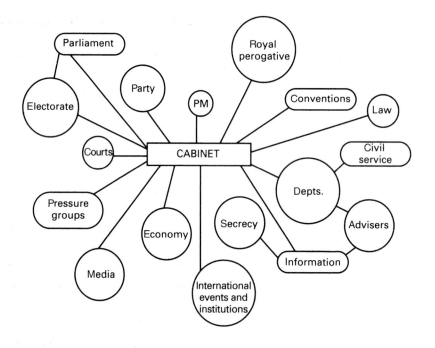

The Prime Minister

By convention, the monarch chooses as Prime Minister the leader of the majority party in the Commons. The first Prime Minister in the modern sense is usually said to be Sir Robert Peel, who held office after the 1832 Reform Act which established the principle of executive accountability through Parliament to the electorate.

▲ *Sir Robert Peel (1788–1850)*

Powers of the Prime Minister

The powers of the Prime Minister, derived from the royal prerogative, rest entirely on convention:

▶ deciding the structure of government, for example, creating, merging or splitting departments

▶ appointing and dismissing all ministers, selecting Cabinet ministers and allocating departmental responsibilities

▶ deciding the agenda for Cabinet meetings, chairing Cabinet meetings, and summing up decisions reached in Cabinet

▶ deciding the number, composition and terms of reference of Cabinet committees; and may chair important committees personally

▶ co-ordinating government policy

▶ political head of the civil service, ultimately responsible for numbers, duties and conditions of work

▶ appointing top civil servants, judiciary, clergy, etc.; awarding peerages, honours and titles

▶ representing the government and country at international summits, etc.

▶ communicating government policy and advice to the monarch through weekly meetings

▶ deciding the date of the general election within the five-year term

▶ deciding the timetable of government legislation in the Commons; a function usually delegated to the Leader of the House, a senior Cabinet minister

▶ leader of the party (this role differs somewhat within different parties).

According to the theory of Cabinet government, the Prime Minister is simply 'first among equals', but a leader who can hire and fire all other ministers is clearly more than that. The conventional list of the PM's powers is extensive, and since the 1960s many commentators have perceived a trend towards Prime Ministerial rather than Cabinet government in Britain. However, the actual powers of a Prime Minister vary considerably according to circumstance; above all, they depend on authority.

Prime Ministers 1900–2000

1900–2	Marquis of Salisbury (Cons.)
1902–5	Arthur Balfour (Cons.)
1905–8	Sir Henry Campbell-Bannerman (Lib.)
1908–16	Herbert Asquith (Lib.)
1916–22	David Lloyd George (Lib.)
	(War) coalition govt. with Cons.
1922–3	Andrew Bonar Law (Cons.)
1923–4	Stanley Baldwin (Cons.)
1924	James MacDonald (Lab.)
	Minority government
1924–9	Stanley Baldwin (Cons.)
1929–35	James MacDonald (Lab.)
	Econ. crisis; coalition 'National Government' 1931-35
1935–7	Stanley Baldwin (Cons.)
1937–40	Neville Chamberlain (Cons.)
1940–5	Winston Churchill (Cons.)
	War coalition government
1945–51	Clement Attlee (Lab.)
1951–5	Sir Winston Churchill (Cons.)
	Resigned 1955; new PM Eden called and won election
1955–7	Sir Anthony Eden (Cons.)
	Resigned over ill-health and Suez
1957–63	Harold Macmillan (Cons.)
	Resigned 1963. No general election
1963–4	Sir Alec Douglas-Home (Cons.)
1964–70	Harold Wilson (Lab.)
	Majority of 4. Re-elected 1966
1970–4	Edward Heath (Cons.)
1974–6	Harold Wilson (Lab.)
	Feb. 1974 minority government
	Oct. 1974 election – majority of 3
	Resigned March 1976 – no general election
1976–9	James Callaghan (Lab.)
	1977–9 minority government. 'Lib-Lab Pact'
	Defeated on vote of censure in Commons
1979–90	Margaret Thatcher (Cons.)
	Resigned 1990. No general election
1990–7	John Major (Cons.)
	Lost his majority by 1997
1997	Tony Blair (Lab.)
	Record 179 majority

Cabinet or Prime Ministerial government?

Former Labour minister Richard Crossman, in the 1960s, was among the first to assert that 'The post-war epoch has seen the final transformation of Cabinet government into Prime Ministerial government'. He borrowed Bagehot's phraseology to argue that the

Cabinet had joined the monarchy in 'dignified impotence', and cited three main reasons for the rise in the power of the PM:

► the rise of disciplined parties

► the creation of the Cabinet Secretariat (1916) – the body of civil servants who administer the machinery of Cabinet, and who are largely under the control of the Prime Minister

► the unification of the civil service under the Prime Minister in 1919, which gave the PM effective control of the Whitehall **bureaucracy**.

Crossman later revised his thinking, but others have taken up the theme, including writers such as John Mackintosh and Hugo Young, and former ministers such as Michael Heseltine (during the Westland affair) and Tony Benn. It is often difficult to assess the real balance of power within the executive because of the exceptional secrecy which shrouds the whole machinery of government and policy-making, but these commentators point to the following.

Factors enhancing Prime Ministerial power

► *Time* – the PM has no departmental responsibilities.

► *Control of Cabinet committees* – These, according to writer Peter Hennessy, are the real 'engine room' of British government. Their number, composition and terms of reference are not fully known, but there are believed to be about 135 committees now – fewer than under previous Prime Ministers such as Attlee. They may contain both ministers and/or civil servants and Prime Minister Tony Blair brought in Liberal Democrats, including Paddy Ashdown, into a Cabinet committee on constitutional reform; the PM also decides whether they make recommendations to the full Cabinet or actually make policy decisions.

Some key Cabinet committees:

– Economic and domestic policy (EDP), chaired by Prime Minister

– Overseas and defence policy (ODP), chaired by Prime Minister

– Home affairs, social policy (EDH), chaired by Leader of the House

– Intelligence and security (IS), chaired by Cabinet Secretary, Sir Richard Wilson.

► *Political and administrative support from political advisers and civil servants* – The PM has effective control of the Cabinet Office – the group of civil servants within the Secretariat who organise Cabinet and committee meetings, draw up and circulate agendas, policy papers, reports and minutes, summon persons and liaise between departments. At its head is the Cabinet Secretary, who is also Head of the Civil Service and who works very closely with the PM. In 1998, Prime Minister Tony Blair beefed up the Cabinet Office and appointed Jack Cunningham as 'enforcer' with power to oversee and co-ordinate all government policy.

There is also the Prime Minister's Office at Number 10, with four sections made up of civil servants and political advisers: these are party political supporters brought in from industry, business, trade unions (with an 'old Labour' PM) and journalism, together with 'spin doctors' – public relations and press spokespersons – to give the PM partisan advice and support on policy options.

► Thatcher was also noted for her use of informal, *ad hoc* groups of policy advisers – ministers, civil servants, outside advisers and others combined – such as the Economic Seminar. These groups bypass both Cabinet and the formal Cabinet committees, and are said to have made key decisions on, for example, abolishing exchange controls (1979) and banning trade unions at GCHQ (1984).

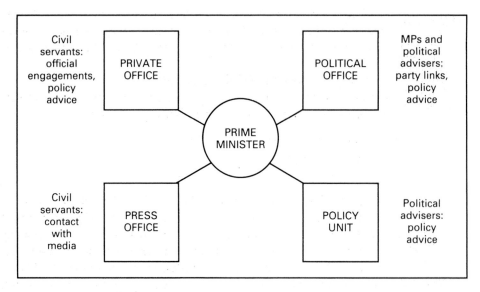

▲ *The Prime Minister's Office at Number 10*

▶ Prime Ministers have other *informal sources* of policy advice such as sympathetic pressure groups (for example, for Thatcher, the Adam Smith Institute; for Major, the Conservative Centre for Policy Studies; for Blair, Demos).

Former Conservative minister Francis Pym has described this network of Prime Ministerial support groups as 'a government within a government'. Critics of Prime Ministerial power fear that these bodies do not simply advise on policy but help to make policy decisions; since they are non-elected, and bypass Cabinet government, this may be seen as 'unconstitutional'.

In 1983 Thatcher abolished the 'Think Tank' – the Central Policy Review Staff (CPRS) – which had been set up within the Cabinet Office by Heath in 1970 to advise Cabinet on long-term policy. It had been the source of some embarrassing leaks, for example, a 1982 Think Tank report on welfare cuts, and perhaps it was deemed unnecessary. However, former Permanent Secretary Sir Douglas Wass (Reith Lectures, 1983) advocated a new Think Tank as an aid to Cabinet rather than Prime Ministerial government.

Many key policy decisions since the Second World War are said to have been made by the Prime Minister (usually with the advice and agreement of a few senior ministers, civil servants, policy advisers, etc.) rather than by the Cabinet as a whole.

Key examples of Prime Ministerial policies

These are said to include: the Budget, nuclear weapons, and intelligence and security, which have never been matters for Cabinet government.

▶ *Chamberlain:* Appeasement (1938)

▶ *Eden:* Suez (1956)

▶ *Wilson:* Devaluation of the pound (1967)

▶ *Thatcher:* the Falklands conflict (1982 – when Cabinet was suspended and replaced by a 'War Cabinet' – actually a Cabinet committee chaired by the PM); abolition of the Greater London and metropolitan councils (1985); the bombing of Libya by US planes from British bases (1986); the *Spycatcher* affair (1986–8); the poll tax (1988); restructuring of the civil service (1988); inner-cities policy (1988), etc. It was astonishingly revealed in 1998 that she had a plan in 1984 (a month after the IRA bombing of the Conservative conference) to shift the Irish border so as to transfer a large proportion of republican Catholics from Northern Ireland to Eire and that ministers such as Geoffrey Howe had to work hard to dissuade her.

▶ *Major:* the Gulf 'War Cabinet' (1991)

▶ *Blair:* Formula One tobacco advertising exemption; gag on four EU MPs over welfare cuts; Amsterdam Treaty; Social Exclusion Unit; personal veto of Chancellor Brown's plan to increase the top rate of income tax in 1998; appointment of friend and Scottish media owner Gus MacDonald as Scottish Industry minister from *outside* Parliament contrary to powerful convention; Blair's 'project' – the creation of a long-term centre-left alliance – to which end he extended consultation with the Liberal

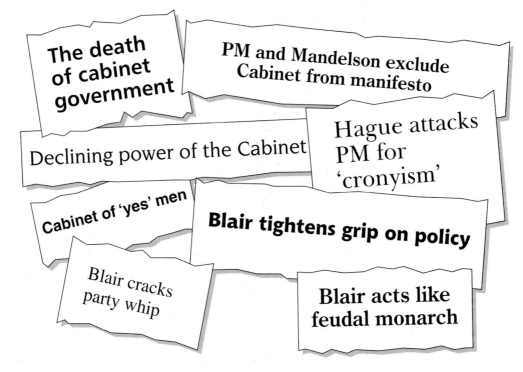

The death of cabinet government

PM and Mandelson exclude Cabinet from manifesto

Declining power of the Cabinet

Hague attacks PM for 'cronyism'

Cabinet of 'yes' men

Blair tightens grip on policy

Blair cracks party whip

Blair acts like feudal monarch

▲ *Prime Ministerial government?*

Democrats to education, health, welfare, foreign and defence policy in 1999 and appointed moderate Conservatives such as Michael Heseltine, Ken Clarke and Chris Patten to various committees and quangos.

Although arguments about Prime Ministerial government predate Thatcher, her style and image of leadership – variously described as 'strong' and 'authoritarian' – intensified the debate, especially since she was the first Prime Minister to have lent her name to an era (see Jones). However, key Cabinet colleagues such as Nigel Lawson and Geoffrey Howe wearied of her autocratic nature and it ultimately destroyed her. John Major's approach was deliberately more Cabinet-oriented, collegiate and consensual but this, in turn, came to be seen as a weakness and his government became increasingly divided, especially over Europe. Blair displayed his centralising and disciplinarian tendencies over his government and party from the earliest days of his premiership, and critics made much of his 'control freakery', for example, keeping his MPs ruthlessly 'on message' via pager from Millbank, reliance on powerful spin doctors such as Alastair Campbell and Jonathan Powell, promotion of loyalists in reshuffles – what critics call his 'culture of cronyism', etc.

Suggested reforms to curb the powers of the Prime Minister include:

▶ a 'constitutional premiership' – outlining and limiting the powers of the PM (and perhaps also the Cabinet) in law

▶ election of the Cabinet by the parliamentary party

▶ transferring the PM's powers of patronage to the Commons

▶ more political advisers for ministers

▶ ministers choosing their own senior departmental civil servants

▶ a Think Tank to serve Cabinet as a whole

▶ less power and authority for the PM's spin doctors.

The growing emphasis in British politics and the media on party leaders' individual personalities, styles and images has led some (for example, Foley) to suggest that British government is becoming 'presidential'. However, a presidential system is based on separation of the executive and legislature; in the USA the President is separately elected by the people, and neither he nor his appointed executive team (also called Cabinet) are allowed to be members of Congress (the US equivalent of Parliament). The President may therefore lack a majority in Congress, and may thus be weaker than a British Prime Minister, for example, Bill Clinton's Health Bill fiasco and his historic **impeachment** hearings by the Senate in 1999. An outright 'presidential system' therefore has additional checks and balances which are lacking in British 'parliamentary government'.

In the looser sense, however, Tony Blair has undoubtedly displayed a more 'presidential' *style* of leadership than most, i.e. a carefully cultivated and exceptionally personal, populist, 'hands on' style and image. Former Conservative frontbencher Michael Howard has spoken of 'a trend towards presidency away from parliamentary democracy'. Examples include Blair's claiming of a personal mandate for the creation and success of 'new' Labour, his walkabout with Cherie upon his victory in 1997 (and Cherie herself personifying the 'first lady' syndrome, for example, her attendance at the 1999 music Brit Awards), his 'call me Tony' relationship with ministers and officials, his welfare road shows, 'people's Princess' speech on the death of Diana, Princess of Wales, personal intervention in the Northern Ireland and Middle East peace talks, his 'cool Britannia' soirees at No. 10, going live on the Internet, personal slogans such as the 'third way', etc. When he added his voice in 1999 – not in Parliament but on BBC Radio 2's Jimmy

Young programme – to the media hue and cry over England football manager Glen Hoddle's comments on reincarnation and disability, he was criticised (for example, by John Major) for headline grabbing and promoting 'mob mentality'.

Constraints on Prime Ministerial government

► *Authority* is the essential precondition of Prime Ministerial power. It derives from the electorate, the Commons, the Crown and, above all, the party. Unlike an American president, a British Prime Minister depends on party support and loyalty (for example, Thatcher, who was ousted by her party in 1990 despite having a safe arithmetical majority in the Commons).

► Every Prime Ministerial power is also a *responsibility*; if it is misused, the PM may lose authority and even risk losing office: for example, Eden over Suez, Macmillan's so-called 'night of the long knives' when he sacked seven Cabinet ministers at once (1962), Heath over the miners' strike (1974), Thatcher over Europe and the poll tax and Major over his failure to control party divisions and 'sleaze'.

► There are *constraints on the PM's appointment and dismissal of ministers*: they should come from Parliament, should represent all regions of the country, should reflect the range of political feeling in the party and retain party support (Peter Mandelson and Geoffrey Robinson in 1998 did not) and they should, preferably, be honest and competent. Such constraints in a parliamentary system contrast with the unlimited patronage powers of an American President which may generate a 'spoils system'. A Prime Minister must also 'be a good butcher'; on the other hand, too many reshuffles suggest misjudgement, disunity or incompetence.

► *Cabinet revolts* are rare, but significant: for example, against Wilson's devaluation of the pound (1967) and Thatcher's proposed sale of British Leyland to US General Motors (1986).

► *Backbench revolts*: for example, against Major's second rise in VAT on domestic fuel (1995); Blair's cut in lone parents' benefits (1997).

► *The Lords*: for example, they forced Major to climb down over Sky TV sports coverage buy-up and forced limited concessions from Blair over Scottish university tuition fees.

► *Pressure groups* may be a key constraint: for example, the miners against Heath in 1974 and the public sector trade unions against Callaghan in the 'winter of discontent' 1978–9; the anti-gun group Snowdrop persuaded Major to ban handguns after the Dunblane massacre, and the Countryside Alliance frightened Blair off banning fox hunting.

► *The media and civil service* may be a hindrance as well as a help, but a Prime Minister's effective power at any time depends on a wide variety of circumstances: personality and charisma, health and energy, size of majority, length of time in office and proximity of a general election, the state of the economy, international events (such as war), popularity and competence of the Opposition (especially their Leader), etc.

► *The EU* is clearly a growing constraint on the policy-making power of any PM (for example, the beef ban) and may also affect his or her authority if relations are clumsy (for example, Thatcher).

► A Labour Prime Minister used to be subject to additional *party constraints*, notably the National Executive Committee and annual conference, but these are increasingly weak and sidelined under Blair. Also, Labour Shadow Cabinets are elected by fellow Labour MPs, and will expect ministerial offices in a new government – but can fairly quickly be reshuffled.

To quote former Prime Minister Herbert Asquith: 'The office of the Prime Minister is what its holder chooses and is able to make of it'. This stresses the flexibility of Prime Ministerial power, but also its limitations.

In sum, to expect or assume either Cabinet government or Prime Ministerial government, in any literal sense, may be too simplistic. The tasks of modern government are too many for a group of 20 or so busy (and more or less transient) ministers – never mind one person. Policy-making is a more or less pluralist process, dispersed throughout what Madgwick calls 'the central executive territory' – though the diverse groups of ministers, civil servants, advisers and experts involved may often be directed or even dominated by the Prime Minister. The key problems arising are:

- the secrecy surrounding the policy-making process
- the fear that PM-dominated policy-making may produce unbalanced or ill-judged policies, unchecked by Cabinet or Commons (given the strength of party discipline)
- the fear that policy decisions are made by non-elected, unaccountable groups and individuals
- the perceived decline in ministerial accountability to Parliament and to the voters.

ESSAYS

1 *Theme:* Monarchy

Q? Are monarchy and democracy compatible?

(Cambridge, June 1986, Paper 1)

---

3 Write a timed essay incorporating the points listed in the plan below (and adding your own arguments, names and examples). Note that the title does not specify Britain; consider various types and styles of monarchy, for example, Sweden, Middle East, some African tribal societies, etc. Also bear in mind different interpretations of 'democracy' – see Chapter 2.

 Essay plan

a) Definitions . . . depends on type of monarchy (for example, absolute or constitutional) and type of democracy (for example, direct or indirect)

b) Not compatible:

- If absolute monarchy – not 'people power'
- Not elected
- Aristocratic hierarchy against the interests of the majority
- Promotes privilege and deference
- Consent created by media and political socialisation
- May mask significant conflicts of interest in society
- Royal prerogative (whether used by monarch, PM and ministers or others) may by-pass Parliament and breach the 'rule of law'
- Promotes 'absolute premiership' – 'prime ministerial government'

c) Compatible:

  ▶ Constitutional monarchy – subordinate to the ballot box

  ▶ Need not preclude 'people power'

  ▶ Sources of authority other than election: tradition, rules of the constitution, charisma, experience and expertise, lack of power

  ▶ Consent

  ▶ Promotes 'national interest' – unites country, enhances economy and tourism, etc.

  ▶ Constitutional check against 'elective dictatorship'

  ▶ Alternatives? For example, elected 'impartial' president over PM and government (as in Eire), or fusion of 'efficient' and 'dignified' roles of executive in single premier (as in USA) – problems

d) Conclusion: Compatible, especially with indirect democracy; but British monarchy – and PM, royal prerogative, etc. – in need of reform: for example, written constitution, 'constitutional premiership'.

Note: If you wish to conclude that they are not compatible, swap sections (b) and (c); always put your own case last.

2 *Theme:* Prime Minister

Q? 'The powers of the Prime Minister do not explain his authority.' Discuss.

(London, Feb. 1976, Paper 1)

A✓ Examiners' comments

'There are two conceptual points which need clarification for a good answer to this question: the difference between power and authority, and the idea that power is an ambiguous concept, i.e. that "the growing institutional power of the Prime Minister" as described by John Mackintosh does not in fact seem to guarantee effective power to influence events or opinion. Clarification of one of these concepts should earn an E or D grade; a C grade would require both. For an A or B grade to be awarded some thoughtful exemplification would be needed of the apparent paradox of politics that a man or government can have a lot of power without much authority, or a lot of authority without much formal power.'

Short plan

a) Definitions: power (P) versus authority (A) . . .

  (Much P, little A: military junta. Much A, little P: British monarch.)

b) Sources of PM's authority: electorate, party, Parliament, Crown, charisma? (Weber), state of economy, media . . .

c) Therefore A → (leads to) P rather than vice versa.

  (Briefly list conventional powers; examples of practical limits.)

  Loss of A → loss of P: Eden, Heath, Thatcher, Major . . . Revolts . . .

d) But good use of P may increase A: Churchill?

  And misuse of P may decrease A: for example, Macmillan 1962; Thatcher and GCHQ, Westland, Libyan bombing, EU, etc.; Blair and Ecclestone affair, cronyism and 'control freakery', etc.

e) Conclusion: generally agree: A explains P, not vice versa.

  But use/misuse of P may then enhance or diminish A.

3 *Theme:* **Prime Ministerial government?**

Stimulus response questions

This type of exam question presents a prose passage, diagram or set of data (for example, electoral statistics), and asks students a number of questions on and around the issues raised in the passage. It is not simply 'data response', i.e. full information for all of the answers will not be found in the passage itself; students must know and show wider knowledge and evaluative skills in their answers. Sometimes marks allocated will be shown against each part-question, but if not, the question will be marked as a whole, and students must judge how much time and attention to devote to each part of the whole question. You should therefore read it all through carefully first and consider how much and what information to put where; do not repeat yourself in different parts of the whole answer.

Q? *Read the passage below, then answer the questions which follow.*

> Those who argue that in Britain today we still have 'Cabinet government' point to the considerable practical constraints which operate on any Prime Minister's exercise of power; and also to the extra constraints which party imposes on a Labour Prime Minister compared with a Conservative Prime Minister. Those who assert 'Prime Ministerial government', however – such as Tony Benn – argue that the powers of a modern Prime Minister are immense because they derive directly from the Crown and constitutionally do not require approval from Parliament. Such critics point to a PM's powers of patronage, powers to control the very structure and policies of government, the security services, the flow of information, international relations, war and peace, and even the precise date on which the people may be allowed to go to the ballot box. This, say the critics, is the real danger of the British Crown and monarchy today: not the flummery and family trivia which fills the pages of the tabloids, but the personal autocracy which it allows and empowers at the very heart of British democracy.

a) What constraints may, in practice, limit the powers of a Prime Minister?

b) Why and how might a Labour Prime Minister be more constrained by the party than a Conservative Prime Minister?

c) Comment on the view outlined at the end of the passage about the role of the British Crown and monarchy today.

d) Should Prime Ministerial power be lessened or not? If so, how?

(Simulated example)

A✓ Suggested answer

a) The many practical constraints on the powers of the PM centre on the need for authority from the people, Parliament, the party and the royal prerogative.

The power of the PM to choose ministers is usually limited by the fact that they must come from Parliament (although a safe seat or a peerage may be given to a favoured individual, for example, Labour's Baroness Blackstone; and Blair brought Gus MacDonald into government although he was not in Parliament at all). Ministers should represent a balanced team in terms of age, experience, geography and shades of thinking within the party if they are not to become alienated from the back-benchers.

There are also clear constraints on the dismissal of ministers. Though a PM should 'be a good butcher', if she or he sacks too many ministers too frequently it implies poor judgement in the first place, and the PM's authority will be undermined, as in

Macmillan's 'night of the long knives' in 1962 when he sacked seven Cabinet ministers overnight.

Cabinet revolts limit a PM's policy-making power. They are not common and it may often look like 'PM government' simply because a Cabinet is happy to accept PM leadership. When they do occur they may suggest misjudgement or mismanagement by a PM, for example, in 1982 when the Cabinet refused to discuss a leaked Think Tank report advocating large NHS cuts before the 1983 election. However, a Cabinet may be obstructive in the short term but a PM may 'win' in the end, for example Thatcher and student loans.

The backbenchers may also be a constraint (for example, VAT 1996), though they risk loss of promotion prospects. Parliament as a whole should be a key constraint; and the Lords have been more active in opposing government bills since the 1980s, but their power is limited.

Extra-parliamentary groups are also a constraint, though the power of the trade unions particularly has been curbed since the 1980s.

The EU is a particular constraint, for example, the beef ban.

The real policy-making power of a PM depends on circumstances: the state of the economy, the size of the government's majority, the proximity of a general election, international events, the health, character and length of tenure of the PM him/herself, etc.

b) A Labour Shadow Cabinet is elected by Labour MPs, not chosen by the leader, and a Labour leader is obliged to take it with him into office; however, he can reshuffle after a year, and always has the freedom to allocate portfolios and to dismiss individual shadow/ministers. A Labour leader has to contend with the NEC and Conference which, according to party rules, have policy-making power. The NEC is the collective party head – writing the manifesto, appointing party officials, supervising party discipline, etc. – and has no direct equivalent in the Conservative Party. Nor is the Conservative conference a policy-making body as such, but rather a sounding board for party opinion and a rally around the leader.

Moreover, the Conservative Party historically has a stronger philosophical tradition of loyalty to its leader, whereas the Labour Party used to lay greater stress on intraparty democracy (which can mean more visible disunity).

However, that did not stop the Conservatives forcing Thatcher out of office. Also, PM Tony Blair has markedly strengthened and centralised his control within the Labour Party, downgrading the powers of Conference and the NEC. Finally, the institutional powers of a Prime Minister often, in practice, over-ride theoretical party constraints, so the differences between a Labour and Conservative PM are not great in practice.

c) The end of the passage suggests that (though the monarch as an individual may be beyond reproach) the conventional transfer of powers from the Crown to Prime Minister creates a Prime Ministerial autocracy, and that it is this constitutional arrangement which is the real 'danger' to British democracy.

On the one hand, the transfer of prerogative powers from monarch to ministers is intended to make the exercise of those powers democratic and accountable, because most ministers are chosen from the majority party in the Commons and are collectively accountable to Parliament, for example, through debates, votes, Question Time, committees, votes of censure, etc. This arrangement also lifts the monarch personally out of political controversy and party politics. He or she still has some limited power: for example, choice of PM in a hung Parliament, dismissal of a PM (for example, Gough Whitlam in Australia 1975), and granting of certain honours. For the most part, however, the role of the monarch today is largely symbolic and cere-monial – 'dignified' rather than 'efficient' as Bagehot put it. To that extent, the arrangement enhances 'representative and responsible government' and 'constitu-tional monarchy'.

On the other hand, the sweeping prerogative powers outlined in the passage are exercised, by ministers and especially Prime Minister, merely by convention. They therefore lack legal definition and limits, and may in practice be very flexible. A Prime Minister who can hire and fire all other ministers is clearly more than *primus inter pares*; the potential scope for corruption in the exercise of patronage is consid-erable (for example, Lloyd George's 'sale of honours' and 'Tony's cronies'); and PMs can apparently break some conventional rules with impunity (for example, the Westland affair).

d) I would conclude that the powers of a Prime Minister should be lessened, because Prime Ministerial autocracy is less democratically accountable to Parliament and the people than is collective Cabinet government; and because policies which are not debated and discussed by the whole Cabinet may prove to be 'banana skins' for the government – i.e. ill-judged, inept and unpopular or unworkable, for example, GCHQ, the poll tax, student tuition fees, etc.

One solution would be a 'constitutional premiership' (Benn) where the powers of a Prime Minister are written and limited in law. Also, the MPs of the governing party could elect the Cabinet and approve portfolios. Cabinet ministers could choose their own top civil servants and have their own *cabinets* – bigger teams of advisers – as Kinnock advocated. Freedom of information legislation would reduce the secrecy of the policy-making process and hence should enhance Cabinet government. Finally, a PM's powers of patronage should be transferred to the Commons (together with the replacement of the Lords by an elected second chamber), and new arrange-ments could be made for fixed-term general elections. These reforms combined would substantially remove the possibility of Prime Ministerial government and enhance the democratic accountability of government as a whole.

---

5 Write at least one of the following essays. Always write a brief plan first.

a) 'In theory monarchy is indefensible in modern government; in practice no-one has invented a better system.' Discuss.

(Oxford, Summer 1986, Paper 1)

b) To what extent does the British Cabinet system conform to the prin-ciple of 'collective responsibility'? Does this principle have any value?

(Oxford and Cambridge, June 1986, Paper 2)

c) Compare and contrast the powers exercised by British Prime Ministers since 1976.

(Oxford and Cambridge, June 1997, Paper 1)

d) 'The Cabinet has increasingly become a reporting and reviewing body, rather than a decision-taker.' Discuss.

(London, June 1996, Paper 1)

e) 'The Prime Minister has to all intents and purposes turned into a President.' Discuss.

(London, Jan. 1998, Paper 1)

GUIDE TO EXERCISES

Page 114

1 a) To legitimise the powers and actions of PM and ministers; to maintain flexibility; plus inertia.

b) 'Hung Parliament' – choice of PM.

If PM refuses to resign when government is defeated in the legislature on a vote of censure or major policy: for example, Australia 1975 – Labour PM Gough Whitlam refused to resign when defeated on his Budget; the Governor-General, acting for the Crown, dismissed him and replaced him with Opposition leader Malcolm Fraser, who immediately called a general election and won it, thus legitimising the Crown's action.

When to grant dissolution of Parliament: for example, after defeat of a new minority government; in war, etc.

c) Its use by ministers by-passes the elected Commons, and thus ministerial responsibility to Parliament is undermined; it breaches the central principle of the 'rule of law' that everyone is equal under the law; it may allow the security services to break the law with impunity.

Page 116

2 Short answer question: *When do ministers resign?*

Ministers resign largely in accordance with two key conventions of the constitution: collective and individual ministerial responsibility.

Collective responsibility rests on the assumption that Cabinet is a collective policy-making body, accountable to Parliament and hence public for its policies; therefore all ministers should publicly support and defend government policy or should resign. For example, Michael Heseltine, Nigel Lawson and Geoffrey Howe all resigned from Thatcher governments over disagreements with her about European policy, and Malcolm Chisholm resigned from Blair's government in 1997 over cuts in lone parents' benefits.

However, such resignations are relatively rare: John Major's 'bastards' – Portillo, Lilley and Redwood – did not resign despite open disagreements over Europe (though Redwood did resign to stand unsuccessfully against Major in 1995).

Also, government should collectively resign if defeated in the Commons on a vote of no confidence, for example, Callaghan's minority Labour government in 1979.

Individual ministerial responsibility means that a minister with portfolio – i.e. a head of department – is accountable for the actions of his department and should resign in the event of serious departmental error – even if that error was committed by civil servants, since they are non-elected, non-political, anonymous administrators and therefore should not be publicly accountable. Leon Brittan was blamed and resigned over the Westland affair in the 1980s and Chancellor Norman Lamont was – belatedly and reluctantly – forced to resign in 1993 over the UK's fall-out from the ERM the previous year. However, such resignations are very rare: Michael Howard's Home Office policies were ruled illegal fifteen times in the 1990s but he never resigned. Instead, he sacked civil servant Derek Lewis (who later won an unfair dismissal case). William Waldegrave and Nicholas Lyell were criticised by the Scott Report over the arms to Iraq affair but did not resign; instead, PM John Major changed the written guidelines to read 'ministers must not *knowingly* mislead Parliament', thus allowing ministers increasingly to blame their civil servants for not keeping them informed, as Robin Cook did in 1998/9 over arms to Sierra Leone.

Resignations over personal misdemeanour (usually sex, financial scandal and/or dishonesty) are much more common. John Major lost twelve ministers in this way, for example, David Mellor (sex), Neil Hamilton (cash for questions) and Jonathan Aitken (dishonesty). By 1999 Blair's government had lost Ron Davies over dishonesty about an alleged gay sexual encounter on Clapham Common, and Peter Mandelson and Geoffrey Robinson over a non-declared personal loan when Mandelson's department was investigating Robinson's personal finances. All of these ministers went reluctantly, under sustained pressure from the media, party, public opinion and therefore ultimately also from the PM.

In sum, both conventions are only erratically enforced, which calls into question the democratic accountability of government ministers for their policies and actions.

REFERENCES

Bagehot, Walter (1963) *The English Constitution* (1867), Fontana
Benn, Tony (1980) 'The case for a constitutional premiership', *Parliamentary Affairs*, Vol. xxxiii, No. 1, Winter
Crossman, Richard (1963) Introduction to Bagehot's *The English Constitution*, Fontana
Foley, Michael (1993) *The Rise of the British Presidency*, Manchester University Press
Hennessy, Peter (1990) *Whitehall*, Fontana
Jones, Bill (ed.) (1994) *Political Issues in Britain Today*, Manchester University Press
Mackintosh, John (1988) in Richards, P.G. (ed.) (1988) *The Government and Politics of Britain*, Hutchinson
Madgwick, Peter (1986) 'Prime ministerial power revisited', *Social Studies Review*, May
Pym, Francis (1984) *The Politics of Consent*, Hamilton
Young, Hugo (1990) *One of Us*, Macmillan

7 The civil service

KEY ISSUES

▶ Theory and practice of 'bureaucracy'
   The Rayner and Ibbs reforms; further reforms
▶ Power and influence
   Constraints on personal and political freedoms
▶ Neutrality; 'politicisation'
   A political civil service?
▶ Secrecy and 'open government' – arguments and reforms
   Declining permanence and anonymity; declining ministerial responsibility

TOPIC NOTES

Key facts and concepts

Civil servants are non-elected administrators and officials of the government. There are around 500,000 of them, and they form a hierarchy within each government department. At the top are the *higher civil service*: the Permanent Secretaries and other 'mandarins' (as they are often called, after the Chinese bureaucrats of old). Their functions include: giving information and policy advice to ministers, preparing policy papers and speeches, keeping the minister's official diaries and dealing with correspondence, organising and minuting meetings, anticipating parliamentary questions and preparing answers for ministers, consulting with outside interest groups, and running the departments. Further down the ladder are the administrative and clerical officials who administer the policies of government in Whitehall and around the country.

As *permanent*, non-elected, career officials who serve under successive governments of any party, civil servants are required to be neutral, i.e. they should not let political or personal bias influence their work. Non-elected civil servants are also not supposed to have policy-making power, though their advice – based on experience, and the possible costs, technical and administrative feasibility of different policy options, etc. – may legitimately influence ministers' decisions. Thus civil servants are meant to be anonymous, i.e. not publicly accountable for the work of the department; the minister in charge is

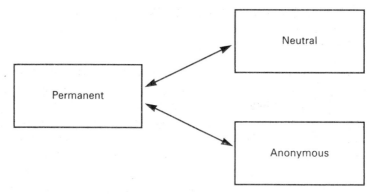

▲ *The British civil servant?*

answerable to Parliament and public for government policy and administration, according to the convention of ministerial responsibility.

There are many restrictive rules designed to protect the neutrality, anonymity and integrity of civil servants (see the list below); most were confirmed by the Masterman Committee on the Political Activities of Civil Servants 1949, and reviewed by the Armitage Committee 1978, and the last two points in the list were introduced post-1979.

► Though all civil servants may vote, none may stand for political office.

► Though they may be members of the mainstream parties, none may be members or sympathisers of communist or fascist organisations, and the top ranks may not be politically active (for example, campaigning for any party or pressure group).

► Before the 'fall of the wall', some could not travel 'behind the iron curtain' to socialist countries without permission.

► Some officials, for example, in the Ministry of Defence and Foreign Office, may be subject to 'positive vetting', i.e. a secret investigation of their private lives and political sympathies.

► They are all bound by the Official Secrets Act.

► They may not speak to the media or write publicly about their work without permission.

► For two years after leaving office, they should seek permission to work for private companies with which their department may have had dealings.

► Officials in the Ministry of Defence were barred by the Thatcher administration from being members of the Campaign for Nuclear Disarmament.

► Officials at Government Communications Headquarters (GCHQ) – the government's 'spy centre' – were barred in 1984 from belonging to trade unions, but this right was restored by Prime Minister Tony Blair.

Prior to the Thatcher era, the main post-war reform of the civil service was based on the Fulton Report (1968), which created a more unified, streamlined, specialised and politically independent civil service. However, the civil service was still frequently criticised and Thatcher, especially, viewed it as ripe for reform.

Criticisms and reforms

Bureaucracy and efficiency

Bureaucracy means the large-scale professional administration of any organisation, business or government. It is, in theory, characterised by appointment rather than election, permanence, hierarchy, consistent rules and procedures, impartial and impersonal methods, specialisation of functions, and division between the work and private lives of bureaucrats to prevent corruption or bias. The British civil service is sometimes said to be too bureaucratic, i.e. too inflexible, rule-bound, slow, costly, self-protective and obstructive – a negative image of 'faceless bureaucrats' and excessive 'red tape'. Sir John Hoskyns, a former policy adviser to Thatcher, accused the Whitehall machine in the early 1980s of lacking direction, drive and imagination: 'In organisational terms government is a creature without a brain' (lecture to Institute of Directors, 28 September 1983).

The New Right Conservative government under Thatcher sought to 'roll back the frontiers of state' and 'cut the bureaucracy' in accordance with its *laissez-faire* philosophy and its wish to cut public spending. Civil service numbers were reduced by over 100,000 to under 500,000, and politically sympathetic businessmen and industrialists were brought in to devise ways of making the civil service more efficient and management-minded. Sir Derek Rayner of Marks & Spencer set up an Efficiency Unit, a Management Information System for Ministers (MINIS) and a Financial Management Initiative (FMI). His successor as head of the Efficiency Unit, Sir Robin Ibbs of ICI, introduced the structural separation of the higher civil service – the policy advisers – from the administrators, who were to be devolved into semi-autonomous 'executive agencies' headed by chief executives with considerable freedom and flexibility of management. This reform was called Next Steps.

Criticisms of these proposals centred on fears of loss of:

▶ political (ministerial) accountability for policy administration

▶ co-ordination between policy advice and decision-making, and the administration of those policies

▶ incentive for administrative officials whose prospects of promotion to the top civil service may be reduced

▶ efficiency and morale in departments where staff cuts were high

▶ economies of scale, resulting in higher costs

▶ confidentiality within the administrative machine.

In theory, the principle of individual ministerial responsibility was preserved, together with Treasury control of budgets. Nevertheless, even by the end of 1990 over 30 executive agencies had been created, involving 80,000 civil servants, with around 30 more in the pipeline for the following year, and the Treasury and Civil Service Select Committee could already describe Next Steps as 'the most radical reform of the public service this century'. It has proceeded apace throughout the 1990s with almost three-quarters of the civil service organised into executive agencies by the end of the century.

There has clearly been some blurring of the question of political responsibility, the prime example in the 1990s being Conservative Home Secretary Michael Howard who sacked the chief executive of the prison service, Derek Lewis, over a series of prison crises rather than resigning himself, by asserting a constitutional distinction between 'policy' and 'operational' decisions.

The Labour government has continued the Next Steps programme, Major's Citizen's Charter and commercialisation of the civil service, with occasional outright privatisation. Also, many areas of decision-making and administration – for example, the planning of the Millenium Dome – which would once have been the responsibility of civil servants have now been passed to quangos (quasi-autonomous, non-governmental organisations) – committees appointed by government but technically not part of government. This allows scope for a *de facto* 'spoils system' or what in Britain is more often called 'cronyism', i.e. politicisation of what should be impartial appointments and decisions.

Power and influence

As non-elected officials, civil servants may influence ministers' policy decisions but they should not, in theory, have power themselves. However, critics such as Kellner and Crowther-Hunt argue that they derive power from many sources:

▶ their large numbers, compared with ministers, who are busy with parliamentary and constituency as well as executive duties

▶ their permanence, compared with ministers who average two years in any one office

▶ their experience and expertise, deriving from permanence and also from access to information which even ministers may be denied because of the exceptional secrecy of the British system of government. For example, civil servants – especially the Permanent Secretary of the Foreign Office, Sir John Kerr – were strongly criticised for withholding information from ministers about the arms to Sierra Leone deal, by an internal inquiry, a Commons committee and Foreign Secretary Robin Cook himself (1998–99)

▶ their departmental structure which, according to Crossman and others, may foster a common departmental outlook, for example, pro-farmers in the Agriculture department, which ministers find hard to counter

▶ their network of inter-departmental committees which parallels the Cabinet committee network and which may enable officials effectively to predetermine policy options before they reach ministers

▶ their effective control of the administrative processes, including the administration of any reforms to the machinery of Whitehall itself, such as the Rayner and Ibbs proposals

▶ their close involvement in national security and intelligence matters, for example, in key Cabinet committees from which most ministers are entirely excluded

▶ their extensive powers of patronage over thousands of titles and appointments which are nominally the responsibility of the PM

▶ British membership of the EU, which has increased the workload of ministers and has also necessitated much more preparation and co-ordination of policies by officials.

To quote former Cabinet Secretary Lord William Armstrong: 'The biggest and most pervasive influence is in setting the framework within which questions of policy are raised.

It would have been enormously difficult for my minister to change the framework, and to that extent we had great power' (quoted in *The Times*, 15 November 1976).

If civil servants have significant power to shape policy, it may not be realistic to expect individual ministers to take full responsibility for all policy decisions; and the apparent decline in ministerial resignations over policy and administrative errors (see Chapter 6) may reflect this.

A counter-argument is that complaints of excessive civil service power may simply suggest ministerial weakness or incompetence; many writers stress that officials like decisive and firm-minded ministers; and many former ministers such as Dennis Healey and Peter Walker share this view.

Sample short answer question and answer

Q? Distinguish between the power and authority of ministers and civil servants.

A✓ Power is the ability to do, or make others do, what you want regardless of consent. Authority implies legitimacy based on consent and respect. Ministers derive their authority from party, Parliament, PM and conventions, which give them the rightful power to make policy decisions and to run their departments. This should be enhanced by their civil servants and political advisers. However, ministers' power and authority may be constrained by backbench revolts (for example, second VAT rise), the Lords (for example, London referendum), the courts (for example, *ultra vires* rulings), pressure groups (for example, the farmers), the media (for example, the Cook/Regan affair) and by the state of the economy and by international events such as Iraq.

Civil servants in theory have no policy-making power, being permanent, neutral and anonymous Crown servants. However, critics such as Benn, Kellner and Crowther-Hunt have suggested that they derive power from their sheer numbers, permanence, experience and expertise, patronage and role on committees and in the EU. This can be bolstered by the secrecy of the system. Civil servants do have legitimate authority to advise and administer policy, deriving from their appointment and promotion by the Prime Minister on the basis of meritocratic examination and assessment. They may lose authority and even be sacked if they are perceived by government as a political challenge, for example, Sir Patrick Brown and Anne Bullen.

Neutrality and 'politicisation'

Others, however, allege that civil servants are both powerful and partisan; but the theme of these criticisms has changed over time.

▶ From the first majority Labour government of 1945 through to the 1970s, Labour ministers tended to argue that senior officials were anti-Labour and pro-Conservative because of their narrow class and educational background (70 per cent public schools and Oxbridge). Crossman argued that civil servants were deliberately obstructive, for example, of Labour's nationalisation plans; and Barbara Castle has said that senior officials added clauses to the industrial relations White Paper 'In Place of Strife' (1969) trying to curb the trade unions, against the express wish of ministers. Hence the appointment by many ministers since 1974 of party political advisers from academia, industry and trade unions, to counter or bypass unsympathetic civil servants. It has been suggested, however (for example, by former Conservative minister Michael

Heseltine in Young and Sloman), that the real obstruction to radical Labour policies came from right-wing Labour Prime Ministers such as Wilson and Callaghan.

▶ In the 1970s and 1980s ministers of both main parties often argued that their offi- cials were not party political as such, but were centrist and hostile to radicalism, whether of the left or the right. Benn wrote of 'established Whitehall policy' promoting consensus politics, and Nicholas Ridley said that his Conservative govern- ment's privatisation plans were met with official 'procrastination, inactivity and sabo- tage'. Even former Permanent Secretary Sir Anthony Part has said that 'the civil service always hopes that it's influencing ministers to the common ground' (quoted in *The Times*, 5 December 1980).

Civil service centrism, if it exists, may derive from a particular official perception of the 'national interest', or simply from a desire for continuity of policy for long-term stability, administrative convenience, bureaucratic self-interest or political safety.

▶ Writers such as Simpson (and many Labour politicians) argued that senior officials were 'politicised' under Thatcher to act – against their constitutional neutrality – in support of the Conservative government. Critics point to:

- the premature dismissal of former Cabinet Secretary Sir Ian Bancroft – a rare event in the top ranks of the civil service

- the close involvement of his successor, Sir Robert Armstrong, in the Westland affair, and in the *Spycatcher* case where he spoke for the government in the Australian courts and admitted to being 'economical with the truth'

- the alleged involvement of other top officials in party political matters: for example, Thatcher's press secretary Bernard Ingham and private secretary Charles Powell in Westland, and Ingham in party meetings about the government's defence policies. Critics – including civil servants themselves – also cite the publi- cation by officials of material 'promoting' (rather than simply explaining) contro- versial policies such as the poll tax and NHS reforms; and the improper use of MI5 staff and information in a party political campaign to discredit CND, according to former MI5 official Cathy Massiter

- the unusual degree of personal interest which Mrs Thatcher took in senior offi- cial appointments, and her well-known tendency to ask 'Is he one of us?' Critics cite Treasury Permanent Secretary Peter Middleton and Defence Permanent Secretary Clive Whitmore as 'political appointments'. (They also stress that, simply because of her long premiership, Thatcher oversaw the appointments of virtually all of the 27 top Permanent Secretaries.) Even the professional body of top civil servants, the First Division Association, said, 'There is evidence that the tradi- tional even-handedness of very senior officials is being undermined' (quoted in *The Financial Times*, 27 February 1985)

- Some political opponents (for example, Roy Jenkins in a speech in the Lords in 1988) linked the alleged 'politicisation' of the civil service to a perceived 'Thatcherite' onslaught on other Establishment and traditionally conservative insti- tutions such as the Church of England, the BBC, the universities and the judiciary.

The Westland affair of the mid-1980s, especially, demonstrated that the line between 'political' ministers and 'neutral' civil servants is a very fine one indeed. However, the specific allegation of political motivation in appointments is hard to prove or disprove. Mrs Thatcher and others said that she simply sought people with drive and energy, and disliked the tradition of Buggins' Turn, i.e. promotion by seniority; this might have fuelled some resentment amongst senior officials. Moreover, people like Armstrong and Ingham

▲ *Sir Richard Wilson, Cabinet Secretary (1999)*

all worked with previous Labour governments for many years. The 'politicisation' argument is therefore rarely clear-cut; but note that it stresses Prime Ministerial more than civil service power.

Civil service 'politicisation' was hardly an issue under the Major government but returned sharply to the fore after the 1997 election. Two days after coming to power, Blair issued an order in council (a Prime Ministerial edict) giving his spin doctors Alastair Campbell and Jonathan Powell authority over the civil service, and giving them civil service status 'except those aspects which relate to impartiality and objectivity' (said Cabinet Secretary, Sir Richard Wilson) – a strange new constitutional (or unconstitutional?) hybrid. Campbell famously issued a memo instructing civil servants to 'raise their game' in selling the government's virtues in stories to the media. Two senior civil servants – Sir Patrick Brown and Anne Bullen – were sacked for being 'Conservative political appointments'. By mid-1998 all top civil service press officers had been replaced by party spin doctors and top civil servants had complained to the Commons Public Administration Committee of 'creeping politicisation'. Blair has also streamlined and centralised the Government Information Service under the control of Number 10.

On the other hand, however, John Major's government established a code of conduct and a commissioner for civil servants who believed that their ministers were pressuring them to act improperly; and Blair's government gave these reforms legal force.

---

1 Some commentators perceive or predict a loss of civil service anonymity and/or permanence, arising either from 'politicisation' or from other constitutional and political developments.

    a) Suggest possible reasons and evidence for loss of (i) anonymity and (ii) permanence, now or in the future.

b) What might be the implications of any such trends for ministerial responsibility?

Some of those who believe that the senior civil service is or was being covertly politicised, for example, Tony Benn and Clive Ponting, advocate reform of the executive to enhance traditional civil service neutrality, anonymity and ministerial responsibility (both collective and individual). Others – for example, the First Division Association, John Hoskyns and Dr William Plowden, a former senior civil servant and Director General of the Royal Institute of Public Administration – have instead suggested introducing an overtly political higher civil service (perhaps the top three ranks only), along the lines of the US system where officials are party political appointees who come and go with the government of the day.

---

2 a) Write a list of possible reforms which might enhance the traditional roles and relationships of civil servants and ministers.

b) Write a case for, and a case against, appointing top civil servants on an overtly party political basis.

Secrecy

The criticism of excessive secrecy is levelled not just against the civil service, but against the whole machinery of British government. Crossman called it 'the British disease'; examples include:

▶ The Official Secrets Act 1911: intended originally to be temporary, it was passed by Parliament in a single day at the height of a German spy scare, and its most contentious clause was Section 2, which made secret all official information, however harmless. The Franks Committee 1972 recommended repeal of Section 2, but as late as 1984 it was used to prosecute and imprison a junior civil servant, Sarah Tisdall, for passing to *The Guardian* the date of arrival of Cruise missiles in Britain. However, when senior civil servant Clive Ponting was prosecuted in 1985 for passing to Tam Dalyell MP details of the sinking of the *Belgrano* during the Falklands conflict, he was acquitted; and Section 2 seemed so discredited as to be almost unenforceable. Instead, the government then tried to use the civil law of confidentiality to suppress embarrassing information, such as the book *Spycatcher* by former MI5 official Peter Wright.

A Conservative backbencher, Richard Shepherd, introduced a private member's bill in 1988 to reform the secrecy laws – not in any radical way – but the government imposed an unprecedented three-line whip against it, and it was defeated. The Government then produced its own Official Secrets Act 1989; it replaces the blanket 1911 Section 2 with six broad categories of information where unauthorised disclosure may be prosecuted; but it does not permit a public interest defence for exposing wrong-doing (Ponting's defence) nor a defence of prior publication (*Spycatcher*). In 1997, former MI6 agent Richard Tomlinson was jailed for a year for trying to write a book about his work.

▶ The Public Records Act 1958: forbids the publication of any government papers for a minimum of 30 years (the so-called '30-year rule').

► The government's use, or attempted use, of Public Interest Immunity Certificates (PIICs) in many important cases such as arms to Iraq, allows them to withhold information from the courts and places them above 'the rule of law'. In 1999 a Mr Nick Mullen was released on appeal after serving eight years as a suspected terrorist because, it was finally revealed, the authorities had used PIICs to hide from the original court hearing the fact that he had been illegally kidnapped from Zimbabwe (and denied access to a lawyer) by MI6 and the police to bring him to trial in England. Officials from the police, security services, Foreign and Home Offices had all colluded to lie about the case to Parliament and the media. Lord Justice Rose described their conduct as 'so unworthy and shameful that it was an affront to the public conscience to allow the prosecution to proceed' and that there had been 'a blatant and extremely serious failure to adhere to the rule of law'.

CHALLENGE TO TRIAL SECRETS

Britain could be forced to change the way crucial facts are kept secret at trials after the European Commission on Human Rights ruled yesterday that two men convicted in 1990 of murder were denied a fair trial. The commission said unanimously that the men's right to a fair trial had been breached when confidential information was withheld from the trial judge under public-interest immunity procedures.

The commission said that Raphael Rowe and Michael Davis, convicted of the murder of a hairdresser and of robberies close to the M25, were also treated unfairly by the Court of Appeal. It had not heard representations from their lawyers about whether the secret material should be disclosed, and the proceedings were in private. The Government said that it would fight the case at the full hearing and had no plans to change the law.

(The Times, 23 March 1999)

► Ministers may alternatively seek court injunctions banning the release of official documents, as Home Secretary Jack Straw did over the leak of the Macpherson report on the Stephen Lawrence case in 1999.

► The British executive and media together also operate a system of voluntary self-censorship based on non-legal guidelines known as the 'D-Notice system' (D for defence), which is unique in peacetime for a 'liberal democracy'.

► The secrecy of the policy-making processes, Cabinet committee system and Cabinet meetings themselves, as well as the restrictions surrounding official information given to Parliament, and the publication of former ministers' memoirs (since the Crossman Diaries, 1975), etc.

► The secrecy of the lobby system, where ministers and civil servants give political correspondents daily briefings whose sources could not be named (hence the use of phrases like 'sources close to Downing Street', which usually meant the Prime Minister's Press Secretary). However, the Labour government post-1997 relaxed this rule.

► The 1998 bill setting up the Welsh Assembly decreed that elected assembly members would be bound by the Official Secrets Act, which caused uproar.

► There have also been frequent allegations of the improper withholding of information by government from Parliament: for example, the sinking of the *Belgrano* during the Falklands conflict (1982), the Zircon spy satellite project (1986), the Westland affair (1986), the payment of 'sweeteners' to British Aerospace to buy Rover (1990), the development of new nuclear weapons such as Chevaline and Trident, the BSE scandal (1986), the arms to Iraq affair (1988) and the arms to Sierra Leone affair (1998), etc.

More open government has therefore long been advocated, and there have been some recent changes. Many Cabinet committees were publicly listed from the early 1990s; the Scott Inquiry into the arms to Iraq affair exposed ministerial wrong-doing (though no one resigned); the lobby system is now 'sourced'; TV cameras have been allowed into the Foreign Office; the 1998 Budget was preceded by an informative Green Paper; the Nolan Inquiry opened up MPs' personal interests and earnings to public scrutiny and party funding will also be more open in future, as will be the monarch's accounts; even MI5 jobs have been publicly advertised since 1996. Above all, the Labour government came to power in 1997 on a promise of a Freedom of Information Act for the first time in British history – although the bill was much delayed and watered down. It remains to be seen how genuinely radical this will be.

Sample short answer question and answer

Q? How has British government become more open since the 1980s?

A✓ 1980s:

▶ Televising of Parliament and especially select committees
▶ Creation of National Audit Office 1985
▶ Security Services Act 1988 – gave them legal footing
▶ Official Secrets Act 1989 – repealed blanket Section Two
▶ Public acknowledgement and info. about Cabinet committee system
▶ Increasing judicial review of executive action
▶ Growing number of political auto/biographies

1990s:

▶ Judicial committees, for example, Scott, Nolan, Macpherson, Phillips, Saville
▶ Nolan/Neill reforms and Commissioner for Standards
▶ Advertising jobs on quangos and in MI5
▶ Green Budget, i.e. consultative document
▶ Freedom of Information law
▶ Lobby system now on the record
▶ Publication of royal accounts
▶ TV cameras in Foreign Office
▶ Statutory civil service code of ethics and Commissioner
▶ Reformed calculation of unemployment statistics

---

3 Suggest a case for, and a case against, developing more open government in Britain.

ESSAYS

1 *Theme:* Civil service power
Consider the two titles below.

Q? Is the civil service really 'secret government' as some assert?

(London, June 1982, Paper 1)

Q? Does the power of the modern Civil Service mean that the concept of ministerial responsibility is a sham?

(Oxford and Cambridge, July 1983, Paper O)

A✓ Notes for guidance

The theme of these two titles is very similar: that the civil service have policy-making power, contrary to theory and to appearances.

The first title suggests that this power is 'secret', i.e. hidden behind the cloak of ministerial responsibility. The general secrecy of the system is relevant in so far as it may bolster civil service power; but 'secrecy' as such is not the core issue here.

The second title goes further to suggest that ministerial responsibility is a 'sham', implying a deliberate pretence. Consider whether the accusation may be levelled against civil servants and/or ministers. It also refers to the 'modern' civil service, perhaps implying some change (increase) over time in the role and power of officials – discuss possible reasons and evidence for any such change.

For both titles, bear in mind the need to discuss the following points:

▶ the theory of civil service influence and ministerial power

▶ names and arguments of those who defend the civil service and deny civil service 'power'. If you disagree with the titles, this section should go at the end of the essay

▶ names of critics who allege civil service power

▶ perceived sources of civil service power

▶ different types of power, for example, through policy advice or administration

▶ suggested examples of 'civil service policy-making'

▶ allegations of civil service political bias, and their changing nature

▶ the apparent decline in ministerial resignations over policy and administrative errors, with examples; does this imply that civil service 'power' is not 'secret' but is formally recognised, i.e. no 'sham'? Consider also examples where ministerial responsibility has been upheld

▶ the perceived decline in civil service anonymity, with examples; does this also imply no 'secret government' or 'sham'?

▶ the alleged 'politicisation' of the civil service by Thatcher and Blair; does this imply civil service pliability and/or power?

▶ the implications of Whitehall reforms (for example, Ibbs) for civil service/ministerial power and accountability

▶ if critical of the *status quo*, suggest reform(s): either to enhance the 'traditional' role of the civil service, or to make them overtly accountable for their 'power'.

2 *Theme:* Civil service reform

Q? 'Given the dominance of civil servants in policy implementation one might question whether radical reform of the civil service could ever be achieved.' Evaluate recent attempts to reform the civil service in the light of this statement.

(JMB, June 1986, Paper 2)

A✓ Examiners' comments

'This popular question was found by candidates to be difficult. There were two reasons for this: (a) linking together the two parts of what was not an easy question; (b) lack of understanding on the part of many candidates of the term "implementation". Consequently many candidates really produced two answers within one: one discussing minister/civil service relationships without any real focus on implementation; the second discussing civil service reform, without any real focus on civil service power (never mind implementation). In consequence a measure of latitude was exercised in marking this question, particularly to reward candidates who were well-prepared but yet still found difficulty in focusing on the specific question.'

Additional essay tips

▶ The title quote states that civil servants effectively control the execution of policy, including reform of Whitehall; and that they might use their administrative power to obstruct reform of the civil service itself.

▶ The focus on reform also implies defects, past or present; briefly outline the main criticisms which reformers have sought to address.

▶ 'Recent reforms' to be evaluated should include: the Fulton Report, and – since the 1980s – cuts in civil service numbers, abolition of the Civil Service Department, banning of trade unions at GCHQ, the Rayner reforms, the restructuring which followed Ibbs' proposals, alleged 'politicisation' of senior civil servants and freedom of information.

▶ Stress role of PM; and consider possible reasons for resistance to reform.

Q? Discuss the constitutional significance of recent changes in the Civil Service.

(London, June 1996, Paper 1)

A✓ Sample essay answer

The most significant post-war civil service reforms started with the Fulton Report in the 1960s. Many of these were reversed in the 1980s by Thatcher, who radically altered the civil service structure. Tony Blair has continued this trend. The constitutional role of the civil service rests on three main conventions: permanence, neutrality and anonymity. In recent years all three of these doctrines have been threatened.

Neutrality in the civil service has undergone the most serious constitutional changes. These changes were mainly instigated by Thatcher in the 1980s. She, it is said, deliberately made political appointments – for example, Whitmore and Middleton. She abolished the Civil Service Department (CSD) which made all the top appointments and promotions; these powers were brought directly under Prime Ministerial control. She would ask 'Is he one of us?' when deciding senior appointments. She even sacked the former Cabinet Secretary Ian Bancroft for not 'playing ball' with her, and then merged the two top Civil Service jobs of Cabinet Secretary and Head of the Home Civil Service in the person of Robert Armstrong. So arguably Thatcher centralised control of the civil service around herself and directly politicised it at the expense of neutrality.

Armstrong was sent to plead the government's case in the *Spycatcher* case in Australia, where he admitted to being economical with the truth. This directly politicised him because he was stating government policy, and it also undermined his anonymity. Thatcher's Press Secretary, Bernard Ingham, was also at times very publicly defensive of the 'Iron Lady'. Both of these two, with Charles Powell, Thatcher's PPS during the Westland affair, sought to undermine Michael Heseltine. This – as well as bolstering Prime Ministerial government – directly threatened their neutrality and anonymity and was arguably a major constitutional change to the civil service.

Thatcher also banned trade unions at GCHQ, the government's 'spy centre'. This could be seen as promoting neutrality as it sought to limit political participation and activism. It also arguably enhanced their anonymity as they had no forum to talk publicly as a collective. On the other hand, this was done at the expense of their civil liberties, contrary to the principles of liberal democracy, and it was politically motivated.

Under Thatcher, civil servants were known to participate in policy-making, contrary to constitutional theory. Thatcher told the civil service to find her a tax which would penalise Labour councils. They came up with the poll tax, by-passing Cabinet government. This is unconstitutional and seriously threatened civil service neutrality as it directly embroiled them in political activity, as well as further enhancing Prime Ministerial government.

The arms to Iraq affair exposed how civil servants could be made to cover up ministers' wrong-doings and not report them, since the change in policy was not reported to Parliament. Sir Robin Butler said that most of the documents 'were below my eyesight level'. In response to this, in 1995, Major set up a new civil service code of ethics and Commissioner to whom civil servants could go and complain of ministers' wrongdoings. Blair has gone a stage further and entrenched these in law. These are rare examples of changes which should enhance, rather than undermine, the traditional roles of the civil service.

Finally, under the Conservative government, Heseltine asked the civil service to find suitable 'cheerleaders' for the party, i.e. find party donors (1996). This directly embroiled the civil service in party politics. The then Cabinet Secretary Sir Robin Butler put his foot down and stopped this, indicating that the civil service can respond to improper politicisation.

However, unconstitutional behaviour has continued under Blair's government, with Blair's attempted appointment of a senior party official, Jonathan Powell, as his PPS (i.e. as a senior civil servant). This, again, was blocked by the Cabinet Secretary but it shows attempted politicisation in the civil service. Also, Alastair Campbell, Blair's press spokesman, wrote to the civil service press officers and told them to 'raise their game' in selling stories to the media – another threat to both their neutrality and anonymity. Blair, on only his second day as Prime Minister, issued an order in council which gave Campbell and Powell direct executive power over the civil service – both politicisation of the civil service and Prime Ministerial government.

Civil service permanence has also come under threat. Anne Bullen was sacked for allegedly being a Conservative political appointee, as was Sir Patrick Brown. Previously, Thatcher sacked 100,000 civil servants in the Rayner and Ibbs' reforms. The civil service is no longer a job for life. This could further undermine their neutrality, if they are asked to push party policy, as they may fear for their jobs and feel obliged to comply. In Major's government, Michael Howard's 'naming and blaming' and sacking of Derek Lewis over errors in the prison service – an Ibbs' executive agency – undermined individual ministerial responsibility and civil service neutrality, anonymity and permanence. Butler said at the time that ministers should not be held accountable for civil service errors in executive agencies – a major constitutional change, as it negates individual ministerial responsibility in large parts of the government machine.

Their constitutional rule of being anonymous has also come under threat recently. When Robin Cook allowed TV cameras in the Foreign Office – though it enhanced open government – it directly exposed the workings of the civil service to the public gaze.

In sum, the core civil service doctrines of permanence, neutrality and anonymity – and ministerial responsibility – have been seriously threatened. Reforms are needed to counter this. We could politicise the senior civil service and remove neutrality, i.e. change them with each new government. We could even elect the Cabinet Secretary. This would overtly eliminate neutrality, anonymity and permanence. Alternatively, we could clearly demarcate the roles of civil servants and policy advisers, making the former responsible only for advising and implementing policy to restore the traditional ethos of the Crown servants. This is the principle which Blair is using to justify his substantial increase in Downing Street advisers. However, his reforms clearly promote Prime Ministerial government and are no guarantee of constitutionality.

3 *Theme:* A political civil service?

Q? State a case for and a case against having a more political, that is a less politically neutral, civil service.

(London, Feb. 1976, Paper 1)

A✓ Examiners' comments

'A bare pass would be achieved by a simple and lop-sided advocacy of either "the civil service frustrates the intentions of the party manifesto" or "politics must at all costs be kept out of administration or we will have no objectivity and a spoils system". A candidate will fail if he is not even lop-sided but tries to fly on one wing alone. These "for and against" questions are designed to test empathy and the ability to present reasons and justifications on both sides. The average candidate will see the difficulties on both sides: lack of drive and thrust, but the danger of a political bureaucracy leading to a one-party state. The candidate who gains either grade A or B will know something of political advisers and will see that the distinction between "involvement" and "neutrality" is not obvious; like lawyers, civil servants support their clients in a most partisan way. The good candidate will also distinguish between civil servants supporting or criticising a Minister privately and having a public voice.'

Student's essay

In theory the British civil service, specifically the most senior officials, the mandarins (who make up around 600 of the civil service) should be permanent, anonymous and neutral. The permanence means that it is a career job and that the mandarins must serve under successive governments. The anonymity of the civil service means that they are not publicly accountable and accountable only privately to their ministers, the PM, the Ombudsman or the departmental committees, they are not permitted to talk to the media about their work or personal views. The bulk of this question, however, is concerned with their neutrality. This means that they should be impartial, non-party political and, as Sir Douglas Wass put it, they should be loyal, but not enthusiastic to the minister or policy of the day.

The argument in favour of a political civil service centres around the criticism that the civil service has been 'politicised'. It is argued that this occurred in Mrs Thatcher's term of office, specific examples being former Cabinet Secretary Sir Robert Armstrong, who acted on behalf of the government in the *Spycatcher* court hearings and admitted to being 'economical with the truth'; and press secretary Bernard Ingham. Tony Blair and his spin doctors are accused of continuing to politicise top civil servants. The likes of

Plowden and Ponting, as well as the First Division Association (the civil service union), have argued that in Britain we already have a political civil service and that it should be made open, rather than continue with an arguable 'myth' of civil service neutrality.

In addition to the arguments that the civil service is already political are the actual arguments in favour of a political system of civil service. It has been argued by critics of the present system that the 'neutral' officials are too 'pliable' and indifferent in their government administration (Bancroft). They have been seen to be equally supportive of the policies of one government and then another government that may propose opposing ideas. Whilst this may be seen as a fulfilment of the neutral and permanent theories of the civil service, it may mean that little attention is placed upon the immediate concerns of the day. It is also argued by Nevil Johnson that this apparent indifference shows a lack of integrity on the part of the civil service; and if they were overtly politicised they would have greater motivation.

Those in favour of politicising the civil service look to the USA and France. It is arguable that such systems allow for greater commitment on the part of the bureaucrats and that they enhance the strength and 'efficiency' of the government of the day. In such a system the bureaucrats come and go with the government of the day so that their loyalties are not divided.

The arguments against politicising concentrate on the lack of continuity and the dangers of a 'one-party state'. Whilst for example Tony Benn may criticise the present system in Britain, he regards the American political bureaucracy as a 'spoils system'. Critics of politicising the civil service argue that a political civil service entails lack of job security, since once the government of the day is defeated in an election, the officials would lose their jobs. This might entail a reduction in the quality of officials since the job prospects are not good. Therefore it might be difficult to attract qualified individuals. Critics of politicisation also concentrate on the fact that a lack of permanence and continuity means that the officials cannot gain any expertise and are as ill-equipped as their ministers. The critics of a political civil service (for example, Wass) also state that it may prevent long-term planning that the present system may enjoy.

I conclude that the drawbacks of politicising the civil service are too dangerous, and take Wass's arguments that there should be an Opposition civil service (on temporary secondment) to prevent a possible one-party system due to too much bias in government. I also propose a constitutional premiership so that the officials are more accountable to their own ministers and less dependent upon the will of the particular PM involved.

---

4 In the light of the examiners' comments above, and your own knowledge of the subject, try to assess, mark and grade the student's essay as if you were the examiner. The essay is reprinted as the student wrote it, under timed conditions.

Q? **4** *Theme:* **Open government**
Discuss the arguments for and against the introduction of a Freedom of Information Act in Britain.

(JMB, June 1986, Paper 1)

Short plan for guidance

Range of current secrecy provisions; examples . . .

Critics of present degree of secrecy . . .

Case against a Freedom of Information Act:

▶ All governments are reluctant to increase checks against themselves.

▶ Freedom of Information Act would increase powers of non-elected – and some say 'unrepresentative' – judges in deciding extent of open government.

▶ Could inhibit honest advice from officials to ministers.

▶ Could lead to 'political' appointment of officials to avoid public knowledge of internal friction or unsympathetic advice.

▶ Open government may undermine ministerial responsibility to Parliament if actions of civil servants become more public.

▶ Could make government less efficient. Lord Bancroft: 'Government is difficult enough without having to halt continually while people peer up the governmental kilts.'

▶ Could be costly to administer.

▶ Existing provisions – for example, data protection laws, Green Papers, departmental committees, etc. – are adequate.

Case for a Freedom of Information Act:

▶ Present secrecy laws run counter to principle of 'open government' and informed choice in 'liberal democracy'.

▶ Public 'right to know' stressed by judges, for example, in *Spycatcher* case.

▶ Range of existing secrecy provisions may discredit law and make it hard to protect genuine secrets.

▶ Secrecy may undermine ministerial responsibility to Parliament if MPs lack information about government policies.

▶ Flexibility of present law allows government to define limits of 'national security'; but a government concerned with protecting itself may not be best placed to decide what should properly be kept secret. Lord Donaldson: '...very easy for the government to confuse the national interest with the government interest'.

▶ Double standards of present system – where ministers may leak on an unattributable basis, but civil servants may be prosecuted – fuels resentment in civil service and may encourage leaks by officials.

▶ Civil servants who suspect government malpractice – for example, Ponting – have had no recourse but to leak and/or to resign.

▶ Excessive secrecy may undermine the authority of government in the eyes of the public.

▶ Excessive secrecy may hide waste, inefficiency or corruption – for example, loss of £212 million through mismanagement in Crown Agents Affair (Fay Report 1977); loss of £3.5 billion each year through long-term mismanagement and fraud in the Ministry of Defence (Public Accounts Committee Report 1998).

▶ Pursuit of excessive secrecy – for example, through the courts – may waste taxpayers' money in legal costs.

▶ Pressure groups need more official information to represent their members/causes adequately; and media need information to inform the public and scrutinise government.

▶ Academic research about British government and politics hampered by undue secrecy.

▶ Opinion polls indicate majority support for freedom of information.

▶ More informed debate about policies may produce better policies, and/or more consensus politics.

▶ Freedom of information legislation appears to work well in USA, etc.

Conclusion: Arguments for Freedom of Information Act outweigh those against.

Note: If you wish to conclude against a Freedom of Information Act, put the 'case against' last.

---

5 Write at least one of the following essays. Always write a brief plan first.

a) In 1995, at the time of the sacking of the Head of the Prison Service Agency, Derek Lewis, by the Home Secretary, Michael Howard, a distinction was drawn between responsibility for 'policy' and 'operational' responsibility.

Consider how such a distinction accords with the constitutional convention of individual ministerial responsibility. How far, and in what ways, has the introduction of agencies and market testing changed the roles and relationships of ministers and civil servants?

(AEB, Summer 1997, Paper 1)

b) 'Government in Britain is afflicted by a culture of secrecy, and the notion of accountability is increasingly ignored.' In the light of recent events (such as the Scott Inquiry), do you accept this analysis?

(Oxford and Cambridge, June 1997, Paper 1)

c) Discuss the main ways in which senior civil servants contribute to the political process in Britain.

(Cambridge, June 1989, Paper 1)

d) Have recent changes in the Civil Service been so radical as to 're-invent' British government?

(London, Jan. 1998, Paper 1)

e) Is government secrecy compatible with democracy?

(Oxford, Summer 1980, Paper II)

GUIDE TO EXERCISES

Page 138

1 a) (i) Decline in civil service anonymity:

- More accountable to Parliament since creation of Ombudsman (1967) and departmental select committees (1979)

- Senior officials are increasingly public spokesmen for the government in the media and the courts, for example, Armstrong in the *Spycatcher* case

- Officials are more often publicly named and sometimes blamed for policy errors: for example, by administrative tribunal over collapse of Vehicle and General Insurance Co. (1971); Westland (1986); arms to Sierra Leone (1998/9)

- More media coverage and communication: for example, Peter Hennessy's *Whitehall*, ministerial and official memoirs

- Financial Management Initiative (1982), and creation of executive agencies (1988), were both designed to give senior officials more **autonomy** over budgets and management, which may suggest more direct accountability of officials for example, to Parliament

- Leaks by officials publicly prosecuted, for example, Tisdall and Ponting.

(ii) Decline in civil service permanence:

- Cuts in numbers – loss of job security

- Sacking of Bancroft

- Perception of 'political' appointments may prompt replacement of key senior officials by a new government or PM (for example, Sir Patrick Brown and Anne Bullen), producing a political civil service *de facto*

- Restructuring might ultimately lead to privatisation of some administrative units, and loss of civil service status and permanence for those staff.

b) May reduce ministerial accountability to Parliament.

Page 139

2 a) Possible reforms:

- Ministers (rather than PM and civil servants themselves) appointing and dismissing their own officials

- More political advisers for ministers (perhaps in advisory bodies like the French *cabinets*)

- More access by ministers and advisers to official committees and files

- More open government

- Control of Cabinet Office by Cabinet (rather than by PM)

- Greater adherence to convention of individual ministerial responsibility

- Stronger parliamentary control of executive – for example, more power and publicity for Ombudsman and select committees

- Withdrawal from EU (Benn)

b) Case for and against a political civil service: see essay 3 on page 145.

Page 141

3 Case for and against 'open government': see essay 4 on page 146.

REFERENCES

Bancroft, Lord (1983) 'In defence of the mandarins', *The Guardian*, 2 October
Castle, Barbara (1984) *The Castle Diaries, 1974–76*
Crossman, R.H.S. (1979) *The Crossman Diaries*, Condensed version, ed. A. Howard, Magnum Books
Hailsham, Lord (1978) *The Dilemma of Democracy*, Collins
Hennessy, Peter (1990) *Whitehall*, Fontana
Johnson, Nevil (1977) *In Search of the Constitution*, Methuen
Kellner, P. and Crowther-Hunt, N. (1980) *The Civil Servants*, MacDonald & Jane's
Simpson, David (1989) *Politicisation of the Civil Service*, Longman
Young, H. and Sloman, A. (1982) *No, Minister: An Inquiry into the Civil Service*, BBC

8 Local government and devolution

KEY ISSUES

▶ Local government:
  Functions of local government and councillors
  Accountability of local government
  Pros and cons of local government
  Central–local government relations
  Local government versus parliamentary democracy
  Local government finance
  Controls on local government
▶ Devolution

TOPIC NOTES

Key facts and concepts

Local government entails the election of local people to run local services, such as education, housing, refuse collection, social services, planning and transport, leisure and recreation, police, etc. The structure of local government in the UK is a mixture of single-tier and two-tier local authorities. It has been reorganised frequently by central government through parliamentary statute – for example, in the mid-1970s, mid-1980s and mid-1990s – partly in a search for greater efficiency and accountability, but also sometimes for less laudable motives of party conflict and political control.

The structure and major functions of local government

The Local Government Act 1985, enacted on 1 April 1986, abolished the Greater London Council and the six metropolitan county councils (Greater Manchester, South and West Yorkshire, West Midlands, Merseyside, Tyne and Wear). Conservative central government argued that they were too costly and remote from the local communities. Their functions passed either to the 32 London borough councils, or to district councils in the metropolitan areas, or to joint boards of district and borough councillors, or to quangos (for example, London Regional Transport Board), or to central government. London was therefore the only European capital without a city-wide elected executive. The GLC and metropolitan councils fought strongly against abolition, arguing that they were more democratic, efficient and co-ordinated than the new arrangements which, they said, would actually be more costly. All of the abolished councils were Labour-led, and the issue was very much party-political.

Since abolition was a Conservative manifesto proposal in the 1983 election, the government argued that it had a mandate to carry out the policy, although public opinion polls indicated around 70 per cent of voters were opposed to it. The May 1985 local elections were thus a possible obstacle to abolition, since they were bound to be treated as a referendum on abolition, and the Conservatives were likely to fare badly; the government therefore proposed to bring forward abolition and to give powers to nominated district and borough councillors until the new arrangements were established. This proposal – enshrined in the Local Government (Interim Provisions) Bill 1984, known as the 'Paving Bill' – was defeated by the Lords on the grounds that it had no mandate (unlike abolition itself). The government therefore simply deferred the elections.

In 1992 a Local Government Commission was established to make proposals for further reorganisation based on the criteria of efficiency, accountability, responsiveness and localness, with central government clearly favouring unitary rather than two-tier structures. However, the process was controversial, with the larger county and smaller district councils fighting to survive. The result, by the end of the 1990s, was a mixture of unitary authorities for some regions of England (46 in all, for example, the Isle of Wight) and the retention of a two-tier system for other regions. In 1996 in Wales, a two-tier system was replaced by 21 unitary authorities and in Scotland by 28.

The question of reform is certainly not dead. The 1997 Labour government promised to introduce an elected London council and mayor and in 1998 a local, single-question referendum produced a two-thirds majority in favour. The nature of the referendum was, however, controversial because many voters wanted a council but not a mayor, or vice versa, but were not given the choice.

There are currently around 20,000 county, district and borough councillors. They are elected for fixed four-year terms to local areas known as wards (rather than constituencies). In London, all borough seats are contested together every four years. In the 36 metropolitan boroughs one-third of the seats are contested each year, with county council elections in the fourth year. The non-metropolitan district and unitary councils choose either method. Councillors are part-time and are paid expenses and attendance allowances only; they therefore tend to be atypical of the electorate, many of whom lack the time or money for local political involvement. Around 25 per cent of councillors are women. Councillors are usually party political like MPs, but there are many more independents (around 15 per cent), and there are many 'hung' councils where no one party has an absolute majority.

The functions and powers of local councillors

What are the functions and powers of a local councillor? How do they differ from those of an MP?

A councillor is a member of a local executive body, whereas an MP is a member of the national legislature. Both are elected to represent a local area; but a ward is smaller than a constituency and, whereas a councillor is purely local, an MP is expected to represent both constituency and national interests (according to the Burkean view). An MP is a legislator, and local councils – like everyone else – should work within the law of the land ('rule of law'). MPs may pass laws – such as the Local Government Act 1985 – which alter the powers of local councils or even abolish them completely. MPs are also meant to scrutinise and control the executive, both central and local; councillors are therefore subordinate to MPs. The only kind of law which councillors may make is delegated legislation, for example, local government by-laws. Their functions are executive rather than legislative – providing local services such as education, housing, refuse collection, fire and police, roads and harbours, leisure and social services. Some of these are 'mandatory', i.e. local government is obliged by law to carry out certain functions, such as housing the homeless; others are 'permissive', i.e. optional – such as providing local libraries and nurseries. Under both Conservative and Labour governments in the 1990s, the desire has been to change the role of local councils from that of directly funding and providing local services to being *enabling authorities* with different ways of delivering services, for example, through partnerships with the private sector and contracting out of some services, including outright privatisation.

Local government is advised and administered by appointed officials who are full-time, paid and permanent. As with the central civil service, the distinction between advice, administration and policy-making may be blurred, and the officials are sometimes accused of having power without public accountability. The issue of 'politicisation' is perhaps even stronger at local than at national level.

1 List five advantages, and five disadvantages, of local government.

Local government finance

Local government spending – for example, on building and running schools, council housing, roads, and providing services like homes for older people, parks and gardens, plus the administrative costs of local government itself – totals around £30 billion, nearly one quarter of all public expenditure.

Capital spending, for example, on new roads, is financed by borrowing from central government and banks, etc., and by selling assets such as land.

Revenue (day-to-day running costs, wages, etc.) is financed by:

▶ *Grants* from central government. These have increased to provide over 60 per cent of local revenue, together with increasing central control under the community charge and council tax systems (see below).

▶ *Payments for services*, for example, council house rents.

▶ Until 1989–90, local rates were levied on business and domestic properties. These were replaced (1989 in Scotland, 1990 in England and Wales) by the community charge or poll tax – a flat-rate charge paid by every adult, unconnected with property. This measure – the Local Government Finance Act 1988 – was highly controversial because it was unrelated to voters' ability to pay. It sparked a widespread campaign of civil disobedience (illegal non-payment), culminating in a violent anti-poll tax demonstration in London in 1990. It was one of the issues that helped to bring down Margaret Thatcher as Prime Minister in 1990 and her successor, John Major, was quick to replace it with a banded property tax per household with a 25 per cent discount for single people and exemptions for students – the *council tax*.

Like the poll tax, the council tax may be 'capped', i.e. central government can impose a limit on the maximum levied, which contradicts the principle of local responsibility and accountability for spending levels. This also undermines the 'mandate' of local authorities, and some councillors have said that they could not then afford to provide mandatory services. Capping was also perceived by critics as being motivated by party politics (like the abolition of the Labour-led GLC and Metropolitan councils): for example, in 1995 they enabled Conservative-controlled Berkshire to escape capping despite a 20.6 per cent spending increase, while Labour-controlled Brent with a 1.4 per cent rise in spending was capped. However, the Labour government since 1998 has relaxed, though not abolished, capping.

Business rates have been removed from local authority control and replaced by the *uniform business rate*, centrally fixed and collected then redistributed to councils in the form of grants. There is, therefore, still a strong element of central financial control.

Controls on local government

Parliament

Local authorities are created by statute, and all powers must be granted by law. There were 58 items of local government legislation in the ten years after 1979.

Courts

Courts may rule local authorities *ultra vires*, i.e. acting beyond their legal powers. For example, in the 1981 GLC 'Fares Fair' case, the courts ruled public transport fare cuts illegal under the Transport (London) Act 1969 which required 'economical' services (interpreted by the courts to mean 'non-subsidised'). There was more controversy in the mid-1980s when Liverpool and Lambeth councillors over-stepped the rate-capping limits, were surcharged for illegal expenditure, bankrupted and hence barred from office for five years.

(However, the courts can also, of course, rule against central government's actions and in favour of local government: for example, in 1985 when the Environment Department took money away from the GLC prior to abolition to set up London Regional Transport, the High Court ruled that £50 million too much had been taken, which the judge described as 'unlawful, irrational and procedurally improper'. The difference here was that central government used its majority in Parliament to re-write and even backdate the law to legalise its own illegality.)

Central government

Central government intervenes to control overall public spending – hence, for example, compulsory competitive tendering of some local services such as refuse collection; to ensure consistency of standards across the country, for example, in education; and to co-ordinate local functions such as planning. Methods include:

▶ financial control: grants, audits (via the Audit Commission for Local Authorities in England and Wales, established in 1983 and appointed by the Environment Secretary), capping, powers of veto over capital spending projects, etc.

▶ ministerial approval required in many areas, for example, education (the Education Reform Act 1988 granted the Secretary of State 366 new powers)

▶ inspection by relevant department, for example, police, fire, education

▶ appeals against local authority action, for example, to the Environment Secretary against planning decisions

▶ inquiries, for example, the Widdicombe Inquiry into the Conduct of Local Authority Business, whose 1985 report resulted in legislation curbing 'twin-tracking' where an officer of one authority is an elected member of another; barring around 70,000 local government officers from public political activity; the prohibition of 'political' advertising by local authorities (such as the GLC's campaign against abolition, which cost £10 million); a ban on the appointment of all party political advisers by local authorities; and a compulsory register of councillors' financial interests

▶ the Commissioners for Local Administration – three local ombudsmen established in 1972 – who investigate public complaints of maladministration against local authorities

▶ central government can remove local authorities' power ('default') as in 1972 when Labour-controlled Clay Cross Council refused to increase council house rents as required by the Housing Finance Act of that year, the Conservative government sent in a Housing Commissioner. Or, through Parliamentary legislation, whole local authorities can themselves be abolished.

It may be argued that this undermines local democracy and the mandate of local authorities; but local elections are often about national parties, policies and issues; and the voter turnout is usually low – around 40 per cent – perhaps, of course, precisely because local councils are seen as weak and insignificant. Local government may be even more prone to sleaze and corruption than central government and therefore in need of external control. For example, in the 1980s Westminster council was embroiled in the 'homes for votes' scandal (which started in 1987 and became public in 1989): this involved the targeting of council house sales to increase potential Conservative voters in key marginal areas, at a cost to the public purse of over £20 million. The district auditor in his report condemned the policy as 'disgraceful and unlawful **gerrymandering**'. Protracted legal proceedings followed. By 1998 the former council leader Dame Shirley Porter had allegedly moved a personal fund of £70 million offshore to avoid paying a £26.5 million court surcharge for 'wilful misconduct'.

The consequences of growing central control of local government since 1979 have been growing legal and financial constraints, loss of local power and increasing centralisation. For example, the Local Government Act 1988 extended compulsory competitive tendering (CCT) of some services, for example, refuse collection, street cleaning, and catering; it also included the controversial Clause 28 (a backbench amendment) forbidding local authorities from 'promoting' homosexuality. The forced sale of council houses has been operative since 1980, but local authorities are not allowed to spend most of the resulting revenue. There has been legislation allowing council tenants and schools to opt out of local government control, the imposition of non-elected Housing Action Trusts (HATs) to run some urban council estates (Housing Act 1988), the establishment of city technology colleges outside of local authority control, the abolition of the Inner London Education Authority (ILEA) in 1990, vouchers for nursery schools, compulsory exam league tables and the removal of 'failing schools' from local authority control. Many of the changes were imposed rather than being the product of local or political consensus. They were made easier by a long-running Conservative party and press campaign against the so-called 'loony left' in local Labour councils until 1997.

GOLDSMITHS' MEDIA RESEARCH GROUP
The Press and the Loony Left

A NEW STYLE of investigative journalism has developed which itself needs investigating. A small number of partisan newspapers have produced a series of bizarre reports – about left-wing councils in London – which have either been conjured out of thin air or have contained more artificial additives than true ingredients.

One recurrent theme of these reports is that 'loony left' councils are hypersensitive to imagined racial and sexist slurs to a point bordering on paranoia. For example, the London Standard (February 27, 1986) published a startling report that Hackney council had officially renamed manholes as 'access chambers'. The report featured an irate engineer, Tom Jordan, who allegedly had received a memorandum from the council containing the new decree.

The report was pure fiction. The council had not authorised the renaming of manholes, nor sent out a memorandum to that effect. It did not even employ an engineer called Tom Jordan. But this did not prevent the story from being recycled in nine other newspapers, including the pro-Labour Daily Mirror, where Keith Waterhouse denounced Hackney councillors as 'barking mad'.

The source of the story was the Fleet Street News Agency. The editor at the time was Leif Kalfayan (now at the Daily Mail) who claims that 'Tom Jordan' was

tracked down 'at some engineering depot that we got out of the directory enquiries or the telephone book'. The story, he insists, originated from the Hackney Gazette, which Tim Cooper, the newspaper's local government correspondent, strongly denies. The Hackney Gazette has never carried the story.

In a similar vein, the Sun (November 22, 1986) disclosed that Camden council had ordered its employees not to call each other 'sunshine' because the council supposed it to be racist. The article alleged that council chiefs had sent a memorandum to 'key members of the social services department' banning the word, and that a white worker who had called a black colleague 'sunshine' faced dismissal.

Again this report (which was recycled by the Daily Mail) was fiction; no memorandum on this subject had been issued by the council and no white worker faced the sack for calling a black colleague 'sunshine'. The author of the Sun article, Dina Malik, refused our invitation to justify what she wrote. But her report would appear to be a garbled version of an incident that occurred more than a year before in which a black worker had been called to a disciplinary hearing for

a number of reasons, including calling his white manager 'sunshine' in a derogatory manner.

Another recurring tabloid theme is that left-wing councils are obsessively preoccupied with minority interests at the expense of those of the white, heterosexual majority. Working to this prepared story line, the Sun (February 20, 1987) ran a major investigative report headlined 'Freebie trip for blacks but white kids must pay. Barmy Brent does it again' (which was again recycled in the Daily Mail). The Sun article alleged that 'a loony left council is splashing out at least £9,000 to send a group of black teenagers on an expenses-paid jaunt to Communist Cuba.' The report was seemingly corroborated by 'youth worker Shirley Williams' who said 'blacks are getting the subsidised places because we really only want to take them'.

The report is untrue. A voluntary organisation, Caribbean Exchange, has been trying to raise funds for the trip. But Brent council has not offered to subsidise the trip, and the Caribbean Exchange is no more part of the council than the local boy scouts and girl guides, which are also affiliated to its Youth and Communities Service.

The story which got the widest

publicity and which has come to encapsulate the tabloid image of the 'loony left' was the alleged banning of the nursery rhyme Baa Baa Black Sheep. The story appears to have surfaced originally in the Daily Star (February 15, 1986), which claimed that Beavers Play Group in Hackney had suppressed the rhyme. This was reworked by the Sun (February 20, 1986) into 'loony left-wing councillors have banned children from reciting the nursery rhyme'.

In fact, the council had not banned the rhyme. All that happened is that the parent-run Beavers Play Group had sometimes sung a humorous alternative version of the rhyme, beginning 'Baa Baa White Sheep ...' and ending 'and one for the little boy (or girl) with holes in his (or her) socks', as well as singing the conventional version of the rhyme.

The story was given a new twist by Anthony Doran in the Daily Mail (October 9, 1986), who reported that Haringey council had banned the rhyme at a racism awareness course which play leaders in the borough had been instructed to attend. This report was repeated in a large number of other papers. In fact, the council issued no such ban. It is not even clear that the rhyme was even discussed at the racism course,

where attendance was voluntary.

Out of all the papers which repeated the story, only the Yorkshire Evening Press had the grace to print a retraction, acknowledging that it had relied on 'an inaccurate report'.

Perhaps the final irony is that the story eventually became almost true, although in another borough. Nursery teachers did effectively ban the rhyme at one Islington school, perhaps believing, due to press publicity, that it was the policy of left-wing councils to forbid it. But on this occasion, Islington council's denial that it had banned the rhyme or promoted its ban was widely reported.

Coverage of London councils has been particularly inaccurate and distorted in four papers – the Sun, Daily Mail, Mail on Sunday and the London Evening Standard. Their more lurid and misleading reports on 'loony left' authorities have been regularly repeated in local newspapers up and down the country. They have also been incorporated into briefings issued by the Conservative Party Central Office. These four papers have thus played a key role in mass-producing the 'London effect'. The local elections on Thursday may show whether this effect extends beyond London.

(The Guardian, 4 May 1987)

However, some central government initiatives have decentralised power. The Conservative governments of the 1980s and 1990s argued that their reforms of housing and education gave more direct power to tenants and parents and the community care initiative of the early 1990s gave a greater role and funding to local social services (though it has since been widely criticised for failures to control the mentally ill in the community). Labour has relaxed council tax capping and replaced compulsory competitive tendering with a system known as 'best value', which will not involve compulsory privatisation and will involve more consultation with local people about range and quality of services rather than focusing purely on commercial considerations.

Some local councils have also taken the initiative on decentralisation: for example, in 1999 Milton Keynes held a local referendum on the amount of increase in the council tax. This may be seen as a boost for direct democracy or as an evasion of political responsibility by councillors – or both.

The clearest example recently of executive decentralisation has been the creation by the Labour government, by referendum (1998) as well as statute, of an elected London authority and mayor to replace the GLC. Although two-thirds of those who voted supported the proposal, turnout was only 34 per cent – perhaps because many saw the result as a foregone conclusion. The first elections were delayed until May 2000: the government pleaded legislative log-jam; critics suspected 'stop Ken Livingstone as mayor' machinations. When the London Bill began its passage through the Commons in January 1999 it listed 115 powers residing with the Environment Secretary but said nothing on the procedures for putting up party candidates for London mayor.

These first local government elections to be held by partial proportional representation will produce one member from each of 14 'mega-boroughs' and a further 11 members chosen proportionally from a London-wide list. The London authority will have responsibility for the Metropolitan Police, London Transport (but government will by then have established public-private partnerships to finance London Transport), a regional development authority for London, the fire services, strategic roads and major planning decisions; it will have powers to levy charges on London boroughs for police and fire services and perhaps also road charging. It will also have powers to approve or amend the mayor's budget.

The upheavals in local government over the last three decades, combined with voter apathy and party political disagreement about the role of local government, pose questions about the structures and functions of local government in the next century. Some New Right analysts (for example, the Adam Smith Institute) argue that the local authority of the future should be a residual enabling authority with most services contracted out to the private sector. Other Conservatives (such as Michael Heseltine) want local authorities to retain substantial planning and co-ordinating functions within a market framework. Liberal Democrats advocate more community-oriented councils with more participation by, and accountability to, local voters. The Labour government seems to lean to greater decentralisation – for example, proposing powerful elected mayors for the regions and cities of England – but this goes hand in hand with tight curbs on local spending, plans to allow private companies to take over 'failing' schools and local authorities (something even Thatcher didn't countenance) and strenuous efforts to prevent 'Red Ken' Livingstone becoming London mayor and 'old' Labour Rhodri Morgan becoming Welsh first minister. Critics perceive this as 'decentralisation on our terms'.

The independent Commission for Local Democracy (1995) mourned 'the emasculation of local democracy since the war' which has contributed to low electoral turnouts and reduced representation of communities. It recommended radical changes to both the structure of local government and its relationship with the centre. The introduction of legislative devolution in 1999 may encourage this.

Legislative devolution

Devolution means the delegation – passing down – of some legislative and/or executive functions of central powers to local bodies, while the national power remains responsible for major national issues such as defence, foreign affairs and macro-economics. The local bodies are subordinate to the central legislature or executive, which can readily retrieve their powers. The system remains unitary because the centre is still sovereign. **Federalism**, on the other hand, entails greater local autonomy. Here the regions allocate certain national powers such as defence and foreign affairs to a central body, and they are in theory equal to it. The local powers have autonomy within their own, defined areas of decision-making. Thus central government cannot increase its powers at the expense of the regions or federal states. The courts arbitrate in cases of conflict. The USA and Australia are examples of federal systems. **Separatism** means complete political independence.

The United Kingdom has long had elements of *executive devolution* in local government, and Scotland and Wales have their own Secretaries of State with Cabinet status. Scotland's legal and educational systems are also quite distinct. Until 1999 there was, however, no *legislative devolution*; Westminster was the sole UK legislature since the suspension in 1972 of the Northern Irish Parliament (Stormont) and the introduction of 'direct rule' from Westminster because of the growing political conflict in Northern Ireland at that time.

Encouraged by the rise of nationalist feeling in Scotland and Wales since the late 1960s, Labour and the Liberal Democrats have, since the 1970s, advocated legislative devolution for Scotland and Wales, and the Liberal Democrats also proposed elected local legislatures for the regions of England. A Labour government in 1977 introduced a Devolution Bill, and held referenda on the issue in Scotland and Wales in 1979. Wales voted against; Scotland voted in favour, but the 'yes' vote amounted to only 32.5 per cent of the total electorate, and the bill required approval by at least 40 per cent of the electorate (a backbench amendment) so the issue was dropped.

Over the next two decades support for the Scottish and Welsh Nationalist parties increased, but the Conservative governments of that period were firmly opposed to devolution. In 1997, the Conservatives won no seats at all in Scotland or in Wales, and Labour came to power with a mandate to hold new referenda on the question of devolution.

Scotland

Scotland held a two-question referendum in September 1997: 74 per cent voted in favour of a Scottish Parliament and 60 per cent agreed that it should have tax-varying powers of up to 3p in the pound (turnout was 60 per cent). The Scottish Parliament came into being in May 1999 with 129 members elected by the Additional Member System: 73 elected by first-past-the-post and 56 'top-up' MSPs elected from regional party lists using the eight European parliamentary constituencies.

Left-wing Labour MP Dennis Canavan stood against the official Labour candidate for the Scottish Parliament after being forced off the party list for (he claims) being too radical.

The new Scottish executive is responsible for the following policy areas:

- ▶ health
- ▶ education and training
- ▶ local government, housing and social work
- ▶ economic development
- ▶ employment
- ▶ transport
- ▶ law and home affairs
- ▶ police
- ▶ environment
- ▶ energy
- ▶ agriculture, forestry and fishing
- ▶ culture, sport and the arts
- ▶ administration of certain EU laws in Scotland (for example, civil nuclear emergency planning).

Westminster remains responsible for foreign affairs including relations with the EU, defence and national security, macro-economic and fiscal matters, immigration, railways, shipping, airlines, pensions, employment law, broadcasting and telecommunications and much else. Overall, the Scotland Act lists 19 pages of powers that are reserved to Westminster.

The arrangements for Scotland did not address the 'West Lothian question' (so-called because it was first raised by the MP for that area, Tam Dalyell): that Scottish MPs at Westminster (already over-represented numerically) would continue to have law-making powers over areas of English policy such as health and education, while English MPs would have no such power over Scotland because the Scottish Parliament would be legislating on such matters.

Scotland also has a disproportionate share of Cabinet ministers and of central government finances. As English voters become increasingly aware of such imbalances, it may fuel calls for reduced voting rights for Scottish MPs at Westminster, fewer Scottish MPs at Westminster and/or elected assemblies for the regions of England to parallel the Scottish Parliament.

Wales

In Wales, the government held the referendum one week after the Scottish vote, in the hope of giving the 'yes' side a boost. Despite this, the 'yes' vote scraped a 0.6 per cent majority on only a 50 per cent turnout. It quickly came to be known as *yr ie bychan* – 'the little yes'. The vote was geographically split, with the eastern areas giving a decisive 'no' vote and the 'yes' vote increasing the further the areas were from the English border. Although there has long been a sense of national Welsh culture, centred especially on the Welsh language, there is far less support for political **nationalism** in Wales than in Scotland because of the perceived economic and political benefits of the Union. The 60-member Welsh assembly will therefore be much weaker than the Scottish Parliament, with control over the spending of the £7 billion Welsh Office budget but no taxation or law-making powers.

Labour

Devolution: strengthening the Union

The United Kingdom is a partnership enriched by distinct national identities and traditions. Scotland has its own systems of education, law and local government. Wales has its language and cultural traditions. We will meet the demand for decentralisation of power to Scotland and Wales, once established in referendums.

Subsidiarity is as sound a principle in Britain as it is in Europe. Our proposal is for devolution, not federation. A sovereign Westminster Parliament will devolve power to Scotland and Wales. The Union will be strengthened and the threat of separatism removed.

As soon as possible after the election, we will enact legislation to allow the people of Scotland and Wales to vote in separate referendums on our proposals, which will be set out in White Papers. These referendums will take place not later than the autumn of 1997. A simple majority of those voting in each referendum will be the majority required. Popular endorsement will strengthen the legitimacy of our proposals and speed their passage through Parliament.

For Scotland we propose the creation of a parliament with law-making powers, firmly based on the agreement reached in the Scottish Constitutional Convention, including defined and limited financial powers to vary revenue and elected by an additional member system. In the Scottish referendum we will seek separate endorsement of the proposal to create a parliament, and of the proposal to give it defined and limited financial powers to vary revenue. The Scottish parliament will extend democratic control over the responsibilities currently exercised administratively by the Scottish Office. The responsibilities of the UK Parliament will remain over UK policy, for example economic, defence and foreign policy.

The Welsh assembly will provide democratic control of the existing Welsh Office functions. It will have secondary legislative powers and will be specifically empowered to reform and democratise the quango state. It will be elected by an additional member system. Following majorities in the referendums, we will introduce in the first year of the Parliament legislation on the substantive devolution proposals outlined in our white papers.

Conservative

The Union

The Union between Scotland, Wales, Northern Ireland and England underpins our nation's stability. The Conservative commitment to the United Kingdom does not mean ignoring the distinctive individuality of the different nations. On the contrary, we have gone further in recognising that diversity than any previous government. We are publishing manifestos for Wales and Scotland.

While preserving the role of parliament at the centre of the Union, we have given new powers to the Scottish Grand Committee – enabling Scottish and Welsh MPs to call Ministers to account and debate legislation which affects those countries – something that would be impossible with separate Assemblies. For the first time, Welsh members of Parliament can ask their questions to Ministers in Welsh in Wales. Most recently we have similarly extended the basic powers of the Northern Ireland Grand Committee.

We believe this is the right way to go. By contrast, the development of new assemblies in Scotland and Wales would create strains which could well pull apart the Union. That would create a new layer of government, which would be hungry for power. It would risk rivalry and conflict between these parliaments or assemblies and the parliament at Westminster. And it would raise serious questions about whether the representation of Scottish and Welsh MPs at Westminster – and their role in matters affecting English affairs – could remain unchanged.

Nor do we believe it would be in the interest of the Scottish or Welsh people. A Scottish tax-raising parliament, for example, could well affect the choice of where new investment locates in the United Kingdom.

In a world where people want security, nothing would be more dangerous than to unravel a constitution that binds our nation together and the institutions that bring us stability. We will continue to fight for the strength and diversity that benefits all of us as a proud union of nations.

▲ *The 1997 manifestos of the main political parties on devolution*

Liberal Democrat

Giving government back to the people

Far too much power has been concentrated in Westminster and Whitehall. Democratic government should be as close to ordinary people as possible.

We will:

• Introduce Home Rule for Scotland, with the creation of a Scottish Parliament, elected by proportional representation, and able to raise and reduce income tax.

• Introduce Home Rule for Wales, with the creation of a Welsh Senedd, elected by proportional representation, and able to raise and reduce income tax.

• Strengthen local government. We will establish a 'power of general competence', giving councils wider scope for action. We will allow local authorities to raise more of their funds locally, give them greater discretion over spending and allow them, within strict limits, to go directly to the markets to raise finance for capital projects. We will, in the long term, replace Council Tax with a Local Income Tax, and replace the Uniform Business Rate with a fairer system of business rates, raised through local councils and set in accordance with local priorities.

Northern Ireland

Peace in Northern Ireland depends on containing and ultimately removing the entrenched hostility between the two main communities in Northern Ireland.

We will:

• Establish a power-sharing executive for Northern Ireland, elected under a fair and proportional system of voting. We will press for a new constitutional settlement based on the protection of individual rights through a Bill of Rights, incorporating the European Convention.

• Give individuals more power and political responsibility. We will introduce a fair and proportional voting system for all elections, and reform and strengthen local government in the province.

• Ensure respect for civil liberties. We will introduce an independent procedure for investigating complaints against the security forces, and reform the Diplock system so that three judges instead of one preside over non-jury trials. We will urgently implement the North Report's recommendations for an independent commission to supervise parades and marches.

• Promote economic growth. We will strengthen the all-Ireland economy through the creation of effective cross-border agencies. We will invest in education and promote inward investment.

• Build on the Joint Declaration and the Framework Document, by working with the Irish government to create agreement between as many of the constitutional parties as possible. Sinn Fein can only be admitted to this process if, in accordance with the Mitchell principle, they and the IRA turn their backs on terrorism. Meanwhile, we must remain vigilant and keep in place the present means for countering terrorism.

▲ *The 1997 manifestos of the main political parties on devolution (continued)*

The Welsh Assembly is also elected by the AMS system, with 40 first-past-the-post and 20 party list members. It operates on a local government style committee system with executive rather than legislative or fiscal powers – in effect, taking over the role of the Welsh Office in deciding how Westminster legislation is implemented in Wales, in the following policy areas:

▶ economic development

▶ agriculture

▶ industry and training

▶ education

▶ local government services

▶ health and social services

▶ housing

▶ the environment

▶ planning and transport

▶ sport and heritage.

In February 1999, the Welsh Labour Party elected its leader for the Welsh Assembly – in effect, the future Welsh First Secretary. Blair's favoured candidate, Alun Michael, beat traditionalist, 'people's choice' Rhodri Morgan by 5 per cent. Although Morgan won the overwhelming support of the rank-and-file members and all of the trade unions which balloted their members, Michael won the backing of the Welsh MPs and MEPs and, above all, the **block votes** of the remaining union leaders. Some critics therefore saw the result as a 'stitch up' by the party machine – and as an ironic outcome, given 'new' Labour's customary hostility to the trade union block vote system elsewhere in the party.

Northern Ireland

At around the same time (1998) but for different reasons – namely, the Northern Ireland peace process – an assembly for Northern Ireland was re-established at Stormont (for the first time since its abolition in 1972) following the peace deal on 10 April (Good Friday) 1998. The peace deal provided for a Northern Ireland Assembly of 108 seats elected by proportional representation; a 12-member executive chosen from within and by the assembly in proportion to the parties' strength in the assembly (thus, for example, Sinn Fein were guaranteed two seats on the executive); also a North–South executive council to be set up some months later, in return for which Eire gave up its constitutional claim to the North. There was also provision for a wider British-Irish Intergovernmental Council representing all five parliaments of the UK and Eire, and for decommissioning of weapons and prisoner releases within two years.

In May 1998 a rapid referendum on the peace deal was held throughout Ireland and unsurprisingly won substantial support:

▶ Northern Ireland: 71 per cent 'yes' versus 29 per cent 'no' on 81 per cent turnout = 58 per cent in favour

▶ Eire: 94 per cent 'yes' versus 6 per cent 'no' on 56 per cent turnout = 53 per cent in favour.

In June, elections were held for the Northern Ireland assembly and in July the executive was elected from the assembly: the first minister was leading Unionist David Trimble and his deputy was leading Nationalist Seamus Mallon.

England

In April 1999 the government set up regional economic development agencies for the eight English regions outside London, thinking that would be enough to redress the balance at least until the next election, but there were already growing calls for elected English regional assemblies. For example, in March 1999, even before the Scottish Parliament was established, a movement was set up calling for a regional assembly for Yorkshire. Some ministers such as John Prescott wanted these to be part of the framework for an element of regional representation from all parts of the UK in a reformed second chamber at Westminster.

At the same time, if Scottish voters do not feel that their situation has significantly improved after some time, they may start to demand greater local autonomy, federalism or even independence. One 1998 poll indicated that 65 per cent of Scots believe that Scotland will be independent by 2013. This was one reason why the Conservatives and others used to reject devolution, fearing that it might be the first step down the slippery slope towards the break-up of the UK.

ESSAYS

1 *Theme:* **Local government**

Look at these two questions.

Q? Account for recent attempts by central government to assert greater control over local government.

(London, June 1986, Paper 1)

Q? Discuss the arguments for and against recent extensions of central control over local government.

(London, June 1987, Paper 1)

A✓ **Notes for guidance**

Whereas the first title above requires a list of reasons for growing central government control over local government, the second title requires an evaluation of the arguments *for* and *against* such growing control, and is therefore more difficult.

---

2 Consider the list of points below, all of which could form an answer to the second title above. Which would *not* be necessary for the first title?

a) Methods and examples of growing central control over local government: rate-capping, community charge-capping, uniform business rate, **surcharging** of councillors through the courts, abolition of GLC and metropolitan counties, compulsory tendering of some services, removal and restraint of powers in education and housing, city technology colleges, Housing Action Trusts (HATs), etc.

b) The UK is a unitary state – central power may always give or take power to and from the regions.

c) Central government intervenes at local level to ensure:

- ► control of overall public spending

- ► consistency of provision of services across the country

- ► co-ordination of local functions and services.

d) Local government may thwart the mandate of central government – and the latter is stronger because turnout at local elections is low.

e) Prior to rates reform, only a minority of voters paid rates and local government was insufficiently accountable for its spending. Local businesses also paid disproportionate costs.

f) Local authorities have sometimes gone beyond their local mandate to involve themselves in national issues such as defence.

g) Two or more tiers of local government may be excessively costly, bureaucratic and remote from local communities.

h) Local government may avoid necessary but painful financial measures in pursuit of political popularity; it may therefore be very costly and inefficient.

i) Local government has a mandate from local electors.

j) Local government provides checks and balances against 'elective dictatorship' of majority central government in a sovereign, unitary Parliament.

k) Local government elections provide a test of public opinion between general elections.

l) Local government allows democratic participation at local level.

m) Local government provides a training and recruitment ground for central government and Parliament.

n) Local government knows local needs.

o) Local government provides services relatively cost-effectively; transfer of powers to the centre or to quangos, etc. may increase costs, reduce democratic accountability and ignore local needs.

p) Central government intervention may simply be party political.

Q? How and why is local democracy limited in the UK?

(London, June 1988, Paper 1)

A✓ **Examiners' comments**

'Most candidates demonstrated a reasonable knowledge of how local democracy is limited in the United Kingdom, with the better answers pointing to recent examples such as rate capping and the abolition of the metropolitan counties. The "why" part of the question produced some good answers couched in terms of the unitary nature of the UK constitution. High marks were available for those who understood the conflict between local and national democracy. A good example of how the second part should have been tackled was given by one candidate who began as follows:

"Local democracy in the UK is limited primarily because the UK is a unitary state. That is to say, all power is derived from the centre and may be taken back if the government so decides. This century local government has been given the responsibility for education and housing by central government, but the central government has also taken back from local government responsibility for running local hospitals."

The candidate then went on to discuss the problem of conflicting mandates and the need for central government to ensure uniformity of provision and to control public expenditure.'

Q? Why not abolish local government altogether?

(Cambridge, June 1985, Paper 1)

A✓ **Notes for guidance**

Like many other titles, this one centres largely on the broad arguments for and against local government, outlined above. The introduction should point out – with examples – that local government in the UK has been increasingly limited in function and weak in its powers, and that there is a case for carrying this shift of power through to its logical conclusion. However, this may be effectively to say that central government has curtailed local government so much that it is virtually impotent, and may as well be abolished altogether – a self-fulfilling prophecy which may be logical, but may not be 'democratic'.

Q? How great could the powers of regional parliaments become without there ceasing to be a British state?

(London, Feb. 1976, Paper 1)

A✓ Examiners' comments

'The answer should turn on some clear understanding of "state". The weakest possible definition would not be compatible with Scotland described as "simply a member of the Commonwealth"; legal separation followed by practical integration could still retain a weak sense of the state. In a strong sense, it implies the continuing power to act decisively in defence, foreign relations and in response to internal crises; this could well be threatened by various levels of "home rule". Some of these notions must be specified, even hypothetically, for the award of a grade B or an A.'

Skeletal essay plan

▶ History of calls for legislative devolution – to regions of England as well as to Scotland, Wales and Northern Ireland . . .

▶ The concept of 'state': definitions and problems . . .

▶ Degrees of devolved power: local law making; local spending; local revenue-raising; lack of 'over-ride' by Westminster; capacity to legislate for administrative/legal/political/financial autonomy

▶ Possibility that limited devolution – and resulting local dissatisfaction – may generate calls for greater autonomy and hence ultimate break-up of UK – 'thin end of the wedge' argument.

▶ *Conclusion:* Essence of 'state' is political sovereignty, i.e. control of defence, national security, international relations and military matters. In practical terms, ultimate control of purse-strings is key to political control by centre. (It is, of course, debatable whether there *should* continue to be a British state; there is a case for complete separatism, at least of the four countries of the UK, if not the regions of England.)

Q? Discuss the changing nature of the relationship between central and local government.

(London, June 1992, Paper 1)

A✓ Sample essay answer

Local government entails the election of local people to run local services such as education, housing, refuse collection, etc. The relationship of local government to the centre has always been one of subordination, in a unitary constitution, but it is widely perceived that there has been increasing centralisation over the last twenty years. Margaret Thatcher's Conservative governments were particularly active in this respect; there were 58 items of local government legislation in 1979–89.

On the one hand, however, this trend is not entirely new: for example, local ombudsmen were introduced by central government in 1972 to scrutinise local councils; and in the same year, Labour-controlled Clay Cross council famously lost its battle against the Conservative central government over rent increases.

Moreover, not all of the changes during the 1980s and 1990s amounted to centralisation. Past Conservative governments would argue that the opting out of schools and hospitals from council control was done through grassroots 'people power' by the votes of parents and staff, and the abolition of the GLC and metropolitan county councils resulted in many of their powers and functions being devolved down to borough and district councils, rather than up. Labour has relaxed council tax capping and replaced compulsory competitive tendering (CCT) with a system known as 'best value' which will involve more consultation with local people. The clearest example of executive decen-tralisation has been the creation by the Labour government, by referendum as well as statute, of an elected London authority and mayor to replace the GLC.

Local authorities still have some real power, for example to fix council taxes (within capping limits), choose spending priorities (again as far as legislation allows), pass by-laws through delegated legislation, etc. Some local councils have also taken the initiative on decentralisation: for example, in 1999 Milton Keynes held a local referendum on the amount of increase in the council tax.

However, the bulk of the changes in the relationship between central and local govern-ment have been imposed from above and have resulted in a reduction of the powers and roles of local government and a transfer of power to the centre.

The impact on local government financing has been particularly marked, with 80 per cent of all local government revenue now coming from and controlled by central govern-ment. The Audit Commission, created in 1983 and appointed by the Environment Secretary, oversees all local government expenditure. Spending curbs have been imposed from the centre, first through cuts and 'holdback' of the Rate Support Grant, then by rate capping – now council tax capping – and surcharging and disqualification of over-spending councillors, for example, Liverpool in 1986. The Local Government Finance Act 1988 introduced the ill-fated poll tax, and also the Uniform Business Rate which is set, collected and distributed by central government to local government. All of these changes have had a centralising effect on the relationship between central and local government.

Similarly, in 1980 central government began forcing local authorities to sell council houses but prohibited them from spending the resulting revenue. Non-elected Housing Action Trusts were imposed to run some urban housing estates. The 1985 Widdicombe Inquiry resulted in legislation banning 'political' advertising and political advisers and imposing a compulsory register of financial interests for local, but not central, government. The abolition of the GLC and six metropolitan councils resulted in many of their powers and functions being transferred up to government ministers or centrally appointed quangos and committees. There was also a shift of power to the centre in the field of education, with the abolition of the ILEA and the introduction of the Education Act 1988 which gave the Secretary of State for Education 366 new powers of control. Clause 28 of the Local Government Act of the same year, which prohibited the 'promotion' of homosexuality in schools, was especially controversial. In other services such as refuse collection and street cleaning, compulsory competitive tendering was imposed.

Conservative central governments argued that these changes were necessary to curb local government over-spending (especially by 'loony left' Labour councils such as Lambeth and Haringey) and to improve the efficiency and accountability of local government. The centre had a mandate to cut public spending at local as well as national level and – especially given the low turnouts for local elections – central government's mandate was stronger. The changes were also intended to streamline, standardise and co-ordinate provision of services across the country.

The demerits of the changes, however, have outweighed the merits. A single-party majority government (especially one with Labour's massive majority), in a sovereign parliament with a flexible constitution, always threatens to become an 'elective dicta-torship' (Hailsham), and the changing nature of the relationship between central and local government since 1979 has increased this danger. Strong local government is one of the criteria of pluralism in a liberal democracy, and a valuable part of the checks and balances against central government, as well as being a vital channel of democratic participation and representation in its own right. The representative claims of Westminster and Whitehall are debatable, especially without PR. Local authorities have their own mandate to provide local services which meet the needs and wants of local people, and centralisation has actually undermined the accountability of local government to its voters. Some local authorities now claim that they lack the revenue to provide even mandatory services such as housing. The 'loony left' stories of the 1980s were said by, for example, Goldsmith's Media Research Group to be largely a Conservative tabloid fiction. There was evidence (for example, from independent accountants Coopers and Lybrand) that abolition of the GLC and metropolitan county councils cost five times more money than it saved.

Labour came to power in 1997 on a promise to restore local democracy, and such a reversal of the centralising trend would enhance Britain's claim to be a liberal democracy. The EU's insistence on 'subsidiarity', i.e. the principle that diverse political powers should reside at the lowest possible level within and between member states, may also help to promote local democracy in the twenty-first century.

---

3 Write at least one of the following essays. Always write a brief plan first.

a) 'The main trouble with local government is that it is neither democratic nor properly accountable.' Discuss in the light of recent problems.

(London, June 1985, Paper 1)

b) 'In the past twenty years there has been a significant reduction in local democracy in Britain.' Do you agree?

(Oxford and Cambridge, June 1997, Paper 1)

c) Should local government be given greater independence from central government control?

(Oxford, Summer 1986, Paper 1)

d) Discuss the arguments for and against devolution to Scotland and Wales.

(London, June 1998, Paper 1)

e) In the past, writers of politics textbooks often claimed that the characteristics of the political culture in the UK were 'homogeneity, consensus and deference'. They believed the same values largely applied throughout the UK – in England, Scotland, Wales and Northern Ireland.

Is it still possible to understand the UK political culture in such terms? In what ways, and for what reasons, have the norms and values of the political culture changed within the UK in the past thirty years?

(AEB, Summer 1997, Paper 2)

GUIDE TO EXERCISES

Page 154

1 Advantages of local government:

- Knows local needs
- Allows element of local democracy, accountability and political participation
- Imposes checks and balances on centre
- Upholds liberal democratic principles of decentralisation and pluralism
- Some areas, for example, Scotland, not well represented at Westminster
- Provides training and recruitment ground for centre
- May be more cost-effective than central bureaucracy

Disadvantages of local government:

- May thwart (stronger?) mandate of central government
- May mean inconsistent and unco-ordinated provision of services across the country
- May be unduly costly
- May mean local 'elective dictatorship' of one strong and/or radical and/or irresponsible party on a minority vote
- Strong local government is contrary to the constitutional principles of a unitary state

Page 163

2 There are 15 points listed altogether; the last eight would not be necessary in answer to the first title.

REFERENCES

Alexander, Alan (1989) 'The decline of local government', *Contemporary Record*, Vol. 2, No. 6, Summer

Falconer, Peter and Jones, Alistair (1998) 'Electing a Scottish Parliament', *Talking Politics*, Vol. 11, No. 2, Winter

Houlihan, Barrie (1986) *The Politics of Local Government*, Longman

McNaughton, Neil (1998) *Local and Regional Government in Britain*, Hodder & Stoughton

Norris, Paul (1998) 'Northern Ireland: The long road to peace', *Talking Politics*, Vol. 11, No. 1, Autumn

Rallings, Colin and Thrasher, Michael (1998) 'The 1998 local election results and democracy', *Talking Politics*, Vol. 11, No. 1, Autumn

Wilson, David J. (1990) 'More power to the centre? The changing nature of central government/local authority relationships', *Talking Politics*, Vol. 3, No. 1, Autumn

9 The legal system and civil rights

KEY ISSUES

▶ The law:

The 'rule of law': theory and practice

Civil disobedience: arguments for and against

▶ The courts:

The courts and Parliament

The courts and the executive

The judges

Judicial independence and impartiality

▶ The police:

Public order and politics

Powers, impartiality and accountability

▶ Civil rights and freedoms:

Degrees, limits and trends

Relationships between freedom and equality

A Bill of Rights: arguments for and against

TOPIC NOTES

Key facts and concepts

The law

Laws are the rules of state which – unlike conventions – are enforceable in the courts. There are many different types of law (see Chapter 2), including statute law, common law, case law, EU law and delegated legislation.

---

1 Give a precise definition and topical example of each of the five types of law mentioned above.

Broadly, all of these types of law fall under one or other of the following headings.

▶ *Civil law* concerns disputes between individuals or groups in society. The aggrieved individual (or company, etc.) decides whether to take proceedings, and the aim is compensation.

▶ *Criminal law* concerns offences against society or state, and the aim of proceedings is punishment. The offence may be the same, for example, assault, but under criminal law the Crown Prosecution Service (CPS) may take action even if the victim does not desire it. The legal processes are different and are often in different types of courts, for example county courts and the High Court for civil cases, and magistrates' courts and Crown courts for criminal cases. Civil cases, such as divorce or bankruptcy, are rarely heard before a jury. Jury trial is a feature of criminal cases in the Crown courts; but 98 per cent of all criminal cases begin and end in a lower magistrate's court, with no jury. Moreover, under successive statutes such as the Criminal Justice Acts of 1988, 1991, 1994 and 1998, a growing number of criminal charges, such as obstruction, breach of the peace and common assault, have lost the right to jury trial in the Crown courts, despite the widely-held principle that 'trial by one's peers is the lamp that shows that freedom lives' (to quote former judge Lord Devlin).

The 'rule of law'

The phrase, the 'rule of law' (see Chapter 2) was coined by A.V. Dicey (1885), and the concept, which seeks to equate law and justice, is said to be central to any constitutional democracy. However, it is best seen as a statement of an ideal (or as a list of ideal principles), to which many legal systems may aspire; but, in Britain and other countries, all of its key principles are consistently breached in practice.

---

2 a) List six basic principles of the 'rule of law'.

b) Give at least two examples of breaches of each principle in the English legal system.

Law, justice and morality

Something is 'legal' if it is in accordance with the law of the land; whereas something is 'just' if it is deemed fair and equitable. The idea of the 'rule of law' seeks to equate law and justice, but sometimes the law may be regarded as unjust: for example, the poll tax, legal immunities of diplomats, legal tax avoidance, retrospective (backdated) law, imprisonment before trial (remand), the high costs of litigation, etc. Conversely, an action may be seen as 'just', though illegal: for example, personal retribution – 'an eye for an eye'; breaking the law to prevent a greater crime; the Robin Hood principle (stealing from the rich to give to the poor); illegal political protest, for example the Newbury by-pass protesters; 'just' violence against an 'unjust' state (one man's 'terrorist' is another man's 'freedom fighter'), etc.

Similarly, an action that is deemed 'moral' – ethically right and proper – may be illegal: such as 'draft-dodging' (refusing conscription into the army, for example on religious grounds); anti-nuclear protests such as trespassing in nuclear bases; euthanasia ('mercy-killing'); Sikhs refusing to wear motorcycle helmets in place of their turbans, etc. Or an 'immoral' action may be legal: for example suicide, adultery, divorce or abortion.

All three concepts are subjective; even whether an action is legal or illegal is often a matter of debate between senior judges, as the divisions among the Law Lords over the extradition of Chile's former General Pinochet (1998) demonstrated. However, perceived conflicts between law, justice and morality are sometimes used to justify **civil disobedience**: deliberate, peaceful law-breaking as an act of public, political protest. Some examples are: cannabis 'smoke-ins' in Hyde Park; the obstruction by the pressure group Greenpeace of nuclear waste discharges into the North Sea and its occupation of the Brent Spar oil platform; the refusal by some local councils, for example Liverpool and Lambeth, to obey central government's 'rate-capping' laws; public refusals to pay the poll tax; secondary picketing by trade unions such as the National Union of Seamen; and the freeing of animals from research laboratories by the Animal Liberation Front.

---

3 a) Find five further examples of civil disobedience by pressure groups or individuals.

b) What arguments were used to justify the action in each case?

c) List three key arguments for, and three arguments against, civil disobedience.

The courts

The civil and criminal courts in England and Wales are summarised in the diagram below.

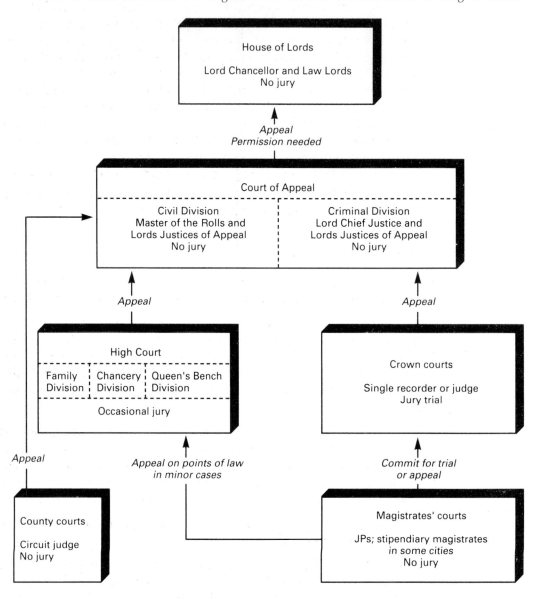

▲ *Civil and criminal courts in England and Wales*

Besides the British courts, Britain is a member of two separate European courts:

▶ the European Court of Justice (ECJ) at Luxembourg, which enforces European Union law, for example, against Britain's discriminatory retirement ages for men and women, pollution of British beaches, the beef ban, the 48-hour maximum working week, etc.

▶ the European Court of Human Rights (ECHR) at Strasbourg, which is nothing to do with the EU. It enforces the 1950 European Convention for the Protection of Human Rights, ratified by 40 countries including the UK. However, its rulings are not formally binding in the way that EU law is: for example, in 1990 the ECHR ruled illegal the detention without charge of three men over four days under the Prevention of Terrorism Act but the British government said that it would ignore the ruling (derogation).

The ECHR has ruled against British governments on phone tapping by government agencies, corporal punishment in state schools, torture of prisoners in Northern Ireland, press censorship, discrimination against women and ethnic minorities, lengthy detention without charge of prisoners under the anti-terrorism laws, the killing of three unarmed IRA suspects in Gibraltar by the SAS in 1988, discrimination against gays on the age of consent (1997) and many other matters. The 1997 Labour government was first ruled illegal by the ECHR in 1998 for trying to prohibit pressure groups from leafletting the public about parliamentary candidates' personal views on abortion. British governments by the late 1990s had lost more cases at Strasbourg than any others, largely because until 1998 Britain had no domestic Bill of Rights, did not enforce the European Convention in its own courts, and because much government action is still based simply on convention rather than on law.

However, the Labour government enshrined the European Convention into British law as the Human Rights Act 1998, to take effect in the year 2000.

The courts and Parliament

Parliament is sovereign – the British courts therefore cannot, in theory, challenge the law of Parliament; they can only interpret and enforce statute law as it is written.

However, EU law takes precedence over UK law and, where they conflict, the British courts are required to enforce EU law. This was established by the *Factortame* case of 1990 (about the rights of Spanish trawlers to fish in British waters, contrary to the Merchant Shipping Act 1988). Parliament remains technically sovereign in that it could pass an Act expressly overriding European law or, indeed, could withdraw from the EU altogether – unlikely in practice.

Secondly, Parliament's law may be unclear or ambiguous; in a test case, the judges must interpret the law precisely, which can allow a very 'creative' judicial role amounting effectively to 'law-making'. The courts and Parliament may clash when the courts interpret a statute in a way which Parliament did not intend. Parliament may then, of course, re-write the law; it can thus 'legalise illegality' or set aside court decisions.

Lord Denning – formerly a very senior (and maverick) judge – argued that judges should be able to veto parliamentary statutes:

> 'Every judge on his appointment discards all politics and all prejudices. You need have no fear. The judges of England have always in the past – and I hope always will – be vigilant in guarding our freedoms. Someone must be trusted. Let it be the judges.'
>
> *(Dimbleby Lecture, 'Misuse of power', 1980)*

He gave the hypothetical example of any attempt by the Commons to abolish the House of Lords – which seemed, to some critics, to demonstrate the very 'politics and prejudices' he sought to deny. Also, without a written constitution or Bill of Rights at the time of his lecture, there were no clear, consistent and overriding constitutional principles against which judges could challenge parliamentary statutes.

The new British Bill of Rights will, however, undoubtedly extend the role of the judges; but it expressly maintains the principle of parliamentary sovereignty and says that the judges cannot set aside parliamentary statutes in the event of conflicts – they can only point out such conflicts and leave it for Parliament to resolve them or not.

The courts and the executive

Administrative law is the whole package of laws which apply to executive and other public bodies. There is no distinct body of administrative law or courts in Britain (unlike, for example, France). However, the ordinary courts may hear civil or criminal actions against central or local government members or departments. They may declare the orders or actions of a minister or department to be *ultra vires*, i.e. beyond their legal powers – either because of what was done or because of the way in which it was done.

Such **judicial review** of executive action has increased markedly since three significant rulings against the government in 1976, concerning attempts to ban Laker Skytrain, to stop people buying TV licences early to avoid a price increase, and to hasten the introduction of comprehensive schools in Tameside.

Those were all rulings against a Labour government, but the later Conservative governments have been over-ruled by the British courts more often than any others – for example, Peter Lilley's Social Security Department reducing the benefits of a blind student and notably Michael Howard's Home Office being ruled illegal 15 times in the 1990s, for example, over cuts in compensation for crime victims, illegal deportation of asylum seekers, refusal of Mohamed Al Fayed's **citizenship**, etc.

However, any central government usually has a majority in a sovereign Parliament, and therefore if it is ruled illegal by the courts it may use Parliament to rewrite the law and so legalise itself. It may even backdate the rewritten law so that the government was never technically illegal – so-called 'retrospective law'. Some examples are: Environment Secretary Nicholas Ridley taking £50 million too much from the GLC to finance the new London Regional Transport body (1985), increasing toll charges for the Severn Bridge (1986), and authorising the building of the Okehampton by-pass through Dartmoor National Park (1986); DHSS Secretary Norman Fowler imposing cuts in board and lodging allowances, cuts in opticians' fees (1986), and the Local Government Act 1987 retrospectively legalised central government's grant allocations to local authorities – which, it was discovered, had been technically illegal since 1981. Labour Chancellor Gordon Brown's 1998 budget contained a retrospective law closing an offshore tax loophole.

The courts' control of central government is therefore limited, and is bound up with the issue of parliamentary sovereignty. It is also debatable how far non-elected and arguably unrepresentative judges *should* control 'democratic' public bodies. This issue has also been central to judicial rulings against local councils: for example, GLC's 'Fares

Number of cases of judicial review

Year	No. of cases
1968	87
1970s	Average 280 cases per annum
1980s	Average 980 cases per annum
1990	2,129
1991	2,089
1992	2,439
1993	2,886
1994	3,200
1995	3,650
1996	3,955
1997	4,200

Fair' policy (1982), and the 'surcharging' of Liverpool and Lambeth councillors who breached the rate-capping laws (1985).

Nevertheless, such cases of judicial review continue to rise, perhaps because the judges are less 'executive-minded' nowadays, or because citizens are increasingly aware of their legal rights against government and/or because governments are increasingly careless about adhering to the letter of the law. The 1997 Labour government, for example, was ruled illegal in the British courts over its ban on the domestic sale of beef on the bone less than a year after coming to office.

The judges

There is a hierarchy of judges in the British courts, from magistrates (JPs) who are lay-people rather than trained lawyers, through recorders (part-time judges), and judges in the Crown courts up to the most senior judges (Law Lords) in the House of Lords.

The independence of the judiciary

According to the 'rule of law', justice should be an end in itself, and judges should not be subject to political pressure from the legislature or executive, nor should they be partial or prejudiced in their interpretation or enforcement of the law. To this end:

► the judiciary should be separate from the other branches of government, in accordance with Montesquieu's principle of the 'separation of powers'

► judicial appointments should be based on merit, not on political patronage

► senior judges have security of tenure: under the Act of Settlement 1701, they can only be removed by a resolution in both Houses of Parliament (which has never yet happened)

► judges receive fixed salaries paid from the Consolidated Fund and not subject to political debate in Parliament

► judges' decisions should not be questioned in Parliament

► judges' remarks in court (like those of lawyers, witnesses and jury members) are not liable to legal actions for damages.

---

4 How far are these principles of judicial independence upheld? Can you give specific instances where any principles are, or have been, breached?

Many commentators, such as J.A.G. Griffith, question how far judges are, or can be, 'non-political'. This concept has at least four dimensions: separation of powers; freedom from external political pressure; lack of personal or political prejudice; and lack of involvement in any political role. Judges are often said to be unavoidably 'political', in one sense or another, for the following reasons.

► Judges' social background – 97 per cent male, 88 per cent public school and Oxbridge – their above-average age, and the nature of their legal training (still steeped in nineteenth-century Victorian values), all of which may foster a conservative, if not Conservative (i.e. party political), outlook. Judges' comments especially on class, race and gender have often caused controversy. In 1998 the government declared that new judges, as well as police and prison officers, must declare Freemasonry membership. However, on the issue of personal interest or bias there was an unprecedented case in 1998 where the Law Lords overturned their own previous ruling in favour of the extradition of former Chilean leader General Pinochet for war crimes, because of the undeclared connection of one of the Law Lords, Lord Hoffman, with a relevant pressure group, Amnesty International.

▶ Overlaps between judiciary, legislature and executive – for example the Lord Chancellor and Law Lords; the Lord Chancellor's appointment of senior judges (the Labour government reneged on a pre-election promise to transfer the Lord Chancellor's powers of appointment to a judicial appointments commission); commissions of inquiry headed by judges (for example, the Scott Inquiry into arms to Iraq, Macpherson Inquiry into the Stephen Lawrence affair, Phillips Inquiry into BSE, Saville Inquiry (1998) into the 1972 events of 'Bloody Sunday' in Northern Ireland), etc.

▶ 'Judges are part of the machinery of authority within the State and as such cannot avoid the making of political decisions' (Griffith, 1991, page 272). Also as 'part of the state', judges may have a particular view of the 'national interest'; in cases of dispute between state and citizen, they may 'show themselves more executive-minded than the executive' (Lord Atkin) – especially on issues of national security and official secrecy such as the banning of trade unions at GCHQ, and the Tisdall and Ponting cases; and also in key industrial disputes such as the 1984–5 miners' strike.

▶ Judges must review executive actions under administrative law – an unavoidably 'political' role whichever way they rule – for example, Labour being ruled illegal over its ban on the sale of beef on the bone.

▶ The Law Lords have also been given the politically fraught task of ruling on any conflicts between the Scottish and Westminster Parliaments.

▶ Judges must enforce statutes which sometimes seem overtly party political: for example, the Employment and Trade Union Acts of the 1980s and 1990s, the rate- and charge-capping legislation, etc.

▶ Marxists such as Miliband argue that the whole legal system in a capitalist country like Britain is necessarily class-based, and that judges are – unavoidably – part of the political 'superstructure' which protects private property and profit for a minority ruling class.

▲ Judging the judges

The 'political' nature of the judiciary is both enhanced and highlighted by 'judicial creativity'. Either judges must interpret statute law or, where none exists, they must make and enforce common law. For example, in a famous test case 1962 a man called Shaw published a directory of prostitutes; and the Law Lords invented an interesting new common law of 'conspiracy to corrupt public morals' under which to convict him.

The other side of the coin of judicial 'independence' is judicial unaccountability. Election of judges, either by the general public or by an electoral college of lawyers, is therefore sometimes suggested. Note that this would very likely make judges more, rather than less, political. Appointment by an independent commission, rather than by the Lord Chancellor and Prime Minister, is a more likely possibility for the future.

The police

There are 127,000 police in Britain (of whom around 10 per cent are women and 2 per cent are black). Their job is to enforce the criminal law 'on the ground': to prevent crime, apprehend criminals and maintain public order. Their numbers, pay and powers have increased substantially since the 1980s: for example, the Police Act 1997 gave them powers to enter private premises, plant bugs, inspect files, etc. with no external authorisation; and the 1998 anti-terrorism laws allow individuals to be convicted of belonging to terrorist organisations purely on the opinion of a single police officer. Essay questions on this topic focus on the following issues.

Public order

This concept implies legal, peaceful, controllable behaviour especially of crowds in public places, for example, pickets, marches and demonstrations. The maintenance of public order is therefore the most overtly 'political' role of the police. The Public Order Act 1936 outlawed quasi-military organisations and unofficial political uniforms (for example, fascist blackshirts); it bans 'offensive weapons' (which the police have taken to include nail files, combs and keys); and it covers threatening, abusive or insulting language, breach of the peace, public nuisance and obstruction of the highway or of the police. The Public Order Act 1986 provides new definitions and sentences for disorderly behaviour, unlawful assembly, affray and rioting; it requires organisers of marches to give the police seven days' notice; and it allows senior police officers to stipulate the time, place and numbers involved in meetings and marches, and to ban demonstrations if they threaten public disorder or 'serious disruption to the local community'. The danger of such discretionary policing powers, according to some observers such as the pressure group Liberty, is that they may be exercised in an inconsistent, arbitrary or excessive way, for example, against young people, blacks, environmental protesters, travellers and 'hippies'.

Controversy has surrounded policing tactics in many public order incidents: for example, during an anti-National Front demonstration in 1979, teacher Blair Peach was killed by a Special Patrol Group officer, but no one was disciplined or prosecuted. After riots in Brixton and Toxteth (1981) and in Handsworth and Tottenham (1985), the police allegedly broke into people's homes, unlawfully assaulted people and detained children for days without informing their families. During the miners' strike (1984–5) there were over 500 official complaints against the police of illegal detention, assault, criminal damage to homes, strip-searching of miners' wives and tapping of union members' phones – but no prosecutions or disciplinary charges resulted. In blocking the Peace

Convoy at Stonehenge in 1985, the police attacked women and children and wantonly destroyed their property according to the owner of the land, Lord Cardigan. Twenty-four of the 'travellers' finally won over £25,000 damages against Wiltshire police in 1991. Following a peaceful demonstration at Manchester University (1985), police allegedly arrested and assaulted student Stephen Shaw, burnt him with cigarettes and repeatedly threatened him until he fled the country. In 1986 officers from a police patrol van assaulted five innocent schoolboys in Holloway Road. Violent policing of the Wapping picket lines in the same year was described by critics as a 'police riot'; and violence at the anti-poll tax demonstration in 1990 was allegedly instigated by the police.

There is also concern about assaults and deaths in police custody: for example, Joy Gardner whose head was bound with 13 feet of masking tape as a restraint so that she suffocated (1996); Roger Sylvester who died in 1999 after restraint by eight officers. The misuse of firearms and shooting of innocent people by the police is also criticised: for example, in the 1980s Steven Waldorf (mistaken for a robber) was shot at least 14 times whilst sitting in his car; six-year-old John Shorthouse was killed in his bed whilst police were searching for his father; and Cherry Groce was shot and paralysed in her home while police were looking for her son. A number of deaths have also followed police use of CS spray in the late 1990s. (No police convictions resulted from any of the above cases.) Better police training is often recommended by critics.

Yard pays £376,000 to wronged citizens

Met faces riot charges

Police pay £350 damages for woman's 'terror' ride

Injured, fined

Police 'at fault' in student clash

Police guilty of hippy attack

▲ *Discretionary policing – use or abuse of power?*

Impartiality

Like judges, the police are supposed to enforce the law impartially. However, the Scarman Report found police **racialism** to be one factor underlying the 1981 Brixton riots, and a study of the London Metropolitan Police by the Policy Studies Institute in 1983 found routine racialism, sexism, a 'cult of violence', a disregard for the law and the rules of police procedure, and a readiness to cover-up for colleagues' wrong-doing. There are still frequent accusations of internal as well as external racialism: for example, over a dozen legal cases of alleged discrimination against past or present officers within the Met ongoing at any one time in 1998–9.

Police Constable Blakelock was killed during a riot on the Broadwater Farm estate in Tottenham in 1987. In the ensuing trial of Winston Silcott and two others, the judge criticised the 'oppressive behaviour' of the police handling the interrogations, and all three were acquitted and freed on appeal in 1991.

Home Office statistics support the possibility of police bias, especially racial: for example, blacks are five times more likely than whites to be stopped and searched on suspicion in proportion to their 6 per cent share of the population. The notorious failure to convict anyone of the racial killing of black teenager Stephen Lawrence in 1993 was attributed to police racialism as well as ineptitude and possible corruption; and it took the police two years to accept that the burning to death of Michael Menson on a London street in 1996 was a racial killing, i.e. that he did not set fire to himself as the police had said. According to Lee Jasper, director of the black pressure group 1990 Trust, speaking in 1999, 'Blacks are under-policed as victims of crime and over-policed when going about their law-abiding business'.

Cases such as these prompted the Labour government, in the Crime and Disorder Act 1998, to give the courts and local authorities new powers to deal with racial crimes and racial harassment; and all public bodies, including the police, must now monitor employment and promotion of staff by ethnic group. The (little known) exemption of the police and other public authorities from the Race Relations Acts is to be repealed in the wake of the Stephen Lawrence case. Also in 1998, the European Court of Human Rights ruled against the police's blanket immunity against negligence claims; this should, therefore, be enacted in British law.

There has, further, been persistent evidence of police corruption since the 1970s: in 1999, half of the 43 police forces in England and Wales had officers facing charges of theft, drug trafficking, destroying evidence, planting evidence and even armed robbery. There were dozens of convictions against Stoke Newington officers in the mid-1990s and ongoing investigations and convictions for fabrication of evidence against the Metropolitan Police Flying Squad in 1999. A leaked memo from the director of the National Criminal Intelligence Service in 1998 described the problem as akin to that 'in some third world countries'.

The so-called 'numbers cases' were the most notorious miscarriages of justice over the last three decades. The Guildford Four – Gerard Conlon and others – were released in 1989 after wrongly serving 14 years for IRA pub bombings. The similar case of the Birmingham Six has caused equal disquiet. Some officers involved in that case were in the West Midlands Serious Crime Squad, which was disbanded by its own Chief Constable in 1989 after repeated findings of fabrication of evidence, false confessions, assault and intimidation resulting in dubious convictions.

As a consequence of such cases, the Conservative government in 1997 set up the Criminal Cases Review Commission; by its second anniversary, it was swamped with over 2,000 cases of alleged wrongful convictions.

The Labour government has promised further reforms to ensure that corrupt police face quicker dismissal with less scope to hide behind paid sick leave and early retirement on full pensions. However, the Police Federation (the staff association for junior ranks) is a powerful and litigious organisation: it wins over £20 million per year in damages from legal actions in support of junior officers.

Writer Stuart Hall has also noted the growth of a powerful 'bobby lobby' since the 1970s, with the Police Federation issuing press adverts advocating capital punishment,

▲ *The Birmingham Six, with the MP Chris Mullen, on the day of their release, 15 March 1991*

and the Association of Chief Police Officers campaigning actively for tougher public order laws, stiffer sentencing and more police weaponry – all politically sensitive proposals.

There were increasingly frequent references in the 1980s and early 1990s to the growth of a **police state** in Britain, from commentators as diverse as Arthur Scargill, Lord Scarman, Lord Gifford QC and the Bishop of Durham. This concept implies a state where the law is arbitrarily enforced by the police who are themselves largely above the law, authoritarian and militaristic, with extensive powers of stop, search, detention, interrogation, use of force and secret surveillance, operating in support of government and state and with the tacit or open support of government and judiciary. (See also Roger Scruton's definition below.)

---

police state. A state in which political stability has come to be, or to seem to be, dependent upon police supervision of the ordinary citizen, and in which the police are given powers suitable to that. The police force is extended, and operates secretly, with powers to detain for interrogation without charge, to search, to interrupt correspondence and to tap telephone calls, and in general to keep detailed records on citizens accused of no crime, in order to enforce measures designed to extinguish all opposition to the government and its institutions. The powers here may not be legally granted, but that is not normally an obstacle, since there is a presumption that there is no rule of law in these circumstances, and the acquisition of large *de facto* powers by the police will simply be one large aspect of a widespread defiance of natural justice.

(Roger Scruton, Dictionary of Political Thought*)*

Writers such as Robert Reiner have noted some disturbing trends in British policing: increasing numbers and powers, use of force, militarisation, politicisation, centralisation, arbitrary and discriminatory law enforcement, lack of accountability, and secret surveillance of legal groups such as trade unions, CND and Liberty. However, the degree of police power and accountability is perceptibly different in Britain from, for example, the dark days of South Africa or Chile.

Accountability

The local nature of UK policing has been modified by the creation of a National Crime Squad in 1998. Otherwise, the 43 regional police forces in England and Wales are controlled by:

▶ the *Home Secretary*, at the national level

▶ at local level, each regional force except London is linked to a *local council police committee* which used to comprise two-thirds elected councillors and one-third non-elected magistrates. Since 1994, the police authorities each have 17 members: nine councillors, three magistrates and five 'independent' members who should 'represent the interests of a wide range of people within the community in a police area' – in effect, however, they are Home Office appointees. These committees are partially responsible – together with central government and the local Chief Constables – for police pay, equipment, overall structure and strategy. However, some committees (such as Manchester and Merseyside) have objected to their lack of control, for example, over police acquisition of plastic bullets and CS gas

▶ *civil and criminal law* – the Metropolitan police alone pay out over £1 million per year in civil cases of wrongful arrest, assault and malicious prosecution; and two officers, Hamish Montgomery and Patrick Shevlin, were given life sentences in 1988 for the killing of Owen Roberts in police custody. The Police and Criminal Evidence Act (PACE) 1984 extended police powers of stop and search, seizure of evidence, detention without charge (for up to 96 hours) and interrogation; but it also codified and set limits on those powers in statute law for the first time

▶ the *Police Complaints Authority (PCA)*, established under the 1984 Act – technically independent in that none of its members are police officers; but all of its investigations are still carried out by the police themselves, an arrangement which even the Police Federation has come to oppose because of public mistrust of the system. Over 45,000 complaints of assault, illegal detention, malicious prosecution, etc. were made against the police in 1998, but under 0.3 per cent resulted in disciplinary proceedings.

Civil rights and freedoms

Rights are entitlements – for example, to some kind of freedom or equality. **Natural rights** are those to which, according to some philosophers, everyone is entitled; civil rights are those granted to citizens by a particular state or government, and they may differ widely from one society to another.

Different political ideologies adopt different views on rights and freedoms: liberals tend to stress individual rights and **positive freedoms** which should be enhanced by state action if necessary – for example, the right to own private property, and the freedom from sexual or racial discrimination, protected by law. Socialists tend to stress collective rights (for example, freedom of assembly or industrial action for trade unions), and economic, political or social equalities; and socialists are (more or less) opposed to private property.

Freedom and equality may conflict; for example, the freedom to choose between private or public health or education (a liberal tenet) may conflict with the goal of equal access to health care or equal educational opportunities (a socialist tenet). Similarly, progressive taxation in pursuit of greater economic equality or welfare may conflict with the freedom of individuals to spend their own money as they wish.

Conflict may also arise between individual and collective freedoms: for example, the collective right to strike against the individual's right to strike-break was a source of acute conflict within mining families and communities during the 1984–5 dispute.

Law, by its nature, may both enhance and constrain freedom: for example, it may protect the individual against violence, theft or discrimination, but it also limits individual freedom of action in those spheres. Is discrimination – sexual, religious or racial – an individual right or a social wrong?

Some laws in Britain are often seen as excessive constraints on individual or collective freedoms, and this view is sometimes used to justify civil disobedience. For example, civil servants Sarah Tisdall and Clive Ponting in 1984 both deliberately breached Section 2 of the 1911 Official Secrets Act; and trade unions such as the miners, seamen and print-workers have been taken to court over 'secondary picketing', illegal since 1980. The Criminal Justice Act 1994, which effectively removed the right to silence, was particularly controversial.

▲ *In 1994 protestors against the new Criminal Justice Act climbed onto the roof of the Houses of Parliament*

5 Consider the following list of rights and freedoms. For each, say what limits currently exist in British law and practice. What limits, if any, do you think there should be on each, and why? Do some rights conflict with others? Can you add to the list?

a) The right to life

b) The right to death

c) Freedom of assembly

d) Freedom of movement

e) The right to strike

f) Freedom of speech

g) Freedom of information

h) Freedom of the media

i) The right to privacy

j) Freedom of religious conscience

k) Freedom from arbitrary arrest or imprisonment

l) Freedom from discrimination

m) Legal equality

n) Political equality

o) Equal educational opportunities

p) The right to work

q) The right to housing

Note: Consider, for example, the law or practice on: murder; abortion; euthanasia; treason and sedition; libel and slander; official secrets; obscenity and pornography; race relations and sexual discrimination; immigration; political and religious 'extremism'; personal privacy; personal morality; homosexuality; the electoral deposit; a minimum wage; conditions of work; trade union membership; picketing; remand; the 'sus' laws (suspicion); the costs of litigation; state and public schooling; corporal punishment; unemployment; homelessness; poverty and welfare.

A Bill of Rights for Britain?

In Britain, until the enforcement of a domestic Bill of Rights in 2000, few rights were guaranteed in law; such rights as citizens had tended to be negative, i.e. they were allowed to do something if there was no law against it. The Human Rights Act 1998 incorporates the European Convention on Human Rights into UK law, and it will come into force in 2000 after British judges have undergone relevant training. However, in cases of conflict between the Bill of Rights and ordinary parliamentary statute, the judges will be required to enforce statute (to maintain the concept of parliamentary sovereignty); they can only point out any such conflicts to Parliament for possible action (or not).

Rights under the European Convention on Human Rights

Convention:

Article 2	Right to life
Article 3	Freedom from torture or inhuman or degrading treatment or punishment
Article 4	Freedom from slavery or forced labour
Article 5	Right to liberty and security of person
Article 6	Right to a fair trial by an impartial tribunal
Article 7	Freedom from retroactive criminal laws
Article 8	Right to respect for private and family life, home and correspondence
Article 9	Freedom of thought, conscience and religion
Article 10	Freedom of expression
Article 11	Freedom of peaceful assembly and association, including the right to join a trade union
Article 12	Right to marry and found family
Article 13	Right to an effective remedy before a national authority
Article 14	Freedom from discrimination

Protocol 1:

Article 1	Right to a peaceful enjoyment of possessions
Article 2	Right to education; and to education in conformity with religious and philosophical convictions
Article 3	Right to take part in free elections by secret ballot

Protocol 4:

Article 1	Freedom from imprisonment for debt
Article 2	Freedom of movement of persons
Article 3	Right to enter and stay in one's country
Article 4	Freedom from collective expulsion

Examples of British cases heard by the European Court of Human Rights

▶ Illegal imprisonment of poll tax non-payers

▶ Corporal punishment in state schools

▶ Press censorship (for example, in the *Sunday Times* thalidomide drug story and the *Spycatcher* cases)

▶ Phone tapping by government agencies

▶ Retrospective seizure of drug dealers' assets

▶ Prisoners' conditions and treatment in Britain and torture of prisoners in Northern Ireland

▶ Birching of criminal offenders in the Isle of Man

▶ Discrimination against homosexuals in Northern Ireland

▶ Discrimination against women, ethnic minorities and immigrants

▶ The rights of workers against closed shops

Case for a Bill of Rights

▶ According to some observers (for example, pressure groups such as Liberty and Charter 88), basic civil liberties in Britain are always under threat with a majority government in a sovereign Parliament in effective control of a flexible, unwritten constitution. They point to new and draconian 'anti-terrorism' laws passed through Parliament in a single day in 1998 which are being extended to cover environmentalists and animal rights activists, etc. They say that the growing political emphasis on law and order in the 1980s and 1990s (for example, the introduction of child jails for 12–14-year-olds in 1998), together with growing police powers, bureaucracy and a conservative judiciary, have all added to the threat.

▶ The situation in Northern Ireland – where rights of political activity and legal equality, residence, movement, privacy, jury trial, freedom from arbitrary detention and from 'cruel and inhuman punishment', etc. were long abridged – demonstrated the fragility of basic liberties in the UK.

▶ The 'rule of law' demands a clear statement of citizens' rights and duties, which has been lacking in Britain.

▶ A Bill of Rights will impose more legal limits on governments' actions, which are often guided only by convention and are therefore effectively above or beyond the law.

▶ With no domestic Bill of Rights, recourse to the European Court of Human Rights was often necessary, but very time-consuming and costly (though this option will, of course, still be available when Britain has its own Bill of Rights).

▶ Since Britain is already a signatory of the European Convention, it is simple and logical to incorporate it into domestic law.

Case against a Bill of Rights

▶ Which rights should be entrenched? How general or specific should they be? Political consensus is hard to achieve.

▶ How entrenched should a Bill of Rights be? Should it have the status of an ordinary statute? Critics feared excessive rigidity, but the fact that ordinary parliamentary statute law will take precedence over the provisions of the British Bill of Rights is now perhaps causing greater concern.

▶ Many existing laws will conflict with it, for example, the Police Act, Prevention of Terrorism Acts, Criminal Justice Acts, etc. (though this is precisely why defenders of civil rights want to see them entrenched). The issue of privacy versus freedom of information is especially fraught.

▶ All governments are reluctant to increase constraints against themselves and against the state.

▶ It could be hard to reconcile majority and minority rights, or collective versus individual rights, or freedom and equality.

▶ Left-wingers are suspicious of a Bill of Rights which may entrench 'liberal' principles such as property rights and undermine 'socialist' principles such as trade union rights.

▶ Many (such as Griffith) do not, in Lord Denning's words, 'trust the judges' to interpret and enforce a Bill of Rights in a liberal and progressive way, because they see judges as unrepresentative, conservative and 'executive-minded'. A domestic Bill of Rights will inevitably transfer some power from elected MPs to non-elected judges, and it could also make judges more overtly 'political'.

▶ Every Bill of Rights has some qualifying clause allowing for the restriction of rights, for example, 'in the national interest', and some are scarcely worth the paper on which they are written.

▶ Rights in Britain are said by some to be adequately protected through Parliament and the Ombudsman, the 'rule of law', the courts (including the European Courts), administrative tribunals, pressure groups and the media, etc.

ESSAYS

1 *Theme:* Law-breaking

Note the different scope of the five questions below (all taken from the London Board): from those which cover law-breaking in all its forms, through those which focus more narrowly on civil disobedience, i.e. peaceful, political law-breaking, to those which concern only violent law-breaking.

a) **Q?** Are there circumstances in which we should break the law?

(London, Feb. 1976, Paper 1)

A✓   Examiners' comments

'This question must not be turned into either a "good old rule of law" or a "conscience is king" rhapsody. "Circumstances" is the key word. Some general rules must be advanced (minimal), plausible examples given (average), and some attempt at defining criteria to judge between law and justice would carry more marks. The better candidate will attempt to define what is meant by "law" and will see that both the example of breaking a general rule and of enduring needlessly a lawful injustice are to be considered.'

b) **Q?** What forms of protest against government do you consider legitimate, and what forms illegitimate?

(London, June 1984, Paper 1)

A✓   Examiners' comments

'Many candidates attempted this question and were able to offer an account of different forms of dissent. Difficulties arose over distinguishing the basis of legitimacy and most candidates concentrated their answers on legality. The better candidates were able to raise problems concerning the issues that Greenpeace posed at Sellafield – about protest that breaks the law but that raises the question that, while such protest may be unlawful, is it necessarily illegitimate?'

c) **Q?** Is there ever a case for civil disobedience?

(London, June 1979, Page 1)

d) **Q?** Can any recent instance of direct action by a pressure group in defiance of the law be justified?

(London, June 1985, Paper 1)

e) **Q?** How tolerant should we be towards threats to overthrow the state by violence?

(London, June 1978, Paper 1)

Additional essay tips on questions (a)–(e)

a) 'Should' is a strong word, implying not simply a right but a duty to break the law.

b) This question seeks a personal evaluation of various methods of political protest, with some explicit and reasoned line-drawing: for example, 'I would condone illegal "leaking" of official secrets to expose wrong-doing, but I would not condone unprovoked violence against the police because . . .', etc.

c) This question requires a balanced assessment of both the 'case for' and the 'case against' civil disobedience; but the word 'ever' would make it hard to conclude with a blanket 'no'.

d) This question specifies law-breaking by pressure groups; examples of law-breaking by other individuals and organisations would not be relevant, however accurate or topical they may be. Several examples of illegal action by different pressure groups may be discussed here; not just one.

e) 'We' may mean the state, society or both; and a distinction could be made between real and uttered 'threats'. Where more than one interpretation of a question seems possible, always point this out explicitly in the introduction; and always cover every possible interpretation in your answer, to gain most marks.

2 *Theme:* The judges

Q? Are British judges 'more executive-minded than the executive' (Lord Acton)?

(Simulated question)

A✓ **Extended essay plan**

Introduction:

▶ Title implies that British judiciary favours government and state in disputes between state and citizen

▶ Role of judges: to interpret and enforce law in an independent and impartial manner, including 'administrative law' in relation to government itself.

Case for title:

▶ Alleged breaches of judicial independence, for example, overlaps such as Lord Chancellor, 'political' appointments such as Lord Donaldson

▶ Griffith's argument that judges 'are part of the machinery of authority within the state'

▶ Cases where judges have backed government against citizens: ABC, Harriet Harman, Ponting, Tisdall, GCHQ, miners' strike, Prison Officers' Association, 'numbers cases', Lord Mackay on employment tribunal appeals

▶ Griffith's argument that judges are not only executive-minded but conservative and Conservative-minded, given their socio-economic background, legal training and age, etc.

Case against title:

▶ Theory and practice of judicial independence; safeguards, for example, security of tenure, non-political appointment, judicial immunity

▶ Frequency of judicial rulings against government since mid-1970s: examples – (against Labour) Laker Skytrain, TV licenses, Tameside comprehensive school; (against Conservatives) Judge Smedley in Matrix Churchill case, contempt of court (Baker), pit closures (Heseltine), Pergau Dam (Hurd), cuts in criminal victim compensation, child deportation, arbitrary and secretive parole and appeal decisions (all Michael Howard)

- ▶ The courts have often upheld civil liberties against government policies, for example, of teachers' boycott and privatised workers' new terms and conditions, and against anti-union contracts

- ▶ Senior judges in the 1990s seem increasingly 'liberal minded' and prepared openly to criticise government policies: examples – crits. of law reform proposals (Judge Woolf), juvenile imprisonment (Judge Tumin), legal aid cuts (Lord Taylor), miscarriages of justice (Judge May)

- ▶ Judicial inquiries are thorough and balanced: examples – Scott (arms to Iraq), Nolan (standards in public life)

- ▶ Many senior judges, for example, Lords Taylor, Bingham and Browne-Wilkinson, advocate a domestic Bill of Rights, contrary to Conservative government policy.

Conclusion:
Disagree – title too simplistic, especially since 1990. However, scope for reforms in judicial recruitment and training, plus domestic Bill of Rights.

3 *Theme:* **The Police**

Q? How and why have the powers of the police changed in Britain since the 1970s?

(London, Jan. 1988, Paper 1)

A✓ **Extended essay plan**

Introduction:
Role of police: preservation of law and order, protection of life and property, apprehending of offenders. Role has changed since 1970s, particularly with Thatcherism – growing police numbers, resources and powers.

Why?
Incidents and events have influenced government into strengthening powers and role: for example, rising crime rates, Northern Ireland (until 1995), miners' strike 1984–5, 1980s' inner city riots in Liverpool, Toxteth, Brixton, Handsworth and Tottenham, football violence, Stonehenge, Wapping, poll tax disturbance, hunt saboteurs, protests against motorways, live animal exports and Criminal Justice Act.

Causes of growth in crime and disorder:
- ▶ Conservative view: Disintegration of family life, lack of discipline in schools, inadequate policing and punishment of offenders, etc.
- ▶ Labour view: rising unemployment and poverty, growing gap between rich and poor, 'loadsamoney' culture, racism, youth alienation, 'bad' policies, etc.

How?
- ▶ Growing *de jure* powers of police:

Prevention of Terrorism Act 1976 on . . .

Police and Criminal Evidence Act 1984 . . .

Public Order Act 1986 . . .

Trade Union Acts of 1980s . . .

Criminal Justice Act 1994 . . .

Police Act 1997 . . . (anti-terrorism laws 1998 . . .)

Changing *de facto* powers and role of police:

'Politicisation' . . .

'Bobby lobby' . . .

'Militarisation' . . .

Arming of police . . .

Centralisation of control . . .

Racism . . .

Surveillance of pressure groups and non-conformists . . .

Conclusion:

Need to make police more accountable to law and local democracy. Reforms: better police training, liberalise criminal justice laws, a police ombudsman, new House of Commons' select committee on policing and civil liberties.

4 *Theme:* Civil rights

Q? Besides Parliament, what bodies best preserve and enhance civil liberties?

(London, June 1978, Paper 1)

A✓ **Essay plan**

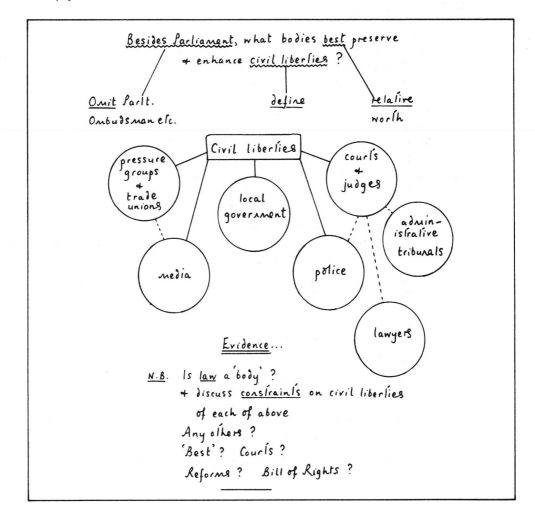

How adequately do British judges protect civil liberties?

(London, June 1993, Paper 1)

A✓ Extended essay plan

Notes: 'How adequately . . .?' always requires case for and against. Always put last the case which you most support. Since the title says 'judges' and not 'courts', you may include not only court cases, but judicial statements expressed outside of court. Both sides will require examples to back up the arguments. You should logically lean, in your conclusion, towards the side with the most examples. However, for the examples listed below, consider how many could go on *either* or *both sides* of the argument because they raise conflicting civil liberties.

Introduction:

▶ 'Civil liberties': citizens' entitlements and freedoms under the law. Examples: freedom of expression/information, freedom of association, assembly and movement, freedom from arbitrary arrest or detention, freedom from discrimination, freedom of conscience, right to privacy, right to work, etc.

▶ Role of judges: to interpret and enforce the law in an independent and impartial manner, according to 'the rule of law'. Possible conflicts: judges cannot challenge the validity of the law except through interpretation; and they must protect the rights of both citizen and state according to law.

Case against saying that judges protect civil liberties:
Sometimes the law itself may constrain civil liberties; or, according to critics such as Griffith, the judges may be biased and conservative in their role.

Examples:

▶ 'Numbers cases' prior to release (1970s and 1980s)

▶ Ban on trade unions at GCHQ (1984)

▶ Miners' strike cases (1984)

▶ Government secrecy upheld by judges in Tisdall and Ponting cases (1985)

▶ Case against three 'Birmingham Six' case detectives dropped by court for fear of prejudicial media coverage (1993)

▶ Courts upheld Home Secretary's claim that Prison Officers' Association was not a trade union, therefore was not permitted to take strike action (1993)

▶ Two Rastafarian parents imprisoned for refusing insulin to diabetic daughter on grounds of religious conscience (1993)

▶ Eight men imprisoned for private and consensual acts of sado-masochism (1993)

▶ Lord Chancellor pressured judges to cut employment tribunal appeals to save government money (1994)

▶ Court upheld enforcement of 'closed' visits to IRA prisoners (1995).

Case for saying that judges protect civil liberties:
British 'liberal democratic' theory implies that law and courts should protect civil liberties.

Examples:

▶ Home Secretary ruled in contempt of court over deportation case (1991)

▶ Scott Inquiry into arms for Iraq (1991)

▶ Judge Smedley disallowed government secrecy in Matrix Churchill trial (1992)

▶ Lord Taylor advocated Bill of Rights in Dimbleby Lecture (1992)

▶ Procedure of coal pit closures ruled illegal (1992)

▶ Court upheld right to die of Hillsborough victim Tony Bland (1993)

▶ Lord Woolf and other senior judges criticised government's law reform proposals (1993)

▶ Appeal Court upheld teachers' national exam boycott (1993)

▶ Appeal Court ruled anti-union contracts illegal (1993)

▶ High Court ruled that privatised workers' terms and conditions must not be changed for worse (1993)

▶ Judge Tumin criticised excessive juvenile imprisonment (1993)

▶ Lord Taylor criticised Lord Chancellor's legal aid cuts (1993)

▶ Law Lords led fight in Lords against Criminal Justice Bill 1994

▶ Secret government deal over Pergau Dam ruled illegal (1995)

▶ Home Secretary ruled illegal over secrecy re parole and appeals decisions, delays in prisoner releases, cuts in crime victim compensation and deportation of child asylum seeker (1995).

Conclusion:

On balance, British judges seem increasingly concerned to uphold civil liberties, especially in the 1990s with a new and perhaps more progressive body of senior judges in action. However, attempts – especially by government – to curb civil liberties are still common; some Parliamentary legislation itself is constraining of civil liberties, notably the 1980s' trade union legislation and the 1994 Criminal Justice Act; and British judges (as they themselves have pointed out) are handicapped by the fact that Britain had no domestic Bill of Rights until 2000.

Many senior judges, as well as pressure groups like Liberty, therefore advocate incorporating the European Convention on Human Rights into British law. Also, legislation on freedom of information and greater legislative controls on the prerogative powers of government ministers would help to enhance civil liberties in Britain. Broadening the recruitment and training of the judiciary is also often recommended.

---

6 Write at least one of the following essays. Always write a brief plan first.

a) What are the main threats to the rule of law in contemporary Britain?

(Cambridge, June 1986, Paper 1)

b) 'The obligation to obey the law is always conditional – even in a democracy.' Discuss.

(Oxford and Cambridge, June 1990, Paper 1)

c) Outline and assess recent government policy over law and order.

(Oxford and Cambridge, June 1997, Paper 1)

d) Should the police be more subject to democratic control?

(Oxford, Summer 1986, Paper 1)

e) (i) What do you consider to be the most important civil liberties?
(ii) How well are civil liberties protected in the United Kingdom?

(London, June 1998, Paper 1)

f) What rights do UK citizens possess? Assess the effectiveness of the various procedures for complaint, and redress, open to individuals if they believe they are the victims of unfairness, incompetence or injustice on the part of a government.

(AEB, Summer 1997, Paper 1)

GUIDE TO EXERCISES

Page 170

1 • Statute law: Acts of Parliament, for example, Criminal Justice Act 1998

   • Common law: 'common custom of the realm', established and enforced by the judges since the twelfth century, for example, public rights to common land and footpaths

   • Case law: 'Judge-made law' – judicial interpretations of statute, common and other forms of law which set a precedent for future cases, for example, the Pinochet extradition case 1998/9

   • EU law: European Union legislation, which takes precedence over all domestic law, for example, world wide beef ban

   • Delegated legislation: law made by bodies other than Parliament under authority passed down (delegated) by Parliament, for example, local authority by-laws

Page 170

2   Principles and breaches of the 'rule of law':

   • Everyone, including government, should be equally subject to the same law. Exceptions: legal immunities of diplomats, MPs, etc.; cost of litigation – 'The law, like the Ritz Hotel, is open to all' (Lord Justice Darling); exemption of police from Race Relations Acts.

   • There should be a clear statement of people's rights and duties under the law. Exceptions: quantity and complexity of law; retrospective law – for example, a retrospective ban on tax exemption for overseas earners (1998); plethora of conventions.

   • There should be fair, consistent and open court procedures. Exceptions: inconsistent sentencing; secret trials, for example, Bettany spy trial (1984); different rules for different courts, for example, administrative and deportation tribunals and coroners' courts.

   • Justice should be an end in itself, with no arbitrary law or government. Exceptions: alleged police bias, for example, in enforcing public order laws; retrospective law; delegated legislation, for example, Social Security Act 1986.

   • No one should be subject to legal penalty unless she or he has broken the law – innocent till proven guilty. Exceptions: remand before trial; the 'sus' laws; effective removal of right to silence in CJA 1994; 'trial by media' (for example, *The Daily Mail* (1997) giving names and pictures of five unconvicted men as 'murderers' of black teenager Stephen Lawrence); seizure of defendants' assets before conviction.

- There should be an independent and impartial judiciary. Exceptions: lack of separation of powers; political patronage; alleged judicial bias – for example, in 1998 the Law Lords for the first time overruled *themselves* because of Lord Hoffman's undeclared Amnesty connection in the Pinochet extradition hearing.

Page 171

3   c) Arguments for/against civil disobedience:
- The law is/not democratic.
- There are/not legal and effective methods of protest.
- The law does/not protect our rights and freedoms.

Page 175

4   Independence of judiciary; breaches of principles:
- Lord Chancellor, Law Lords, judges heading executive inquiries, for example, Lord Justice Woolf on prison riots
- Allegations of political patronage, for example, Lord John Donaldson's promotion from 1979 by Conservative PM
- Rowdy debates in Parliament over large pay increases for judges, for example, in 1985
- Labour MP Martin Flannery referred to 'tame Tory judges' in 1984–5 miners' strike; Mrs Thatcher criticised low sentence imposed on child rapist by Judge Stanley Price in 1982.

REFERENCES

Denning, Lord (1980) Dimbleby Lecture: 'Misuse of power'
Griffith, J.A.G. (1991) *The Politics of the Judiciary*, Fontana
Hain, Peter (1984) *Political Trials in Britain*, Penguin
Hall, Stuart *et al.* (1979) *Policing the Crisis*, Macmillan
Miliband, Ralph (1969) *The State in Capitalist Society*, Quartet
Reiner, Robert (1984) 'Is Britain turning into a police state?', *New Society*, 2 August
Scruton, Roger (1983) *A Dictionary of Political Thought*, Pan

10 Public opinion, pressure groups and media

TOPIC NOTES

Key facts and concepts

Public opinion

In a democracy it is usually assumed that government should be responsive to public opinion; but this is a very difficult concept to define or measure. It is best defined as the majority view on a given issue at a given time; but if opinion is divided several ways there may be no 'majority' view; or the view of a vocal or powerful minority may dominate.

Public opinion may be expressed or assessed through elections, referenda (for example, in 1975 on remaining in the EU; and in 1998 in Scotland, Wales and Northern Ireland on devolution), through letters to the press or to MPs, pressure group activity, opinion polls or direct action.

However, a distorted impression of public opinion may be conveyed, for example, by tactical voting, abstention, unequal degrees of political activism by different sections of the public (for example, the middle classes tend to be more politically active than the working class). *Public opinion polls* may question an unrepresentative sample of people; they may offer limited options as answers; or they may shape the very thing they are trying to measure, simply by posing questions about an issue which some people may never have considered before. Political parties often carry out their own polls; and they may publish misleading results in an effort to boost their own vote. It is sometimes suggested that even professional opinion polls should be banned in the days before an election, because they may influence the result of the election itself: for example, if one party seems very strong – or very weak – its supporters may not bother to vote at all.

Referenda provide an element of 'direct democracy' in a representative system (even though, in Britain, they are invariably only 'advisory' to maintain the semblance of parliamentary sovereignty). They can be educative, increasing public awareness and understanding of an issue because all sides are likely to bombard the voters with information and argument. They help to legitimise the resulting policy decision and to promote consensus behind it within both government and public.

On the other hand, referenda may oversimplify a complex issue by reducing voter choice to a simple 'yes' or 'no, for example, on the question of proportional representation. They may also reduce voter choice by merging two or more issues in one question, for example, in the referendum on an elected London council and mayor in 1998. Voters may be subject to very one-sided campaigns – for example, in the 1975 European and 1998 Scottish referenda – or to misleading propaganda rather than informative facts. The vote may be so close as to call into doubt the legitimacy of the policy; for example, the referendum on Welsh devolution was won by under 1 per cent. Cynics may go so far as to suggest that governments will only offer referenda where it suits them and when they are sure they are going to win – i.e. referenda may be used simply to legitimise what governments intend to do anyway, whilst at the same time allowing governments to evade responsibility and blame the voters for any unpopular consequences. They are also, of course, time-consuming and costly.

Though public opinion is difficult to define or measure, it may influence Parliament or government: for example, the so-called 'greening' of the Conservative governments from the late 1980s, when they paid increasing attention to environmental issues, reflecting growing public concern and pressure group activity.

However, it may be argued that politicians should not follow every whim of public opinion, because it may be ill-informed, selfish, fickle, emotional or irrational. Parliament's consistent rejection of capital punishment since the 1960s may be one example of this.

Sample short answer question and answer

Q? Distinguish between political influence and political power.

A✓ 'Influence' is persuasive effect on others' ideas or actions; it may or may not be intended, organised or perceived, but it is based on reasoned agreement, respect, etc., and is therefore closer to authority than to power. 'Power' is the ability to make decisions, to act, or to get others to do something through threat or use of sanctions – rewards or punishments, even force or violence. It implies coercion rather than consent. If farmers or water workers can cut off food or water supplies, that is power; whereas a persuasive publicity campaign by Comic Relief or CND is simply influence.

Pressure groups

Pressure groups are organisations which seek to promote a cause or to protect a section of society, often by influencing government, Parliament or the public. Unlike parties, they do not stand candidates for election, and their aims and membership are often narrower; but they do often have close links with political parties.

Two main types of pressure group are:

▶ *promotional or cause groups*, which seek to promote a specific cause, for example, Countryside Alliance (rural issues), Shelter (housing), Friends of the Earth (environment)

▶ *protective or sectional or interest groups*, which seek to protect the interests of their own members as a particular section of society, for example, trade unions and professional associations such as the NUM (National Union of Mineworkers), the Law Society (solicitors), the CBI (Confederation of British Industry), etc.

Some groups are hybrid, i.e. a mixture of both types: for example, the Automobile Association and Royal Automobile Club, seek to protect their own members and to promote the cause of motoring and the wider interests of all motorists.

Some pressure groups may be temporary and disband if they achieve their aims, for example, preventing nuclear waste-dumping in a local area.

Pressure groups may also be subdivided into *insider* and *outsider groups*, depending on the closeness of their relationships with government, civil servants and other key policy-makers.

Power and influence

There has been a huge growth in the number and influence of pressure groups in the twentieth century for a number of reasons:

▶ the principle of public participation and influence in political decision-making, established with universal suffrage

▶ the weakness of individual as opposed to collective influence and organisation

▶ the expanding role of government and state in public affairs, and rising public expectations of government intervention and activity

▶ new pressure groups being formed to oppose existing ones, for example, FOREST (Freedom Organisation for the Enjoyment of Smoking Tobacco) to counter the anti-smoking group ASH (Action on Smoking and Health); pro- and anti-abortion groups, etc.

Pressure groups vary enormously in power and influence, depending on their type, size, membership, financial resources, links with parties, methods, media coverage and current trends in government policy (for example, CND became the fastest growing pressure group in the country in the early 1980s as US and British governments pursued a strongly pro-nuclear line and built up stocks of Cruise and other nuclear weapons). Large groups are not necessarily the most powerful. Protective groups tend to have more sanctions available to them than promotional groups, and hence more power, for example, the members of a key economic interest group may withdraw their labour or capital. Promotional groups may have considerable *influence* on public opinion or on government policy: for example, a large demonstration by the Countryside Alliance in 1997 persuaded the Labour government to renege on its manifesto promise to abolish fox-hunting; but even the largest promotional group – such as CND – lacks *power* to change government policy.

Methods used by pressure groups

The most powerful groups – such as the National Farmers' Union – often have direct links with government and civil service, in a relationship of mutual need, for example, for information, expertise and influence. Such groups rarely need to resort to public lobbying, street demonstrations, etc.; the most powerful and influential groups are therefore often, paradoxically, the least visible. A few groups, such as the farmers, have the statutory right to be consulted on relevant legislation and policy initiatives. Examples of the farming lobby's influence were: the forced resignation of junior health minister Edwina Currie, followed by new government subsidies to egg producers, after her statistically accurate remark in 1988 that 'most egg production' in this country was contaminated by salmonella; and the huge extra subsidies given to the beef farmers in the 1990s to compensate them for lost sales due to the BSE scandal.

Many pressure groups increasingly target the EU – some, indeed, have even transferred their headquarters to Brussels – in recognition of the increasing decision-making power of the EU. Many also target quangos, local government and the media as increasingly influential institutions.

Many groups work through Parliament and MPs by:

▶ *financing political parties* – the Labour Party, historically, has been funded largely by trade unions such as the TGWU, while the Conservative Party has been funded mainly by business and industry. However, since 1997, Labour has won increasing business support and finance and has been deliberately distancing itself more from the unions

▶ *lobbying MPs in Parliament* – through letters, leaflets, petitions, free gifts, dinners, trips and parties, and personal 'consultancy fees' to MPs. Since the 'cash for questions' scandal of the 1990s, MPs are bound by much stricter rules of declaration than previously

▶ *sponsoring MPs* – many trade unions pay some part of a local Labour party's election campaign costs in return for support by a Labour MP, for example, Dennis Skinner is sponsored by the National Union of Mineworkers

▶ *drafting and promoting private members' bills* – for example, David Steel's 1967 Abortion Act was largely drafted by the Abortion Law Reform Association, and successive amendment bills (for example, by John Corrie, David Alton and Anne Widdicombe) were backed by anti-abortion groups such as the Society for the Protection of the Unborn Child (SPUC)

▶ *seeking to influence government legislation* – for example, the Lord's Day Observance Society mobilised Conservative MPs into opposing Sunday trading in 1986

▶ *hiring professional lobbyists*, such as Hill and Knowlton or Political Planning Services, to promote a cause among MPs, for which clients may pay around £30,000 per year. There are now over 60 such organisations in Britain.

Often a last resort for the least powerful but most visible cause groups is to seek to influence government indirectly through the mobilisation of public opinion: for example, Child Poverty Action Group, Shelter and Greenpeace. Methods used include conducting or publicising opinion polls, petitions, pickets, leaflets and letters, media adverts, demonstrations and staged public events, such as Greenpeace dumping four tons of genetically-modified soya beans outside the gates of Downing Street in 1999 in protest over Blair's backing for GM foods. Concern is sometimes expressed where pressure groups' publicity tactics are emotive, obstructive, illegal or violent.

Pressure groups may use civil disobedience (see Chapter 9) to gain publicity for their cause: for example, CND members trespassing and cutting the perimeter wire at nuclear bases, refusing to pay taxes towards nuclear weapons and staging mass street 'die-ins' (obstruction). Sometimes groups resort to the threat or use of violence: for example, the Animal Liberation Front planting bombs at animal experimentation centres and at shops which sell fur products. Such groups would argue that it is fair to counter violence with violence; and such methods may also win more publicity and response than legal, peaceful methods – which raises questions about the role and responsibility of the media in their coverage of public participation and protest.

---

1 Select any *four* pressure groups – two protective and two promotional. Write brief notes on each, under the following headings:

▶ Aims

▶ Characteristics: size, type of membership, sources of finance, links with political parties

▶ Methods

▶ 'Successful' or 'unsuccessful'? By what criteria?

▶ Reasons for success or failure.

Trade unions

A trade union is a protective organisation of workers which aims to protect its members' pay and working conditions. There are several types:

▶ craft unions – for example, the National Graphical Association (NGA)

▶ industrial unions – for example, the National Union of Mineworkers (NUM)

▶ general unions – for example, the Transport and General Workers' Union (TGWU)

▶ white-collar unions – for example, the National Association of Local Government Officers (NALGO).

Generally, the more skilled and specialised its members, the more 'powerful' is the union.

▶ *Arthur Scargill, radical NUM President*

Power

In the 1960s and 1970s, during the period of consensus politics, trade unions were closely involved with governments – both Labour and Conservative – in shaping economic and industrial policy. Examples of trade union influence or power during this period were:

▶ the Labour government's abandonment of the 1969 White Paper 'In Place of Strife' in the face of trade union opposition

▶ the 1974 miners' strike which is often credited with bringing down the Heath government

▶ the Labour Party's repeal in 1974 of the Industrial Relations Act 1971, and abolition of the Industrial Relations Court, in response to strong trade union opposition

▶ the participation of the trade unions in the Social Contract 1974–8

▶ the 1978–9 'winter of discontent' – public sector strikes over pay restraint, which contributed to Callaghan's defeat in the 1979 election

▶ the involvement of the trade unions in bodies such as the Advisory, Conciliation and Arbitration Service (ACAS).

This **corporatist** approach was rejected by the Thatcher governments of the 1980s.

The theme of exam essay questions on this topic has therefore changed over the last two decades from the 'excessive power' of trade unions to their 'loss of power'. This is because economic recession and high unemployment in the late 1970s and 1980s, together with a series of legislative changes, combined to weaken most trade unions – by 1999, membership was down 5 million from its peak in 1979 – and both Conservative and Labour governments in the 1990s largely rejected any return to corporatism.

Legislation in the 1980s

▶ *Employment Act 1980* – Limited sympathy and secondary action, i.e. action other than that between workers and their own employers, at their own place of work, in a dispute only about pay or conditions of work.

▶ *Employment Act 1982* – Prohibited sympathy and secondary action, secondary and mass picketing. Required secret ballots for maintaining a **closed shop** (where 80 per cent must be in favour). Rendered trade unions liable for damages for breach of contract arising from industrial action.

▶ *Trade Union Act 1984* – Required secret ballots before industrial action, and for maintaining a political fund (i.e. contributions to the Labour Party). Allowed fines and **sequestration**, i.e. freezing and seizure of union funds by courts for illegal action or contempt of court.

▶ *Employment Act 1988* – Required unions balloting on industrial action in separate workplaces to win a majority vote in every workplace. Prohibited unions from disciplining strike-breakers even if a clear majority have voted for strike action. Employers still allowed to sack strikers even after a ballot in favour of action. Established a trade union Commissioner to fund cases against unions in courts. Required periodic re-election by secret ballot of all union officers.

▶ *Employment Act 1989* – Prohibited the pre-entry closed shop.

The defeat of the miners in 1985, after a year-long strike over pit closures, was seen by the government and trade unions alike as a watershed in the decline of trade unions' power and rights. (In the four years from the end of the strike to March 1989, for example, the South Wales mining industry was reduced from 28 pits and 24,000 men to 9 pits and 6,000 men.)

Another turning point was Murdoch's 1986 'Wapping revolution', when he moved *The Sunday Times* and *News of the World* from Fleet Street to Wapping to be printed by new computer technology, eliminating the old crafts of the printers and excluding the unions. Five and a half thousand workers were dismissed; there were mass secondary pickets and demonstrations at Wapping; these were illegal under the 1980 and 1982 Employment Acts, therefore the SOGAT union had all of its funds sequestrated. (Nineteen-year-old picket Michael Delaney was hit and killed by one of TNT's 32-tonne lorries; although the jury returned a verdict of unlawful killing, the DPP said that there was no case to answer. Eighteen police officers were prosecuted for excessive violence on the picket lines, but all of the charges were dropped after long delays in bringing the cases to court.)

The most powerful 'trade unions' now are the professional associations such as the Bar (barristers), Law Society (solicitors) and British Medical Association (doctors), which have a legal monopoly on their own professional services, regulate entry to their own professions, and often have the dual function of protecting and disciplining their own members. Concern about the latter aspect of their role, and the possible conflicts of interest which may arise from it, prompted the setting up in 1991 of an ombudsman for the legal services.

The 1997 Labour government chose not to reverse the 1980s' anti-union legislation; indeed, in 1998, Home Secretary Jack Straw refused to grant trade union recognition to the Prison Officers' Association and banned their pay protest meetings using the Public Order Act 1986 and Criminal Justice Act 1994.

The Labour government has, however, restored rights of trade union membership at GCHQ and allowed compensation for sacked GCHQ workers; and it has legislated for trade union recognition in large workplaces provided that 40 per cent of all eligible workers vote in agreement (Employment Relations Act 1999).

The superficial appearance of the shift in the role of the trade unions has been of an emphasis away from industrial action to an emphasis on provision of public services – what left-wing critics call 'credit card trade unionism'. However, trade unionists themselves would argue that the aim has always been provision of services (such as legal aid in tribunal cases and retirement homes for sick miners); and that they cannot provide efficient service unless they protect their members' terms and conditions of work and also protect investment into their own industries. Nevertheless, strikes have fallen from 2,600 per year in the 1970s to one tenth of that number in the 1990s. This can be described either favourably as a tribute to 'Thatcher's legacy' or critically as the result of 'a climate of fear and intimidation'.

---

2 What is meant by the following terms (all of which are related to the issue of trade unions):

a) block vote?

b) closed shop?

c) corporatism?

d) functional representation?

e) sequestration?

Mass media

The main theme of essays on the media is how far they 'shape public opinion or the political agenda' (see the *Essays* section at end of this chapter). Questions are also asked on the related themes of ownership, control and possible bias of the media. The main viewpoints on the topic are the liberal or pluralist views on the one hand, and the radical-critical, socialist or Marxist views on the other.

A distinction must be made between the press and broadcasting media; TV and radio are obliged by law to be non-party political, whereas the press are not. However, some radical left-wing critics (for example, Miliband and Tunstall) perceive a broader, and consistent, conservative bias in all mainstream media, including TV and radio. They attribute this largely to the concentrated and 'establishment' nature of media ownership and control. Given the high cost of launching a new mass medium (for example, it cost £20 million to launch *The Independent* in 1986), the owners tend to come from from a narrow economic and social background which is not inclined to radicalism.

"... *and now Murdoch's put in a bid for the Monopolies Commission* ..."

(The Guardian, 7 July 1987)

Ownership and influence

Media ownership is also becoming more, rather than less concentrated, with growing overlaps between different forms of media. Three conglomerates currently control 80 per cent of newspaper circulation: Rupert Murdoch's News International, Mirror Newspaper Group and United Newspapers. Murdoch also owns Sky TV and the Mirror Group has an interest in Central TV. This should be curbed by anti-monopoly regulation but, for example, when Rupert Murdoch took over Times Newspapers from Thomson in 1981, and *Today* in 1987, the government refused reference to the Monopoly and Mergers Commission, and approved the mergers. The high costs of the 'new technology revolution' in the media – direct printing by computer, satellite, cable and digital broadcasting – may raise costs and narrow ownership still further.

It is therefore unsurprising, according to socialist critics such as Tunstall, that the British press was for decades largely and overtly Conservative; one famous example being *The Sun*'s headline after the 1992 general election, 'It's the Sun wot won it' (for the Conservatives). Neil Kinnock agreed and Conservative treasurer, Lord MacAlpine, thanked the tabloids for their help.

Such newspapers only turned to the Labour Party when Labour adopted largely Conservative policies for the 1997 election. The most notable convert to the Labour cause was the Murdoch empire – perhaps partially persuaded by Labour's support for the 'predatory' press pricing of newspapers such as *The Times*, which the new Labour government pushed through Parliament in the Competition Act 1998. See the table below.

1997 General Election: Percentage of readers who voted for main parties

Dailies	Sun	Mirror	Star	Mail	Express	Telegraph	Guardian	Times	Independent	FT
C	30	14	17	49	49	57	8	42	16	48
Lab	52	72	66	29	29	20	67	28	47	29
Lib Dem	12	11	12	14	16	17	22	25	30	19

Sundays	NoW	Mirror	People	Mail	Express	Times	Telegraph	Observer	IoS
C	28	18	21	49	53	43	26	11	14
Lab	55	67	62	28	27	30	19	63	48
Lib Dem	11	12	11	15	14	21	17	22	32

Source: MORI

As the newspapers delivered their endorsements at the end of the campaign, Tony Blair won more for Labour – 11 out of 19 – than at any time in living memory.
Dailies for Blair: *The Sun, The Mirror, Daily Star, The Guardian* and *The Independent* (both suggesting tactical voting against Tories), *Financial Times*. Total sales: 8 million.
Sundays for Blair: *News of the World, Sunday Mirror, The People, The Observer* and *Independent on Sunday* (both again suggesting tactical voting). Sales: 9.6 million.
Dailies for Major: *Daily Mail, The Express, The Daily Telegraph.* Total sales: 4.5 million.
Sundays for Major: *The Express on Sunday, Mail on Sunday, The Sunday Times, The Sunday Telegraph.* Sales: 5.5 million.
Eurosceptic: *The Times* suggested voting for Eurosceptic candidates from six parties.

(The Times Guide to the House of Commons *(1997) Times Books)*

Influence on the political agenda

Labour has since been accused of being obsessed with its media image; talk of reliance on spin doctors, Millbank pagers and 'control freakery' became a running theme of satire and the Speaker of the Commons repeatedly had to ask the government to announce policy decisions first to Parliament and not to the media (for example, Child Support Agency reforms and the defence review in 1998). The Labour government has even been accused of allowing its policy agenda to be dictated by the press, notably on (not) joining the euro in the first wave. Increasingly, also, Labour spin doctors have become the message rather than simply the messengers: for example, in 1999 Chancellor

Gordon Brown's spin doctor Charlie Whelan was forced to resign over allegations that he was involved in the leak about Peter Mandelson's undeclared loan from Geoffrey Robinson which had forced their resignations from government a few days earlier.

As one academic writer has put it:

> 'Without ideological certainties to guide either the politicians or the voters, the mass media move to centre stage as the link between the two . . . It gives rise to the idea of the "public relations state" engaging in a more or less permanent publicity campaign for all its activities.'
>
> *(Ralph Negrine (1997) 'Politics and the media',* Politics Review, *Vol. 6, No. 4, April)*

Marxist critics such Miliband argue, however, that the party orientations of the media are irrelevant, since all are broadly supportive of the *status quo*. Pluralist views, conversely, stress the diversity of the media, from publications on the extreme left advocating orthodox communist ideology to those advancing neo-Nazi, racialist views on the extreme right.

Political controls on the media

Note (and point out explicitly in essays) that 'political' controls may include economic sanctions which are used for 'political' ends, for example, to influence or dictate the political or social content of the media.

Ownership
Lord Beaverbrook to the Royal Commission on the Press 1949: 'I run the Daily Express purely for the purpose of making propaganda, and for no other motive'. Also Stanley Baldwin's criticism of Lords Beaverbrook and Rothermere in 1931, that they sought 'power without responsibility, the prerogative of the harlot throughout the ages'.

Advertising
Over £70 million per year worth of advertising is sold in the two-minute break in ITV's late evening news. Advertising may prompt direct pressure on media content – for example, in 1980 W.D. & H.O. Wills withdrew £500,000 of advertising from *The Sunday Times* because of an anti-smoking article by the paper's health correspondent. Or it may prompt indirect pressure through the 'ratings' battle – for example, when *The Star* plummeted downmarket in 1987, Tesco withdrew its advertising, circulation fell, and the Express group changed its policy.

Censorship by distributors
W.H. Smith long refused to stock *Private Eye* and *Gay News* on the grounds that they were 'abhorrent, though lawful'.

Direct censorship by government
For example: Northern Ireland, Falklands, Gulf War – curbs on news reports, pictures, MoD disinformation, etc.

Government pressure
For example, through the penalty imposed on the BBC licence fee in 1979 after BBC interviews with the IRA and INLA; through threat of grant cuts, for example, by Eden over BBC coverage of Suez. Also the postponing of *Real Lives* by BBC in 1985 after letter from Home Secretary Leon Brittan; criticism of BBC by Norman Tebbit over

coverage of Libya in 1986; strong government pressure and alleged manipulation of information over Thames TV's *Death on the Rock* (about shooting of unarmed IRA members in Gibraltar). Such pressure is not new, nor confined to one party: for example, Harold Wilson persuaded the BBC not to show *Steptoe and Son* on the night of the 1964 election in case it kept Labour voters at home. In 1999 Prime Minister Tony Blair criticised the national media for 'trivialising' news coverage and said that he would target his messages more directly at the regional and local press in future.

Allegedly 'political' appointments

For example, BBC chairman Marmaduke Hussey and director general Michael Checkland; Lord Chalfont, deputy chairman of IBA ('The most flagrant example yet of the politicisation of government appointments', said Lord Bonham Carter, formerly on BBC board of governors); Lord Rees-Mogg, chairman of Broadcasting Standards Council set up in 1990; Greg Dyke as BBC chairman in 1999.

Legal constraints

▶ Broadcasting laws allow the Home Secretary complete control over all broadcasting content; thus, for example, Home Office curbs in 1988 on direct reporting of Irish activists, criticised particularly because it covered legal political parties such as Sinn Fein, was challenged in the courts by them, as well as by the National Union of Journalists, on the grounds that it prevented the broadcasting media from upholding their legal obligation of balance and impartiality. The ban was finally lifted in 1995.

▶ Any public or private body or person may seek an injunction in the courts prohibiting media publication under the wider laws listed below.

▶ Official Secrets Act (under which police raided BBC Scotland in 1987 to seize tapes on the *Secret Society* programme about Zircon project; MI5 vet some broadcasting staff and have agents permanently employed within the national broadcasting companies)

▶ Prevention of Terrorism Act (renewed annually)

▶ Police and Criminal Evidence Act 1984 (under which journalists have been obliged to hand over unpublished photographs for example, of the Wapping disturbances and riots)

▶ Police Act 1997: grants the police new powers of unauthorised entry into private premises, bugging and seizure of evidence

▶ The new privacy law introduced under the UK Bill of Rights will constrain public, but not private, authorities, for example, the BBC but not the press. Thus, for example, the role of the 'paparazzi' (press rat-pack) in the death of Diana, Princess of Wales, and the press hounding of other public figures will not necessarily be addressed

▶ Libel laws

▶ Contempt of Court Act 1981

▶ Obscenity laws

▶ Race Relations Acts

▶ Laws of sedition, incitement to disaffection and treason, etc.

Self-censorship

A combination of all of the above has generated much self-censorship, especially by broadcasters: for example:

▶ 1926 General Strike (when BBC head Lord Reith said, 'Since the BBC is a national institution and since the government in this crisis is acting for the people . . . the

BBC is for the government in the crisis too . . . They know they can trust us not to be really impartial')

▶ 1936 abdication crisis

▶ 1956 Suez affair

▶ 1982 Falklands conflict

▶ 1991 Gulf war

▶ 1963 Profumo affair

▶ cancellation of E.P. Thompson's 1981 anti-nuclear Dimbleby lecture

▶ the BBC banning for 20 years the anti-nuclear film *The War Game* as 'too horrific, especially for viewers of limited intelligence'

▶ over thirty programmes on Northern Ireland dropped since 1969

▶ *The Untouchables*, about links between senior police and a notorious gangster, banned by the BBC and eventually shown by Granada

▶ BBC postponing and vetting of *Secret Society* series in 1987

▶ former minister John Biffen's description, in BBC interview Feb. 1989, of No. 10 press secretary Bernard Ingham as 'merely the sewer, not the sewerage' – cut out of broadcast by senior editor

▶ many plays about sensitive topics postponed, cut or banned, for example, *Tumbledown* (Falklands), *Mates* (teenage homosexuality), *Leftover People* (unemployment)

▶ references on the BBC to (1998) Labour minister Peter Mandelson's alleged homosexuality

▶ a BBC Omnibus programme on media censorship, censored to exclude references to previous censorship.

Radical critics therefore cite Ernest Bevin's comment in a Cabinet debate about media censorship decades ago: 'Why bother to muzzle sheep?'

The lobby system

The lobby system, whereby political journalists meet politicians and civil servants at Westminster for daily 'unattributable briefings', has been criticised, for example by Hennessy for its secretiveness, mutual dependency and scope for news manipulation and misinformation (for example, budget leaks). However, it has become more open since 1997.

The Press Complaints Commission

The Press Complaints Commission which replaced the Press Council in 1990 as a voluntary self-regulating body investigates complaints of bias, cheque-book journalism, invasion of privacy, etc., and may censure newspapers. Critics fear that it may be a watchdog without teeth, and that statutory control of the press may be necessary.

ESSAYS

1 *Theme:* **Public opinion**

Q? Can the refusal of an elected assembly to reintroduce capital punishment, when the majority of the electorate appear to favour such a measure, be reconciled with democratic principles?

(Oxford and Cambridge, July 1984, Paper 1)

A✓ Guidance on essay plan

Introduction should go straight to the key concept of 'democratic principles' – open to diverse interpretations: direct 'people-power' or indirect representation, of people's views or interests – which may not coincide; individual v. minority v. majority v. national views or interests; different interpretations of 'representative' and 'responsible' government.

The next section should be specific and empirical: seek out (in your local library) and give concrete opinion poll figures on the issue of capital punishment; and also give precise details and figures on the periodic debates and votes on the issue in the Commons over the past ten years (see *Hansard*).

Case for elected assembly going against opinion poll findings
Note: Put this case first only if you are going to disagree with it.

a) Opinion poll findings may be wrong, because of poor sampling, (mis)leading wording, etc.

b) If assembly is indeed going against public opinion – case for, in general terms (i.e. regardless of issue):

▶ Public opinion may be ill-informed, misinformed, emotional, irrational or fickle.

▶ MPs are not meant to be delegates of voters, but 'responsible' representatives using their own judgement in the national interest (Burkean view).

▶ Especially on moral issues such as capital punishment, MPs are expected and allowed to obey their own consciences – hence private members' bills and free votes.

▶ Liberal democracy stresses the views and rights of individuals and minorities, not just 'tyranny of the majority'.

c) Case for refusal to reintroduce capital punishment, in specific terms:

▶ To condemn killing, and punish it by killing, is illogical; and, for Christians and others, immoral.

▶ 'Deterrence' argument is unsupported by all available statistics in every country where capital punishment has been abolished or reintroduced (UN studies, etc.). Moreover, since most homicides are unpremeditated family/domestic/ 'passionate' crimes, no scope for deterrence or repetition. Many others committed by mentally sick and deranged; and one-third of all those who murder then commit suicide, so again death seems no deterrence.

▶ Selective capital punishment – for example, for the murder of police officers – produced unworkable anomalies under the old 1957 Homicide Act (for example, if a robber missed a policeman and shot a passer-by).

▶ For the tiny category of 'terrorist' murders, legal definition of terms would be an acute problem; selective capital punishment would punish the motive rather than the act itself, and would give 'terrorists' the special political status which they have long demanded; state execution would make martyrs of them and may provoke widespread sympathetic and/or violent responses.

▶ Juries may be unwilling to convict – especially on majority rather than unanimous verdicts – if death sentence was likely.

▶ Judicial errors – for example, the hangings of Timothy Evans, James Hanratty, Walter Rowland, Craig and Bentley – cannot be remedied.

Case against elected assembly going against opinion poll findings
Note: Put this case last only if you are going to agree with it:

---

3 Write your own 'case against', focusing on the central issue of 'democratic principles'; ensure that it is reasoned, well-evidenced, analytical and unemotional.

On arguments for capital punishment, one valuable source is the *Hansard* record of debates on the issue in the House of Commons. Note that you may offer a 'mixed' conclusion, i.e. that an elected assembly may be right to go against majority opinion, though you personally advocate capital punishment; or vice-versa.

Always put your own case(s) last.

Q? Discuss the role of opinion polls in British politics.

(JMB, June 1984, Paper 1)

A✓ Examiners' comments
'Here weaker candidates tended to describe the detailed mechanics of sampling and failed to discuss the role of public opinion polls. Many mentioned their influence upon the Prime Minister's choice of election date. The best considered the influence of opinion polls upon voting behaviour, mentioned calls for banning publication in the days immediately before elections and were aware of the use of private polls by political parties. Some even brought in their use by pressure groups.'

Consider the table on page 208 on the polls during the 1997 general election campaign.

2 *Theme*: Pressure groups

Q? Do pressure groups undermine or support democratic government?

(London, June 1998, Paper 1)

---

4 Find specific and topical examples for each of the points made in the Notes for Guidance below.

A✓ Notes for guidance

Arguments that pressure groups 'support democratic government':
▶ They enhance pluralism: competing centres of power, representation and choice. Especially true where pro- and anti- groups co-exist; all shades of opinion represented.
▶ They 'fill the gaps' in the party system, for example, by promoting causes which cut across party lines, especially on local or 'moral' issues such as abortion, capital punishment, etc.
▶ They provide channels of collective influence and power for the public where individual action (including voting) may be relatively weak or ineffectual.
▶ They provide channels of direct participation for the public, going beyond mere indirect representation through Parliament.

1997 Election: The campaign polls

Fieldwork dates	Agency	Publication date	Sample size	C	Lab	LD	Other	Lead	Swing 92–97
19–21 Mar	Gallup (S Telegraph*)	23 Mar	985	29	54.5	10.5	6	−25.5	−16.75
20–24 Mar	Harris (Independent)	28 Mar	1,096	30	54	11	6	−24	−16.0
21–24 Mar	MORI (Times)	27 Mar	1,932	29	50	14	7	−21	−14.5
27–31 Mar	Harris (Independent)	4 Apr	1,091	28	52	14	6	−24	−16.0
26 Mar–2 Apr	Gallup (D Telegraph*)	4 Apr	1,126	31	52	11	6	−21	−14.5
29–31 Mar	ICM (Guardian*)	2 Apr	1,200	32	46	17	5	−14	−11.0
1 Apr	MORI (Times)	3 Apr	1,118	28	55	11	6	−27	−17.5
1–3 Apr	Gallup (C4 News*)	9 Apr	1,035	30	54	11	5	−24	−16.0
2–3 Apr	MORI (Ind on S/S Mirror+)	6 Apr	1,069	30	55	9	6	−25	−16.5
2–4 Apr	ICM (Observer*+)	6 Apr	1,793	33	48	14	5	−15	−11.5
3 Apr	NOP (S Times)	6 Apr	1,575	28	52	12	8	−24	−16.0
4 Apr	NOP (Reuters)	7 Apr	1,088	30	51	11	8	−21	−14.5
4–6 Apr	Gallup (D Telegraph*)	7 Apr	1,026	32	53	10	5	−21	−14.5
4–7 Apr	Harris (Independent)	11 Apr	1,138	28	52	14	6	−24	−16.0
6–7 Apr	ICM (Guardian*)	9 Apr	1,022	34	46	15	5	−12	−10
7–9 Apr	Gallup (D Telegraph*)	10 Apr	1,019	30	53	11	6	−23	−15.5
8 Apr	MORI (Times)	10 Apr	1,114	34	49	12	5	−15	−11.5
9–11 Apr	CM (Observer*+)	13 Apr	1,002	32	48	15	5	−16	−12.0
9–12 Apr	Gallup (S Telegraph*)	13 Apr	1,043	33	49	12	5	−16	−12.0
11 Apr	NOP (S Times)	13 Apr	1,595	28	48	17	7	−20	−14.0
11–14 Apr	MOORI (Eve Standard)	15 Apr	1,778	29	50	15	6	−21	−14.5
11–14 Apr	Harris (Independent)	18 Apr	1,136	31	49	13	6	−18	−13.0
12–15 Apr	Gallup (D Telegraph*)	16 Apr	1,025	30	51	12	7	−21	−14.5
13–14 Apr	ICM (Guardian*)	16 Apr	1,007	31	45	19	5	−14	−11.0
15 Apr	MORI (Times)	17 Apr	1,137	32	49	13	6	−17	−12.5
15–18 Apr	Gallup (D Telegraph*)	19 Apr	1,018	32	50	13	5	−18	−13.0
16–18 Apr	ICM (Observer*+)	20 Apr	1,000	32	47	16	5	−15	−11.5
18 Apr	NOP (S Times)	20 Apr	1,595	31	45	17	7	−14	−11.0
17–21 Apr	Harris (Independent)	25 Apr	1,177	30	48	15	7	−18	−13.0
18–21 Apr	Gallup (D Telegraph*)	22 Apr	1,294	32	48	12	8	−16	−12.0
18–22 Apr	Gallup (C4 News*)	23 Apr	1,120	31	50	13	6	−19	−13.5
20–21 Apr	ICM (Guardian*)	23 Apr	1,004	37	42	14	6	−5	−6.5
22 Apr	MORI (Times)	24 Apr	1,133	27	48	17	8	−21	−14.5
21–23 Apr	Gallup (D Telegraph*)	24 Apr	1,069	30	50	12	8	−20	−14.0
23–24 Apr	MORI (Ind on S/S Mirror+)	7 Apr 9	41	29	53	12	6	−24	−16.0
23–25 Apr	Gallup (D Telegraph*)	26 Apr	1,012	32	48	14	6	−16	−12.0
23–25 Apr	ICM (Observer*+)	27 Apr	1,000	32	47	16	5	−15	−11.5
25 Apr	NOP (S Times)	27 Apr	1,588	29	47	16	9	−18	−13.0
24–28 Apr	Gallup (C4 News*)	29 Apr	1,466	31	49	14	6	−18	−13.0
25–27 Apr	Gallup (D Telegraph*)	28 Apr	1,028	30	49	14	6	−19	−13.5
27–29 Apr	Harris (Independent)	1 May	1,154	31	48	15	6	−17	−12.5
28–29 Apr	Gallup (D Telegraph*)	30 Apr	1,038	31	51	13	6	−20	−14.0
29 Apr	NOP (Reuters)	30 Apr	1,093	28	50	14	8	−22	−15.0
29–30	Apr MORI (Times)	1 May	2,304	28	48	16	8	−20	−14.0
29–30	Apr ICM (Guardian*)	1 May	1,555	33	43	18	6	−10	−9.0
30 Apr	Gallup (D Telegraph*)	1 May	1,849	33	47	14	6	−14	−11.0
30 Apr	MORI (E Standard+*)	1 May	1,501	29	47	19	5	−18	−13.0
1 May	NOP (ITN@)	1 May	15,761	30	46	18	6	−16	−12.0
1 May	NOP (BBC@)	1 May	17,073	29	47	18	6	−18	−13.0
1 May	**Election result**			**31.4**	**44.4**	**17.2**	**7**	**−13**	**−10.5**

*Telephone survey   +Panel survey   @Exit poll

(The Times Guide to the House of Commons *(1997)* Times Books)

▶ They provide channels of communication between government and electorate.

▶ They seek to represent deprived or inarticulate sections of society (for example, Help the Aged, Child Poverty Action Group).

▶ Protective groups especially are usually internally democratic, in that members elect leaders.

▶ Trade unions especially are representative of large numbers of people (nine million); and their tactics of direct action may be seen as mass, direct democracy or 'people-power'.

▶ Pressure groups provide information, education and expertise for public, Parliament and government; therefore are much consulted by MPs and executive; and may help to enhance open government by exposing events, information and issues.

▶ They provide a check on 'parliamentary sovereignty' and 'elective dictatorship', especially where the electoral system is unrepresentative and parliamentary opposition is weak; hence checks and balances in liberal democracy.

▶ They may promote continuity of policy between successive governments.

▶ They may provide public services, for example, legal aid and advice.

Arguments that pressure groups 'undermine democratic government':
▶ They may by-pass or usurp the elected representatives in Parliament and government; MPs may be reduced to 'lobby-fodder'. (Home Secretary Douglas Hurd in 1986 likened them to sea-serpents, strangling ministers in their coils and distorting the constitutional relationship between government and electorate.)

▶ Their lobbying tactics may amount to near bribery and corruption of MPs.

▶ They may be small, sectional or unrepresentative but influential or powerful, at the expense of majority or 'national' views or interests. Thus Lord Hailsham in his 1983 Hamlyn Lecture described single-purpose pressure groups as 'enemies of liberty'.

▶ They may have a 'closed', excessively close and secretive relationship with the executive, excluding other views and interests; hence 'the embryo of a corporate state' (Benn).

▶ Their collective power may undermine individual rights and interests, contrary to 'liberal democratic' principles.

▶ Promotional groups especially may be internally undemocratic – no election of leaders by members, leadership out of touch with membership, etc. ('iron law of oligarchy'); or they may claim to speak on behalf of others, but without any consultation or mandate to do so, etc.

▶ Groups with constitutional aims may be internally dominated by people who seek to subvert liberal democracy itself.

▶ Their methods may be illegal and/or coercive. (But note that many pressure groups would defend such tactics in theory and practice – see Chapter 9 and next essay question.)

Q? How might civil disobedience as a tactic used by pressure groups be justified within a parliamentary democracy? Discuss, with examples, the effectiveness of such tactics.

(JMB, June 1986, Paper 2)

A✓ Examiners' comments

'This question was also very popular and generally well done, often also with plenty of examples. Some candidates – generally the weaker ones – had difficulty coping with "parliamentary democracy"; others, including those who produced some quite good answers, dealt at length with whether civil disobedience was justifiable, ignoring or de-emphasising "as a tactic used by pressure groups". The examples were predictable although many candidates failed to mention examples such as Wapping.'

Note: See Chapter 9 for discussion of various forms of deliberate law-breaking, including peaceful civil disobedience and political violence.

3 *Theme:* Trade unions

Q? The titles below are from the London Board 1981–96; note the changing theme of the questions, from 'the power of the unions' to 'government reform of the unions' and their 'changing role'.

a) Are there any limits to the political power of trade unions?

(London, June 1981, Paper 2)

b) Comment on the view that the political power of the trade unions is rather less than is commonly supposed.

(London, June 1982, Paper 2)

c) What factors shaped the influence of the trade unions on governments between 1974 and 1984?

(London, June 1984, Paper 2)

d) (i) What steps have Conservative governments taken since 1979 to alter the legal position of trade unions?
   (ii) Assess their impact on the unions.

(London, Jan. 1991, Paper 2)

e) Discuss the changing political influence of the trade unions since 1964.

(London, Jan. 1994, Paper 2)

f) Discuss the changing role of the trade unions since 1979.

(London, Jan. 1996, Paper 2)

Q? Is it more important that individuals should be protected by trade unions or from trade unions?

(Oxford, Summer 1985, Paper 0)

A✓ **Notes for guidance**

Case for protection of individuals by trade unions:

▶ Weakness of individual workers versus employers.

▶ Historical role of unions in advancing working people's conditions of work, health, safety, pay, living standards and pensions.

▶ 'Representative' nature of unions: unlike most promotional groups, members elect leaders, who are usually 'delegates' rather than mere 'representatives'; and together they represent a larger population sector than any other pressure groups (9 million).

▶ Direct action by trade unions, for example, strikes, may be seen as mass, direct 'people-power'.

▶ Visible union or workers' power, for example, strikes, is a negative, uncertain and often self-destructive weapon of last resort, involving loss of pay and job security; it may thus be an indication of relative weakness, i.e. lack of alternative sanctions and power.

▶ Studies, for example, by the Glasgow University Media Group suggest that media coverage of unions and industrial action is consistently biased and hostile. For example, many forms of industrial dispute, presented as strikes, are in fact 'lock-outs' by management (for example, the 1998 dockers' 'strike' was, in fact, a mass dismissal and lock-out); 95 per cent of all strikes are 'wildcat' or unofficial, but are portrayed as if 'bully-boy' union leaders are calling out unwilling members; employers' figures on the 'costs' of strikes are presented uncritically, omitting company 'savings' in wages, raw materials, fuel, etc.

▶ Thus public hostility to unions and industrial action is greater, the less direct experience people have of them (and people also tend to say 'the unions are too powerful', but 'my union is not strong enough on my behalf').

▶ Though workers' negative or disruptive power may be significant and inconvenient, their power may be small if measured in terms of results – closures, unemployment, redundancies, growing income inequalities, balance of decision-making power in workplace between workers and employers.

▶ Contrary to popular myth, Britain was always well down the international league table on strike figures, even in the 1960s and 1970s when trade union power was perceived to be at its height.

---

5 Write the 'case for protection of individuals from trade unions'. Ensure that it is reasoned and well-evidenced.

---

4 *Theme:* **Media**

Q? Consider the essay titles and examiners' comments below.

a) 'There is no equality of access to the media.' Discuss the impact of this on British politics.

(London, Jan. 1998, Paper 2)

b) Analyse the role of the press in influencing political attitudes.

(London, Jan. 1997, Paper 2)

c) 'The mass media shape public opinion on politics.' Discuss.

(London, June 1988, Paper 2)

A✓   **Examiners' comments on question (c)**

'Candidates needed to address the concept of public opinion: does it exist, and how does one measure it? This is fraught with difficulties but high marks were awarded for pointing out some of the problems and for trying to assess accurately the role of the media in relation to public opinion. Too many candidates were determined to discuss media bias (a different question) and committed the fallacy of thinking that if bias was proven then the role of the media in shaping public opinion is also proven. One good conclusion offered by a candidate read as follows:

"However, the media is only one of several inputs that determine political opinion. Class, race, religion and where you live and work all help to shape your political opinions . . . a working class voter in the north is likely to have a Labour view of politics and if his friends and family share the same opinion, the media is unlikely to change it."'

Q?   **The Media and Democracy**

'In order to create profits, media organisations compete for their audiences with the consequent pursuit of the lowest common denominator in public taste. In the case of the tabloids, this means the relegation of hard news to inside pages and the promotion to the front page of trivial stories such as sex scandals, royal family gossip and the comings and goings of soap opera stars.

On television, the same tendency has been apparent with the reduction of current affairs programmes, their demotion from peak viewing times and the dilution of news programmes with more human interest stories. **As a result of this tendency it can be argued that the media's role of educating the nation in a pluralist democracy is being diminished.'**

Source: adapted from BILL JONES, Politics UK (Philip Allan)

Assess the validity of the conclusion in the final sentence above. Apart from the mass media, what other sources provide information about politics for citizens? How important are such sources in influencing public opinion?

(AEB, Summer 1997, Paper 1)

----

6   Incorporate the points below (which are in no particular order) into an ordered answer to the title above.

▶ Definitions of 'influence' and 'power'

▶ Definition of 'political agenda': the issues that people think about and the priorities they give to them

▶ This in turn influences public opinion and the views of the policy-makers. Reciprocal?

▶ The media simply reflect public concerns and interests – for example, *Sunday Sport*, page 3, royals . . . increase circulation. Begs question, how do people develop wants? Socialisation . . .

▶ Diverse roles of media from diverse viewpoints: information, education, communication, entertainment, persuasion, propaganda, social control . . .

▶ Role of advertising: information, persuasion, creating awareness of products and services, creation of wants . . .

▶ Political agenda: derives from pressure and interest groups, politicians and parties, public events, and from what is defined as 'newsworthy' . . ., for example, topic of the moment: child abuse, prison riots, genetic experimentation . . .

Accessible stories, for example, London v. north.

Available pictures

▶ Use of big news agencies, for example, UPI → uniformity of content

▶ Media also influence political institutions and processes – for example, in elections they do not simply cover the campaign, they are the campaign; events and speeches staged and tailored to suit media convenience and accessibility

▶ 20 million watch TV news each day

▶ Jeremy Isaacs, 'Media in the Market Place' (Henry Heatherington Lecture, Dec. 1987) in *New Socialist*, March/April 1988 (update these statistics):

From which sources do you get the info you need about the world?

	1981	1986
TV	53	65
Newspapers	34	23
Radio	11	10

▶ 'Agenda-setting' not conscious conspiracy – unconscious consensual assumptions, hidden agenda, creation of consensus, blurring of news and comment, for example, strikes 'bad' . . .

▶ Negative images: Arthur Scargill, Peter Mandelson, William Hague, Glen Hoddle . . .

▶ Stereotypes, for example, women, muggers, football hooligans . . .

▶ Political content/social engineering of soap operas – constant topic of public conversation

▶ Events are significant part of political agenda whether media cover them or not, for example, riots, N. Ireland

▶ *Sunday Times* 'Insight' team (on deforming drug Thalidomide, Crossman diaries) – disbanded under Murdoch

▶ Sociological approaches: media creation of 'folk devils and moral panics' (Cohen), and 'deviancy amplification': for example, hippies, drugs, football hooligans, lager louts . . .

▶ Direction of public political awareness

▶ Liberal view – pluralist media; 'Fourth Estate'.

New technology will enhance range, choice and pluralism.

Many readers do not recognise political bias in media, for example, 15 per cent of *Sun* readers in mid-1990s thought it was a Labour paper.

Jeremy Isaacs criticises view of people as passive consumers: 'Human beings are not blotting paper who simply sop up the last impression that is left on them . . .' (in *New Socialist*).

▶ Counter: Socialists point to political imbalance of press, unparalleled in western world.

▶ Not the issue for Marxists – all bourgeois agents, servants of ruling class, opium of the people.

▶ Other influences on public opinion: family, friends, work, class, education, age, sex, religion, race, region, past experience . . .

(The Sun, 12 January 1999)

7 Write at least one of the following essays. Always write a brief plan first.

a) Does it matter that citizens are increasingly apathetic about politics?

(Oxford and Cambridge, June 1997, Paper 1)

b) What factors determine the success or failure of British pressure groups?

(Oxford and Cambridge, June 1997, Paper 1)

c) 'The problem in Britain today is not that pressure groups are too powerful but that they have too little say in government.' Discuss.

(Oxford, June 1985, Paper 1)

d) What factors have encouraged the development of pressure group activities on the EU level?

(Cambridge, June 1989, Paper 1)

e) Discuss recent changes in the links between trade unions and the Labour Party.

(London, Jan. 1997, Paper 2)

f) Is it the function of the media to reflect public opinion or to form it?

(Oxford and Cambridge, July 1984, Paper 0)

GUIDE TO EXERCISES

Page 201

2 a) Block vote: method of union voting, for example, at Labour conferences, where a majority union vote for an option results in 100 per cent of that union's votes counting towards that option. Being phased out because of unpopularity.

b) Closed shop: where an individual must belong to the appropriate union or association in order to work at a particular trade or profession. Largely prohibited by 1980s' legislation.

c) Corporatism: tripartite involvement and consultation of workers' and employers' groups with state in economic policy-making. A feature of the era of 'consensus politics'; 'Thatcherism' was anti-corporatist.

d) Functional representation: consultation and/or decision-making through occupational or industrial groups (rather than through, for example, parties). Advocated for the second chamber by Winston Churchill in 1930s.

e) Sequestration: freezing and/or seizure of some or all of a union's assets by the courts, as penalty for contempt of court (introduced in 1984 as alternative to imprisoning union leaders and applied to, for example, NUM and SOGAT).

REFERENCES

Cohen, S. (1971) *Images of Deviance*, Penguin

Glasgow University Media Group (1976) *Bad News*, Routledge and Kegan Paul (also *More Bad News* and *Really Bad News*)

Hennessy, P. (1988) in *The Independent*, 8 February

Miliband, R. (1969) *The State in Capitalist Society*, Quartet

Tunstall, J. (1983) *The Media in Britain*, Constable

11 The European Union

KEY ISSUES

▶ The question of sovereignty

▶ Role and significance of the institutions of the EU

▶ Political parties' views – and divisions – on the EU

▶ Key events in the development of the EU

▶ Future development of the EU

TOPIC NOTES

Key facts and concepts

Six countries formed the (then) *European Economic Community (EEC)* when the Treaty of Rome was signed in 1957: France, Germany, Italy, Luxembourg, the Netherlands and Belgium. Britain, Denmark and Ireland joined on 1 January 1973; Greece joined in 1981; then Spain and Portugal (1986); and most recently Finland, Sweden and Austria (1995). Norway had also planned to join in 1995 but its voters rejected membership in a referendum. There are now 15 member countries (360 million people) and 12 more states have formally applied for membership.

The creation of the EEC was intended to establish a common market, economic and monetary union and an ever closer union among the peoples of Europe. Thus the visions of a single market and a federal Europe date from the 1950s, not the 1980s as is sometimes suggested today. They were inspired by a desire for lasting peace and security after two world wars; awareness of growing economic and social interdependence and a desire for greater international co-operation between European countries; the advantages of large-scale markets; greater world influence; and the wish to challenge the blocs of the USA and the former USSR. The main economic principle enshrined in the Treaty of Rome was free trade – the removal of barriers and the establishment of common tariffs and policies (especially in agriculture, fishing, coal and steel) across Europe. The 1960s also saw the creation of the controversial Common Agricultural Policy (CAP) which by 1999 cost £30 billion per year.

In 1967 the EEC merged with the European Coal and Steel Community and the European Atomic Energy Community to become the *European Community (EC)*. When the Maastricht Treaty came into effect in 1993 this became the *European Union (EU)*. The changing labels are clearly illustrative of the broadening and increasingly integrated embrace of the EU.

The EU is a **supranational** institution, i.e. not just an international fraternity but a sovereign power over member states with a body of law that takes precedence over national law.

Britain initially refused to join for a number of reasons: a sense of superiority and national pride after victory in war; a hankering after lost imperial status; Britain's international status and links with the USA and Commonwealth; a sense of political and geographical difference – an island mentality; xenophobia (and mistrust especially of Germany and France); for the right wing of the Conservative Party especially, fear of loss of sovereignty and national identity; and for the left wing of the Labour Party, dislike of the free market capitalist nature of the EEC. By the 1960s it was clear that the EEC was an established success and Britain applied to join but was twice vetoed by France's President, Charles de Gaulle. Britain eventually joined in 1973, under Ted Heath's Conservative government. When the Labour Party came to power in 1974 they were still very divided on the issue, so Harold Wilson held the first ever national referendum in 1975 on the question of staying in the EC. He lifted collective responsibility and allowed his Cabinet ministers (such as Tony Benn) publicly to divide on the issue. Two-thirds of the country voted to stay in Europe, thus legitimising Wilson's own support for the EC. Elections to the European Parliament were first held in 1979.

The issue of sovereignty

The question of sovereignty is multi-dimensional.

Political sovereignty

This has been the main issue since 1973. It has two dimensions.

▶ *Parliamentary sovereignty* – the linchpin of the British constitution since the English Civil War in the mid-seventeenth century – has been effectively negated by the primacy of EU laws and treaties. Over 60 per cent of UK legislation now originates from the EU. No continental country has (or had) parliamentary sovereignty because they all have written constitutions and supreme courts, therefore this issue matters more to the UK. However, observers might be forgiven for being sceptical about *governments'* expressed concerns about it, since British governments have done more than Europe ever has to undermine Parliament's real power, from within.

▶ Governments and voters are generally more concerned about the loss of *national sovereignty*, i.e. their ability to pursue their own policies without external interference.

Economic sovereignty

Economic sovereignty has become an important issue with the creation of the single European currency in 1999. However, this has actually long been undermined by foreign ownership and investment from Europe and elsewhere and by Britain's dependence especially on the health of the American economy – apparently with little hostility from the traditional right-wing Eurosceptics. Moreover, the Labour government's granting to

1952

First meeting of the Common Assembly of the European Coal and Steel Community (ECSC) comprising six countries: Belgium, France, West Germany, Italy, Luxembourg and the Netherlands. Formed to make war between France and Germany not only 'unthinkable but materially impossible'. The first president of the ECSC's High Authority was Jean Monnet.

1957

Treaty of Rome establishes the European Economic Community (EEC). Konrad Adenauer, German chancellor 1949-63, was an enthusiastic supporter of European construction.

1967

The ECSC, EEC and European Atomic Energy Community (Euratom) formally amalgamated into the European Community (EC).

1968

Customs union erects a common external tariff.

1973

Britain, Republic of Ireland and Denmark join the EC. British Prime Minister Ted Heath played a pivotal role in Britain's decision to join.

1981

British Prime Minister Margaret Thatcher fought a successful campaign for a rebate of the UK's high budget contributions. She also fuelled anti-EC feelings at home and fears of a single European currency despite the economic benefits it promised to bring.

1987

The Single European Act, promoted by Commission president Jacques Delors, established the four freedoms: by the end of 1992 an internal market to be established as 'an area without frontiers in which the free movement of goods and persons, services and capital is ensured.'

1991 Maastricht

The most important single development in the history of the community to date. The Maastricht Treaty was designed to create 'an ever closer union among the peoples of Europe.' It set out a detailed, and controversial, timetable for economic and monetary union, at the latest by 1999, and provided for the development for foreign and defence policies.

British Prime Minister John Major toned down the anti-European rhetoric when he replaced Margaret Thatcher. Britain opted out of the monetary union timetable and the protocol known as the Social Chapter.

1995

Austria, Finland and Sweden finally accede to membership of the EU, but Norway says 'no' in a referendum, to the delight of its fishermen and farmers and the dismay of the capital, Oslo.

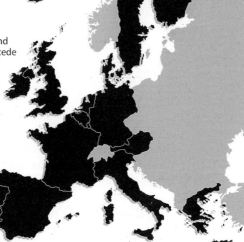

(adapted from The Guardian, *27 March 1999)*

▲ *Britain and the history of the EU*

the Bank of England of independent control of interest rates (immediately after the 1997 general election) was a willing surrender of a key economic power which brought Britain into line with one of the conditions for joining the euro.

A more positive view (Moravcsik) argues that national governments benefit from EU membership, pooling sovereignty to achieve policy goals which would be unattainable alone; and that EU decision-making helps to strengthen national governments by reducing the impact of domestic constraints.

The institutions of the EU

The Council of Ministers

The Council is the ultimate policy-making body, and comprises the Foreign Ministers of each member state, with other ministers in topic sub-committees when appropriate. The preparation of such policy decisions is largely undertaken by civil servants of the member states and of the Commission (see below) which, according to critics such as Tony Benn, gives civil servants real and substantial policy-making power.

Before 1986 Council voting had to be unanimous, i.e. any one country could effectively veto any policy, but the Single European Act 1986 introduced *Qualified Majority Voting (QMV)*, i.e. majority voting where each member state is assigned a weighting according to its size: thus Britain, France and Germany have ten votes each while Luxembourg at the other extreme has two. Sixty-two of the total 87 votes are needed to secure a majority. This has meant a further loss of power by individual countries to Europe. For example, in 1993 Britain was overruled on the principle of a 48-hour working week. In May 1996 British Prime Minister John Major launched a policy of non-co-operation within the EU in protest against the world-wide ban on the sale of British beef (imposed because of continuing fears about the effect on human health of BSE); but the impact of Britain's non-co-operation was limited, mainly because QMV meant that many EU decisions did not require Britain's agreement. This further illustrated the supranational nature of the EU and the restricted power of member states.

The President of the Council is provided by a different country in rotation every six months (for example, Britain's Robin Cook held the Presidency for the first half of 1998).

The European Commission

The Commission is sometimes described as the civil service of the EU. It is actually both more and less than a civil service. It is more because it has real legislative and executive powers. It is less because it does not directly administer policy decisions (usually the member states do that). It is based in Brussels and comprises 20 commissioners – two each from some of the larger countries such as Britain (Neil Kinnock and Chris Patten from July 1999) and one from each of the other countries. They are appointed by their respective governments for five-year renewable terms, and are usually former politicians, diplomats or senior civil servants. They are required to be independent of their national governments and to be European-oriented. Each Commissioner is responsible for a certain EU policy area (for example, Kinnock was responsible for transport). They present policy proposals to the Council of Ministers, have significant powers of delegated legislation – each year the Commission passes 4,000–5,000 pieces of legislation – they carry out decisions made, administer most of the Union's budget and investigate breaches of the rules – thus they can impose fines on offenders and take member states to the European Court of Justice (see page 223). For example, Sir Leon Brittan investigated the British government's payment of sweeteners to induce British Aerospace to buy the Rover Group in 1986, and the European Court of Justice obliged repayment of the £48m.

Each Commissioner has a *cabinet* – a small team of personal advisers and officials appointed by the Commissioners themselves, which allows scope for dubious favouritism.

The Commission has a civil service of about 17,000. Although it is frequently criticised for being overly bureaucratic, it is remarkably small and generally efficient by comparison with the bureaucracy of some member states (for example, Britain's Ministry of Defence alone has 116,000 civil servants).

However, in 1999 the Commission's officials were at the centre of a massive scandal about fraud, corruption, nepotism and cronyism, in which three or four of the Commissioners – notably France's Edith Cresson – were also implicated. In January of that year the EU Parliament came close to sacking all 20 Commissioners (because it lacked the power to dismiss individuals). Following the publication of a highly critical independent report in March which concluded, 'It is difficult to find anyone who has even the slightest sense of responsibility', all 20 Commissioners resigned – an unprecedented crisis in the history of the EU. (Luxembourg) President Jacques Santer was replaced by (Italian) Romano Prodi, a decision made at a summit of the European Council.

Jacques Santer: was he really so bad?

Some men will stop at nothing to hang on to their jobs, says Le Canard Enchaîné. Despite the damning report accusing his commission of gross mismanagement, Jacques Santer, the future 'ex-president' of the European Commission, was trying, up to the last minute, to find some way – any way – of avoiding the need to resign. He telephoned both the French PM, Lionel Jospin, and the French President, Jacques Chirac, to persuade them that the French Commissioner, Edith Cresson, should go but he should stay. When that failed he came up with a new wheeze. None of the Eurocrats should resign, he suggested, but the more blameworthy ones, like Cresson, should have some of their powers reassigned to those who had come in for less criticism. If only he had applied the same energy to his job.

This savaging of Santer is terribly unfair, says Andreas Middel in Die Welt. For under his guidance the EU has done remarkable things. Thanks to him the once controversial idea of bringing home former Eastern bloc countries into the EU has become an accepted reality. Indeed, Santer will go down in history as one of the Founding Fathers of the euro, the man who supervised the smooth transition to the single currency. If he did make mistakes – failing to take the European Parliament seriously enough, for example, these were simply bad habits he inherited from his predecessors.

That only shows how awful most commissioners have been, said Wolfgang Proissl in Die Welt. The problem is not so much corruption but gross mismanagement, catalogued in detail in the report. Yet the commissioners remain complacent. 'We did so well with the euro,' one told Proissl last week as he puffed his cigar, 'and as thanks we get felled for a few irregularities.' Quite so, said Erik Empatz in Le Canard Enchaîné. Our Anglo-Saxon friends are rejoicing at the downfall of Cresson because she awarded a scientific post to her dentist friend and because she once called them a nation of 'homosexuals'. But the real cause for rejoicing is not the fall of individuals such as Cresson or Santer. It is that the feudal nature of the EC – its nepotism, its byzantine system of awarding contracts – may soon be a thing of the past. This crisis has at last established the fact that the Commission is not above the law.

Reproduced with kind permission from The Week *(27 March 1999).*

Subscriptions available on 01454 6200700

The European Council

The European Council, established in 1974, is made up of the heads of each government, and meets twice a year in so-called European Summit meetings – for example, the Maastricht Treaty was signed by John Major at a European Council meeting in December 1991, with opt-outs on the single currency and Social Chapter; and in 1997 Tony Blair signed the Amsterdam Treaty by which the UK signed up to the Social Chapter. The March 1999 summit had a weighty programme covering the crisis of the – then non-existent – European Commission, and Nato's bombing of Serbia, as well as proposals for radical budget reforms. Other summits, however, may be little more than media events.

The European Parliament

This is the only elected body of the EU, but it has relatively little power. It is based in Strasbourg and now has 626 seats, of which Britain – like France and Italy – has 87. Only Germany has more, with 99. Other countries have fewer seats in rough proportion to their populations, ranging down to Luxembourg with six. British Euro-constituencies are much larger than national constituencies with about 500,000 voters in each, and MEPs are elected every five years (latest elections June 1999). The Labour government has changed the electoral system for Euro-elections from first-past-the-post to the closed party list system, a form of PR where the party leaders rather than the voters choose the MEPs to fill the seats. The obvious criticism of this system is that the voter has no say in who are the actual MPs, who are likely to be loyal party placemen. The House of Lords rejected the closed list system for EU elections a record *six* times, but the government in the Commons pushed it through nevertheless. By 1999, some independent-minded and popular Labour MEPs – for example, Christine Oddy (Coventry and North Warwickshire) – were pushed so far down the party lists as to be effectively deselected by the leadership, with the voters having no say in the process.

The Parliament is a forum for debate, is consulted on major policy issues and can suggest amendments which the Commission often accepts, it can veto certain forms of legislation, can modify or reject the EU budget (as it did five times in the 1980s), can question the Council or Commission, can investigate public complaints of European maladministration (with an EU Ombudsman since Maastricht), can veto EU Commissioners' appointments and can, in theory, dismiss the entire Commission by a two-thirds majority – never yet done, but it was pressure from MEPs which forced the Commission's collective resignation in 1999.

The European Parliament's profile is fairly low, many voters are apathetic or cynical about it and turnout at elections is relatively low (averaging under 60 per cent across Europe), with Britain's turnout usually lowest (for example, 23 per cent in 1999). However, the Parliament's success against the Commission in 1999 may embolden it and stimulate voter interest in its activities.

Sample short answer question and answer

Q? a) What are the powers of the European Parliament?

b) Does the European Parliament need reform?

A✓ a) The European Parliament is composed of 626 MEPs. It performs similar functions to the British House of Commons – representation, debate and scrutiny – but it only has limited powers. It can, for example, veto the EU budget – and in the 1980s it rejected the budget five times. It can dismiss the Commission with a two-thirds majority. After the 1999 Commission fraud debacle, this power may be extended to the dismissal of individual Commissioners. The Parliament can also suggest amendments to draft legislation from the Commission, about 70 per cent of which are accepted by the Commission. The Maastricht Treaty gave it more powers, for example to veto certain forms of legislation, to veto Commissioners' appointments and to investigate voters' complaints of maladministration.

b) The Parliament is the only directly elected body of the EU but has limited powers – hence the *democratic deficit* at the heart of the EU. Although the Maastricht Treaty gave it more power, the treaty also entrenched the system of intergovernmental decision-making in the Council of Ministers which, to critics, means a secretive and unaccountable club of national executives making most of the key decisions. Paradoxically, as it stands, the EU strengthens national governments and bureaucracies at the expense of national parliaments and voters. If the European Parliament was to be given more genuine law-making power and ability to scrutinise and control the Commission and Council, that would further democratise the EU on the one hand, and reduce the potential for elective dictatorship within Britain, on the other. Perhaps that is why the British government was almost alone in resisting the granting of more power and influence to the European Parliament during the Maastricht negotiations.

The European Court of Justice

This comprises 15 judges appointed by member states for six-year renewable terms, and is based in Luxembourg. It interprets and enforces EU law, which takes precedence over national law, but it lacks sanctions and relies on the Commission for enforcement. British courts are obliged by the European Communities Act 1972 to refuse to enforce Acts of Parliament which contravene European law (a principle established by the 1990 *Factortame* case about fishing rights in British waters). Even on entry in 1972, the British Parliament had to accept 43 volumes of existing EU legislation.

EU decision making – a summary

At its simplest: the Commission makes a proposal; the Parliament offers its opinion; the Council of Ministers makes a decision; the Court of Justice interprets and enforces the decision; the member countries administer the decision.

The impact of the EU on British political parties

Membership of the EU has profoundly divided the British political parties, Labour especially in the 1970s and the Conservatives especially in the 1980s and 1990s. Left-wing Labour MPs especially have always been hostile to the EU, which they perceive as a capitalist club. The defection of four leading right-wing Labour MPs to found the (short-lived) Social Democratic Party in 1981 was partly a response to Labour's then policy of withdrawal from the EC.

The Conservatives, under Margaret Thatcher, became increasingly suspicious of the EC in the 1980s as they saw it extending beyond a free trade community to a supra-

EC 'rewrites' British constitution

The European Court of Justice ruled yesterday that courts in Britain must suspend Acts of Parliament where rights of citizens guaranteed by EC law may be at risk.

The Luxembourg court's decision paves the way for a wholly new constitutional and legal experience for the UK legal system, strengthening the hand of businesses and individuals to seek effective justice under Community law in the British courts.

One Luxembourg source said yesterday that it amounted to a rewriting of the British constitution.

It means that claimants able to show prima facie breaches of EC law will be entitled to seek immediate injunctions to prevent hardship pending rulings on their cases. Until now, they have had no remedy for losses that can be suffered during the lengthy wait for a ruling in their favour by the European Court.

Yesterday's decision stemmed from litigation against the Government by the Spanish fishing industry over the Merchant Fishing Act 1988, which introduced a ban on so-called 'quota hopping' by Spanish-owned vessels fishing in British waters under British flags.

The companies claim the Act has forced them to lay up more than 90 vessels, exposing them to financial ruin. The Government had accused the Spanish companies of 'plundering' fish allocated to Britain under the EC's Common Fisheries Policy.

The House of Lords refused to grant the Spanish companies an injunction suspending the Act pending a ruling

UK courts empowered to overrule Parliament

from Luxembourg, on the ground that it had no power to do so. But yesterday the EC judges said that the Law Lords were wrong and ordered them to apply the ruling.

The judges said any law that prevented, even temporarily, Community rules from having full force was incompatible with the essence of EC law.

The Luxembourg decision, which court officials emphasised would have no bearing on the final ruling on the merits of the case, also overrides the English rule that a temporary injunction cannot be made against the Crown.

The ruling comes after last month's opinion by Giuseppe Tesauro, the EC Advocate General, who said the case was of 'unquestionable importance' to the relationship between EC law and national courts.

Michael Hutchings, an EC law expert of the London solicitors Lowell White Durrant, said: 'It is clearly a fundamental case. It says for the first time that it is a principle of UK law as influenced by the European Court that Parliament is not supreme in every circumstance; if action by Parliament or by the Government through subordinate legislation is contrary to EC law, the UK courts have power to suspend it.

'That gives the House of Lords a similar function to that of the Supreme Court in the United States [which can strike down laws as unconstitutional]

with the difference that here we are applying a system of law which is inferior to Parliament.'

In other European states, such as West Germany, the operation of legislation can be stayed pending a challenge to its constitutionality.

But, although judicial review has been developed by the UK courts to challenge the exercise of official and administrative powers, and while UK law has developed to embrace EC rulings and court decisions, there is no tradition in Britain of reviewing primary legislation passed by Parliament.

The court's ruling that British courts have a duty to grant 'interim relief' in appropriate circumstances for claimants, pending full adjudication of cases, is confined to claims invoking EC rights which are, in Euro-court terminology, 'directly applicable' in national courts of member states.

But it is likely to be of wide significance since such rights cover all those in the Treaty of Rome - such as free movement of goods and persons, the freedom to provide services and establish businesses, and sex equality - and those in certain EC directives.

The ruling will not give the right to receive interim payments of damages or compensation. UK courts will apply UK law to decide whether an injunction should be granted on the facts of the particular case.

Mr Hutchings said the decision would be particularly significant in the business sphere. 'The crucial point is that the remedy needs to be rapid, otherwise the claimant may be put out of business.'

(The Independent, 30 June 1990)

national political power (which, in fact, it always was). Since 1990, divisions over Europe have been primarily responsible for: Thatcher's prime ministerial defeat; the temporary withdrawal of the whip from several Conservative Euro-rebels which eradicated Major's small majority; John Redwood's leadership challenge against John Major in 1995; the defection from the Conservative Party of pro-European MPs such as Emma Nicholson and Alan Howarth; the beef ban and Britain's damaging non-co-operation policy of 1996. (Opposition to EU membership also generated the brief creation of James Goldsmith's Referendum Party and Alan Sked's Independence Party for the 1997 election, both of which slightly dented the Conservative vote.) Even after the 1997 election, the Conservatives remained divided: in 1998, pro-European Peter Temple-Morris MP (who had already lost the Conservative whip) joined Labour, MEP James Moorhouse defected to the Liberal Democrats and two more MEPs (John Stevens and Brendan Donnelly) quit the party over its hostility to the single currency after the euro was born in January 1999.

Blair's Labour government is now more Europhile – especially as the social dimension of EU policy making expands – and is currently (1999) pursuing the national changeover plan, making preparations to adapt to, and very likely eventually join, the euro.

Of the three main parties, only the Liberal Democrats are fully committed to the development of a federal Europe.

Key events in the development of the EU

The Single European Act (SEA) 1986

The SEA developed the idea of a single European market with a commitment to advancing economic integration. The Single European Market officially came into being on 1 January 1993, establishing the four freedoms of movement for goods, capital, services and persons, although Britain refused to scrap frontier controls over the movement of persons (the Schengen Accord).

The Maastricht Treaty 1991

The Maastricht Treaty created a European Union with common citizenship, and set out a timetable and procedure for creating European Monetary Union (EMU).

The creation of the EU, with its implications for further loss of national political and economic sovereignty, was highly controversial. Moreover, Germany had reunified in October 1990 and some of the other member states (and their voters) viewed this with suspicion – they feared that growing European integration would be dominated by an overpowerful Germany. The Danish referendum of 1992 rejected the treaty and another had to be held in May 1993 to reverse that decision. The process of ratification in the British House of Commons was very fraught and was only achieved when John Major made the issue a vote of confidence in July 1993. He also ensured the deletion of every reference to federalism (the 'F-word') from the treaty and its replacement with the goal of an ever closer union, because federalism has been used inaccurately by Euro-sceptics to imply the complete absorption of member countries into a European monolith. In fact, as students of Politics will already know, federalism means the ordered division of sovereignty between central and local powers with constitutional guarantees of mutual spheres of autonomy. Thus the treaty established the principle of **subsidiarity** whereby decisions should be taken at the lowest possible level compatible with efficiency and democracy. This was an attempt to return to member states some power previously lost to Brussels; and Scottish and Welsh nationalists argued that it also implied greater devolution of power within the UK (as was enacted in 1997). The treaty also created an advisory Committee of the Regions with 189 nominated members including 24 from the UK, to give the regions of Europe – including Scotland and Wales – more say in the future of the EU.

The single currency

The Maastricht Treaty – the most important single development in the history of the EU to date – bound member states to work towards EMU, i.e. a future single currency (to be known as the euro) starting in 1999, with the exception of Britain (and Denmark) which secured an opt-out – a variable geometry approach. Common interest rates for the participating economies will be decided by a European Central Bank based in Frankfurt.

The first stage for each country was to enter its currency into the Exchange Rate Mechanism (ERM) whereby currency values are tied to each other within certain bands of flexibility. Britain joined the ERM in 1990, but was humiliatingly forced out on 16 September 1992 (so-called Black Wednesday) when currency speculation on the international financial markets forced the devaluation of the pound below the floor of its ERM band. Chancellor Norman Lamont eventually – and reluctantly – resigned over Britain's fall-out.

National economies can join the euro only when they meet certain *convergence criteria*: a country's budget deficit should not be more than 3 per cent of GDP; public debt should not exceed 60 per cent of GDP; the rate of inflation should not be higher than 1.5 per cent above that of the best three countries; the interest rates of the national currencies should be within (quite flexible) normal bands; and unemployment (20 million across Europe in the late 1990s) must not be too high. Eleven member countries joined euroland in 1999.

Case for a single currency:

▶ European integration and a truly single market require a single currency.

▶ It would enhance Europe's competitiveness against the USA and Japan.

▶ Currency transaction costs would be eliminated.

▶ The currency speculators would be weakened.

▶ Business stability and certainty would be enhanced.

Case against a single currency:

▶ Practical difficulties of aligning very diverse economies and currencies of member states.

▶ Loss of national sovereignty.

▶ Loss of governments' ability to adjust currency values against external shocks.

▶ Loss of wealth, employment and power from weaker to stronger member countries, including probable domination by the German deutschmark and central Bundesbank.

(The Guardian, *19 March 1999*)

The Social Chapter

The Maastricht Treaty also bound member states – except Britain, which again secured an opt-out – to the Social Chapter, an agreement incorporating into the treaty the 1989 Social Charter on minimum employment wages and rights, sexual equality, freedom of information and other social improvements throughout the EU. The then Conservative government's main argument against it was that such added constraints and costs on British businesses would increase unemployment and decrease profits. The Labour government signed up to the Social Chapter in 1997.

Maastricht's other pillars

The two other pillars of the treaty were based on intergovernmental co-operation rather than supranational integration, and also on unanimous voting rather than QMV, therefore the British government did not feel threatened by them.

▶ The Maastricht Treaty's second pillar deals with *foreign and defence policy co-operation*; but this was undermined by the EU's disunity and impotence over Bosnia in 1995, and also by the then British Defence Secretary Michael Portillo's wariness of Europe and his Europhobic speech to the 1995 Conservative conference.

▶ The third pillar concerns co-operation on *interior and justice affairs*, for example, toughening rules against drug smuggling, terrorism, immigration and asylum seekers from outside Europe, but relaxing restraints against movement of persons within Europe. To critics, this raised the prospect of a 'Fortress Europe'; nevertheless, the latter part of the agreement caused junior Conservative minister Charles Wardle to resign in 1995.

The Amsterdam Treaty 1997

This agreement (signed by Tony Blair) added an employment chapter and provided for the gradual introduction of common policies on immigration, asylum and visa laws. It also extended QMV to such areas as employment, sexual equality, public health and customs co-operation.

The future – a Europe of nation states or a United States of Europe?

The main British parties have always been divided on the question of Europe; Thatcher's growing distaste for it substantially contributed to her downfall in 1990, and the Conservative government's small majority from 1995–7 gave disproportionate influence to the small number of Euro-rebels in the party, nine of whom temporarily lost the whip (i.e. were sacked from or left the party) in 1994–5 over the issue. Blair's Labour government is more Europhile and is currently (1999) pursuing the national changeover plan making preparations to adapt to, and very likely eventually to join, the euro.

By contrast, most other EU countries are more pro-Europe and many other countries, such as Cyprus and Malta, and including Eastern European countries such as Poland and Hungary since the end of the Cold War in 1990, are very keen to join the EU, taking the possible total up to at least 27. It seems likely that the Union will both deepen and widen by the turn of the century, and Britain will have to decide whether it genuinely wishes to be at the heart of Europe or to be sidelined and left behind.

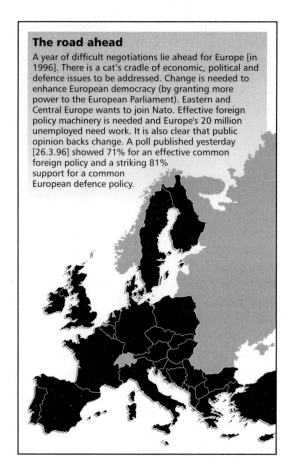

The road ahead

A year of difficult negotiations lie ahead for Europe [in 1996]. There is a cat's cradle of economic, political and defence issues to be addressed. Change is needed to enhance European democracy (by granting more power to the European Parliament). Eastern and Central Europe wants to join Nato. Effective foreign policy machinery is needed and Europe's 20 million unemployed need work. It is also clear that public opinion backs change. A poll published yesterday [26.3.96] showed 71% for an effective common foreign policy and a striking 81% support for a common European defence policy.

(adapted from The Guardian, *27 March 1996)*

---

1 Quiz: answer all of the questions which follow. (Score out of a total of 35.)

a) When was the EEC formed? (1)

b) Which of the bodies in the diagram opposite is the dominant decision-maker? (1)

c) In which of these institutions would **(i)** the British Prime Minister and **(ii)** the British Foreign Secretary attend meetings? (2)

d) Name one British Commissioner for Europe. (1)

e) In which cities are **(i)** the European Parliament and **(ii)** the European Court of Justice situated? (2)

f) Name the three newest member countries of the European Union. (3)

g) Give one sentence definitions of the following terms:

(i) Sovereignty

(ii) Subsidiarity

(iii) Supranationalism. (3)

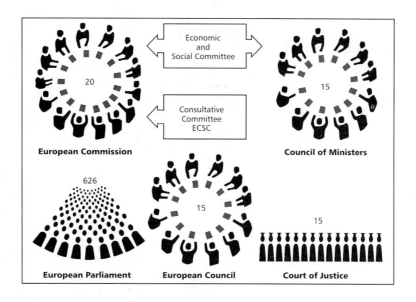

h) Give two reasons why the idea of a more united Europe gained strength in the post-1945 era. (2)

i) Give two reasons why Britain initially refused to join this process. (2)

j) In what year did Britain join the (then) EEC? (1)

k) In what year was the British referendum on staying in Europe? (1)

l) In what year were elections to the European Parliament first held? (1)

m) (i) What is QMV? (1)

(ii) When was it introduced? (1)

(iii) What impact has QMV had on the balance of power between Europe and individual member states? (1)

n) Why has the left wing of the Labour Party traditionally been hostile to the European Union? (1)

o) Why has the right wing of the Conservative Party been hostile to Europe? (1)

p) What do the following initials stand for?

(i) EMU

(ii) ERM

(iii) ECU. (3)

q) When (in what year) and why did Black Wednesday happen? (2)

r) Give one argument for, and one argument against, a single European currency. (2)

s) When was the Maastricht Treaty signed? (1)

t) (i) What is the Social Chapter? (1)

(ii) Suggest one reason why the Conservative government chose to opt out of it. (1)

ESSAYS

Q? Discuss the impact of the European Union on British political processes.

(London, specimen paper, 1997)

A✓ Summary sample answer

The EU (then the Common Market) was formed in 1957 by six countries. It now has 15 member states.

The UK joined in 1973. This meant that the British Parliament lost legal or legislative sovereignty both *de jure* and *de facto* (i.e. both in theory and in practice) in areas where European law took precedence. This loss of sovereignty has since increased, with the growing scope of European intervention and with reforms of European voting procedures. The most important reform was the change from unanimous voting in the Council of Ministers, i.e. any one country could effectively veto any policy, to Qualified Majority Voting, under the Single European Act 1986. For example, in 1993 Britain was overruled on the principle of a 48-hour working week.

In 1975 a national referendum was held on Britain's continuing membership of the then EC. Technically, this was merely advisory, and so in theory Parliament's legal sovereignty was not affected. In practice, however, Parliament could scarcely have ignored the referendum result. Similarly, in theory, Parliament could legislate to leave the EU at any time, but in political practice that seems difficult and unlikely.

From another perspective, the primacy of EU law has curbed the dangers of elective dictatorship of a single party majority UK government within a sovereign Parliament, for example, forcing the government to reform pensions law and rights for part-time workers.

Since British and European courts are required to enforce European law rather than domestic law where there is conflict between the two, Parliament has also lost some legal sovereignty to the British courts as well as to the ECJ.

Elections to the European Parliament were first held in 1979, adding a new layer of democracy to the British political system, but the European Parliament – the only elected institution of the EU – is still relatively weak. Since the main decision-making bodies of the EU – the Council of Ministers and the European Commission – are not elected, membership of the EU has also meant some loss of the political sovereignty of the British electorate.

The sheer quantity and impact of EU law upon Britain has given the British constitution an increasingly codified and rigid character, as well as modifying its unitary nature.

Membership of the EU has increased the powers of the British Prime Minister: for example, in membership of the European Council with its twice-yearly summits; in signing EU agreements such as Maastricht and Amsterdam; and in appointing European Commissioners and civil servants. The EU can also clearly influence the Prime Minister's thinking: for example, at a 1998 summit Tony Blair moved perceptibly left on the issues of increased spending for jobs and growth and on common defence, foreign and security policies.

Membership of the EU has also increased the policy-making powers of Foreign Ministers in the Council of Ministers; and it is widely held to have increased the power of civil servants.

Most obviously, membership of the EU has profoundly divided the British political parties, Labour especially in the 1970s and the Conservatives especially in the 1980s and 1990s. The defection of four leading Labour MPs to found the (short-lived) Social Democratic Party in 1981 was partly a response to Labour's then policy of withdrawal from the EC. Since 1990, divisions over Europe have been primarily responsible for Thatcher's prime ministerial defeat, the temporary withdrawal of the whip from several Conservative Euro-rebels, John Redwood's leadership challenge against John Major in 1995, the defection from the Conservative Party of MPs such as Emma Nicholson and Alan Howarth, and the beef ban and Britain's damaging non-co-operation policy of 1996. Even after the 1997 election, the Conservatives remained divided: in 1998, pro-European Peter Temple-Morris MP (who had already lost the Conservative whip) joined Labour, MEP James Moorhouse defected to the Liberal Democrats and two more MEPs (John Stevens and Brendan Donnelly) quit the party over its hostility to the single currency after the euro was born in January 1999.

There is the possibility of future referendums, for example on the question of a single European currency.

The EU court has protected some civil liberties against British law, for example in relation to retirement ages, food and water standards and employment rights of transsexuals.

Finally, many British pressure groups are increasingly focusing their attention on EU rather than on domestic decision-making institutions – a reliable indicator of the shifting balance of power and influence. For example, the Committee of Professional Agricultural Organisations (COPA), comprising most of the national farmers' organisations, including Britain's National Farmers' Union, is based in Brussels where it can effectively lobby the relevant EU institutions, especially the Commission. Similarly, most British local authorities – especially those who receive EU financial aid – now have a European office to maintain effective contacts, again, especially with the Commission; and local authority by-laws (for example, on weights and measures) are often based on EU regulations.

Q? a) Define the concept of sovereignty.

b) Outline two ways in which the EU has limited UK sovereignty.

(London, June 1998, Paper 1)

A✓ Notes for guidance

a) Sovereignty means the legitimate location of power of last resort over any community. It may be defined purely in legal terms as the power to make binding laws which no other body can set aside or overrule. It may also be viewed as the autonomous power of a community to govern itself – a territorial concept relating to the powers of independent nation states. Reference may also be made to the political sovereignty of the electorate to rule themselves and elect and remove governments, i.e. the people power at the root of the legitimacy of Parliament and government which justifies the democratic claims of a political system. The location of sovereignty is not always easy to pinpoint, for example, in federal systems such as the USA.

b) The most obvious legal limitations should be addressed: that by signing EU treaties – Rome, SEA, Maastricht, Amsterdam – the UK has subordinated itself to the dictates of EU laws, regulations and directives. The *Factortame* case could be cited as an example, together with its implications for the qualitatively new role of the British courts in being able to veto UK statutes. Loss of control over many areas of economic policy could be cited, for example, agriculture, tariffs and trade, the beef ban, the single currency in future, etc. Other areas could be mentioned such as fishing, environment, conditions of work (the 48-hour working week, the minimum wage, etc.). Territorial sovereignty has been limited by the four freedoms and the erosion of state boundaries. Degrees of loss of sovereignty, with the introduction and extension of QMV, could also be mentioned.

---

2 Write at least one of the following essays. Always write a brief plan first.

   a) Is national sovereignty compatible with membership of the EU?

(Simulated question)

   b) What are the advantages and disadvantages to Britain of its membership of the EU?

(Simulated question)

   c) Discuss the impact of the European Union upon British institutions.

(London, Jan. 1998, Paper 1)

   d) The impact of membership of the European Union has been to challenge the essential elements of the British constitution. Discuss.

(London, June 1997, Paper 1)

   e) Discuss the views of the British political parties on the EU.

(Simulated question)

   f) Identify the similarities and differences in the relationships between constituents and their respective MPs and MEPs. In what ways, and for what reasons, does the service offered to constituents by MEPs differ from that offered by MPs?

(AEB, Summer 1997, Paper 1)

GUIDE TO EXERCISES

Page 228

1 a) 1957

   b) The Council of Ministers

   c) (i) The European Council; (i) The Council of Ministers

   d) Neil Kinnock, Chris Patten

   e) (i) Strasbourg and Brussels; (ii) Luxembourg

   f) Finland, Sweden, Austria

   g) (i) Ultimate authority and power

      (ii) The principle established by the Maastricht Treaty that, within the EU, decisions should be taken at the lowest possible level compatible with efficiency and democracy

      (iii) The creation of a sovereign authority over and above member states

h) Desire for peace and security after two wars; awareness of growing economic and social interdependence and desire for greater international cooperation; advantages of large-scale markets; greater world influence; challenge to USSR and E. Europe

i) A sense of superiority and national pride after victory in war; hankering after imperial status; international status and links with USA and Commonwealth; sense of political and geographical difference; Labour dislike of capitalist aspects of EU; xenophobia

j) 1973

k) 1975

l) 1979

m) (i) Qualified Majority Voting, in the Council of Ministers

(ii) The Single European Act 1986

(iii) Member states have lost further power to the Council

n) They see it as a bastion of free market capitalism

o) They fear loss of sovereignty and national identity

p) (i) Economic and Monetary Union

(ii) Exchange Rate Mechanism

(iii) European Currency Unit

q) 16 September 1992; currency speculation on the financial markets forced the devaluation of the pound below the floor of its ERM band

r) *For:* European economic integration requires a single currency; it would enhance Europe's competitiveness against USA and Japan; currency transaction costs would be eliminated; the currency speculators would be weakened; business stability and certainty would be enhanced

Against: Loss of national sovereignty; loss of governments' ability to adjust currency value against external shocks; loss of wealth, employment and power from weaker to stronger member countries

s) December 1991

t) (i) Agreement on minimum employment rights, sexual equality, freedom of information and other social improvements throughout the EU

(ii) The government argued that it would increase unemployment

REFERENCES

Moravcsik, A. (1993) 'Preferences and power in the EC', *Journal of Common Market Studies*, Vol. 31, No. 4

Nugent, Neill (1992) *The Government and Politics of the European Community*, Macmillan

Pilkington, Colin (1995) *Britain in the European Union Today*, Manchester University Press

12 British Parliamentary democracy: A revision chapter

SOME KEY ISSUES

- ▶ Majority government in sovereign Parliament with a flexible constitution – 'elective dictatorship'?
- ▶ How democratic and representative is the British political system?
- ▶ How pluralist is the British state?
- ▶ How effective is Parliament in law-making, controlling the executive and representing the people?
- ▶ Does Britain have Prime Ministerial government?
- ▶ Are the civil service too powerful or too pliable?
- ▶ How representative, accountable and effective is local government?
- ▶ 'The rule of law' – a myth?
- ▶ Civil liberties – how well are they protected?
- ▶ Pressure groups – how do they compare with political parties?
- ▶ Do the media reflect ruling class interests?
- ▶ The EU – does it challenge the constitution?
- ▶ The British constitution – an ongoing object of dispute?

REVISION EXERCISES

Review Chapters 2–11 before attempting these exercises.

1 Give one-sentence definitions of each of the following:

   a) Sovereignty

   b) Parliamentary government

   c) A 'safe seat'

d) A private bill

e) Parliamentary privilege

f) The royal prerogative

g) Mandate

h) Minority government

i) Coalition government

j) Cabinet government

k) *Ultra vires*

l) Constitutionalism

m) Unconstitutional action

n) Anti-constitutional action

o) Case law

p) Delegated legislation

q) Convention

r) Civil disobedience

s) Civil rights

t) Political power

u) Political influence

v) Pluralism

w) Welfare state

x) Bureaucracy

y) Devolution.

2 Quick Quiz. Briefly answer the following questions:

a) Who coined the phrase 'elective dictatorship'?

b) Why is the House of Lords not a 'supreme court' in the American sense (i.e. what is the difference between them)?

c) Who first used the word 'wets', and to describe whom?

d) Distinguish between the functions of standing and select committees of the House of Commons.

e) Which one of the following is attached to the EU – the European Court of Human Rights or the European Court of Justice?

f) Which statute created a UK Bill of Rights (to take effect in the year 2000)?

g) How much is the current deposit for parliamentary candidates; and what percentage of the vote must they win in order not to lose their deposits?

h) List five methods by which Parliament seeks to hold the executive to account.

i) Who coined the phrase 'the rule of law'?

j) Which government department is responsible for:

(i) roads?

(ii) prisons?

(iii) food safety?

k) When was 'one person one vote' established for everyone over 21?

l) When was the last Official Secrets Act passed?

m) Name the two ministers most involved in the arms to Iraq controversy.

n) Complete: 'Sarah Tisdall leaked details of .... to .... ; Clive Ponting leaked details of .... to .... Only one of them was convicted and imprisoned, namely ....'

o) Which key piece of constitutional case law established the British courts' authority to override parliamentary statute in favour of EU law?

3 True or false?

a) By convention, ministers must be MPs in the Commons.

b) A 'constitution' is the body of laws by which a state is governed.

c) There are approximately 100 members of the government.

d) Parliament can abolish the monarchy at will.

e) The two elements in 'parliamentary government' are the House of Commons and the House of Lords.

f) 'Administrative law' is the law which applies to executive and public bodies.

g) Civil servants must be neutral, so cannot vote.

h) Unlike civil servants, political advisers are not required to be politically neutral.

i) 'Parliamentary sovereignty' means that no court can challenge the law of Parliament.

j) The Speaker is an MP of the House of Commons.

k) All government bills must be introduced first in the House of Commons.

l) Backdating a law, i.e. applying it before the date when it was actually made, is illegal.

m) The death penalty still exists in Britain.

n) A 'joint committee' is one comprising both government and opposition MPs.

o) The monarch, in her private capacity, is above the law.

p) The police are forbidden to strike.

q) All Conservative Party members elect the party leader.

r) The 'ten o'clock adjournment' of the House of Commons is when all the MPs go home.

s) Cabinet committees consist only of Cabinet ministers.

t) The Ombudsman is an MP of the House of Commons.

4 Give at least three specific and topical examples of each of the following:

a)   Defeats of government by the House of Lords

b)   'Expertise' in the House of Lords

c)   Disproportionality of the first-past-the-post electoral system

d)   Other 'defects' of first-past-the-post

e)   Backbench revolts (successful and unsuccessful)

f)   Private members' bills (successful and unsuccessful)

g)   Sponsored MPs

h)   'Consensus politics' (party policies)

i)   'Adversary politics' (party policies)

j)   Two-party system (for example, in House of Commons)

k)   Multi-party politics in Britain

l)   Role of departmental select committees

m)   Parliamentary privilege (use or abuse)

n)   External checks on Parliament

o)   Prime Ministerial government

p)   Cabinet government

q)   Collective Cabinet responsibility

r)   Individual ministerial responsibility

s)   Political advisers to ministers/PM

t)   Civil service influence on policy

u)   Secrecy in British government

v)   Breaches of 'rule of law'

w)   Constitutional law

x)   Alleged judicial 'bias'

y)   Courts' control of executive

z)   Civil disobedience

aa)   Police/public order incidents

bb)   Promotional and sectional pressure group methods

cc) Media influence on public opinion

dd) Recent changes to British constitution.

5 Stimulus response question (simulated)

Study the following passage and then answer questions (a) to (e).

According to writers such as Norton (*The Constitution in Flux*), uncritical acceptance of the British constitution ceased in the 1970s, for a number of reasons: governments' inability to cope with growing economic problems; political pressures such as the rise of nationalism in Scotland and Wales, the 'troubles' in Northern Ireland, the indeterminate results of the two 1974 general elections and, paradoxically, growing fears of 'elective dictatorship' (Hailsham, 1976) in Britain. Suggestions for reform included a reformed second chamber, electoral reform for the Commons, devolution, freedom of information and a Bill of Rights. None of these had been enacted by 1997, but the Labour government of that year came to power on a series of manifesto promises of radical constitutional reform. However, some of these reforms have been enacted more quickly and keenly than others and they have, paradoxically, been accompanied by a growing centralisation of government control over key aspects of the party and political machinery.

a) Name the nationalist parties in:

   (i) Scotland   (1)

   (ii) Wales.   (1)

b) Briefly describe the outcome of:

   (i) the February 1974 election   (1)

   (ii) the October 1974 election.   (1)

c) (i) What is meant by the phrase 'elective dictatorship'?   (2)

   (ii) Why might fears of 'elective dictatorship' seem paradoxical in the light of the 1974 election results?   (2)

d) Select any one of the five reforms mentioned in the passage, and give arguments for and against it.   (6)

e) Explain and illustrate the last sentence of the extract.   (6)

ESSAYS

Q? 1 *Theme: 'Elective dictatorship'?*

What control does the government exercise over Parliament?

(Oxford, Summer 1981, Paper 1)

A✓ Notes for guidance

▶ Party discipline (via whips and natural party loyalty), usually over majority in House of Commons

▶ Control of timetable (through Leader of House)

▶ Selection of most legislative proposals, including those on power of Parliament itself (for example, reform of Lords 1999)

▶ Guillotine on bills in committee and closure on bills in debate

▶ Control of official information – financial details, defence projects, for example, Zircon, refusal to answer questions on grounds of 'national security'

▶ Can ignore select committee recommendations

▶ Can prevent civil servants from giving evidence to committees

▶ Can ignore Ombudsman's recommendations

▶ Can reject Lords' amendments

▶ Can reject recommendations of Boundary Commissioners

▶ Can reform procedures of Commons, for example, PM's Question Time

▶ Powers of PM: creation of new peers, appointment of Lords spiritual, appointment of 'payroll' ministers from Parliament, choosing date of general election within five-year term.

2 *Theme:* Democracy and representation

Q? 'Knowledge is power.' Comment, with regard to the extent of secrecy in British government.

(London, Jan. 1985, Paper 1)

A✓ **Notes for guidance**

Link *every* paragraph to the phrase 'knowledge is power' *and* to the issue of secrecy.

▶ Cases where knowledge → power, or lack of knowledge → lack of power:
  – PM and ministers
  – Civil service
  – MPs (lack power to control executive)
  – Public (lack 'people-power' – democracy – if lack knowledge for informed choices)
  – Constraints on knowledge: for example, Public Records Act 1958, D-Notice system, Official Secrets Act, Security Service Act, PIICs, conventions shielding Cabinet committees, policy-making processes, civil service advice to ministers, etc.

▶ But also:
  – Power may generate knowledge: PM, ministers and civil servants
  – Knowledge without power: for example, monarchy; some pressure groups, such as Greenpeace, have influence rather than power
  – Power without knowledge: for example, military; some pressure groups, for example, strike power of trade unions.

▶ Therefore the statement 'knowledge is power' is substantially true; means that secrecy is a constraint on democracy or 'people-power', and also on pluralism. Hence, need for reforms, for example, freedom of information. However, the statement is not always true: despite the degree of secrecy, it is possible to have some forms of power without knowledge, and vice-versa.

3 *Theme:* Pluralism

Q? 'The differences within parties are often just as important as the differences between them.' Discuss.

(London, June 1987, Paper 1)

Examiners' comments

'Although candidates were able to tackle part of this question well, i.e. the differences within parties, very few bothered to address themselves to the question as a whole, i.e. weighing up whether the differences within parties were as important as the differences between them. Candidates must try, even if only briefly, to relate their material to the question as a whole, otherwise the question remains only partially answered. Candidates too often homed in on the Labour Party and ignored the Conservative Party, which again made it more difficult to answer the question set and gave the impression of an unbalanced answer.'

Additional essay tips

Also consider the relative significance of the following:

► Differences within parties:
  - 'New' versus 'old' Labour
  - Splits within Cabinet
  - Backbench revolts
  - Pro- versus anti-Europe factions especially in Conservative Party and especially before 1997 election
  - 'New' versus 'old' (traditional Tory) right in Conservative Party
  - Defections of MPs
  - Party splits to create new parties (for example, SDP 1981).

► Differences between parties:
  - Policy differences – essential basis of pluralism and choice in liberal democracy
  - 'Consensus politics' and 'adversary politics'
  - Organisational differences, for example, financial resources, internal democracy
  - Splits within and between centre parties in late 1980s.

4 *Theme:* Role of Parliament

Q? What are the major functions of Parliament, and how effectively are they performed today?

(Simulated question)

A✓ **Short plan for guidance**

a) Major functions of Parliament:

  ► To make law

  ► To control the executive

  ► To represent the people

  ► These incorporate the subsidiary functions of: debate; controlling the raising and spending of public money; educating and informing the public; redress of grievances; protecting the rights of the individual; training and recruitment ground for ministers.

b) Taking each main function in turn:

  (Point out that enhancing Parliament's effectiveness at one function, for example, law-making, may limit its effectiveness at another function, for example, control of the executive.)

  ► Law-making: effectiveness enhanced by: greater time and weaker party discipline of Lords versus Commons; committees of Lords and Commons; special standing committees; 10-minute limit to some speeches, introduced in 1985; private members' bills; use of closure and guillotine

▶ Effectiveness limited by: lack of authority and power of non-elected Lords; government's control of legislative programme; filibustering; lack of time for private members' bills; delegated legislation; part-time MPs; EU; devolution

▶ Control of executive: effectiveness enhanced by: government defeats by Lords; cross-benchers in Lords; backbench revolts; opportunities for opposition and backbenchers, for example, Question Time, Opposition Days, 10 o'clock adjournment debates; departmental select committees; Ombudsman; Comptroller and Auditor General and Public Accounts Committee

▶ Effectiveness limited by: lack of power of Lords; party discipline in Commons and size of government's majority; government control of timetable; use of closure and guillotine; weaknesses of select committees and Ombudsman; MPs' lack of information, for example, on finance and 'national security'; and MPs' lack of office, secretarial and research facilities

▶ Representation of the people: effectiveness enhanced by: universal suffrage and election of MPs; broadening social background of MPs; good use of parliamentary privilege; reform of Lords; televising of Lords and Commons; use of referenda; Nolan/Neill reforms; devolution

▶ Effectiveness limited by: unrepresentative Lords; non-proportional electoral system for Commons; abuses of parliamentary privilege; sleazy MPs; power and influence of unrepresentative pressure groups; passing of 'bad' law, for example, constraining civil liberties or freedom of information.

Conclusion: not very effective, especially in controlling the executive and representing the people. Reforms: elected second chamber, PR for first chamber, weaker party discipline, freedom of information, more powers and resources for select committees and Ombudsman, entrenched Bill of Rights.

---

6 Find topical examples to illustrate as many of the above points as possible.

Q? **5** *Theme:* **Role of PM**

'The Prime Minister has to all intents and purposes turned into a President.' Discuss.

(London, Jan. 1998, Paper 1)

A✓ **Examiners' comments**

'This was a very popular question, occasionally with the entire entry from a large centre attempting it. Many candidates focused on the powers of the Prime Minister without adequate reference to the role of a President. The overwhelming number of candidates were able to identify the basis upon which the question was being asked. The term "prime ministerial" was used by many, with better candidates being able to locate the source of the term.

Many candidates concentrated on the power of Mrs Thatcher in the 1980s, with higher level candidates comparing her style with that of her successor, John Major. One candidate wrote:

"Margaret Thatcher dominated the political agenda with the sheer force of her personality. In this way she led her Cabinet and was dismissive of opposition from within the government. John Major, by contrast, had a more consensual style and promoted discussion within the Cabinet and was keen to secure agreement of all colleagues in difficult times. A good example of this would be in the immediate aftermath of the ERM crisis in 1992."

The stronger candidates highlighted the manner in which the media focus in on the Prime Minister at the expense of other politicians, general elections being portrayed as gladiatorial contests akin to presidential elections. The very best candidates, however, were able to evaluate the constitutional differences between the role of a Prime Minister and that of a President, for example:

"The Prime Minister cannot be compared to a President from the point of view of the formal roles within their respective political systems. The Prime Minister is formally a member of the legislature and indeed is answerable to it. The President of the USA is not answerable to Congress and is separately elected from it...It may be argued that the UK Prime Minister has more power than the President in the USA because the former, with a large parliamentary majority, has no written constitution to limit his field of action."

The better candidates were also able to question the nature of the presidency in different countries, some having an executive presidency and others having ceremonial presidencies.'

6 *Theme:* Role of civil service

Q? Are senior civil servants too powerful, or are they too pliable?

(London, June 1984, Paper 1)

A✓ **Student's essay**

The senior civil servants are the top permanent secretaries and the 600 or so 'mandarins'. A civil servant's duty is to help administer the work of the executive and to advise on policy. The relationship of civil servants to ministers is idealised by Sir Douglas Wass as being 'loyal but not enthusiastic'. The key characteristics of the civil service are its permanence, neutrality (i.e. non-party political) and anonymity. They are not meant to have policy-making power, but in practice the enormous workload of the government means that many decisions are effectively made by civil servants, for example, the drafting of delegated legislation and compiling the honours list – and it would appear to be more than mere coincidence that 60 per cent of all the honours are awarded to civil servants.

Left-wing Labour ex-ministers such as Tony Benn and Michael Meacher have argued since the 1960s that civil servants are too powerful, and can effectively tie the hands of their ministers. Benn argues that their power comes from their sheer numbers compared with ministers, their permanence (ministers on average last about two years in one post), their expertise (especially in relation to a new government), and their control of information – producing, says Benn, 'misinformation' such as juggling British or NATO troop figures to justify increased expenditure on defence. Meacher lists four specific 'ploys' used by civil servants to manipulate ministers: the 'rules of the game' ploy, 'expert advice' ploy, *fait accompli* and 'timing of papers' ploy. The excessive secrecy of the British system, and bureaucratic 'red tape', are said to exacerbate this. To counter civil service monopoly of information Meacher says ministers should have more advisers. The EU especially has substantially increased the decision/policy-making role of British civil servants.

It is sometimes argued that civil service power is used to protect civil service interests – hence the Crowther-Hunt accusation of its 'Fulton-mindedness' in 1968, happy to accept reforms beneficial to itself but obstructive of those it disliked – the clash between 'the political will and the administrative won't'. It used to be argued that civil service power was used against left-wing Labour policies such as nationalisation (said Crossman and Barbara Castle), because the senior civil service was inherently right-wing – 70 per cent public school and Oxbridge, etc. It is more often argued, however, that the civil service is anti-radical, whether left or right – for example, Conservative ex-minister Nicholas Ridley accused them in the 1980s of obstructing privatisation through 'procrastination, inactivity and sabotage'; and former Industry Permanent Secretary Sir Anthony Part admitted that the civil service seeks to influence ministers towards 'the common ground'. This may be a perception of the public good, or simply pursuit of administrative convenience.

However, not everyone agrees that civil servants are too powerful. The view that 'Benn achieved nothing precisely because Wilson intended him to achieve nothing' (Heseltine) is not implausible. Recent critics of the civil service have argued that it is 'too pliable' and too supportive of the government. Mrs Thatcher was accused of trying to 'politicise' the top ranks of the civil service to the detriment of their traditional neutral status – for example, the involvement of Armstrong, Ingham and Powell in the Westland affair, and Armstrong's 'batting for the government' (Hennessy) in the *Spycatcher* trial. Tony Blair has given his spin doctors, Alastair Campbell and Jonathan Powell, authority over the civil service and, indeed, has replaced many civil service press officers with party spin doctors, leading civil servants formally to complain to the Commons Public Administration Committee of ongoing politicisation. The structural reforms of the civil service – job cuts and Ibbs' executive agencies, etc. – threaten their job security and may make them more pliable, i.e. manipulable because they are fearful for their jobs.

I would argue in conclusion that the civil service are both too pliable – too supportive of government and especially Prime Minister – and too powerful, with that power being used to enhance 'elective dictatorship' and PM power. I would advocate more open government and more ministerial – as opposed to prime ministerial – control of civil service appointments and powers.

Marker's comments on above essay

'This essay was awarded B+. Structure, relevance and use of evidence were good. However, there was some imbalance between the "powerful" and "pliable" sections of argument; the points made in the essay but not accepted in the conclusion were not explicitly refuted; and there was no consideration of whether the civil service is manipulated by bodies other than the PM, for example, pressure and interest groups. (A survey of 350 organisations in 1998 found that 29 per cent of them considered civil servants to be "the most important channel of influence" – ministers scored 32 per cent and Parliament a mere 8 per cent.)'

7 *Theme:* Local government

Q? Does central government have too much or too little control over local government?

(Simulated question)

A✓ Notes for guidance

Answers should recognise the centralising trends in the relationships between central and local government since the Second World War, and especially in the 1980s and 1990s – for example:

▶ the abolition of various councils

▶ the growing financial controls imposed from the centre (capping), etc.

▶ the compulsory tendering and privatisation of many local services – refuse collection, school meals, cleaning, etc.

▶ the compulsory 'opting out' of schools and housing services.

Good candidates might relate these to the centralising and authoritarian dimension of New Right Thatcherite philosophy, and/or to the profound conflicts in the 1980s between radical right-wing central governments and radical left-wing local authorities.

However, up-to-date answers should also recognise some reversal of these tendencies under the Labour government, for example, the relaxation of capping, the provisions for local referenda, and promises of new and stronger local authorities and mayors.

The cases for 'too much' or 'too little' turn essentially on the merits and demerits of local government: enhanced local democracy and provision for diverse local needs, etc., versus thwarting of central government's mandate and expensive and inefficient extra layers of bureaucracy, etc.

8 *Theme:* 'The rule of law'

Q? What are the main threats to the rule of law in contemporary Britain?

(Cambridge, June 1986, Paper 1)

A✓ Short plan for guidance
Principles of rule of law/threats:

▶ Legal equality:
  – Exemptions, for example, monarch, MPs, diplomats, etc.
  – Government 'above law', for example, GCHQ case law, use of PIICs
  – 'Bias' of judges/police, for example, 'numbers' and Stephen Lawrence cases
  – Cost of litigation; limited legal aid

▶ No arbitrary law or government:
  – Constitution and executive power based largely on convention rather than on law
  – 'Elective dictatorship' of majority government in 'sovereign' Parliament with flexible constitution
  – Retrospective law, for example, in 1998 budget
  – Flexible public order, criminal justice and anti-terrorism laws
  – 'Sus' laws

▶ Clear law:
  – Sheer quantity of law
  – Lack of legal guidelines, for example, phone-tapping (1984 European Court of Human Rights case)
  – Uncertain/ambiguous law, for example, public order laws
  – Contradictory law, for example, legal duties and financial constraints on local authorities. (Will increase with UK Bill of Rights)

▶ Innocent till proven guilty:
  – Remand
  – 'Sus' laws
  – 'Trial by media', for example Stephen Lawrence suspects

▶ Trial by fair and independent judges and courts of law:

- Overlaps between judiciary, legislature and executive
- Judicial 'bias'
- Alleged political interference in cases, for example, Tisdall, Ponting
- Inconsistent granting of bail and sentencing
- Jury vetting

9 *Theme:* Civil liberties

Q? a) What do you consider to be the most important civil liberties?

b) How well are civil liberties protected in the United Kingdom?

(London, June 1998, Paper 1)

A✓ Examiners' comments

'Very few responses were forthcoming on this question, which is somewhat worrying as this is so crucial and topical. There was some understanding shown of past problems between government and judiciary including cases such as GCHQ, Michael Howard appeals, etc. Some strong candidates were aware that the judiciary appears more liberal (but very few examples were quoted) and the growth of judicial review was mentioned. The main weakness was simply a lack of any in-depth knowledge of cases and recent changes.'

Additional essay tips

Hence the importance of keeping a current events diary! Do note significant court cases (for example, the Law Lords granting the legal right to protest on a public highway (1999) for the first time, the judge's comments in the Nick Mullen case – see Chapter 9 – etc.) and do include the European courts. Cite other institutions and processes which may protect and/or constrain civil liberties, with examples for each: Parliament, executive, police, media, pressure groups, elections, etc. Note that the 'UK' includes Northern Ireland which may warrant special mention.

10 *Theme:* Pressure groups

Q? 'Many pressure groups work through political parties, but they can all be clearly distinguished from them.' Discuss.

(London, Jan. 1988, Paper 1)

A✓ Notes for guidance

A 'quote – discuss' format requires balanced assessment of every assertion in every part of the title. Therefore consider: pressure groups which do and do not work through or with parties; whether links, overlaps and similarities between pressure groups and parties do or do not erase any clear distinctions between them; whether there may be similarities between pressure groups and parties even where they do not work together; and how far generalisations can be made across 'all' pressure groups. Note and stress every little word when reading and re-reading titles: '*Many* . . . work *through* . . . *but* can *all* be *clearly* distinguished . . .'.

---

7 Construct an essay in answer to the question above using the following skeletal plan.

▶ Definitions and types of parties and pressure groups; examples . . .

▶ Basic differences between parties and pressure groups

▶ Pressure groups working through parties – examples, methods, links, overlaps and similarities

▶ Pressure groups working independently of parties, and vice versa

▶ Differences between pressure groups and parties, with examples

▶ Difficulties of generalising across and among pressure groups and parties – especially large pressure groups and small parties. Consider: aims, methods, membership, internal organisation, size, resources, power, influence, expertise, links with executive/legislature

▶ *Conclusion:* True that many pressure groups work through parties – also vice versa. Often easily distinguished, but title too sweeping – distinctions sometimes very blurred in practice, even where they do not work together as such.

---

11 *Theme:* Media

Q? 'The ruling ideas of any age are the ideas of the ruling class' (Marx and Engels). Discuss with reference to the mass media in Britain.

(Cambridge, June 1985, Paper 1)

A✓ Notes for guidance

The Marxist argument can be summarised as follows.

Almost all of human history has been a series of class societies, from ancient society (masters and slaves) through feudalism (lords and serfs) to modern **capitalism**. In all class societies, there are two main classes (as well as many others): a ruling class and a subject class. The ruling class are those who own and control the means of production (i.e. the factories, etc.) – in capitalism they are called the bourgeoisie. The subject class are those who own only their labour power (i.e. their ability to work) – in capitalism they are called the proletariat. The bourgeoisie exploit the working class – i.e. they buy their labour and use it to create and extract 'surplus value' in the process of production; this is the source of profit in capitalism. There is therefore an inescapable conflict of interests between the two main classes.

Every class has its own 'ideology' – its own set of ideas which reflect and protect its own class interests. The ideology of the ruling class is by far the dominant ideology in society, because the ruling class own and/or control the means by which ideas are transmitted – the media, education systems, political and legal processes, etc. – what Marx called 'the means of mental production'. The personnel of these institutions – politicians, civil servants, etc. – need not be the ruling class as such; but they always and inevitably act as agents of the ruling class, promoting its interests by defending and preserving the existing capitalist system and class hierarchy, by the partial nature and content of the ideas and values which they promote.

Thus 'the ruling ideas of any age are the ideas of the ruling class'. The dominant ideology in capitalism embodies and encourages support of, for example, private property, profit, competition, hierarchy, law and order, **patriotism** and the 'national interest', monarchy and parliamentary democracy (which Marx called 'bourgeois dictatorship', because no major party ever seriously threatens the capitalist system).

Marxism predicts the inevitable abolition of all classes through inevitable revolution. Only then will 'ideology' – class-based ideas and values – disappear.

This essay title therefore requires an evaluation of the role of the mass media in Britain – ownership, control and content – in the context of the Marxist class/ideology theory.

Evidence in support of the Marxist argument could include evidence of the exceptionally concentrated nature of media ownership and control in Britain, and a critique of the media's 'one-sided' treatment of issues such as the monarchy, parliamentary democracy, law and order, defence, the business and City news, a 'national interest', Northern Ireland, property, poverty, trade unions, family, morality, radicalism, socialism and Marxism itself. Good sources are books by the Glasgow University Media Group – for example, *Bad News*, *More Bad News* and *Really Bad News*; also Ralph Miliband – for example, *The State in Capitalist Society*, *Capitalist Democracy in Britain* and *Marxism and Politics*.

Counter-arguments could be based on the pluralist perspective which stresses the diversity of media in liberal democracies, and denies the existence of any ruling class or 'ruling ideas'.

Pluralists would also make a distinction between the party-political bias of the press and the non-party political nature of the broadcasting media. Marxists, however, would not. Interpreting 'the ruling class' as 'the Conservative Party' is much too narrow for Marxist theory, which perceives the Labour Party to be just as much agents of the capitalist system, if not more.

12 *Theme:* The impact of the EU

Q? 'The impact of membership of the European Union has been to challenge the essential elements of the British Constitution.' Discuss.

(London, June 1997, Paper 1)

A✓ Examiners' comments

'One of the least popular essay choices, this question was often done poorly with just a few good answers produced. Most responses were confined to levels 1 and 2. Some of these weaker candidates ignored the constitutional point of the question entirely; many referred to the arguments for and against membership and/or the views of the political parties. Many confused the ECHR with the European Court of Justice. "Loss of sovereignty" was the common theme used by Level 3 candidates, and there was variable knowledge of the consequences of the 1972 European Communities Act. Candidates from a Law background understood and explained *Factortame*, part-time workers, etc. Many commented upon the impact on the House of Lords, the judiciary and the courts; Treaty of Rome Articles 189 and 177 and the view that this temporary transfer of sovereignty "was the will of the British Parliament".'

Notes for guidance

The best approach would be to structure this essay around 'the essential elements of the constitution' as follows:

▶ Unwritten – gradually becoming more written with the plethora of EU law

▶ Flexible – gradually becoming more rigid, for example, the use of referenda for major constitutional changes, instigated by the 1975 EC referendum

▶ Unitary – gradually becoming more federal with the transfer of power above (and below) Westminster

▶ Constitutional monarchy – not significantly changed except that the Queen herself is now a citizen of Europe

▶ Parliamentary sovereignty – effectively negated. Include discussion of the changing role of British courts which must enforce EU law over statute

▶ Parliamentary government – undermined, as government is now subordinate not only to Parliament, for example, the beef ban – and, paradoxically, in some ways now has even more power than before, for example, through EU Council of Ministers

▶ Rule of law – arguably strengthened, with less reliance on conventions and more protection of civil liberties by ECJ

▶ Representative democracy – arguably weakened by 'democratic deficit' within EU institutions; also challenged by referenda

▶ Administrative bureaucracy – changing role as EU gives civil service more real policy-making power.

13 *Theme:* **The constitution**

Q? 'The British constitution itself is now an object of political dispute.' Discuss.

(London, Jan. 1985, Paper 1)

A✓ **Short plan for guidance**

▶ 'Now' implies 'used not to be an object of political dispute'. Has always been debate about parts of system, for example, Lords. However, Philip Norton says whole constitution only came under critical scrutiny from 1970s when it was no longer seen to be 'delivering the goods' – for example, economic decline, rise of nationalist sentiment, indeterminate results of 1974 elections.

▶ Reforms and changes have been many, but until recently piecemeal and multi-directional (i.e. some more progressive than others): for example, Ombudsman, joining EU, use of referenda, Commons select committees, reforms/decline of local government, decline of ministerial responsibility, reforms to and changing role of civil service, changing role of pressure groups, and changes within parties, for example, Labour Party rules and procedures. Since 1997 general election, however, there have been substantive changes: such as devolution, Northern Ireland peace deal, Lords, European electoral system, Bill of Rights, reforms of police, freedom of information, promise of referendum on electoral reform for Commons.

▶ Devolution and the growing impact of membership of the EU especially are *de facto* changing the nature of Britain's constitution, so that it is becoming gradually more written, rigid and federal.

▶ Many, for example Norton, see no need for, or likelihood of, further major change because existing arrangements are seen as adequate with minor modifications; governments are unlikely to increase constraints against themselves, and always have higher priorities, for example, economic policy.

▶ However, there are calls for further progressive change: for example, from civil liberties pressure groups, Liberal Democrats, nationalist parties, and sections of the Conservative and Labour parties themselves. Norton identifies six distinct approaches to constitutional reform: High Tory (no change), Socialist (party-dominated strong government), Marxist (inevitable revolution), Group or Functionalist (incorporation of interest groups), Liberal (individualist) and Traditionalist (limited reform – pro-strong government).

▶ Reasons: perceived 'elective dictatorship', improper use of royal prerogative, ongoing secrecy, lack of clarity and enforceability of constitutional rules, lack of checks and balances within system, for example, weaknesses of Parliament v. executive, Opposition v. government, Cabinet v. PM, local v. central government; perceived 'politicisation', for example, of judiciary, civil service, police, church and education; regional inequalities and imbalances, loss of civil liberties, uncertainty, flexibility and breakability of constitution.

▶ *Conclusion:* Yes.

---

8 Write at least five of the following essays. Always write a brief plan first.

a) What reforms would strengthen the accountability of government to Parliament?

(London, Jan. 1998, Paper 1)

b) How democratic is the UK political system?

(London, Jan. 1999, Paper 1)

c) Examine the view that although there is much focus on elections in the UK, most power is exercised by non-elected appointees. Consider whether non-elected decision-makers are sufficiently accountable for their actions.

(AEB, Summer 1997, Paper 2)

d) In what ways could the role of Parliament be strengthened?

(London, Jan. 1999, Paper 1)

e) 'Prime ministerial power is a myth.' Discuss.

(London, June 1998, Paper 1)

f) To what extent have constitutional conventions concerning politicians and civil servants changed over recent years?

(London, June 1989, Paper 1)

g) 'Centralisation, party politics and the power of officials have combined to destroy democracy in local government.' Discuss.

(Oxford, Summer 1984, Paper 1)

h) What is the 'rule of law'? In what conditions does it flourish, and what are the main threats to its existence?

(Oxford and Cambridge, June 1989, Paper 0)

i) 'The fact that British citizens have the right to take complaints against their government to the European Court of Human Rights at Strasbourg removes the need for a British Bill of Rights.' Discuss.

(JMB, June 1986, Paper 1)

j) Outline arguments for and against the view that 'pressure groups are fundamentally undemocratic since they try to divert governments from the manifesto commitments on which their mandate is based'.

(AEB, Summer 1997, Paper 2)

k) To what extent are mass party organisations really necessary since the growth of the mass media?

(JMB, June 1986, Paper 1)

l) Discuss the impact of the European Union upon British institutions.

(London, Jan. 1998, Paper 1)

m) 'The case for a written constitution has become unanswerable.' Do you agree?

(Oxford, Summer 1990, Paper 1)

GUIDE TO EXERCISES

Page 234

1 a) Sovereignty: ultimate power and authority

b) Parliamentary government: executive chosen from within the legislature and in theory subordinate to it, hence overlap rather than separation of powers

c) A 'safe seat': a constituency which one particular party is virtually certain to win, regardless of the candidate

d) A private bill: a piece of parliamentary legislation which affects specific individual or group interests rather than the whole general public

e) Parliamentary privilege: the exemption of MPs and peers from some ordinary law, under the special laws and customs of Parliament

f) The royal prerogative: the powers of the Crown under common law

g) Mandate: the right or duty of a government, granted by the voters at the ballot box, to carry out its manifesto proposals

h) Minority government: government with under 50 per cent of the seats in the House of Commons

i) Coalition government: government of two or more parties

j) Cabinet government: policy making and responsibility by Cabinet as a collective body, with the Prime Minister *primus inter pares*

k) *Ultra vires*: illegal – as when executive bodies are ruled by the courts to have acted beyond their legal powers

l) Constitutionalism: advocacy or stance of acting within the limits of a body of accepted political rules and principles

m) Unconstitutional action: that which breaks the letter or spirit of the constitution, i.e. any rule, whether in a major or minor way

n) Anti-constitutional action: that which opposes the whole existing constitution and seeks either to replace or abolish it

o) Case law: judge-made law – judicial interpretation of law in a test case, which sets a precedent for future, similar cases

p) Delegated legislation: law made by bodies other than Parliament under legislative power passed down by Parliament

q) Convention: an unwritten, customary rule or practice of the constitution which has no legal force

r) Civil disobedience: deliberate, peaceful, public law-breaking as an act of political protest

s) Civil rights: entitlements which are granted to members of society by a particular government or state, often by law

t) Political power: the ability to do, or to make others do something in the public policy-making sphere, by the threat or use of sanctions such as rewards or punishments

u) Political influence: persuasive effect on others' ideas or actions by example or authority

v) Pluralism: diverse and competing centres of political and economic power – especially, many competing parties

w) Welfare state: provision of money, goods and services by the government to those deemed in need

x) Bureaucracy: professional administration of any large organisation such as business or government

y) Devolution: the passing down of legislative, executive or judicial power from central to regional bodies within a state, with the centre remaining sovereign

Page 235

2 a) Lord Hailsham

b) Two possible answers: the Law Lords are not separate from the legislature as supreme court judges are in the USA; and they cannot veto the legislature as they can in the USA

c) Mrs Thatcher – to describe non-Thatcherite Tories in the Conservative Party such as Francis Pym, James Prior and Ian Gilmour

d) Standing committees scrutinise bills; select committees scrutinise executive policies and activities and investigate specific issues of public concern

e) The European Court of Justice in Luxembourg

f) The Human Rights Act 1998

g) £500; 5 per cent

h) Debates and votes on government bills; Question Time; Opposition days; departmental select committees; the Ombudsman

i) A.V. Dicey (1885)

j) (i) Environment; (ii) Home Office; (iii) Agriculture/Health

k) 1928

l) 1989

m) William Waldegrave and Nicholas Lyell

n) Sarah Tisdall leaked the date of arrival of Cruise missiles in Britain from the USA to the *Guardian* newspaper; Clive Ponting leaked details of the sinking of the *Belgrano* to Labour MP Tam Dalyell. Only one of them was convicted and imprisoned, namely Sarah Tisdall

o) The *Factortame* case, 1990

Page 236

3 a) False – they may be peers in the Lords

b) False – a constitution is a body of rules and principles; not just laws, but also conventions, etc.

c) True

d) True

e) False – the two elements in 'parliamentary government' are the executive and the legislature

f) True

g) False – they may vote but cannot stand for political office

h) True

i) False – international courts, such as the European Court of Justice, can challenge the law of Parliament, and so can British courts when parliamentary statute conflicts with EU law

j) True

k) False – all except money bills may be introduced first in the Commons or Lords

l) False – Parliament may pass retrospective law

m) False – repealed in 1999

n) False – a 'joint committee' is one comprising members of both the Commons and the Lords

o) True

p) True

q) True (since William Hague's 1998 reforms)

r) False – the 'ten o'clock adjournment' is an opportunity for debate on topics chosen by backbenchers

s) False – cabinet committees may include civil servants, outside experts, etc.

t) False – the Ombudsman is a permanent, non-elected official attached to Parliament

Page 237

4 **Note:** These examples should be updated wherever more recent and significant examples are available.

a) War Crimes Bill 1990; sick pay 1991; Sky TV sports coverage 1996

b) Former PMs, for example, Thatcher; Law Lords, for example, Nolan and Neill; businessmen, for example Lord Williams of Elvel

c) 1997 figures of votes versus seats for all main parties (see Chapter 3)

d) No government since 1935 has had an absolute majority of votes cast; many votes are wasted; independents are disadvantaged

e) Sunday shopping 1986; three-line whip on Richard Shepherd's secrecy bill 1989; freezing of child benefit 1990; lone parents' benefit cuts 1997

f) Sidney Silverman's Abolition of Capital Punishment 1965; David Steel's Abortion Act 1967; Michael Foster's anti-fox hunting Bill 1997

g) John Prescott (National Union of Seamen); Dennis Skinner (National Union of Mineworkers)

h) During 1960s and 1970s the two main parties shared similar stances on economic policy, welfare and nuclear weapons. Post-1997 they shared similar policies on taxation, public spending and law and order

i)   In the early 1980s the two main parties disagreed on economic policy, welfare and nuclear weapons. Post-1997 they disagreed on the EU and on constitutional reform

j)   Almost 90 per cent of MPs are Labour or Conservative; the constitution recognises only 'Her Majesty's Government' and 'Her Majesty's Opposition'; parliamentary procedures such as pairing and Opposition Days

k)   Nine parties in Parliament; 17 per cent vote for the Liberal Democrats in 1997; regional differences in party strengths, for example, in Scotland

l)   Government consulted Social Security committee on its pension reform proposals in 1998; took up Home Affairs committee's suggestion of more use of electronic tagging and other community sentences (1999). Foreign Affairs Committee produced highly critical report on the arms to Sierra Leone affair (1999)

m)   Brian Sedgemore on Johnson Matthey Bank (1986) helped to produce criminal convictions; Dale Campbell-Savours (1987) on *Spycatcher*; Stuart Bell (1995) exposed cash for questions scandal.

n)   EU for example, on equal retirement ages for men and women; pressure groups for example, the Countryside Alliance on fox hunting 1997; media for example, on cash for questions.

o)   Thatcher: Falklands; abolition of GLC; Westland; bombing of Libya; poll tax.

Blair: Formula One tobacco advertising exemption; gag on four EU MPs over welfare cuts; Amsterdam Treaty; Social Exclusion Unit; personal veto of Chancellor Brown's plan to increase the top rate of income tax in 1998

p)   Cabinet policy decisions are said to include: refusal to discuss 1982 Think Tank report on NHS reform; refusal to lift rent controls 1986; refusal to sell British Leyland to General Motors 1987; refusal to introduce school vouchers 1987–8; and Major's government was conspicuously Cabinet-oriented

q)   Resignations of Nigel Lawson and Sir Geoffrey Howe over Thatcher's stance on EC 1989 and 1990; resignation of Malcolm Chisholm over lone parents' benefit cuts 1997

r)   Ron Davies over alleged sexual impropriety, and Peter Mandelson and Geoffrey Robinson over financial impropriety 1998

s)   Alastair Campbell and Jonathan Powell (Tony Blair); Charlie Whelan (until 1999) and Ed Balls (Gordon Brown)

t)   Westland; poll tax; role in Cabinet committees such as PSIS; arms to Sierra Leone; much EU policy

u)   Public Records Act 1958 (30-year rule); Official Secrets Act 1989; use of PIICs; D-Notice system. Plus Tisdall, Ponting, *Spycatcher*, arms to Iraq, BSE, arms to Sierra Leone

v)   Cost of litigation; 'numbers' cases; Stephen Lawrence case; use of secrecy certificates (PIICs) in cases, for example, Nick Mullen (1999); Home Secretary's judicial sentencing powers, for example, Bulger boys case (1999)

w)   Official Secrets Act 1989; Criminal Justice Act 1994; Scotland Act 1997; anti-terrorism laws 1998; case law in Pinochet and right of protest cases (1999)

x)   Tisdall, Ponting, GCHQ, trade union, 'numbers' and Pinochet cases

y)   *Ultra vires* rulings: board and lodging allowance cuts, Ridley versus GLC, Young versus Lambeth on poll tax capping 1990, ban on beef on the bone 1998

z) Greenham Common women, Committee of 100's refusal to pay poll tax, Newbury by-pass protesters, Kurdish protesters 1999

aa) Miners' strike 1984–5, Stonehenge 1985, Wapping 1986, poll tax 'riot' 1990

bb) Animal rights groups – from posters to bombs; Comic Relief media campaigns; farmers' demonstration at Brussels 1999

cc) Cash for questions; food safety 1998–9; Nato's bombing of Serbia 1999

dd) Amsterdam Treaty 1997; Scottish and Welsh devolution 1997; Northern Ireland peace agreement 1998; Human Rights Act 1998; closed lists for EU elections 1999; reform of Lords 1999; *de facto* changes such as Blair's presidentialism and politicisation of the civil service

Page 238

5 Stimulus response question – suggested answer (in note form).

a) (i) Scottish Nationalist Party

(ii) Plaid Cymru

b) (i) Minority Labour government under Harold Wilson (with fewer votes than Conservatives)

(ii) Labour government under Wilson with small majority of three seats (which was lost by 1977)

c) (i) 'Elective dictatorship' (Hailsham, 1976) implies strong majority executive in effective control of sovereign Parliament, with a flexible constitution – usually on minority vote – but virtually unassailable between elections

(ii) 1974 elections results produced either minority government or one with a very small majority, which would suggest weak executive; nevertheless, Hailsham asserted 'elective dictatorship' against 1976 Labour government

d) Bill of Rights:

Case against: Power of interpretation and enforcement would be in hands of judges who may be unrepresentative, unaccountable and conservative; it would be hard to reconcile individual/collective or minority/majority rights; every Bill of Rights has a 'get-out' clause which may render it worthless.

Case for: It limits dangers of 'elective dictatorship' of strong government in sovereign Parliament with flexible constitution, and lack of checks and balances in system; constitution and power of government resting largely on conventions – need legal limits and safeguards; UK already signatory of European Convention – would be more logical and efficient to incorporate it into British law; growing constraints on civil liberties, for example, police and public order laws, secrecy and constraints on media, Northern Ireland, changes in British criminal justice system, for example, decline of jury trial, abolition of right to silence, etc. On balance, case for is stronger.

e) Bills and referenda paving the way for devolution in Scotland, Wales and Northern Ireland were rapidly enacted by Labour in 1997–8. Reform of the Lords – removing most of the hereditary peers but without deciding any second stage, more radical reform – was also pushed through quite rapidly. It is worth noting that these reforms would both benefit Labour, as will the introduction of the closed list system for EU elections where (all) party leaderships can pick loyal placemen to fill the seats.

However, freedom of information – potentially threatening to any government – was long delayed, as was electoral reform for Westminster which would inevitably reduce Labour's huge majority. The British Bill of Rights will come into force in 2000 but will not take precedence over ordinary statute law and its provisions could, therefore, often be ignored.

At the same time, Tony Blair has been accused of 'control freakery' because of his disciplinary control over his party, with frequent rule changes and even sackings to suppress dissent.

13 Countdown to the exam

KEY POINTS

▶ Before the exam:
How to revise
Just before the exam
▶ In the exam
▶ After the exam

BEFORE THE EXAM

How to revise

Revising – 'seeing again' – means reviewing the topics, reorganising your information in a relevant and useful way and rethinking the issues and arguments as required by the exam. Like all study, it should not be passive note-cramming, but active exam preparation and practice. For Politics A-level you should start revising about six weeks before the exam – even if you are still doing new work on the course itself.

▶ First, check the exact dates of your exams.

▶ If you have not already done so (see Chapter 1), write a list – in logical order – of the topics which you must cover for the exam. Use your syllabus for guidance, and ask your teacher to check it. Organise your files according to the topic list, with separate sections or pockets for each topic, clearly labelled.

▶ Devise a weekly timetable for the six weeks leading up to the exam, showing when each topic is to be revised. Do not do only as many topics as there are essay questions to be answered! The examiners often cover two or three topics in one question; and your favourite topic may come up in the form of a difficult question – or not at all. If you have four questions to answer on one paper, do at least eight or nine topics in depth, and do not wholly neglect the others. Look very carefully through past exam questions for any topic/theme patterns.

▶ At the beginning of each new week, devise a daily timetable for the rest of that week. This should show everything you plan to do: the different balance of time on different topics, depending on your own preferences and weak areas; methods of revision, for example, noting/timed essays/stimulus questions/current events; other subjects and exams to be revised; eating, sleeping and leisure. Make it realistic and flexible – do not aim to start revising at 8 a.m. if you are a night person. Plan for

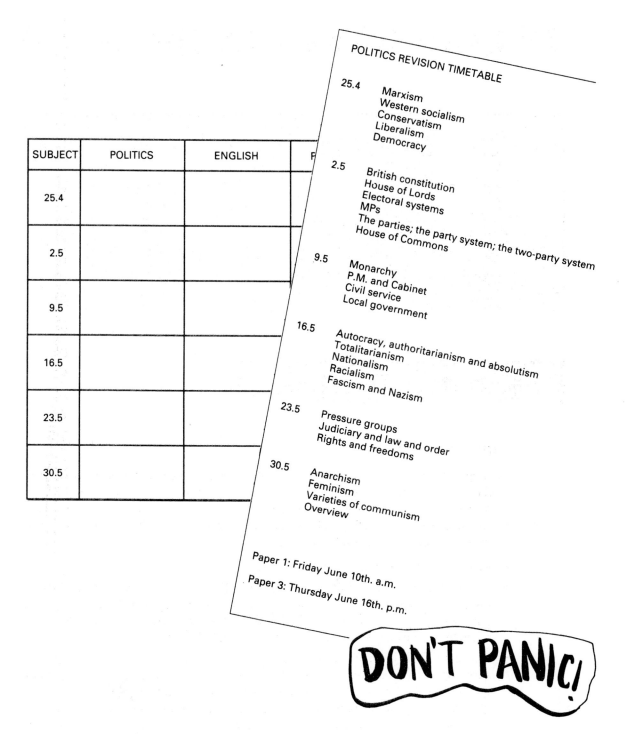

SUBJECT	POLITICS	ENGLISH	F
25.4			
2.5			
9.5			
16.5			
23.5			
30.5			

POLITICS REVISION TIMETABLE

25.4
Marxism
Western socialism
Conservatism
Liberalism
Democracy

2.5
British constitution
House of Lords
Electoral systems
MPs
The parties; the party system; the two-party system
House of Commons

9.5
Monarchy
P.M. and Cabinet
Civil service
Local government

16.5
Autocracy, authoritarianism and absolutism
Totalitarianism
Nationalism
Racialism
Fascism and Nazism

23.5
Pressure groups
Judiciary and law and order
Rights and freedoms

30.5
Anarchism
Feminism
Varieties of communism
Overview

Paper 1: Friday June 10th. a.m.
Paper 3: Thursday June 16th. p.m.

DON'T PANIC!

▲ *A weekly timetable*

short, but frequent and productive sessions of work – the sense of achievement is greater as you tick off more tasks done.

Revising is sometimes tedious, and often requires willpower. When the TV beckons or the telephone tempts you, imagine the day when you will be sitting in front of the exam paper itself, or the day of the results. Remember that the constant choice between success or failure is now yours alone. It is not you versus teachers or parents – it is you

WEEK 25/4

	MON	TUES	WED	THURS	FRI	SAT	SUN
7.00	Sleep	sleep	Sleep	Z z	z z z	z z z	zzzz
8.00	Up	—>	—>	—>	—>	Sleep	Sleep
9.00	Current events		Current events	Philos.	Eng.	Up	Up
10.00	Marxism (N)	Eng.	Review pol.	Philos.	Eng.	Current events	
11.00	Eng.	Review pol.	Philos.			Dem. (E)	Eng.
12.00	Eng.	W. Soc. (N/S)	Philos.	Eng.	Review pol.	Philos.	Eng.
1.00	Lunch						—>
2.00	Marxism (S/P)	W. Soc. (P/E)		Eng.	Dem (N)		Review pol.
3.00	Marxism (E)		Eng.	Eng.	Dem. (N)	Philos.	Review pol.
4.00		Eng.	Cons. (N/S)	Review pol.	Dem. (S/P)	Philos.	Review pol.
5.00			Cons. (E/P)	Lib. (N)			
6.00	Dinner						—>
7.00		Philos.	Out	Lib. (S)	Out	Out	Philos.
8.00	Philos.	Philos.		Lib./Cons. (P/E)			Philos.
9.00	Philos.						Philos.
10.00							

(N) = Notes (S) = Short answers (P) = Plans (E) = Essays

▲ *A daily timetable*

versus the exam – win! It is better to be working and fed-up (but confident and even smug) than not working and guilt-ridden or panic-stricken about it.

Write your own list of do's and don'ts for a trouble-free exam programme. See Chapter 1 for points on study skills, hints on factual learning, note-taking, essay-writing and exam techniques.

Find a good, quiet, comfortable place to work – not in front of the TV! Be honest – is your environment helping you to study or providing welcome distractions? Look after yourself in the weeks leading up to the exam and stay healthy (see Chapter 1), at least until the post-exam celebrations.

Start each revision session with something easy, routine and confidence-building, such as reviewing a checklist of basic facts, definitions or examples from the previous session. Then:

▶ Take out the notes on that day's topic and keep them in a separate folder whilst revising (less daunting that way). Sort them into a logical order, and throw away any messy, redundant or outdated notes.

▶ Go thoroughly through a list of all past questions on the topic. Jot down the four or five recurring 'angles' on the topic and keep a constant look-out for points relevant to each angle as you read around the topic. Always read, note, learn and test yourself with an eye to past exam questions, to ensure relevant answers. If you try to learn chunks of material verbatim, you will recite them in the same way, they will be irrelevant to the question, and you will fare badly.

ASK YOUR TEACHER FOR COPIES OF PAST EXAMINERS' REPORTS

▶ Try to condense each topic to a one-sheet note summary of key essay angles and related terms, concepts and definitions, facts and dates, names, arguments, quotations and examples. Actively reorganise your material to suit your needs. Skim and dip-read critically; weigh up issues, assertions, opinions and evidence in your own mind.

▶ Go through your current events diary (see Chapter 1) and rewrite lists of key examples under topic headings.

Most important

▶ Do a comprehensive sample of past questions (of all types in your exam) on each topic: short answers, stimulus questions, essay plans, timed essays. Be ruthless on timed work; do not get into the habit of going even slightly over time. Do not do all the easy titles, or those you have done well before. When you come across a problem title, ask your teacher about it, then try a brief plan and have it checked.

▶ Work hard on the different timing and techniques required by different types of questions. Look critically over your own past work – read it aloud and listen to the wording and style, correct factual errors, write in missing facts and examples, and ask your teacher what you need to do to go up one grade.

▶ Decide your own chosen stance on every key angle of every topic at this stage, not in the exam itself. How should Parliament be improved, and why? Are you going to opt for PR or not? What kind of PR and why? Are you going to say that Britain has prime ministerial government or not? What reforms would you suggest and why? Are you going to say that local government is too weak or not? Do you advocate a Bill of Rights – why/why not? (Review Chapters 2–12 for the key issues/angles on each topic.)

▶ You should occasionally attempt a full mock exam. If not coerced into it, volunteer – your teacher should be ecstatic! Remember that it does not matter how badly you do; with practice, the next effort – and the exam itself – will be better.

▶ Assess your own weaknesses and aim to eliminate them one by one:

? Factual learning ✔
? Essay planning ✗
? Structure ✗
? Relevance ✔
? Argument ✔
? Evidence ✗
? Timing ✗
? Handwriting ✔
? Waffle ✔

▶ When you get very bored, read the paper or a weekly journal such as the *New Statesman* or *Economist*, watch the TV news and political satire and brush up on current events.

Just before the exam

▶ Carefully check the time and place of your exams. If you have never been there, make an advance visit to locate the place and check how long the journey will take at that time of day.

▶ If you fall ill or have any kind of accident or upset, tell your school or college immediately. Even if you sit the exam, they may think it appropriate to notify the exam board, and special consideration may be given in the marking of your script. *Do not wait until after the exam before saying that you were not on top form.*

▶ On the day before the exam, lay out all necessities – clothes (check the weather forecast), good pens, rulers, watch, tissues, sweets, etc. NO correcting fluid – it will probably be confiscated anyway. Decide your own exam timetable in advance – timing and order of answers, whether you are going to do a compulsory question first or an easy question first, etc. (hence mock exam practice).

IN THE EXAM

▶ Synchronise your watch with the clock in the exam hall.

TIME YOURSELF RUTHLESSLY

▶ Breathe deeply; aim for cool, calm, concentration. Ignore everything around you – clicking pens, jangling bracelets, hysterics and all.

▶ Read the rubric, and follow it.

▶ Pick your titles, but then read through them all once more, slowly, word for word – you may have chosen a nasty title on your pet topic, and neglected a much better title. Do not start an essay and then change your mind half-way through – that will waste too much precious time.

▶ Keep referring back to the title constantly, especially before you write the conclusion.

▶ If panic or memory-failure threatens, move on to something else, then move back later.

▶ Do not try to fool the examiner with invented quotations, half-finished answers, and illegible scrawl when you've forgotten how to spell a name – they know all the tricks!

▶ Try very hard to balance your timing across all questions. The example below shows that a good first answer cannot compensate for a bad final answer (check first and last grades especially – which student gets the better overall grade?). If you mistime, do the last question in brief, detailed note form with an explicit conclusion – do not write half an essay.

Student A	Student B
19	15
15	14
9	12
4	12
47%	53%

▶ If you have any spare time at the end, do read over your work and make amendments – even if messy, they will gain marks. Do not stare into space and do not walk out, no matter how keen you are to get away – every available moment is precious.

▶ If you feel ill during the exam, tell the invigilator (supervisor) at the time, even if you stay to complete the exam.

AFTER THE EXAM

Most students prefer to avoid detailed postmortems on the exam and everything they might have said but did not. Instead, now is the time to reflect on how much you have gained from studying Politics, besides an A-level: political gumption, critical acumen, sound knowledge of current events and issues – and the satisfaction that you can have topical and philosophical arguments with family and friends, and win.

This should not arise, but if the exam result is not good, you may want to ask the exam board for a report or remark. Usually this must be done through your school or college, according to the board's regulations and procedures; discuss it with your teacher as soon as possible.

If you have worked through this book thoroughly you should not need it, but – good luck!

Glossary

administrative law   the body of laws which apply to executive and other public bodies

adversary politics   a period when the two main parties have polarised philosophies and policies

anarchism   rejection of all forms of coercive power, especially of state

anti-constitutional   seeking the complete overthrow of the constitution

anti-parliamentary   seeking the complete overthrow of the parliamentary system

authoritarianism   a system of rule based on coercive power rather than consent

authority   rightful, legitimate power based on consent

autonomy   self-government, independence from external control

bias   prejudice or partisanship that sways or distorts mind and judgement

bicameral legislature   a Parliament with two chambers/houses

bill of rights   a legal document enshrining citizens' entitlements against each other and the state

block vote   method of trade union voting at Labour conferences where a majority union vote for an option results in 100 per cent of that union's votes counting towards that option

bureaucracy   the large scale, professional administration of any organisation, business or government

by-election   an election held in a single constituency (for example, when an MP dies)

cabinet government   collective policy-making and accountability by all senior ministers, with the Prime Minister *primus inter pares* (first among equals)

capitalism   an industrialised economic system based on private ownership of the means of production for private profit

case law   judge-made law as interpreted by the courts in significant test cases

charisma   personal magnetism and charm as a basis for personal authority

citizenship   legal membership of and recognition by a state of an individual, entailing mutual rights and duties

civil disobedience   law-breaking, usually peaceful and public, as a deliberate act of political protest

civil/legal rights   citizen's entitlements (for example, to freedom or equality) granted by the state

class   a social group sharing the same economic characteristics of wealth or income. Marxist definition: a group sharing the same relationship to the means of production

closed shop   an occupation or workplace where an individual must belong to the appropriate union or association in order to work at that particular trade or profession

coalition government   two or more parties in executive office

coercion   compulsory force

collectivism   broadly, a belief in the primacy of some kind of group or collective over the individual; narrowly, a 'left wing' belief in collective economic ownership and equality

collective ministerial responsibility   based on the assumption of collective Cabinet policy making, therefore all ministers are collectively accountable for government policies, and should publicly and unanimously support those policies or should resign

common law   law based on custom and precedent rather than on statute.

communism   theory of economic equality through common ownership of property and wealth, for example, Marxism

consensus politics   a period when the two main parties share similar policies, for example, the 1960s' economic boom

constitution   a set of rules and principles by which a state is governed

constitutionalism   advocacy of, or acting within, a set of clear and enforceable rules which set limits to power of state and government

constitutional law   law that regulates the powers of the various branches of the state

constitutional monarchy   an impartial and largely symbolic hereditary head of state whose powers are largely exercised by ministers, subject to the will of Parliament and the people

conventions   unwritten rules of the constitution which have become so through traditional practice, but which have no legal force

corporatism   the tripartite involvement and consultation of government, employers and workers in economic planning and policy making in a private enterprise economy to promote industrial harmony, productivity and profit

cross-benchers   peers in the Lords who are independent of any party

delegate   an elected representative who acts in accordance with the wishes of the voters

delegated legislation   law made by bodies other than Parliament (for example, local authority by-laws) under power passed down by the sovereign Parliament

devolution   the passing down of limited executive or legislative powers from the sovereign centre to subordinate local bodies, i.e. a more limited form of decentralisation than federalism. Neither entails complete local autonomy

elective dictatorship   Hailsham's thesis of excessive executive power, between elections, over Parliament and public

elitism   belief in rule by a superior minority as desirable and/or inevitable

extra-parliamentary   any political body or activity outside of Parliament

faction   a group within a party which favours and seeks to promote a particular school of thought within the party's broader ideology

fascism   a right-wing, totalitarian regime based on dictatorship, monism, elitism, extreme nationalism and state-controlled capitalism

federalism   division of power between central and local executive and legislative bodies, with both, in theory, supreme in their particular fields, i.e. there is shared sovereignty and the centre cannot override the local bodies. Contrasts with a unitary system where there can be **devolution** but no genuine regional **autonomy**

feminism   a perception of women's inequality and a desire to reduce or eradicate it

flexible constitution   one that needs no special legal process for change, i.e. not rigid

franchise   the right to vote

functional representation   political representation and decision making based on occupational, industrial or interest groups rather than on parties

gerrymandering   the manipulation of electoral boundaries for party political advantage

government   narrowly: the executive, policy making branch of state; broadly: the whole machinery of state – legislature, executive and judiciary

green paper   a consultative document of diverse ideas and options published prior to a bill; more tentative than a white paper

guillotine   a time limit on parliamentary debate of a bill in the committee stage, imposed by the government

ideology   a comprehensive and more or less coherent package of doctrines, beliefs and values which provides a guide to political action

impartiality   objectivity and the absence of bias

impeachment   a formal process for removing from office a politician, for example, for wrongdoing

imperialism   the political and/or economic takeover and control of one country by another

individualism   a belief in the primacy of the individual over any group, society or state

individual ministerial responsibility   based on the assumption that ministerial heads of department are the chosen representatives of the people (while the non-elected civil servants are anonymous administrators), therefore ministers should be publicly accountable for the actions of their department and of themselves and should resign in the event of serious departmental or personal error

influence   persuasive effect on others' ideas or actions

judicial review   court hearings against actions of central or local government or other public authorities

justice   fairness and equity

laissez-faire   free market private enterprise economy with minimal state intervention

law   rules of state enforceable by the courts

legitimacy   rightful authority

liberal democracy   a system of individual representation and protection of individual rights based on free, regular and competitive elections

limited government   government whose powers are constrained by constitutional rules and other checks and balances

mandate   authority to govern granted by the electorate; strictly, the authority or obligation of the government to implement its manifesto proposals

manifesto   a booklet of policy proposals issued by each party before a general election

mechanistic theory   likens state and society to a machine created by individuals to serve them, with parts interchangeable and more important than the whole

meritocracy   a system where people rise to the top and rule due to personal skill, intelligence and effort (term coined by Michael Young, *The Rise of the Meritocracy*, 1958)

minority government   executive with fewer than 50 per cent of seats in House of Commons

monism   the opposite of pluralism; a unitary state with a single ideology, party and leader – a feature of totalitarianism

morality   ethical ideas of good and evil, right and wrong

nation   a group of people who share a sense of common culture, based on common ties of language, religion, history, race and/or territory and who usually want to seek or maintain a nation state

nationalism   a sense of common culture based on, for example, language, religion, traditions and history, usually entailing desire for (maintenance of) a nation-state

natural/human rights   entitlements which should, in theory, accrue to everyone simply by virtue of being human

negative freedom   unrestrained liberty, without state help or hindrance

New Right   Thatcherite conservatives (as distinct from traditional political conservatives) who advocate a free market economy (derived from nineteenth-century *laissez-faire* liberalism) combined with strong moral and social authoritarianism

oligarchy   political elitism, or rule by the few

ombudsman   an official of Parliament who investigates public complaints of government maladministration

open government   non-secretive government – public access to official papers, policy making processes and decisions

organic theory   likens state and society to a natural organism whose parts are unequal but interdependent and harmonious and less important than the whole

parliamentary government   a system based on overlap rather than separation of powers, i.e. the executive is chosen from the legislature and is in theory sub-ordinate and accountable to the legislature – as opposed to a presidential system

parliamentary privilege   the exemption of MPs and peers from some ordinary laws, notably slander and libel

parliamentary sovereignty   Parliament has supreme law-making power, and can make, amend or repeal any law without challenge from any domestic body. Thus it cannot be ruled illegal or unconstitutional, it can legalise illegality and no Parliament can bind its successors. However, it is (since 1973) formally overridden by the EU

party system   political representation and power on the basis of formal, organised groups of people who put up candidates for election on a common policy programme

paternalism   the exercise of 'fatherly' power or authority over others to protect them from harm or to promote their welfare, usually usurping individual responsibility and freedom of choice – a doctrine of traditional conservatism

patriarchy   a power structure dominated by men in both the public, political sphere and the private, family sphere

patriotism   love of one's country, which may or may not be a nation-state

patronage   powers of appointment – granting of jobs, honours or titles

pluralism   diverse and competing centres of power, especially many parties and pres-sure groups, many centres of economic power and various checks and balances throughout the system. Contrasts with monism/totalitarianism

police state   a state where control is maintained by arbitrary and oppressive law enforcement – or illegal repression – by the police who are themselves largely above the law with extensive powers of detention, secret surveillance and use of force, i.e. no 'rule of law'

political elite   a small, dominant, usually privileged decision-making and power-holding group

positive freedom   real ability to achieve one's autonomy and potential, with state help where necessary (for example, through welfare, civil rights legislation, etc.)

power   the ability to do, or make others do, something based on the capacity to coerce

pragmatism   practical adaptation to concrete circumstances, rather than attachment to abstract or rigid theory or ideology

presidential system   a system where the executive is separately elected from the legis-lature and the two bodies are in theory equal, possessing checks and balances against each other

pressure group   an organisation seeking to promote a cause or protect a section of society often by influencing government, Parliament or public

primary election   election of a candidate before election for political office

private bill   a bill which affects only specific individual or group interests rather than the general public

private member's bill   a bill introduced by an individual backbench MP (of any party) rather than by the government

proportional representation   umbrella label for systems of election which produce seats in proportion to the parties' votes

public bill   a bill which concerns the general public interest

quango   quasi-autonomous non-governmental organisation – a body appointed by government but not a formal part of government, and meant to be impartial, to perform some administrative or regulatory function. There are thousands: for example, the Equal Opportunities Commission, General Medical Council, health service trusts, Oftel, the Jockey Club, etc.

racialism/racism   a perception of innate biological castes within human society which can be ranked in a hierarchy; a perception used to rationalise discrimination and/or domination

reactionary   desire to turn the clock back to an earlier *status quo ante*

referendum   a vote by the electorate directly on a specific issue; may be advisory or binding

representation   a form of indirect democracy reflecting the views, interests and/or typical social background of the electorate

responsible (party) government   executive accountable to Parliament and public (through party system, manifesto and mandate); or wise and sensible government in the best interests of the people

rights   entitlements, for example, to some kind of freedom or equality

rigid constitution   one which requires a special legal process for change

royal prerogative   the legal powers of the Crown

rule of law   a principle which seeks to ensure 'just' law which is applicable to all – thus there should be legal equality, clear, consistent and impartial law and an independent judiciary

safe seat   a constituency which one particular party is virtually certain to win regardless of the candidate

scientism   the application of criteria of scientific method to the study of human society – hence objective, empirical, logical, rational, determinist, classificatory, quantifiable and verifiable

select committees of the House of Commons   all-party committees of backbench MPs whose task is to scrutinise the activities of government departments and issues of public interest

separation of powers   an arrangement (favoured by liberal democratic thinker Montesquieu) whereby the personnel and structures of the legislature, executive and judiciary do not overlap with each other

separatism   (desire for) complete break-away and independence of a local region to form a sovereign state

sequestration   the freezing and/or seizure of a trade union's assets by the courts as a penalty for contempt of court over illegal industrial action

socialisation   the instilling of political attitudes and values through agencies such as family, media, education, peer group, church, etc.

sovereignty   ultimate legal and political power and authority

standing committees of the House of Commons   all-party committees of backbench MPs whose task is to scrutinise and amend bills

state   the formal, abstract, sovereign political power over a given territory, usually comprising legislature, executive and judiciary and usually possessing a legal monopoly of coercive power

subsidiarity   the principle enshrined in the EU Maastricht Treaty that power should be exercised at the lowest possible level compatible with efficiency and democracy

supranationalism   the establishment of a sovereign power over member states

surcharging   the personal fining of a local councillor by the courts to the amount of money illegally spent

toleration   acceptance of diverse views and actions

totalitarianism   a twentieth-century concept (devised by Italian fascism) of total control by a monist state of both the public and private spheres based on mass, active consent as well as coercion

ultra vires   literally 'beyond legal powers' – phrase used when central or local government bodies are ruled illegal by the courts

unconstitutional   breaking any rule of the constitution

unicameral legislature   a Parliament with only one chamber/house

unitary constitution   one based upon a single, sovereign, national legislature

unwritten/uncodified constitution   set of rules and principles of government (some written), but not contained in a single, legal document

veto   the power to block a decision through refusal of consent

welfare state   provision by government and public authorities of money, goods and services to those deemed in need

white paper   a draft bill, for public consultation, before publication of the bill

Recommended reading

General

Childs, David (1986) *Britain Since 1945: A Political History*, Methuen
A chronological survey of political events and administrations since the war, up to 1985.
A good reference book even for students of purely contemporary politics (*see also* Sked
and Cook)

Coxall, Bill and Robins, Lynton (1998) *Contemporary British Politics*, Macmillan
A very comprehensive and detailed textbook on British politics for A-level

Glasgow University Media Group (1976) *Bad News*, Routledge & Kegan Paul; (1980)
More Bad News, Routledge & Kegan Paul; (1982) *Really Bad News*, Writers and Readers
A series of radical – and readable – critiques of media 'bias', based on empirical data

Jones, Bill (ed.) (1994) *Political Issues in Britain Today*, Manchester University Press
A concise, balanced and well-ordered outline of key political issues in the fields of policy,
economics, institutions, defence, and law and order

Jones, Bill and Kavanagh, Dennis (1994) *British Politics Today*, Manchester University
Press
A short book of well-ordered, concise notes under numbered headngs on key topics
and issues

Jones, Bill *et al.* (1998) *Politics UK*, Prentice Hall
A detailed, topical and well-presented textbook on British politics for A-level

Macfarlane, L.J. (1986) *Issues in British Politics Since 1945*, Longman
A short survey of key political issues with a historical slant, including international events
and institutions such as the Falklands and EU

Miliband, Ralph (1969) *The State in Capitalist Society*, Quartet
A classic Marxist analysis of the British state and politics

Norton, Philip (1982) *The Constitution in Flux*, Basil Blackwell
A classic analysis of key political issues such as reform of Parliament, Prime Ministerial
government and a Bill of Rights. Weighty – not introductory reading, but excellent for
essays

Renwick, Alan and Swinburn, Ian (1987) *Basic Political Concepts*, Hutchinson
A well-written and topical book on key political concepts such as power and authority,
order and disorder, rights and representation. Good introductory reading; simple without
being simplistic

Sked, Alan and Cook, Chris (1984) *Post-War Britain: A Political History*, Penguin
A survey of post-war administrations since 1945, one chapter per government. This
edition goes up to 1983

Specific

Denning, Lord (1980) 'Misuse of power', The Dimbleby Lecture
A controversial plea for judicial power over Parliament – 'Someone must be trusted. Let it be the judges.' Discuss!

Griffith, J.A.G. (1991) *The Politics of the Judiciary*, Fontana
A classic, critical thesis of a 'political' judiciary, with a mass of empirical evidence

Hailsham, Lord (1976) 'Elective Dictatorship', The Dimbleby Lecture, in *The Listener*, 21 October
A classic thesis of overweening executive power in modern Britain

Young, H. and Sloman, A. (1982) *No, Minister: An Inquiry into the Civil Service*, BBC
An out-dated but short, readable and revealing 'inside look' at the relationships between ministers and civil servants in the 1960s and 1970s

Reference books

The Fontana Dictionary of Modern Thought (1988)
McLean, Iain (ed.) (1996) *The Oxford Concise Dictionary of Politics*, Oxford University Press
Miller, David (ed.) (1991) *The Blackwell Encyclopaedia of Political Thought*, Basil Blackwell
The Penguin Dictionary of Politics (1988)
Pilkington, Colin (1999) *The 'Politics Today' Companion to the British Constitution*, Manchester University Press
Scruton, Roger (1983) *A Dictionary of Political Thought*, Pan
The Times Guide to the House of Commons (1997) Times Books

Journals

Politics Review
Excellent compilation of articles on key issues by writers such as Drewry, Madgwick and Zander; summaries of political and parliamentary affairs; examiners' comments on students' essay answers and on exam techniques, etc. Readable and well-presented. Four issues each academic year

Talking Politics
Began Autumn 1988, produced by the Politics Association. Three issues each year. Many useful articles by writers such as Bill Jones and Philip Norton

Index

Page references in *italic*
indicate tables or figures

abstentions by voters 50–1
Acts of Parliament 22, 107
additional member system
        (AMS) 45–6, *46*, 60
administrative law 174
adversary politics 40, 263
advertising and the media
        203
age and voting behaviour 49,
        51
alternative vote (AV) 42
alternative vote plus (AV+)
        46, 60
Amsterdam Treaty 1997 226
anarchism 19, 263
anti-constitutional actions
        24–5
anti-parliamentary actions
        263
'Arms to Iraq' affair 97–8,
        108
authoritarianism 263
authority 19, 22, 28
        Parliament 105–6
        PM 123, 125–6
autonomy 149, 263

backbenchers
        private members' bills 63,
            77
        rebellions 27, 30, 62, 63
        see also Members of
            Parliament
bias 20, 179, 263
bicameral legislature 103,
        263
bill of rights 173, 183, 185–6
bills 91, 107
block votes 162, 215
bureaucracy 119, 133–4
        see also civil service
Burke, Edmund 18
by-elections 38

Cabinet 2–3, 110, 114–16,
        129
        Cabinet or PM
            government? 117,
            118–24, 126–8
Cabinet committees 119
Cabinet Office 119
candidates, parliamentary
        61–2
capitalism 263

'capping' 154
case law 23, 192
censorship of the media 203
central government *see*
        government
centralisation of government
        20
charisma 19, 263
citizenship 174, 263
civil disobedience 171,
        186–7, 193, 198, 210
civil law 170
Civil List 114
civil rights 19, 20, 181–3,
        189–91, 245
        Bill of Rights 183, 185–6
        European Convention on
            Human Rights *184*
civil service 110, 131–2, 133,
        149
        European Commission 221
        neutrality 136–9, 145–6
        and PM 119
        power and influence
            134–6, 142, 242–3
        reform 133–4, 143–5, 149
        secrecy 139–41, 146–8
class, social 20, 48–9, 246
classical elitism 20, 33
closed shop 200, 215
coalition governments 35, 43,
        44, 52, 54, 59–60
coercion 17
collective responsibility 68
        ministerial 83, 115, 129
collectivism 49, 263
Common Agricultural Policy
        (CAP) 217
common law 23, 192
Commons *see* House of
        Commons
communism 19, 264
community charge 154
conscience, MP's 67
consensus 17
consensus politics 39
Conservative Party 69–70, *72*
        1997 general election
            40–1, 57–8
        and the constitution 28
        and devolution *160*
        and the EU 223–4
        finance and structure 75
        and House of Lords 87–8,
            89
constituencies 38
constituency parties 62, 65

constituents and MPs 38, 65
constitution 22–3, 248–9
        anti-constitutional actions
            24–5
        changes since 1997 *24*
        government structures
            25–6, *26*
        parliamentary sovereignity
            26–7
        power of the executive 28
        and rule of law 28
        unconstitutional actions
            24
        views of 28
constitutional law 23
constitutional monarchy 111
constitutionalism 19
conventions 23
corporatism 199, 215
corruption, police 179
Council of Ministers, EU 220
council tax 154
councillors, local 153
Court of Justice, EU 222,
        224
courts 172–3, *172*
        and the executive 174–5
        judges 175–7, 187–8,
            190–1, 193
        and local government 155
        and Parliament 173
criminal law 170, 177
cross-benchers 71, 264
Crown *see* monarchy
crown immunity 112
currency, single European
        225–6
current events diaries 7, *8*

decentralisation 157
delegated legislation 91,
        192
delegates 18, 33
democracy 18, 21, 31–2
        in Britain 19–21
        liberal democracy 19
        local 164
        media and 212–14
        monarchy and 124–5
        power and authority 19
devolution 90, 99, 158, 165
        England 162
        Northern Ireland 162
        political parties and *160–1*
        Scotland 158–9, 162
        Wales 159–62
direct democracy 18, 31

dominant party system 69, 82

economic sovereignty 218–20
elections 38
    see also general elections
elective dictatorship 28, 31, 44, 78, 92, 208, 238–9
electoral systems 52–3, 54–5
    first-past-the-post 38–41
    non-proportional alternatives to FPTP 42
    proportional representation 43–6
elitism 18, 20, 33, 34
Employment Acts 200
England and devolution 162
essays 2
    common formats 12–15
    content 10–12, 16
    essay plans 9–10
    the essay question 9
    key words in titles 15–16
ethnic minorities voting behaviour 49, 51
European Commission 220–2
European Convention on Human Rights *184*
European Council 222
European Court of Human Rights (ECHR) 172–3
European Court of Justice (ECJ) 172, 223, *224*
European Economic Community (EEC) 217
European Monetary Union (EMU) 225–6
European Parliament 45, 222–3
European Union (EU) 23, 217–18
    Amsterdam Treaty 1997 227
    Britain and 218, *219*, 230–2, 247–8
    and British political parties 223–4
    the future 227, *228*
    institutions of 220–3
    Maastricht Treaty 1991 225–6
    pressure groups and 197
    Single European Act 1986 225
    sovereignty issue 27, 90, 218–20
examinations
    after 260–2
    examiners' reports 5
    see also essays
executive 25, *26*, 27, 28, 30, 107, 110
    and the courts 174–5

House of Commons and 91–5
    MPs and 63–4
    power of 28–9, 30–1
    see also government
extra-parliamentary interests 54

factions 43, 264
fascism 264
federalism 23, 158, 225, 264
feminism 264
finance
    House of Commons control of 95
    local government 154, 155, 156, 166
    political parties 75–6
first-past-the-post electoral system (FPTP) 38–40
    see also general elections
flexible constitution 23
franchise 37
free trade 217
Freedom of Information Act 141, 146–8
freedoms 181, 182
    see also civil rights
functional representation 89, 215, 264

general elections 38
    1997 40–1, *40*, 46, 49, 57–8, *68*, *202*, *208*
    results 1970–1997 *53*
gerrymandering 156, 264
government 17, 33, 107
    Cabinet or PM? 117, 118–24, 126–8
    and local government 155–8, 163–4, 165–7, 243–4
    majority 27, 30, 35, 38
    minority 28, 30, 35, 38, 43–4, 54
    and the party system 67–9
    representative 18, 19, 26
    responsible 18, 26, 68
    structures 25–6, *26*
    see also executive
green papers 30, 264
guillotine (on bills) 91

House of Commons 107
    controlling the executive 91–5
    law-making 90–1
    representing the people 96–100
House of Lords 30, 86–9, 103–5, 107
human rights 181, *184*, 265
hung Parliaments 43, 44

ideologies 246
impartiality 99, 178–81, 264
impeachment 122, 265
imperialism 265
independents 19, 39, 69
indirect democracy 18, 31
individualism 69, 265
influence 195–6
    civil service 134–6
    media 202–3
    MPs 63
    pressure groups 30, 196–7
    select committees 95

judges 175–7, 187–8, 190–1, 193
judicial reviews 174–5, *174*
judiciary 25, *26*
justice 28
    law, justice and morality 170–1

Labour government (1997–) 27, 70–1
    and EU 224
    and House of Lords 86, 88
    and PR 45
Labour Party 70, *73*
    1997 general election 40, 41
    and devolution *160*
    and the EU 223
    finance and structure 75
    and House of Lords 86, 89
laissez-faire 133, 265
law 19, 22–3, 169–70
    breaking 186–7
    Commons and law-making 90–1
    and freedom 182
    justice and morality 170–1
    local government 154
    'rule of law' 19, 28–9, 170, 192–3, 244–5
legal system 20
    civil rights and 181–6, 186–7, 189–91
    courts 170–7, 187–8, 190–1, 193
    the law 169–71
    police 177–81, 188–9
legislature 25, *26*, 27, 107
    and the executive 30–1
    MPs and 62–3
legitimacy 28
liberal democracy 19–21
Liberal Democrats 39, 71, *74*
    1997 general election 41
    and devolution *161*
    and the EU 224
    and PR 43, 44
    view of the constitution 28

liberals, radical 20
limited government 19, 265
lobby system (media briefing) 100, 140, 205
lobbying of Parliament 20, 197, 198
local government 23, 151, 164
  advantages and disadvantages 168
  central government and 155–8, 163–4, 165–7, 243–4
  courts and 155
  devolution 158–62, 165
  finance 154, 155, 156, 166
  legislation 154, 156
  local councillors 153
  structure and function 151–3
Lords see House of Lords

Maastricht Treaty 1991 *219*, 225–7
majority government 27, 30, 35, 38, 54, 92
mandate 35–6, 44, 67, 83
manifestos 24, 35–6, 64, 67
market socialism 70
Marxism 20–1, 246–7
mass media see media
mechanistic theory 265
media 20, 201, 211–14, 246–7
  influence on political agenda 202–3
  ownership and influence 202
  political controls on 203–5
  and voting behaviour 50
Members of Parliament (MPs) 62, 77
  behaviour in Commons 92
  and constituents 38, 65
  loyalties 64–7
  parliamentary privilege 26, 99
  and the party system 69
  power and influence 78–9
  and pressure groups 197–8
  as representatives 18, 61–2, 64, 83
  roles of 62–4, 82–3
meritocracy 265
ministers 110, 111
  MPs as trainee 64
  responsibility 83, 115–16, 129–30, 142
  see also Cabinet
minority governments 28, 30, 35, 38, 43–4

monarchy 110, 111–14, 124–5
monism 265
morality 265
  law, justice and 170–1

national interest, MPs and 67
national sovereignty 218
nationalism 159, 265
nations 18, 265
natural rights 181, 265
negative freedom 265
neutrality of the civil service 136–9, 145–6
New Labour 70, 71
New Right 70, 265
newspapers
  readers and 1997 General Election *202*
  see also media
Nolan Commission 66
Northern Ireland and devolution 162
note-taking 6

occupation and voting behaviour 48–9
Official Secrets Acts 139, 204
oligarchy 18
ombudsman 30, 265
one-party government 19, 34, 38, 43–4, 82
open government 19, 141, 146–7
opinion polls 195, 206–7, *208*
Opposition 38, 69, 92
Opposition Days 92
organic theory, state 33

Parliament 25–6, *27*, 28, 107, 238–9
  and the courts 173
  factors undermining authority 105–6
  functions 86, 240–1
  House of Commons 90–100
  House of Lords 86–9, 103–5
  legal and actual powers 101–2
  and pressure groups 197–8
  sovereignty 23, 26–7, 28, 34–5, 218
Parliament, European 222–3
parliamentary government 25–6, *27*, 29, 31–2
parliamentary privilege 26, 99
party conferences 65
party list system of PR 44–5, *45*, 60
party system 67–9, 78, 82

see also political parties
paternalism 266
patriarchy 266
patriotism 266
patronage 87, 266
pluralism 19, 22, 34, 79, 239–40
police 177, 188–9
  accountability 181
  impartiality 178–81
  public order 177–8
police state 180, *180*
political elite 20, 33
political parties
  1997 general election *68*
  alternation of in government 79–80
  British and EU 223–4
  consensus and differences 80
  and devolution *160–1*
  finance 75–6, 197
  image and voting behaviour 50
  MPs and 64–5
  party conferences 65
  the party system 67–9, 82
  pluralism 239–40
  structure 75
  see also Conservative Party; Labour Party; Liberal Democrats
politicisation of the civil service 137–9, 145–6
poll tax 154
positive freedoms 181, 266
power 17, 18, 22, 79–80, 195–6
  and authority 19
  civil service 134–6, 142
  MPs 63
  Parliament 101–2
  pressure groups 196–7
  Prime Minister 3–4, 117, 119–21, 122
  select committees 95
  trade unions 199–201
pragmatism 266
preference voting 42, *42*, 44, 60
presidential system 26, 122, 241–2
pressure groups 19, 27, 65, 196, 207–10, 245–6
  methods used by 197–8
  power and influence 30, 196–7
  see also trade unions
primary elections 62, 266
Prime Minister (PM) 107, 110, 112, 116, 241–2
  Cabinet or PM government? 117, 118–24, 126–8

PMs 1990–2000 *118*
power 3–4, 117, 119–21, 122, 125
Prime Minister's Office 119, *120*
private bills 91
private members' bills 63, 91, 197
proportional representation (PR) 39, 43–6, 52–3, 54, 59–60
Public Accounts Committee (PAC) 95
public bills 91
Public Interest Immunity Certificates (PIICs) 97, 140
public opinion 194–6, 198, 205–7, 212
public order 177–8

quangos 134, 266
Question Time 92–3

race and voting behaviour 49, 51
racialism, police 178–9
radical liberals 20
radical socialists 20–1
reactionary 267
referenda 23, 195, 267
regional voting behaviour 49
Register of MPs' Interests 65–7
religion and voting behaviour 50
representation 18, 89, 239
representative government 18, 19, 26, 83
representatives 33, 59
  MPs as 34, 64
responsibility 68
  ministerial 83, 115–16, 129, 142
responsible government 18, 26, 68, 83
revision
  factual learning hints 6–7
  how to revise 256–60
  short answer questions 21
  see also study skills

rights *see* civil rights
rigid constitution 23
Rousseau, Jean-Jacques 18
royal prerogative 111, 112, *113*
'rule of law' 19, 28–9, 170, 192–3, 244–5
ruling classes 20, 246

safe seats 38, 267
Santer, Jacques 221
scientism 267
Scotland and devolution 158–9, 162
Scott inquiry 4, 97–8, 108
second ballot 42
secrecy 20, 30, 139–41, 146–8, 239
select committees 30, 93–5
separation of powers 25, 267
separatism 158, 267
sequestration 200, 215
sex and voting behaviour 49
short answer questions 2, 21
single currency 225–6
single elitism 20, 33
Single European Act (SEA) 1986 225
single European currency 225–6
single transferable vote (STV) 44, 60
single-party government 19, 34, 38, 43–4, 82
Social Chapter 226
social class 20, 48–9, 246
socialisation 114, 267
socialism 70
socialists, radical 20–1
society 18
sovereignty 17, 28, 34, 231
  EU and 218–20, 231–2
  Parliamentary 23, 26–7, 34, 90
sponsorship of MPs 65, 197
standing committees 91
states 17, 18, 33, 165
  functions 107
  organic theory 33

statutes 107, 192
stimulus response questions 2
study skills 1–4
  current events diary 7, *8*
  factual learning 6–7
  note-taking 6
  see also revision
subsidiarity 225
supplementary vote 42
supranationalism 218
surcharging 267

television
  and the House of Commons 99–100
  see also media
timetables, revision 256, *257*, *258*
toleration 267
totalitarianism 267
trade unions 18, 75, 198, 210–11
  and MPs 65
  power 30–1, 199–201
Treaty of Rome 1957 217
two-party system 31, 38, 39, 81–2

ultra vires 155, 267
uncodified/unwritten constitution 22
unconstitutional actions 24
unicameral legislature 103, 268
unitary constitution 23

vetoes 62, 268
voters and voting 18, 37–8
  behaviour 48–51, 55–6
  electoral systems 38–46
  EU Council of Ministers 220
  European Parliament 222
  and party system 69

Wales and devolution 159–61
welfare state 268
white papers 30, 268
women
  MPs 61–2
  voting behaviour 49